Reading the Hebrew Bible
after the Shoah

Marvin A. Sweeney

Reading the Hebrew Bible
after the Shoah

ENGAGING HOLOCAUST THEOLOGY

Fortress Press / Minneapolis

Cover image: © Shutterstock / Gary Paul Lewis
Cover design: Designworks
Book design: Zan Ceeley / Trio Bookworks

Library of Congress Cataloging-in-Publication Data

Sweeney, Marvin A. (Marvin Alan), 1953–
  Reading the Hebrew Bible after the Shoah : engaging Holocaust theology / Marvin A.
Sweeney.
    p. cm.
  Includes bibliographical references and index.
  ISBN 978-0-8006-3849-8 (alk. paper)
  1. Theodicy—Biblical teaching. 2. Holocaust (Jewish theology) 3. Bible. O.T. Penta-
teuch—Criticism, interpretation, etc. I. Title.
  BS1199.T44S94 2008
  296.3'118—dc22

                            2008024120

For
Zev Garber
~

CONTENTS

This has been a particularly challenging volume to write. The challenge lies not so much in the difficulties posed by the scholarly issues addressed here, but more so in the recognition that this study is prompted by one of the greatest crimes committed in the history of Western civilization. I am grateful that my maternal great-grandparents, Kalman and Ida Dorman of the Kiev region and Phillip Mendel (Shraga) and Ada Stein of Vilna (Vilnius), were able to escape the Czarist persecutions of Jews in the late nineteenth and early twentieth centuries to seek a new life in a land that granted the basic liberties that all human beings aspire to enjoy. But I shudder at the loss of the six million Jews murdered during the course of the Shoah or Holocaust, the millions more who perished in pogroms and persecutions prior to and after the Shoah, and those who might yet suffer if the lessons of the Shoah are not learned.

I would like to thank the various individuals who played important roles, whether consciously or not, in the conceptualization and writing of this volume.

My doctoral advisor, Rolf P. Knierim, a Methodist Old Testament scholar who served in the German army during the war, taught me the importance of the field of biblical theology and the methodological rigor necessary to engage it. The late Rabbi J. Jerome Pine of Decatur, Illinois, who trained me for Bar Mitzvah, stimulated my interests in religious observance and moral questions early in my life. Various colleagues have also provided important insights and opportunities for engagement with x the questions posed by the Shoah: John Fitzgerald and Henry Green of the University of Miami; Tammi Schneider, the late D. Z. Phillips, and Lori Anne Ferrell of the Claremont Graduate University; Jack Coogan, Kristin De Troyer, Dennis MacDonald, Susan Nelson, Frank Rogers, and Marjorie Suchocki of the Claremont School of Theology; Rabbi Mel Gottlieb and Tamar Frankiel of the Academy for Jewish Religion, California; Farooq Hamid of the University of California, Riverside; Antony Campbell, S.J., of the Jesuit Theological College, Parkville, Australia; Will Krieger of the University of Rhode Island; Wayne Horowitz of the Hebrew University of Jerusalem, Israel; Fred Greenspahn of Florida Atlantic University; Patricia Tull of Louisville Presbyterian Theological Seminary; and Esther Taus of Temple Beth El, San Pedro, California.

My doctoral student, the Rev. Hye Kyung Park, pursues issues raised in this volume in relation to the theological and social issues posed within her own culture in Korea. She read through the manuscript carefully and constructed the bibliography. She saved me from many oversights, but any remaining problems are attributed only to me. My doctoral students at the Claremont Graduate University, my ministerial and academic students at the Claremont School of Theology, and my rabbinical, cantorial, and chaplaincy students at the Academy for Jewish Religion, California, continue to provide insight in their own engagement in the issues raised in this volume.

My wife, Muna, and our daughter, Leah, always provide the love, support, and challenges necessary for me to carry out such work.

Finally, I would like to thank Zev Garber, Emeritus Professor of Jewish Studies at Los Angeles Valley College, for prompting me through his own work to recognize the theological importance of the Shoah. I met Zev as I was completing my own doctoral program at Claremont in 1983 when I sat in on his Second Temple and rabbinic-period Judaism course at the University of California, Riverside. Since that time, he has been a constant friend, wise mentor, and valued role model as I have pursued my own career in Jewish Studies.

In keeping with the concern for the sanctity of the divine name in various streams of Judaism, I employ the terms YHWH, the L-rd, G-d, and so forth.

Marvin A. Sweeney
San Dimas, California
10 Heshvan, 5768

AB	Anchor Bible
ABD	*Anchor Bible Dictionary,* 6 vols. Ed. David Noel Freedman, Gary A. Herion, David F. Graf, and John David Pleins. New York: Doubleday, 1992.
ABS	Archaeology and Biblical Studies
ACOT	Abingdon Old Testament Commentaries
AGJU	Arbeiten zur Geschichte des antiken Judentums und des Urchristentums
AnBib	Analecta biblica
ANEP	*The Ancient Near East in Pictures Relating to the Old Testament.* Ed. J. B. Pritchard. Princeton: Princeton University Press, 1954.
ANET	*Ancient Near Eastern Texts Relating to the Old Testament.* Ed. J. B. Pritchard. Princeton: Princeton University Press, 1969.
AOTC	Abingdon Old Testament Commentaries
BEATAJ	Beiträge zur Erforschung des Alten Testaments und des antiken Judentum
BETL	Bibliotheca ephemeridum theologicarum lovaniensium
BibOr	Biblica et orientalia
BibSem	The Biblical Seminar
BibThS	Biblisch-theologische Studien
BJS	Biblical and Judaic Studies
BZAW	Beihefte zur Zeitschrift für die alttestamentliche Wissenschaft

CAH	Cambridge Ancient History
CBQ	*The Catholic Biblical Quarterly*
CBR	Currents in Biblical Research
CHJ	*Cambridge History of Judaism*
ChrH	The Chronicler's History
ConBOT	Coniectanea biblica: Old Testament Series
ContCom	Continental Commentaries
CR:BS	*Currents in Research: Biblical Studies*
DDD²	*Dictionary of Deities and Demons in the Bible.* Ed. K. van der Toorn, et al. 2d ed. Leiden: Brill, 1999.
DtrH	Deuteronomistic History
EncJud	*Encyclopaedia Judaica.* Ed. C. Roth, et al. 16 vols. Jerusalem: Keter, n.d.
EvT	*Evangelische Theologie*
FAT	Forschungen zum Alten Testament
Fest.	Festschrift
FOTL	Forms of the Old Testament Literature
FRLANT	Forschungen zur Religionen und Literatur des Alten und Neuen Testaments
GCT	Gender, Culture, Theory
HCOT	Historical Commentary on the Old Testament
HSM	Harvard Semitic Monographs
HSS	Harvard Semitic Studies
HUCA	*Hebrew Union College Annual*
IBT	Interpreting Biblical Texts
IDBSup	*The Interpreter's Dictionary of the Bible Supplementary Volume.* Ed. K. Crim. Nashville: Abingdon, 1976.
JAOS	*Journal of the American Oriental Society*
JBL	*Journal of Biblical Literature*
JPS	Jewish Publication Society
JR	*Journal of Religion*
JSOTSup	Journal for the Study of the Old Testament Supplement Series
JSS	*Journal of Semitic Studies*
LHBOTS	Library of Hebrew Bible/Old Testament Series
NCB	New Century Bible Commentary
NICOT	New International Commentary on the Old Testament
OBT	Overtures to Biblical Theology
OBO	Orbis biblicus et orientalis

OTG	Old Testament Guides
OTL	Old Testament Library
SAC	Studies in Antiquity and Christianity
SBL	Society of Biblical Literature
SBLDS	Society of Biblical Literature Dissertation Series
SBLMS	Society of Biblical Literature Monograph Series
SBLSym	Society of Biblical Literature Symposium Series
SBS	Stuttgarter Bibelstudien
SBT	Studies in Biblical Theology
ScrHier	Scripta hierosolymitana
TSAJ	Texte und Studien zum antiken Judentum
VT	*Vetus Testamentum*
VTSup	Vetus Testamentum Supplements
WBC	Word Biblical Commentary
WMANT	Wissenschaftliche Monographien zum Alten und Neuen Testament
ZAW	*Zeitschrift für die alttestamentliche Wissenschaft*

The Shoah
and Biblical Theology

This volume considers the impact of the Holocaust—or Shoah as it is more properly known—on the reading of the Hebrew Bible in both Judaism and Christianity.[1] The Shoah raises fundamental questions concerning the presence, power, and righteousness of G-d and the presumed guilt and sin of those portrayed as subject to divine judgment in the Hebrew Bible. It is therefore imperative to consider the implications of the questions prompted by the Shoah in relation to the theological interpretation of the Hebrew Bible, recognized as foundational in both the Jewish and Christian traditions. The question is especially important since the Hebrew Bible considers events analogous to the Shoah—for instance, the destruction of the Northern Kingdom of Israel, the destruction of Jerusalem and the Babylonian exile, and the threat of the Persian Empire to exterminate the Jewish community of its time—in relation to its understanding of G-d, Israel/Judah, and the nations of the world at large.

Fundamentally, consideration of the Shoah points to a need to rethink traditional concepts of divine presence, power, and righteousness together with traditional notions of human guilt or sin in relation to G-d. Although many biblical theologians presume that traditional notions of divine power and righteousness and human guilt and sin before G-d constitute the fundamental viewpoint of the Hebrew Bible, sustained examination of the Hebrew Bible in relation to questions posed by the Shoah demonstrates that this viewpoint is only one among a number of

2

viewpoints raised among the books of the Hebrew Bible. Even among those books or writings in the Hebrew Bible that articulate traditional viewpoints of reward for righteousness and punishment for wrongdoing, problems emerge in their respective presentations of this issue, for example, Does G-d always act responsibility in the world? Are acts deemed as sinful in the Hebrew Bible actually sinful? What role must human beings assume when G-d fails to act or when G-d acts sinfully?

Altogether, this study argues that the Hebrew Bible is in dialogue concerning the issue of calamitous evil in the world much as modern theology is currently in dialogue concerning the theological significance of the Shoah. Given the theological problems posed by the Shoah and the debate concerning those problems, it is imperative that human beings take more responsibility as partners with G-d in creation—in dialogue with the Hebrew Bible and their respective religious traditions—to see to the establishment of justice and holiness in the world in which we all live. In the Lurianic Kabbalistic tradition of Judaism, such action is called *tikkun olam*, "repair of the world," insofar as human beings are expected to play the primary role in completing the creation of the world begun by G-d and thereby in restoring the presence of G-d that was shattered by the very act of creation itself.

The Shoah and Its Significance for Theology

Some six million Jews were deliberately and systematically murdered by Nazi Germany and its supporters during the course of the Shoah in World War II.[2] Other groups were also targeted by the Nazis, including gays and lesbians, Gypsies, Slavs, and others, but Jews were singled out for complete eradication on the basis of their birth insofar as Nazi Germany viewed Jews as the primary, irreversible, and relentless enemy that threatened to destroy German and, indeed, human civilization as a whole. Following the appointment of Adolf Hitler, leader of the National Socialist (Nazi) German Workers Party, as chancellor in 1933, Germany embarked upon a program of national restoration and conquest that sought to establish German or Aryan rule over all of Europe and ultimately the world. By identifying Jews as the enemy of the German people and the world at large, Hitler deliberately drew on the long history of Western anti-semitism from the Greco-Roman period through modern times as a means to unify the German or Aryan peoples of the world and to mobilize them to undertake his program of world domination.[3]

Such use of anti-semitism proved shockingly effective as large segments of the German and German-speaking populations of Europe, as well as major elements of other European nations, actively participated in or acquiesced to the extermination of the Jews throughout Europe. German action against Jews began in 1933 with the boycott of Jewish-owned shops and professional services and the opening of the first concentration camp at Dachau. The 1935 Nuremberg Laws stripped Jews of citizenship, prohibited intermarriage and sexual relations with Jews by non-Jews, and restricted Jewish employment of non-Jews. Following the annexation of Austria and the occupation of the Czech *Sudetenland* in 1938, *Kristallnacht* ("the night of broken glass") saw attacks throughout Germany and Austria on synagogues, Jewish businesses, and Jewish homes together with increased arrests of Jews. Forced emigration of German, Austrian, and Czech Jews began in 1939. With the conquest of Poland in 1939, Polish Jews were confined to ghettos, and they were increasingly executed by gunfire, asphyxiation, and other means. By 1941, Jews were transported eastward, and plans were made for mass execution and the disposal of bodies by more efficient and cost-effective means, including gas and crematoria at Auschwitz and other locations. The Wannsee Conference in early 1942 authorized the implementation of the "Final Solution," or extermination of the Jewish population of Europe. The ghettos in which Jews had been confined were emptied, and Jews were transported to death camps where they were systematically executed and their bodies cremated. Some concentration camps were employed as sources of slave labor to support the German economy and war effort. Those who were able worked on starvation rations in inhumane conditions until they were no longer capable. Those unable to work were quickly executed.

By the end of the war, Germany and its collaborators had succeeded in destroying approximately two-thirds of Europe's Jewish population (or one-third of the world Jewish population), which had constituted the primary center of Jewish life prior to the war. In the aftermath of the war, the centers of Jewish life shifted to America and the newly created state of Israel as European Judaism was unable to recover from the Shoah and subsequent Soviet persecution and as the Jewish populations of the Middle East were driven out by newly formed Arab governments following the establishment of modern Israel in 1948.

The relative silence of Christian churches during the Shoah is a particular problem that Christian theology is only now beginning to address.[4] Despite its origins as a Jewish sect, Christianity has a long

4   history of antagonism toward Jews beginning with the New Testament and continuing through medieval and modern times.[5] The charges in Matthew 27 that Jews chose to have the Romans execute Jesus and the statement "may his blood be on us and our children" (Matt 27:25) and the charges in John that Jews are the children of the devil and do the devil's bidding (John 8:44) played—and continue to play—an important role in shaping attitudes toward Jews in the church throughout its history. The rise of Christianity to its status as the state religion of the Roman Empire and its successors beginning with the reign of Constantine (306–337 C.E.) played a key role in defining the power of the church together with that of the state in European society to the detriment of Judaism. Beginning in the patristic period, the church's *adversos Iudaeos* tradition argued that Jews had been judged by G-d for rejecting Christ, and that the church had subsequently emerged as the true people of G-d.[6] The church employed the power of state deliberately to suppress Judaism and pointed to the oppressed state of Jews in Christian society as a means to demonstrate the consequences of failure to acknowledge Christ and church authority. Such a stance played a major role in promoting antagonism against Jews throughout the Christian world. Although the church is not directly responsible for the Nazi campaign to eradicate Jews and Judaism, Hitler viewed himself as fulfilling the task of world history as exemplified in the attitudes of the church toward Jews.

At the outset of Nazi rule in 1933, the Roman Catholic Church in Germany and the Nazi regime signed a concordat that safeguarded the position of the Church within the German nation. The Roman Catholic Church did not challenge the boycott against Jews, the Nuremberg laws, or the *Kristallnacht* pogroms. Although the Church did lend assistance to Jews who had converted to Roman Catholicism, it did not lend aid to Jews in general. The reign of Pope Pius XII, beginning in 1939, is a particular point of controversy due to his failure openly to challenge the Nazi regime and its policies toward Jews. Defenders of the pope maintain that such action would have been unsuccessful and even detrimental to the Jews. The Vatican's move to make wartime documents available for study has not silenced critics, particularly since these documents were selected, edited, and made available only on a limited basis.

The Protestant churches were far less unified than the Roman Catholic Church and represented a variety of viewpoints. In general, Protestants saw Jews as precursors to Christianity insofar as the Old Testament provided the foundation for the New Testament, but they tended to see relatively little role for Jews in the world other than ultimately to recognize

Christ. At the outset of the Nazi regime in 1933, the Protestant churches were unwilling to challenge the Nazis. A circle of Protestant thinkers formed the *Deutsche Christen* (German Christians) who called for enthusiastic support of the Nazis and church reforms, such as the removal of Jewish-born clergy, elimination of the Old Testament, and the portrayal of Jesus as a heroic Aryan. Anti-Nazi Protestant clergy, such as Karl Barth and Dietrich Bonhoeffer (executed by the Nazis late in the war), opposed the Nazi regime and the Germanic program of the *Deutsche Christen*, but such opposition tended to be the exception rather than the rule. Protestant Churches in western Europe (for instance, Denmark, the Netherlands, Norway) and America had far better—albeit still problematic—records.

In the aftermath of the war, theological discussion of the Shoah has grown steadily among both Jewish and Christian theologians.[7] Although slow to start due to the collective shock of the Jewish community at the magnitude and scope of the calamity, Jewish theologians such as Martin Buber and Abraham Joshua Heschel began to probe questions concerning the presence and role of G-d in relation to the Shoah and the task of human beings in its aftermath. Sparked especially by the provocative and groundbreaking work of Richard L. Rubenstein, who raised questions concerning Judaism's ability to maintain traditional viewpoints concerning divine presence and justice in the world, the issue of the Shoah has emerged as one of the dominant concerns of late-twentieth- and early-twenty-first-century Jewish thought. Although likewise slow to begin for much the same reasons as Jewish thinkers, the Roman Catholic and Protestant churches began to recognize the overwhelming significance of the Shoah as a challenge to traditional theological conceptions of divine power and the moral culpability of the church. A growing theological discussion of the implications of the Shoah derived from various sources, such as the work of Barth and Bonhoeffer noted above,[8] the initiatives of Pope John XXIII, and the Second Vatican Council, has begun to make itself felt.

Jewish Theological Discussion of the Shoah

Biblical theology must take account of the extensive Jewish theological discussion of the Shoah, insofar as this discussion raises crucial questions concerning the presence, power, and morality of G-d in relation to the Shoah and the role of human beings in the world when faced with the absence, impotence, or disengagement of G-d.

6   Jewish theological engagement with the Shoah actually began during the war itself as the intentions of the Nazis and the magnitude and scope of their plans became clear. Nevertheless, theological discussion of the Shoah in Jewish circles was somewhat limited insofar as Jews concentrated on efforts to mobilize action on the part of Western governments to intervene in an attempt to stop the genocide. Those efforts were relatively unsuccessful due to the overwhelming demands of the war, the prevalent anti-semitism among the Allies themselves, and the fact that Allied political and military options were limited even when there was sympathy for such efforts. In the aftermath of the war, Jews concentrated their efforts on rebuilding the lives of survivors of the Shoah, generally moving them to the newly created state of Israel or to diaspora communities in North America, South America, and elsewhere. The expulsion of Jews from the newly established Arab nations in the aftermath of the war further preoccupied the Jewish community, as did efforts to support and defend the new state of Israel from Arab assault.[9]

The first sustained theological responses to the Shoah began to appear during the 1950s and 1960s, although they tended to be bound up with the broader questions of Jewish understandings of G-d and human beings. Abraham Joshua Heschel's work, including his 1951 study, *Man Is Not Alone*; his 1955 study, *G-d in Search of Man: A Philosophy of Judaism*; and *The Prophets*, the 1962 English edition of his earlier 1936 doctoral dissertation, *Die Prophetie*, addressed fundamental questions of the relationship between G-d and human beings.[10] Heschel himself escaped from Germany and his native Poland at the outset of the war, although his mother and three sisters perished in the Shoah. Heschel was trained in modern critical biblical scholarship, philosophy, and art and aesthetics, but he was born into a Hasidic dynasty and trained in Hasidic/Kabbalistic tradition as well. His background included a profound understanding of Jewish tradition regarding G-d's ongoing interaction with human beings and the questions of theodicy. One example from that tradition is the *Heikhalot Rabbati*, the major work of early-rabbinic merkavah mysticism, which portrays G-d suggesting, when confronted by R. Nehunyah ben ha-Qanah, that the destruction of the Second Temple was a mistake. Another would be the Lurianic Kabbalah, which portrays creation as a process that compromises the infinite and ideal character of G-d and releases the aspects of evil and finiteness that are inherent in the divine personality. For Heschel, divine vulnerability and G-d's need for human beings became hallmarks of his work. Heschel's fundamental thesis was that anything said by human beings about G-d is inherently inadequate, that is, conceptual or rational knowledge and language do not provide the means for human beings to conceptualize, describe, or understand G-d. Rather, human beings must approach the panentheistic character of G-d that permeates all creation with radical amazement, awe, and engagement when one encounters the holy and transcendent. Such encounters are prompted by G-d's need for human beings or G-d's pathos in which G-d reaches out to human beings with emotion, passion, and feeling.

In Heschel's understanding, G-d is not the object of human knowledge; rather, G-d is the subject and humankind is the object of G-d's knowledge insofar as G-d needs humankind, sends the prophets to seek relationship with human beings, and is profoundly affected with outrage, sorrow, joy, approval, and so forth, by the actions of human beings in the world. The life of holiness sharpens human sensitivity to G-d and prepares humans to undertake the actions necessary to sanctify and perfect the world in which we live based in an intimate relationship with the divine who seeks us in the first place. Heschel's understanding of divine pathos and vulnerability paints a very different picture from the standard portrayal of an all-powerful and all-righteous G-d that rewards righteousness and punishes evil. Such a portrayal points fundamentally to the power and responsibility of humankind to ensure the integrity of our world.

Another early theologian who considered the theological ramifications of the Shoah was Rabbi Leo Baeck. Baeck was a Shoah survivor and prominent German Progressive Rabbi and theologian who moved to the United Kingdom after the war and later taught periodically at Hebrew Union College in the United States. His book *This People Israel: The Meaning of Jewish Existence* was originally written while he was incarcerated at Theresienstadt, published in German in 1955, and posthumously published in English in 1965.[11] Baeck reiterated his earlier position, typical of late-nineteenth- and early-twentieth-century liberal Jewish theologians, that ethics and monotheism stood at the basis of Jewish identity and peoplehood. Baeck maintained that the Shoah resulted from the failure of human morality, and that Jews must exercise the innate human capacity for moral autonomy and redouble their efforts to serve as an example to the rest of the world of morality and adherence to G-d.

Another of the early Jewish thinkers to address the theological problems posed by the Shoah was Martin Buber, professor of Jewish philosophy and mysticism at the Hebrew University of Jerusalem. Buber was already well known for his work *I and Thou*, which posited an intimate relationship of dialogue between G-d and human beings.[12] In his 1965 study *The Eclipse of G-d*, Buber questioned whether it was still possible to enter

8 into dialogue with G-d in the aftermath of the Shoah.[13] His question was prompted by the concept of *hester panim (hestēr pānîm)*, "the hidden face of G-d," in Jewish tradition, which posits that the all-powerful and righteous G-d sometimes chooses to remain hidden in times of crisis. Buber argued that human beings had practiced idolatry by following false gods, that is, humans had turned away from an intimate relationship with G-d in a modern, industrialized, and secular world, and thereby had destroyed their relationship with G-d. Although Buber's work made little reference to the Shoah and took up the broader question of secularism in the modern Western world, it had important ramifications for understanding the Shoah. Buber's work placed the onus on human wrongdoing by charging that human beings were responsible for driving G-d away in their lives.

The work of Ignaz Maybaum, *The Face of G-d after Auschwitz*, was published in 1965.[14] Maybaum was a prominent Austrian Reform Rabbi who served a pulpit in Germany and fled in 1939 to serve as rabbi in London and lecturer on theology at the Leo Baeck College until his retirement in 1963. Like many of the German progressive rabbis of his day, Maybaum is heavily influenced by the thought of Moses Mendelssohn, the eighteenth-century Jewish philosopher whose universalistic world view heralded the Enlightenment for Judaism and prompted Jews to consider the reform or modernization of Judaism and to engage in the surrounding Gentile societies of their day. Maybaum's argument focuses on two major points. First, he denies that the Shoah is a unique event and stresses its continuity with past calamities in Jewish history, such as the destructions of the First and the Second Temples. Second, the Shoah may be explained as a vicarious atonement of the victims of the Shoah for the sake of others.

In developing these two points, Maybaum takes a theological view of human history as a whole that owes much to the thought of Mendelssohn. He maintains that the covenant between G-d and the Jews is intended to make Jews into a unique people whose purpose is to give witness to the existence of G-d and divine involvement and purpose in the world. The role of Jews is to bring Gentiles into a relationship with G-d, which thereby explains the extensive interaction between Jews and Gentiles throughout human history. Jews must speak to Gentiles in a language that they will readily understand, that is, the language of violence and destruction. He therefore proposes two terms that designate events of destruction in world history. The Hebrew term *hurban (ḥurbān)*, "destruction," refers to major catastrophic events that convey a message to both Jews and Gentiles concerning the end of an old era and the beginning of a new one, such as the destruction of the First and Second Temples. The term *gezerah* (*gĕzērâ*), "evil decree," refers to a basically Jewish event that does not hold such significance for the relationship between Jews and Gentiles, such as the Spanish expulsion of 1492 or the Chmielnitzki massacres in Poland and the Ukraine in 1648–1667. Maybaum argues that the Shoah must be recognized as the third *ḥurban* in Jewish and Gentile history insofar as Gentile symbols, such as sacrifice and crucifixion, must be employed so that the significance of the event may be made known. He therefore maintains that Jews are sacrificed and suffer vicariously to raise the conscience of the Gentile world, to bring it to G-d, and to atone for the sins of humankind. The Shoah therefore marks the end of the medieval era in human history and the beginning of the modern age, which will see unprecedented cooperation between modern, that is, nonhalachic, Jews and modern, that is, ecumenical, Christians.

The inadequacy of Maybaum's position was immediately recognized insofar as he posited that Jews were destined to suffer and that the Shoah was theologically justified by the need to save the world. Rabbi Irving Greenberg, an Orthodox scholar at Yeshiva University, countered with the statement, "No statement—theological or otherwise—should be made that would not be credible in the presence of burning children."[15] Despite the clearly problematic nature of Maybaum's position, however, his work does pose fundamental questions of theodicy. Can G-d's love and justice be understood in relation to the Shoah? Is it even possible for the Shoah to be understood as a form of punishment? What sins would justify a punishment of the magnitude of the Shoah? Indeed, Maybaum's work raises the question of whether or not it is still possible to conceive of G-d and the Shoah in relation to the traditional categories of divine power and morality.

These issues were taken up in the following year by Richard L. Rubenstein, whose groundbreaking 1966 work *After Auschwitz: Radical Theology and Contemporary Judaism* raised fundamental questions concerning the traditional views of G-d and human action that had dominated Jewish (and Christian) theological thought.[16] Rubenstein is a Conservative Rabbi who served as the Hillel director at the University of Pittsburgh, professor at Florida State University, and later president of the University of Bridgeport. His entire understanding of Judaism is determined by the Shoah as he states, "The one measure of the adequacy of all contemporary Jewish theology is the seriousness with which they deal with the supreme problem of Jewish history."[17] For Rubenstein, the Shoah poses the major theological problem of Judaism, namely, If G-d is the G-d of history and Judaism/Israel is the chosen people, then what responsibility does G-d

10   bear for the Shoah? Either G-d used the Nazis as a tool to punish Jewish
sin as posited for G-d's use of Assyria and Babylonia in the Bible, or if the
Nazis were not G-d's tool of punishment, then how could G-d allow the
Shoah to happen?

Rubenstein's questions were motivated by a 1961 encounter with a
German Protestant clergyman, Heinrich Grueber, who asserted that the
Shoah was G-d's punishment of the Jews. For Rubenstein, this was "a theological point of no return," insofar as it entails that if G-d is the omnipotent
power of the universe, then the murder of six million Jews is the will of
G-d. He discounts the notion that the Shoah may be explained as punishment for sin. Such an assertion blasphemes against G-d, who is portrayed
as vindictive, and against the victims of the Shoah, who are portrayed as
sinful and deserving of death. Rubenstein asks, What sin would justify such
punishment? Because he is unable to accept such an assertion, he rejects
the classical Jewish theological framework by asserting that there is no G-
d and there is no covenant with Israel. On the basis of such a conclusion,
Rubenstein argues that we must recognize the meaninglessness of human
existence, that there is no divine will or concern, that there is no purpose
to human life in fulfilling a divine plan, and that the world is indifferent to
human beings. Taking an existential theological approach, Rubenstein then
asserts that human beings must themselves create meaning in the world.
With the death of G-d, the existence of the Jewish people then comes to the
forefront as the primary framework for Jewish existence.

Rubenstein maintains that Judaism must therefore be demythologized
by renouncing the idea of G-d and the status of the Jewish people as the
chosen people of G-d. He argues that anti-semitism is the product of the
mythic structures and interrelations of Jewish and Christian theologies.
The Jewish myth of the chosen people or the special nature of the Jews has
singled them out for destruction in the Gentile world. The Christian myth
that the church is the new Israel is in turn rooted in the Jewish myth of
chosenness, especially since the crucifixion of Christ becomes a deicidal
act of the chosen people in Christian scripture and theology. Every time
the Christian myth is retold, it plants the seeds of anti-semitism by charging the chosen people with deicide. Rubenstein maintains that although
the Nazis cannot be considered as a Christian movement, they picked
up this conceptualization from European culture and employed it as a
means to attack Jews—and ultimately Christianity as well—in their efforts
to reinvigorate the Teutonic heritage of northern Europe.

Rubenstein maintains that, insofar as the idea of chosenness is the
root of anti-semitism, Jews must reject chosenness in order to put an end

to anti-semitism. Such an act would enable Christians to look upon Jews in the same light as others. But it also entails that Christians must demythologize their tradition by rejecting the divinity of Jesus as the coming Christ. The future of Judaism thereby lies in seeking meaning not in religious or theological structures but in relation to the world of creation in which we live. This calls for the renewal of Zion. Returning to the soil or natural life in the land of Israel and rebuilding Israel points to the future of Judaism in the aftermath of the Shoah. By reinstating the Temple and its rituals, based on the natural cycles of agricultural life in the land, Rubenstein maintains that Jews could escape from history into the vitality and self-liberating promise of natural life in the land by creating a new sense of Jewish identity based upon national existence in the land of Israel.

Rubenstein's position is clearly based in the prevalent notions of existentialism and concern with secularization evident in the theological discussion of the time that produced the so-called death of G-d movement in the 1960s. Although it correctly points to the problematic of traditional theological notions of divine power and morality, it nevertheless continues to blame the victim for its victimization. In this case, the victim is not Jews themselves as Rubenstein so clearly states, but Judaism that by its very existence prompts anti-semitism and provokes its own destruction. Rubenstein also undercuts the very foundations of Jewish existence; that is, by eliminating G-d, he eliminates the primary foundation of Jewish nationhood in his conceptualization of the restoration of the land of Israel.

Response to Rubenstein's position was not long in coming. Emil Fackenheim, a Reform German Rabbi and theologian who was also a survivor of the Shoah, published his study, *G-d's Presence in History: Jewish Affirmations and Theological Reflections*, in 1970.[18] Fackenheim attempts to steer a middle course between the absolute faith of the pious who see no special theological problem in the Shoah and the negative approach of Rubenstein who maintains divine absence in the Shoah. The former alternative blasphemes against the victims of the Shoah whereas the latter alternative blasphemes against the G-d of the victims. Insofar as he believes in G-d, Fackenheim does not see a future for Judaism in Rubenstein's approach and therefore posits that the major theological problem of the Shoah is how to keep G-d and Israel together. He insists that Judaism must find the presence of G-d at Auschwitz even though we are unable to comprehend what G-d was doing. Fackenheim maintains that G-d was at Auschwitz and that G-d addresses Israel through Auschwitz just as G-d addresses Israel at Sinai.

Fackenheim's understanding of G-d and Auschwitz is heavily indebted to the concept of Israel's experience of G-d in history as articulated by the medieval philosopher Judah ha-Levi. Neither Fackenheim nor ha-Levi see Judaism as a theological system of monotheism and ethics, but instead see Judaism as reflection on and response to the experience of the human encounter with the divine in historical events. Fackenheim offers no reasoned proof for the existence of G-d, because such proof is impossible. Instead, he stresses that one must be prepared to hear G-d in the midst of the overwhelming historical events that constitute Jewish history. The most powerful events are public root events that create Jewish identity and continue to influence it throughout history, such as the exodus and the revelation of Torah at Sinai. But epoch-making events are not formative, and instead challenge the root experiences through new situations that test the resiliency and generality of the root experiences in new situations. Such epoch-making events include the destructions of the First and Second Temples that laid the foundations for new stages in Jewish history, such as the new exodus from Babylon that led to the postexilic restoration and the formation of Rabbinic Judaism.

Fackenheim maintains that Auschwitz is another epoch-making event that calls into question the presence of G-d. Insofar as Jews must affirm the presence of G-d even in the Shoah, the Shoah becomes an address by G-d to Israel that calls for response. Just as the commanding voice of Sinai reveals G-d's address to Israel, so the commanding voice of Auschwitz reveals G-d's will to Israel once again. Insofar as Hitler's goal was to eradicate Jews and Judaism, the response of the post-Shoah Jew is to refuse to hand Hitler "a posthumous victory." After Auschwitz, every Jew is commanded to adhere to G-d, to maintain Jewish identity, and to see to the future of Judaism in both the diaspora and in the newly emerging state of Israel.

Although Fackenheim is correct to observe that Rubenstein's agnostic approach to Judaism robs it of its foundations, his emphasis on faith in G-d is dangerously close to those who see no theological problem in the Shoah. Ultimately, Fackenheim affirms divine purpose in the deliberate murder of six million Jews even if we—like Job—do not know what that purpose is. He sees no moral problem in such an approach to G-d, and provides no end to such divine testing. Why would G-d feel it was necessary to put Judaism through such a trial again? Did Jews sin? Was G-d somehow preoccupied or out of control? When will the next test come and how many will perish then? His position also raises questions concerning divine vulnerability, specifically, If Jews do not respond to the commanding voice of Auschwitz, what then happens to G-d? G-d needs human affirmation to be known in the world. Nevertheless, Fackenheim's theological version of the imperative to rebuild speaks to the existential reality of post-Shoah (and post-Temple) Judaism, that is, nothing will happen unless we commit ourselves to Judaism in the aftermath of the destruction.

A second response to Rubenstein was Eliezer Berkovits's 1971 study, *Faith After the Holocaust.*[19] Berkovits was an Orthodox rabbi and theologian who originally taught in Berlin, but then moved to Sydney, Leeds, Boston, and finally to Chicago, where he taught at the Hebrew Theological College. His approach to the problems posed by the Shoah delves into Jewish tradition, but focuses on the question of how human beings will take responsibility for rebuilding the world in the aftermath of the Shoah.

Berkovits begins by noting that the Shoah is not a unique event in Jewish history. Anti-semitism is a repetitive pattern in Jewish history as the medieval destruction of the Rhineland Jewish community, the Spanish expulsion of the Jews, the Chmielnitzki massacres, the Czarist May Laws, and so many other examples amply illustrate. The classical response to and evaluation of such suffering and martyrdom in Jewish tradition is the notion of *Kiddush ha-Shem (qiddûš haššem)*, the sanctification of the Divine Name. *Kiddush ha-Shem* is an ultimate act of trust in G-d that affirms G-d's righteousness and honors G-d's name even if the justice of the act may be questioned.

Berkovits rejects the notion that the Shoah is due to Jewish sin, that is, *mippenei ḥaṭṭaʾeinu (mippĕnê haṭṭāʾĕnû)*, "because of our sins," in Talmudic discourse. He maintains that the Shoah is an act of absolute injustice on G-d's part and that it represents the biblical concept of *hester panim (hestēr pānîm)*, "the hidden face (of G-d)." In probing the question why G-d hides the divine face, Berkovits maintains that such an act is necessary for human beings to begin to exercise full moral responsibility as partners with G-d in the world of creation. His position draws upon the traditional Jewish concept that the task of the human being is to complete the creation that G-d begins by sanctifying and perfecting the world in which we live. Consequently, G-d must withdraw from the world at times to allow humans the opportunity to develop morally, to exercise free will, and to fulfill the divine purpose for human beings in the world. Human beings must learn the consequences of choice, even when they are tragic. G-d cannot intervene in such cases because intervention would interfere with the learning in which humans must necessarily engage. Jews must

14   focus on the positive side of G-d's presence as well, as exemplified in the creation of modern Israel, because to focus only on the Shoah reveals only one side of G-d's personality.

Such a position provides an appropriate emphasis on the responsibility of human beings for the world in which we live, even in the aftermath of disaster. But Berkovits's position echoes Maybaum insofar as divine withdrawal and the evil that potentially follows becomes a redeeming element. G-d hides the divine face so that human beings might learn to exercise free will responsibly. The Shoah then becomes necessary and justifiable insofar as it advances human moral consciousness. Such legitimization of the Shoah is as unacceptable here as it is in Maybaum's notion of vicarious suffering for the betterment of humankind. Berkovits's position also points to the capriciousness of G-d insofar as a beneficent, active, and righteous divine presence cannot always be presumed in human existence. Nevertheless, it leaves open the question of divine fidelity or reliability, in Hebrew, *ḥesed*, a cornerstone of Jewish tradition concerning G-d's commitment to relationship with Israel. How do human beings reestablish relationship with G-d in the aftermath of such abandonment?

Indeed, the question of G-d's power, righteousness, integrity, and presence in the aftermath of the Shoah has emerged as the key question of Jewish theology in subsequent discussion from the 1970s to the present. Elie Wiesel has been a particularly important figure in bringing the theological issues of the Shoah to public attention by his use of novels and other forms of popular and performance literature. Wiesel recounts his own experiences at Auschwitz in the autobiographical novel, *Night*, in which his witness of the murder of his family and others around him prompts his fundamental questioning of the silence of G-d in the face of mass murder.[20] His recognition of G-d's betrayal of humanity prompts his abandonment of Jewish religious practice and leads him to consider the absurdity of G-d. A second novel, *Dawn*, portrays the protagonist Elisha—apparently named for the Talmudic heretic Elisha ben Abuyah or Aḥer—as a Jewish concentration-camp survivor and member of a Jewish terrorist organization who is selected to execute a British soldier in Mandate Palestine prior to the establishment of the state of Israel.[21] For Wiesel, the establishment of Israel entails the rejection of G-d (cf. Rubenstein above) insofar as Jews are left to fend for themselves in the world. A third novel, *The Accident*, portrays the protagonist Eliezer as an Israeli newspaper correspondent who reflects on the nature of G-d. Eliezer sees G-d as a malevolent being who creates human beings as a means for relief from loneliness (cf. Heschel above) and abuses them as toys for amusement.[22]

Wiesel's play *The Trial of G-d* portrays three Jewish itinerant actors in the village of Shamgorad, which was the site of a pogrom that left only two Jewish survivors, at Purim time in 1649.[23] The *Purimspiel,* or Purim play, depicts a trial of G-d in which a mysterious figure named Sam is the only person who will defend the character of G-d against charges that G-d has neglected and abused the Jewish people. After declaring that G-d is just and that the task of humans is to love and praise G-d, Sam reveals that he is actually Satan who laughs in mockery at those who accepted his defense of G-d.

Arthur Cohen, a modern Jewish theologian, novelist, and art and literary critic, published *The Tremendum* in 1981 in an effort to address the theological problems posed by the Shoah.[24] For Cohen, there is no explanation or meaning for the Shoah. Borrowing language from Rudolf Otto's *The Idea of the Holy,*[25] Cohen posits that the idea of G-d as the *Mysterium Tremendum,* the utter mystery, is countered by the notion of the human *tremendum,* in which human beings and not G-d must be recognized as the true actors in the world. The Shoah, like the destruction of the Temples and other such phenomena, is a caesura in Jewish history that demands examination as an eruption of the dark side of human life in history. It evokes fear for Jews that the Jewish people is not eternal and that Jews are not the chosen people of G-d. The *tremendum* marks an end to classical Jewish theology, which had not advanced since the Talmudic period when G-d was understood to act through Torah and the actions of human beings. Although he posits divine existence, Cohen maintains that Jewish thought must also posit the existence of evil—based in part on the Kabbalistic notion that evil was released within the divine at the time of creation. G-d's presence ebbs and flows together with the presence and actions of humankind in the world. Insofar as divine presence is intimately intertwined with the human, the human being emerges as the key figure who can manifest the presence of G-d in the world—or not. Historical events then emerge as the product of human freedom rather than of divine causality. In Cohen's understanding, G-d is present and involved in human events, and represents the ideal hope of the future, but G-d is influenced and potentially restricted by the human. Ultimately the Shoah emerges as the product of human action in the world.

Finally, an innovative 1993 study by David R. Blumenthal, *Facing the Abusing G-d: A Theology of Protest,* reconsiders traditional theology's notion of G-d by drawing on the experience of victims of child abuse.[26] Blumenthal, best known for his work in Jewish mysticism (which itself focuses especially on the question of theodicy), notes how classical

16 theological responses to the Shoah typically posit that G-d does not exist or that G-d is righteous and that human beings are not. Based on his own expertise in Jewish mysticism, which so frequently points to the inherent vulnerability or evil of the divine personality, Blumenthal asks, What if G-d is not just, particularly since the Shoah itself is a paradigmatic example of injustice in the world? Taking an analogy from contemporary concern with the abusive behavior of spouses, parents, clergy, and so forth, Blumenthal posits that G-d may be viewed as an abuser insofar as the Shoah constitutes abuse perpetrated or permitted by the ultimate figure tasked with the well-being and security of the Jewish people and humankind in general. In such a model, the abusive perpetrator is one who is known to and loved by the victim; the abuse breaches or takes advantage of a relationship based on trust; the abuser blames the victim; and the abusive relationship seeks the continued commitment of love while continuing to perpetrate the abuse. Insofar as the Kabbalistic concept of *tzimtzum* (ṣîmṣûm), "(divine) withdrawal or contraction" at the time of creation, produces the evil side or evil face of G-d in the world, G-d emerges as a presence who is unjust and an abuser in relation to human beings whom G-d created and who are dependent upon G-d. Just as victims of abuse must learn to stand up to the abuser and ultimately to forgive the abuser in order to reintegrate themselves and place their own lives back into order, so Jews must learn to forgive the abusive G-d, not because G-d deserves it in any way, but because such forgiveness of the abuser is the necessary precondition for the recovery of the victim of abuse. In order to illustrate and examine the dynamics of this view, Blumenthal presents study materials for four psalms, including Psalms 128, 44, 109, and 27, which take up different aspects of lamentation and appeals for help to G-d who does not respond in a time of threat. In Blumenthal's understanding, the human victims of the Shoah—whether those who experienced the Shoah themselves or those who are left with the legacy of the Shoah—must take responsibility for their recovery and restoration because G-d—for whatever reason—is unable or unwilling to do so.

As this survey of Jewish theological discussion of the Shoah demonstrates, several key issues emerge. First is the question of divine power and righteousness in relation to the Shoah, that is, Are we still able to posit that G-d is the omnipotent and righteous sovereign of all creation or must we recognize divine vulnerability, impotence, absence, or even malevolence in the aftermath of the Shoah? Second is the question of the guilt of the victims, that is, Insofar as classical theology posits that punishment comes as the result of human wrongdoing and righteousness is rewarded with blessing, must we posit that the victims of the Shoah suffered punishment for their own sins or those of humankind or must we instead recognize that suffering (and reward) is not the necessary result of human moral action? Third, given the apparent inability or unwillingness of G-d to shield human beings from gross injustice, what role must human beings take to protect themselves from such injustice and to ensure the righteousness and sanctity of the world of creation in which we live?

Such questions of the power and righteousness of G-d and the responsibility of human beings lie at the core of theology from antiquity to the present. Indeed, Christian theologians are beginning to recognize these issues as well, insofar as historians of Christianity and theology have begun to reexamine the church's attitudes toward Judaism and its treatment of Jews throughout the history of Christianity. And yet it is striking how little a role the Bible has played in this discussion, especially since the Bible is the foundational holy scripture of both Judaism and Christianity in its various forms. With only a few exceptions, biblical theologians have largely overlooked the significance of the Shoah for biblical interpretation, which is a particularly egregious problem insofar as the Hebrew Bible is intimately concerned with the Babylonian exile and the destruction of Jerusalem and Solomon's Temple. In the case of Christian scripture, the New Testament is bound up with the questions posed by the destruction of the Second Temple as a harbinger of divine action in relation to the origins of Christianity.

In order to understand the problems posed by the failure of biblical theology—particularly Old Testament theology—to account for the Shoah, we may now turn to discussion of the theological interpretation of the Hebrew Bible in the twentieth century.

Biblical Theology and the Shoah

Despite the attention that the Shoah now receives in both Jewish and Christian theological discussion, it is nevertheless striking that the Shoah has played so little a role in biblical theology until relatively recent times.[27] In the case of Judaism, biblical theology itself is only now beginning to establish itself as a legitimate field of Jewish thought and the Shoah is one of the issues that Jewish biblical theologians are beginning to consider. In the case of Christianity, however, the absence of the Shoah as a topic of concern until very recent times is particularly problematic since the

Bible ideally plays the foundational role in defining Protestant Christian thought and an increasingly important role in Roman Catholic theology. In order to provide a foundation for considering the impact of the Shoah on biblical theology, we must briefly consider the state of Christian biblical theology immediately prior to and following World War II.

Christian biblical theology was especially preoccupied with the question of the interrelationship between history and theology in biblical interpretation throughout the twentieth century. Nevertheless, historically oriented biblical theologians were quite capable of constructing biblical theology in a manner that addressed the contemporary world. Particularly noteworthy are the works on Old Testament theology by Walter Eichrodt and Gerhard von Rad, generally identified as the two most important Old Testament theologians of the twentieth century. Although both were known for their preoccupation with the historical reconstruction of ancient Israel and Judah in relation to their overriding theological perspectives, their works provide an opportunity to reflect on Christianity's relationship with Judaism.

Walter Eichrodt is generally recognized as the most important Old Testament theologian prior to World War II. He wrote a still-influential three-volume work in German (two volumes in the English edition) during the years 1933–1939—the very years of the rise of the Nazi state—that took up the concept of covenant as the central concern of the Old Testament.[28] Although Eichrodt was especially concerned with the historical dimensions of the Old Testament text, his concern with the fundamental role of the concept of covenant in the Old Testament points to the larger question of Christianity's relationship with Judaism, insofar as the old covenant of Moses would be followed by the new covenant based on Christ as articulated in the New Testament. Regretfully, Eichrodt's antisemitism is evident in his view of Judaism's "torso-like appearance" in relation to Christianity."[29]

Gerhard von Rad is generally recognized as the most important Old Testament theologian of the latter half of the twentieth century. Von Rad's *heilsgeschichtliche* (sacred historical) treatment of Old Testament theology employed the tradition-historical method to construct a kerygmatic reading of the Old Testament. Historical reconstruction therefore played a key role in his efforts to understand the presentation of G-d's actions in relation to Israel throughout history from the time of creation to the eschatological future.[30] Fundamentally, the Old Testament in von Rad's view presents ancient Israel's witness and response to YHWH's saving acts in world history. Insofar as the Prophets conclude the Old Testament and define the future of G-d's relationship with Israel and humanity at large in von Rad's scheme, the New Testament constitutes the basic substance of that future. Again, the Old Testament emerges as a precursor to the New Testament. Von Rad, while not expressing overt anti-semitism, ignores the role of postbiblical Judaism.

Similar observations may be made concerning other Old Testament theologies of the early- to mid-twentieth centuries, namely, they do not take up the question of Judaism, but instead focus on justifying the New Testament and Christianity in relation to the Old Testament. This is particularly striking when one considers the attention that the Hebrew Bible pays to the question of destruction and exile, that is, the destruction of the Northern Kingdom of Israel by the Assyrians in 722/1 B.C.E., the destruction of Jerusalem and Solomon's Temple together with the Babylonian exile in 587/6 B.C.E., and the attempt by the Persian governmental official Haman to destroy the Jewish people during the reign of Ahasuerus. Although neither the destruction of northern Israel nor the destruction of Jerusalem may be considered as equivalent to the Nazi attempt to exterminate the entire Jewish people, both speak to the question of Jewish suffering at Gentile hands. Even in the aftermath of the Shoah, mid-twentieth-century Old Testament theology simply presupposed that both destructions represented the righteous judgment of G-d. The case of Esther is somewhat different, insofar as it portrays a deliberate attempt to destroy the entire Jewish population of the Persian Empire, but Esther is largely ignored in the works of Eichrodt and von Rad and other biblical theologians. Most interpreters correctly recognize its character as a work of literary fiction and therefore do not take it seriously as a work of history.[31] Esther is considered theologically problematic in the view of those works that do treat the book because G-d does not appear in the Hebrew version of the book and because Esther purportedly demonstrates Jewish hatred toward Gentiles. Of course, such a view unjustifiably pushes aside the fact that the Persian government, under the influence of Ahasuerus's government minister, Haman, attempted to exterminate the entire Jewish people.

Although many recent Old Testament theologies continue to focus on the classic themes of the field and ignore the significance of the Shoah, Jewish theological discussion of the Shoah is beginning to have its impact on Christian theology in general and biblical theology in particular. The groundbreaking 1962 study by Jules Isaac, *The Teaching of Contempt: Christian Roots of Anti-Semitism*, did much to awaken Christian scholars to the role of the New Testament and early Christianity in fomenting anti-Jewish attitudes.[32] Likewise, the 1974 study by Rosemary Radford Ruether, *Faith and Fratricide: The Theological Roots of Anti-Semitism*, demonstrated the role that patristic literature played in developing Christian anti-semitism, although her 1989 volume, *The Wrath of Jonah: The Crisis of Religious Nationalism in the Israeli-Palestinian Conflict*, presents a very distorted view of modern Israel's history that borders on more recent forms of anti-semitism in its attempts to characterize modern Israel in Nazi-like terms.[33] Clark Williamson's 1993 study, *A Guest in the House of Israel: Post-Holocaust Church Theology*, provides a very cogent analysis of contemporary Christian theology and New Testament studies that calls upon scholars to rethink the classic Christian expressions of anti-semitism in systematic theology and biblical exegesis.[34] Katharina von Kellenbach's 1994 *Anti-Judaism in Feminist Religious Writings* points to the emergence of anti-semitism in modern feminist religious thought where Judaism so frequently functions as the paradigm for patriarchy.[35] Tania Oldenhage's 2002 study, *Parables for Our Time: Rereading New Testament Scholarship after the Holocaust*, identifies anti-Semitic impulses in Gospel scholarship throughout the twentieth century and into the present.[36]

The impact of theological discussion of the Shoah is now making itself felt in the field of Old Testament theology. Jon Levenson's 1988 study, *Creation and the Persistence of Evil: The Jewish Drama of Divine Omnipotence*, demonstrates that the problem of theodicy is an ongoing issue throughout the Hebrew Bible insofar as YHWH's righteousness, fidelity, and power are constantly challenged in biblical literature.[37] Interestingly, this study followed his well-known essay, "Why Jews Are Not Interested in Biblical Theology," originally published in 1987, which argued that the anti-semitism so frequently expressed in the field convinced Jews that engagement in the field was not worthwhile.[38] Emil Fackenheim's 1990 study, *The Jewish Bible after the Holocaust: A Rereading*, points to the challenge posed to biblical interpretation by the Shoah, insofar as the significance of the issue has so frequently been overlooked.[39] The book of Esther, for example, posits the absence of G-d when a government attempts to destroy the Jewish people, and the book of Job leaves unanswered the question of justice in the killing of Job's ten children even after his fortunes are restored.

Walter Brueggemann's 1997 *Theology of the Old Testament: Testimony, Dispute, Advocacy* focused in general on the communicative aspect of the Hebrew Bible in its efforts to engage in discourse and dialogue about G-d.[40] As part of his discussion of this discourse, Brueggemann very pointedly examined the problem of the continued existence of evil in the world stating that "an Old Testament theology cannot usefully be organized with reference to the Holocaust," but that it "cannot proceed without acknowledgement of the profound and unutterable disruption of the interpretative enterprise that is embodied in the Holocaust."[41] The issue of the Shoah constitutes "a massive and unanswerable challenge to claims about (YHWH's) sovereignty and fidelity"[42] as it does to similar problems for absolutizing Christian claims concerning Jesus Christ.

Rolf Rendtorff's 2001 *Theologie des Alten Testaments. Eine kanonischer Entwurf*, translated into English in 2005 as *The Canonical Hebrew Bible: A Theology of the Old Testament*,[43] calls for a common Jewish and Christian reading of the Hebrew Bible, insofar as both traditions share the same scripture and must recognize their inherent interrelationship. Such a proposal is problematic insofar as its goal to arrive at a common understanding of the Bible would undermine recognition of the distinctive theological identities of Judaism and Christianity, but it is nevertheless motivated by a concern to overcome the theological anti-semitism that has so poisoned relations between Judaism and Christianity throughout history. Concern with the question of the Shoah also appears in the 2000 volume of essays edited by Tod Linafelt, *Strange Fire: Reading the Bible after the Holocaust*,[44] which considers the impact of the Shoah on biblical interpretation, and in selected commentaries published in *The New Interpreter's Bible*, such as the commentaries on Ezekiel by Katherine Pfisterer Darr and on Lamentations by Kathleen O'Connor.[45] James Crenshaw's *Defending G-d: Biblical Responses to the Problem of Evil*, likewise constitutes an important probe into theological problems posed by the Shoah.[46]

The growing concern with the theological problems posed by the Shoah to traditional conceptions of divine omnipotence, righteousness, engagement, and fidelity appear thus far in a somewhat piecemeal fashion, insofar as the Old Testament theologies by Brueggemann and Rendtorff only provide introductory treatments of the issue and most other studies take up only individual biblical passages, books, or thematic concerns. Nevertheless, study of the issue thus far indicates that the problems posed by the Shoah pose a fundamental challenge not only to our traditional conceptions of G-d, but to our reading of the Bible in general. Insofar as the Hebrew Bible has been so frequently employed as a model for understanding divine righteousness and judgment of a sinful Israel as a prelude to the New Testament, this volume attempts an analysis of the problems posed by the Shoah for reading the Hebrew Bible in its entirety. This study attempts to demonstrate that modern interpreters must raise critical questions concerning our understanding of G-d's power, righteousness, engagement, and fidelity in relationship to Israel/Judah and the world

22 | at large. Far from calling for abandonment of G-d or the respective traditions of Judaism and Christianity, this study argues that the problems posed by the Shoah call for human beings to take on greater responsibility for the sanctity, well-being, and fundamental justice of the world in which we live. Such a task is envisioned by the Hebrew Bible, which views human beings as partners with G-d in completing and fulfilling the world of creation that G-d has granted us.

ONE

Abraham and the Problem of Divine Fidelity

God allowing evil in his creation

Although the questions of theodicy and the character of G-d have emerged as central questions in theological discussion of the Shoah, they have—until recently—had relatively little impact on the study of the ancestral narratives of the Pentateuch. Insofar as Genesis defines the relationship between G-d and the earliest ancestors of Israel, such questions would be foundational for reading the narratives concerning Abraham and Sarah—as well as the other patriarchs and matriarchs—now that interpreters are becoming increasingly aware of the pervasive nature of the question of theodicy as well as the characterization of G-d throughout biblical literature.

Modern critical study of the Abraham traditions in Genesis has evolved considerably over the past century.[1] At the end of the nineteenth century, Wellhausenian literary-critical discussion emphasized the identification of the J, E, and P sources that scholars believed underlay the present form of the pentateuchal narrative. Such concerns addressed the question of the compositional history of the Genesis narrative, but left readers with a relatively fragmented text in which narrative blocks would be isolated from their current literary contexts and reconstructed into a new narrative sequence in relation to other textual blocks deemed to originate in the same source. Source analysis thereby constructed the character of G-d as an anthropomorphic character who interrelated with human beings in the J source; as a somewhat distant figure who communicated with humans through angels and other intermediaries in the E source; or

24   as a wholly/holy other deity who made pronouncements to human beings in the P source.

The tradition-historical analysis pioneered by Gunkel and his followers sometimes emphasized divine deception or playfulness in their efforts to emphasize the folkloric character of the pentateuchal narratives, but these were seen as expressions of the primitive social context that produced early forms of the patriarchal traditions.[2] For all the variety in the presentation of G-d in each source, source and tradition-historical analysis did little to raise fundamental questions concerning the character of G-d or divine righteousness. Although YHWH might appear as somewhat of a deceptive trickster in the J source, biblical scholars tended not to raise fundamental questions about G-d's character. Instead, they generally accepted G-d's sovereignty, righteousness, and fidelity as givens in the text, particularly as the text evolved to its later forms, while giving some leeway to the means by which such qualities were expressed. Historical and archeological scholarship of the early twentieth century likewise did little to challenge the portrayal of divine sovereignty or righteousness, insofar as it was fundamentally concerned with establishing the historicity of the patriarchal narratives rather than with exploring the divine character.[3]

But during the latter half of the twentieth century, exegesis of the ancestral narratives began to change as interpreters began to question the historical paradigms of the early half of the century and to move instead to more sophisticated understandings of the literary and social dimensions of biblical narrative. Source analysis had failed to demonstrate fully coherent narratives for the J and E traditions, and many interpreters noted that the priestly material was hardly monolithic and that priestly or cultic concerns could appear throughout the monarchic period.[4] Concomitant difficulties in reconstructing the historical and social contexts of the ancestral narratives likewise pushed interpreters to reconsider their views of biblical narrative, not simply as factual accounts of historical events, but as nuanced portrayals of figures from the distant past from the standpoint of much later historical settings.[5] Although tradition-historical analysis had proved very promising, the difficulties in reconstructing hypothetical oral tradition prompted scholars to take the present form of the narrative far more seriously as an object of research and reflection.

As a result of these difficulties, scholars increasingly began to consider the final literary form of the Genesis narrative, first from the standpoint of redaction-critical analysis—which attempted to explain the present text as the product of a historical process of composition—and then from the standpoint of synchronic plot and character analysis.[6]

Although such work tended to concentrate on the human characters in the Genesis narrative, interpreters increasingly began to recognize that G-d also functions as a major character within the Genesis narratives and that the characterization of G-d therefore demands scholarly attention.[7] Freed from the presuppositions of historical analysis that the trickster or deceptive nature of G-d's character in Genesis is simply the product of a primitive and theologically unsophisticated stage in Israelite religious development, scholars are now coming to recognize that divine duplicity and deception cannot be dismissed as the product of primitive culture, but must be taken into account in biblical interpretation. Insofar as the Abraham and Sarah traditions revolve around the question of the birth of a son to Sarah and therefore the continuation of the covenant between G-d and Abraham, this points to a fundamental concern with divine fidelity in the Genesis narratives concerning Israel's first ancestors, Abraham and Sarah.

The Toledoth Formulae

In order to examine the characterization of G-d in the Abraham and Sarah traditions, it is first necessary to delineate the textual block in which these traditions appear. Although the Abraham and Sarah traditions appear roughly in Genesis 12–25, literary study of Genesis—and indeed of the entire Pentateuch—points to a formulaic literary feature, the so-called *toledoth* (*tôlĕdōt*) formula, which defines the literary structure of the larger text that includes the Abraham and Sarah narratives. In his foundational study of the P tradition in the Pentateuch, Frank Moore Cross Jr. argues that the P redactors of the Pentateuch employed the *toledoth* formulae to organize the literary structure of the book of Genesis and the itinerary notices to organize the literary structure of the narrative in Exodus, Leviticus, and Numbers.[8] In the first instance, the *toledoth* formula refers to instances in which the formulaic expression, *wĕʾelleh tôlĕdōt [personal name]*, for example "and these are the generations of Terah" (Gen 11:27), and its variations, in which the formula introduces narratives that feature the lifetimes and activities of the descendants of the figure in question. In the second instance, the itinerary formulae refer to the notices concerning the locations of Israel's encampment during its journey from Egypt to Moab immediately prior to its entry into the promised land, for instance, *wayyisʿû bĕnê yiśrāʾēl mēraʿmĕsēs sukkōtāh*, "and the people of Israel journeyed from Rameses to Sukkot" (Exod 12:37).

Cross's hypothesis raises two major issues. First is the role of the initial *toledoth* formula in Gen 2:4a, *ēlleh tôlĕdôt haššāmayim wĕhāᵃreṣ bĕhibbārĕᵃm*, "these are the generations of the heavens and the earth when they were created." Interpreters have been divided on the function of this statement. Some argue that it functions as a summation of the narrative concerning the creation of heaven and earth in Gen 1:1—2:3, whereas others point to its introductory role in relation to the following narratives concerning human origins beginning in Gen 2:4b. Although the references to "heaven and earth" and the use of the term *bĕhibbārĕᵃm*, "when they were created," suggest a retrospective viewpoint that would support the former interpretation, several indicators point to a prospective viewpoint. First is the use of the term *tôlĕdôt*, based on the verb root *yld*, "to give birth," which indicates what is generated from the heavens and the earth, namely, the human beings that are noted in Gen 1:26-28. Second is the literary function of the other *toledoth* formulae, which note the generations of an ancestral figure, and then proceed to discuss that figure's descendants, for instance, the notice concerning Adam in Gen 5:1 introduces a genealogy of Adam's descendants in Gen 5:1—6:8; the notice concerning Noah in Gen 6:9 introduces the narrative concerning Noah and his sons in Gen 6:9—9:29; the notice concerning the sons of Noah in Gen 10:1 introduces genealogies of Noah's sons in Gen 10:1—11:9; the notice concerning Shem in Gen 11:10 introduces a genealogy of Shem's descendants in Gen 11:10-26; the notice concerning Terah in Gen 11:27 introduces the Abraham narratives in Gen 11:27—25:11; the notice concerning Ishmael in Gen 25:12 introduces a genealogy of Ishmael's descendants in Gen 25:12-18; the notice concerning Isaac in Gen 25:19 introduces the Jacob narratives in Gen 25:19—35:29; the notice concerning Esau in Gen 36:1 introduces Esau's genealogy in Gen 36:1—37:1; and the notice concerning Jacob in Gen 37:2 introduces the Joseph narratives in Gen 37:2—50:26. As these examples indicate, Gen 2:4a may have somewhat of retrospective function in relation to Gen 1:1—2:3, but they also point forward to the accounts of Adam (and Eve) as the beginning of a sequence of accounts that take up early human history from the time of creation through the time of Joseph. In the case of the longer narratives—for instance, Adam (Eve), Noah (sons), Terah (Abraham), Isaac (Jacob), and Jacob (Joseph)—the narrative points to the key figures in the development of the people Israel. In the case of the shorter narratives—for instance, Ham and Japhet, Ishmael, and Esau—the narrative points to those lines that spin off from the main characters to develop humankind at large. The resulting structure of Genesis therefore emerges as an introductory narrative concerning the creation of heaven and earth in Gen 1:1—2:3, followed by a sequence of narratives in Gen 2:4—50:26, each introduced by an example of the *toledoth* formula, which takes up the development of Israel within the context of humankind.

The second issue is the role of the itinerary formula in the literary structure of Exodus, Leviticus, and Numbers. Here, the structural role of the itinerary formula is rather straightforward, insofar as the formulae point to the movements of Israel from Egypt to Moab as a basic plot element in the pentateuchal narrative. Thus, the narrative begins in Exod 1:1—12:36 with Israel in Egypt as the site for the initial enslavement and the encounter between YHWH (represented by Moses and Aaron) and Pharaoh that leads to Israelite slaves' release at Rameses. Itinerary formulae, each of which introduces a narrative block that recounts a successive stage in the journey, then follow. Thus, the notice in Exod 12:37 introduces Israel's journey from Rameses to Sukkot in Exod 12:37—13:19 that sees the redemption of the firstborn; Exod 13:20 introduces the journey from Sukkot to Etam in Exod 13:20-22 that highlights YHWH's representation as a pillar of fire and cloud, replicating the image of a Temple altar in operation; Exod 14:1-2 introduces the journey from Etam to the Red/Reed Sea in Exod 14:1—15:21 that focuses on Israel's deliverance at the sea; Exod 15:22 introduces the journey from the sea to the wilderness of Shur/Elim in Exod 15:22-27 that focuses on water in the wilderness; Exod 16:1 introduces the journey from Elim to the wilderness of Sin in Exod 16:1-36 that focuses on quails and manna; Exod 17:1 introduces the journey from Sin to Rephidim in Exod 17:1—18:27 that takes up Amalek and Jethro; Exod 19:1 introduces the journey from Rephidim to Sinai in Exod 19:1—Num 10:10 that takes up the lengthy narrative concerning the revelation at Sinai; Num 10:11-12 introduces the journey from Sinai to the wilderness of Paran in Num 10:11—19:22 that takes up the motif of rebellion in the wilderness; Num 20:1 notes the journey from Paran to the wilderness of Zin/Kadesh in Num 20:1-21 that again notes water from the rock; Num 20:22 introduces the journey from Zin/Kadesh to Mt. Hor in Num 20:22—21:3 that takes up the death of Aaron; Num 21:4 introduces the journey from Hor to Edom/Moab in Num 21:4-35 that sees the defeat of Sihon and Og; and Num 22:1 introduces the arrival at Moab in Num 22:1—36:13 that sees census and organization of the people prior to their entry into the promised land.

Two questions remain open when considering the *toledoth* organization of Genesis and the itinerary organization of Exodus–Numbers. First, What is the relation of Deuteronomy to the preceding material,

28　　particularly since Deuteronomy continues to portray the people of Israel in Moab prior to their entry into the promised land? Second, What is the relationship between the two textual blocks in Genesis and Exodus–Numbers that are organized according to such different principles?

The first question is easily answered. Because Deuteronomy portrays the people of Israel in Moab in keeping with their arrival in Moab in Num 22:1—36:13, Deuteronomy must be subsumed into the structural organization of the itinerary pattern identified in Exodus–Numbers. It is clear that Deuteronomy is not written with this structural pattern in mind; indeed, diachronic research on Deuteronomy points to compositional origins as an independent D source or literary composition that is quite distinct from the JEP material in Exodus–Numbers.[9] Nevertheless, a synchronic reading of Deuteronomy in relation to Exodus–Numbers demands that Deuteronomy be subsumed into the structural organization of Exodus–Deuteronomy insofar as it presents Moses' final addresses to Israel following their arrival in Moab and prior to their entry into the land of Israel. Deuteronomy thereby presents an account of Moses' rehearsal of YHWH's Torah or expectations of Israel as the people take possession of the land.

The second question is far more difficult until one observes the presence of a previously unnoticed *toledoth* formula in Num 3:1, *wĕʾelleh tôlĕdōt ʾahărōn ûmōšeh bĕyôm dibber yhwh ʾet mōšeh bĕhar sînāy*, "And these are the generations of Aaron and Moses on the day that YHWH spoke with Moses on Mt. Sinai."[10] Although this example of the *toledoth* formula falls outside of Genesis, it is tied to the examples from Genesis by its similar formulation and by its increasingly narrow focus on Aaron and Moses as a group within the twelve tribes of Israel (see Gen 37:2), that is, the key Levitical figures, Moses and Aaron, who will provide leadership for Israel during the exodus period (Moses) and as high priests once Israel is settled in the land (the descendants of Aaron; see Numbers 17–18). Whereas interpreters would see little relationship between Num 3:1 and the *toledoth* formulae in Genesis due to the role that diachronic reading strategies play in fragmenting readings of texts, a synchronic reading of this formula in relation to the others demands that it be viewed as a continuation of the sequence begun in Genesis. Thus, it points to the role that the *toledoth* formulae play in delineating the full literary structure of the final synchronic form of the Pentateuch. Although the itinerary notices clearly play an important structural role in Exodus–Deuteronomy, that structure is subsumed to that of the *toledoth* formula. Indeed, the different organizational patterns point to a diachronic literary history that must have led to the formation of the present form of the text, but once that text is formed, synchronic literary patterns then govern its overall structure. Thus, the *toledoth* formulae point to a progression of textual blocks in the Pentateuch that trace the development of Israel within humankind from Adam through Moses and Aaron as the Levitical or priestly leadership of Israel within humanity. The itinerary notices trace the journey of Israel from Egypt to Moses, first as the twelve tribes of Israel (Exod 1:1—Num 2:34) and then under the leadership of Aaron and Moses (Num 3:1—Deut 34:12). The literary structure of the Pentateuch may be presented as follows in chart 1.1 on page 30.

The Abraham and Sarah Narratives

Having delineated the literary structure and perspective of the Pentateuch as a whole, the focus must now turn to the Abraham and Sarah narratives in Gen 11:27—25:11. As noted in the preceding discussion, this textual block is introduced with the *toledoth* formula concerning Terah in Gen 11:27, *wĕ'ēlleh tôlĕdōt teraḥ*, "and these are the generations of Terah." It concludes in Gen 25:11 with the notice, "And after the death of Abraham, G-d blessed his son, Isaac, and Isaac settled by Beer-Lahai-Roi." Another example of the *toledoth* formula, "And these are the generations of Ishmael ben Abraham, whom Hagar the Egyptian, the maidservant of Sarah, bore to Abraham," introduces the following textual block concerning the descendants of Ishmael in Gen 25:12-18.

The block of material concerning Abraham and Sarah in Gen 11:27—25:11 contains a series of episodes concerning important events in the lives of Israel's earliest ancestors. Although it might be tempting to read this block as a simple sequence of episodes, careful attention to the syntactical features of this textual block points to an organizational principle that underlies the narrative. Although the narrative episodes are largely constituted as a sequence of blocks joined together by introductory *waw*-consecutive statements, introductory noun clauses—some joined by conjunctive *waw*'s—point to the basic building blocks of this narrative. The *waw*-consecutive narratives then form the constituent subunits of the blocks introduced by conjunctive-*waw*. Thus, the previously observed introductory noun clause in Gen 11:27aα, *wĕ'ēlleh tôlĕdōt teraḥ*, "and these are the generations of Terah," introduces the narrative concerning Abraham and Sarah in Gen 11:27aβ—25:11 as a whole by identifying the generations of Abraham's father, Terah.

Chart 1.1
Synchronic Literary Structure of the Pentateuch:
History of Creation/Formation of People Israel

I.	Creation of Heaven and Earth	Gen 1:1—2:3
II.	Human Origins	Gen 2:4—4:26
III.	Human Development/Problems	Gen 5:1—6:8
IV.	Noah and the Flood	Gen 6:9—9:29
V.	Spread of Humans over the Earth	Gen 10:1—11:9
VI.	History of the Semites	Gen 11:10-26
VII.	History of Abraham (Isaac)	Gen 11:27—25:11
VIII.	History of Ishmael	Gen 25:12-18
IX.	History of Jacob (Isaac)`	Gen 25:19—35:29
X.	History of Esau	Gen 36:1—37:1
XI.	History of the Twelve Tribes of Israel	Gen 37:2—Num 2:34
	A. Joseph and His Brothers in Egypt	Gen 37:2—50:26
	B. Deliverance from Egyptian Bondage: Rameses	Exod 1:1—12:36
	C. From Rameses to Sukkot: Consecration of Firstborn	Exod 12:37—13:19
	D. From Sukkot to Etam: Pillar of Fire and Cloud	Exod 13:20-22
	E. From Etam to the Sea (Pihahirot/Baal Zephon): Deliverance at Sea	Exod 14:1—15:21
	F. From Reed Sea to Wilderness of Shur/Elim: Water in Wilderness	Exod 15:22-27
	G. From Elim to Wilderness of Sin: Quails and Manna	Exod 16:1-36
	H. From Sin to Rephidim: Amalek and Jethro	Exod 17:1—18:27
	I. From Rephidim to Sinai: Revelation of Torah	Exod 19:1—Num 10:1
	1. arrival at Sinai	*Exod 19:1-2*
	2. revelation from mountain: 10 commandments; covenant code;	
	building of the tabernacle	*Exod 19:3-40:38*
	3. revelation from tabernacle: laws of sacrifice and holiness code	*Leviticus 1–27*
	4. Census and organization of people around tabernacle	*Num 1:1—2:34*
XII.	History of Israel under the Guidance of the Levites	Num 3:1—Deut 34:12
	A. Sanctification of the people led by the Levites	Num 3:1—10:10
	B. From Sinai to Wilderness of Paran/Kibroth Hattaavah:	
	rebellion in the wilderness	Num 10:11—11:35a
	C. From Kibroth Hattaavah to Hazeroth	Num 11:35a—12:15
	D. From Hazeroth to the Wilderness of Paran	Num 12:16—19:22
	E. From Paran to Wilderness of Zin/Kadesh: water from rock	Num 20:1-21
	F. From Zin/Kadesh to Mount Hor: death of Aaron	Num 20:22—21:3
	G. From Mt. Hor to Edom/Moab: defeat of Sihon and Og	Num 21:4-35
	H. Arrival at Moab: Balaam; Census and Organization of People	Num 22:1—36:13
	I. Moses' Final Address to Israel: Repetition of the Torah	Deut 1:1—34:12

The first major block appears in Gen 11:27aβ—14:24. The noun clause in Gen 11:27aβ-b, *teraḥ hôlîd 'et-'abrām 'et-nāḥôr wě'et-hārān wěhārān hôlîd 'et-lôṭ*, "Terah fathered Abraham, Nahor, and Haran, and Haran fathered Lot," introduces a sequence of episodes in Gen 11:28—14:24— each introduced with a *waw*-consecutive clause—that lays out basic events in the early life of Abraham from his birth in Ur of the Chaldeans through his movements to Haran and finally to the lands of Canaan, Egypt, and Canaan once again. The constituent subunits begin with Gen 11:28-32, which begins with the statement, *wayyāmot hārān*, "and Haran died," and relates the birth of Terah's descendants, his moves from Ur to Haran, and his death at Haran. In Gen 12:1-9, the L-rd calls Abram, with Sarai and his nephew Lot, out of Haran and into the land of Canaan. Genesis 12:10-20 begins with the *waw*-consecutive statement, *wayěhî rā'āb bā'āreṣ*, "and there was famine in the land," and relates Abram's journey to Egypt in which he identified Sarai as his sister due to his fear that the Egyptians would kill him for his wife. Genesis 13:1-18 begins with the *waw*-consecutive statement, *wayya 'al 'abrām mimmiṣrayim*, "and Abram went up from Egypt," and relates Lot's decision to move to Sodom leaving Abram in the pastureland of Canaan. Finally, Gen 14:1-24 begins with the *waw*-consecutive statement, *wayěhî bîmê 'amrāpel*, "And it came to pass in the days of Amraphel," and relates Abram's efforts to rescue Lot and the people of Sodom and Gomorrah who were taken captive by Amraphel and the other kings of Mesopotamia.

A second block of material appears in Gen 15:1-21, which begins with the temporal noun clause, *'aḥar hadděbārîm hā'ēlleh*, "after these things," and relates YHWH's offer of a covenant to Abram that includes promises of descendants and possession of the land of Canaan, as well as a vision of the future exodus from Egypt. Although there is no conjunctive particle at the outset of this block, the introductory temporal clause clearly ties this passage to the preceding material while simultaneously setting it off as a signal to the reader that a new concern is at hand. At this point, Genesis 15 marks the transition from Abraham's early travels to the question of a relationship with YHWH. A series of subsequent textual blocks, each introduced by a conjunctive-*waw* noun clause, then explores various facets of this relationship by focusing on Sarah, Isaac, and Abraham's later wives and descendants prior to his death.

The block concerned with Sarah, the mother of Abraham's primary line of descendants identified as Israel, begins in Gen 16:1 with the conjunctive-*waw* statement, *wěsāray 'ēšet 'abrām*, "And Sarai, the wife of Abram (did not bear children to him)." Genesis 16:1-16 narrates Sarai's provision of Hagar to her husband who in turn bears him Ishmael. Subsequent subunits, each introduced with a *waw*-consecutive statement, then take up the issue of a covenant that will include the son promised to Sarah. Genesis 17:1-27 begins with the *waw*-consecutive statement, *wayĕhî 'abrām ben-tiš'îm šānâ wĕtēša' šānîm*, "And Abram was ninety-nine years old," and relates his conclusion of a covenant with YHWH. Genesis 18:1—19:38 begins with the *waw*-consecutive statement, *wayyērā' ēlāyw yhwh*, "And YHWH appeared to him (at the Oaks of Mamre)," and relates the Sodom and Gomorrah narrative in which YHWH destroys the cities as punishment for their purported wickedness and, in doing so, reiterates the promise of a son to Abraham and Sarah. Finally, Gen 20:1-18 begins with the *waw*-consecutive statement, *wayyissa' miššām 'abrāhām*, "And Abraham journeyed from there (to the land of the Negeb)," and relates Abraham's encounter with the Philistine king Abimelech, in which he claimed once again that Sarah was his wife.

The block concerned with Isaac, Abraham's son by Sarah and heir to the covenant, appears in Gen 21:1—23:20. The first subunit of this block appears in Gen 21:1-33, which begins with the conjunctive-*waw* statement, *wayhwh pāqad 'et-śārâ*, "And YHWH acknowledged Sarah," and relates the birth of Isaac and the expulsion of Hagar and Ishmael. Subsequent subunits begin with *waw*-consecutive statements and take up other concerns relevant to Isaac. Genesis 22:1-19 begins with the statement, *wayĕhî 'aḥar haddĕbārîm hāēlleh*, "And it came to pass after these things," and relates the binding of Isaac, in which YHWH tests Abraham by demanding the sacrifice of his son Isaac. Genesis 22:20-24 likewise begins with the statement, *wayĕhî 'aḥărê haddĕbārîm hāēlleh*, "And it came to pass after these things," and relates the birth of children to Abraham's brother Nahor, including Rebekah, who would become Isaac's wife. Finally, Gen 23:1-20 begins with the statement, *wayyihyû ḥayyê śārâ mēâ šānâ wĕeśrîm šānâ wĕšeba' šānîm*, "And Sarah's lifespan was one hundred and twenty-seven years," and relates the death and burial of Sarah.

The block concerned with the concluding events of Abraham's life appears in Gen 24:1—25:6. It begins with the conjunctive-*waw* noun clause at the outset of Gen 24:1-67, *wĕabrāhām zāqēn bā'*, "And Abraham was old," which relates Abraham's efforts to find a wife, that is, Rebekah, for Isaac. Genesis 25:1-6 then follows with an introductory *waw*-consecutive clause, *wayyōsep 'abrāhām*, "And Abraham again (took a wife)," and relates Abraham's marriage to Keturah, the birth of children to her, and arrangements to pass his possessions on to Isaac while granting gifts to his sons by concubines.

Finally, the narrative cycle concerned with Abraham concludes with the summation of Abraham's life in Gen 25:7-11. Like the introductory statement in Gen 11:27aα, Gen 25:7 begins with the noun clause, *wĕēlleh yĕmê šĕnê-ḥayyê 'abrāhām*, "And these are the days of the life of Abraham (one hundred and seventy-five years)." The balance of the unit relates the death of Abraham, his burial by his sons at Machpelah, and Isaac's settlement at Beer-Lehai-Roi.

The formal structure of the Abraham narratives in Gen 11:27—25:11 appears as follows in chart 1.2.

Chart 1.2
The Abraham Narratives:
Gen 11:27—25:11

I. Introduction: These Are the Generations of Terah	**Gen 11:27aα**
II. Abraham's Early Migrations: Ur to Canaan	**11:27aβ—14:24**
A. Terah's migration from Ur to Haran: Birth of Abraham	11:27aβ-32
B. YHWH instructs Abram to move to Canaan	12:1-9
C. Abram moves to Egypt and identifies Sarah as his sister	12:10-20
D. Abram grants Lot land in Sodom while retaining Canaan	13:1-18
E. Abram rescues Lot from Mesopotamian kings	14:1-24
III. Subsequent Events: Covenant and Its Ramifications	**15:1—25:6**
A. YHWH offers covenant to Abram	15:1-21
B. Ramifications for Sarah, Isaac, Abraham	16:1—25:6
1. Sarah	*16:1—20:18*
a. Hagar and the birth of Ishmael 16:1-16	
b. Covenant for projected son of Sarah 17:1-27	
c. Sodom and Gomorrah destroyed; Sarah promised son 18:1—19:38	
d. Sarah identified as Abraham's sister to Abimelech 20:1-18	
2. Isaac	*21:1—23:20*
a. Birth of Isaac; expulsion of Hagar and Ishmael 21:1-33	
b. Binding of Isaac 22:1-19	
c. Birth of Rebekah 22:20-24	
d. Death of Sarah 23:1-20	
3. Abraham	*24:1—25:6*
a. Secure Rebekah as wife for Isaac 24:1-67	
b. Marriage to Keturah and birth of sons 25:1-6	
IV. Summation of Abraham's Life	**25:7-11**

The Characters of YHWH and Abraham

The formal structure of the Abraham and Sarah narratives in Gen 11:27—25:11 demonstrates an interest in the periodization of Abraham's lifetime, but it also points to an important concern with the question of the covenant between YHWH and Abraham. This is evident in the organization of the major textual blocks of the unit, which include the introduction in Gen 11:27aα; a portrayal of Abraham's early migrations in Gen 11:27aβ—14:24; subsequent events, with a particular focus on the covenant and its ramifications in Gen 15:1—25:6; and the summation of Abraham's life in Gen 25:7-11. The emphasis on the covenant in Gen 15:1—25:6 is evident in the introductory subunit in Gen 15:1-21, in which YHWH offers the covenant to Abram, and the subsequent block in Gen 16:1—25:6, which lays out ramifications of the covenant for Sarah, Isaac, and Abraham. The ramifications focus especially on the question of Abraham's heir to the covenant. Upon hearing YHWH's promise of great reward in Genesis 15, Abram questions YHWH as to whether he would have a son to inherit his estate, or whether a substitute would inherit his estate in the absence of a son. The following block of material in Gen 16:1—25:6 then focuses on this very question by pointing to Sarah's continued infertility and the birth of a substitute heir to her handmaiden Hagar in Gen 16:1—20:18; Isaac's birth and near-death in Gen 21:1—23:20; and the specification of the roles of Abraham's sons in Gen 25:1-6, in which Abraham secures a wife for Isaac and stipulates Isaac as the heir to his house.

Insofar as the question of Abraham's heir is key to the Abraham and Sarah narratives in Gen 11:27—25:11, the question of YHWH's character or fidelity, as expressed in the literary tension concerning YHWH's promise of posterity to Abraham, emerges as a fundamental motif that underlies the Abraham and Sarah narratives. Having noted Abram's genealogy and his marriage to Sarai in vv. 27aβ-29, Gen 11:27aβ-32 very pointedly notes Sarai's childlessness in v. 30 before proceeding with the account of Terah's and Abram's migrations from Ur to Haran in vv. 31-32. In this manner, the narrator surreptitiously raises the key concern underlying the covenant between YHWH and Abraham, namely, Will Abraham have a son through whom the covenant may continue? Without a son and thus a future, the covenant becomes moot. Because YHWH is portrayed throughout the narrative as the party most directly responsible for providing Abraham with an heir through his wife Sarah, the question of YHWH's fidelity to promises made to Abraham takes center stage throughout the balance of the narrative.

results (handwritten margin annotation)

The question of YHWH's fidelity then appears throughout each of the following episodes concerned with Abram's migrations in Gen 12:1—14:24. Throughout these episodes, the narrator portrays Abram as an obedient and exemplary servant of YHWH, whereas YHWH emerges as a questionable character who continues to make demands of Abram and whose willingness or ability to stand by promises made to Abram remains in doubt in the perspective the reader. Despite YHWH's promises and demands, YHWH places Abram and Sarah in danger at every turn.

The contrast between YHWH's questionable character and Abram's exemplary character begins at the outset of Gen 12:1-9 in which YHWH instructs Abram to move from Haran to the land of Canaan, "Go forth from your native land and from your father's house to the land that I will show you. I will make of you a great nation, and I will bless you; I will make your name great, and you shall be a blessing. I will bless those who bless you and curse him that curses you; and all the families of the earth shall bless themselves by you." This is quite a remarkable set of demands and promises, and yet it is striking that Abram does not question or resist YHWH. Abram does not know where he is going or why, but he shows complete faithfulness in YHWH, who sends him into the unknown. Indeed, YHWH informs him, "I will give this land to you and your offspring," and at no point does Abram express doubt or refuse to follow YHWH's directions.[11] Abram shows himself to be an obedient servant of YHWH when he follows YHWH's instructions and moves his wife and household to the land of Canaan.

The potential for YHWH's infidelity with regard to Abram and Sarah becomes all the more remarkable in the following narrative in Gen 12:10-20 in which a famine brought about by YHWH afflicts the land of Canaan to which Abram has just moved his family. As author of the natural world of creation in the pentateuchal narrative, YHWH places Abram under threat by allowing the famine to take place, prompting Abram to move down to Egypt to save the lives of his family. Some suggest that Abram shows lack of faith in YHWH by refusing to trust in YHWH's willingness to sustain him despite the famine,[12] but such a contention appears to be apologetic when one considers the threat posed to life by famine in an agricultural, subsistence economy. Others condemn Abram as a man who is entirely self-serving and unconcerned with the potential danger to his wife for declaring that Sarai is his sister because he is afraid that the Egyptians will kill him to take her for her beauty.[13] Still others contend that the designation of the wife as sister is a common ancient Near-ern language convention that expresses the intimacy of the relationship.[14]

36   Although such an observation may well be correct, it misses the point of the narrative that Abram feels threatened in a foreign land and makes his statement as a means to protect himself from the Egyptians. Of course, Gen 20:12 later explains that Sarah is Abraham's half-sister so that his statement is not a lie. Nevertheless, his words enable Pharaoh, the king of Egypt, to take Sarai into his harem while Abram prospers. Readers are not told what happens to Sarai in the royal harem; indeed, the Egyptian royal harem would have to be one of the world's most secure places for women in the ancient world. Ultimately Pharaoh learns the truth, returns Sarai to Abram, and allows Abram to leave unharmed. Despite the questions raised about Abram, the narrative maintains that he perceived himself and his family to be under threat, and that he acted in a manner that in his estimation would best ensure his and his family's safety. In the context of a patriarchal society, Abraham's giving up his wife to another man would be a deep source of shame. Indeed, interpreters generally overlook an important point of the narrative, that is, Sarah's descendants could have been Egyptians. The question of Egyptian offspring for the ancestors will appear again in Genesis.[15] There is actually little threat to Sarah in this narrative; the threat comes in relation to the identity of offspring for her and for Abraham.

    The portrayal of Abram's exemplary character and the question of YHWH's fidelity to Abram continue in Gen 13:1-18, which portrays Abram tending sheep in the Negeb wilderness with his nephew, Lot. Because of Abram's prosperity, the flocks grow numerous. Ultimately, the shepherds of Abram and the shepherds of Lot fight among themselves as they compete for pastureland. In order to avoid the quarrel, Abram tells Lot to choose which part of the land he would like. Lot looks for the well-watered and greener land of Sodom and the Jordan Valley, and chooses it for himself, leaving Abram to live on the land that was left over. This is a very remarkable and unselfish act by Abram when considered in the context of an ancient patriarchal society in which Abram as the senior male had the right to choose the best land for himself. Although neither Abram nor Lot would yet know that Sodom and Gomorrah would be destroyed, the narrative allows Abram's magnanimity to shine through. The narrative clues given to the reader in Gen 13:10, 13, tell the reader what YHWH already knows, namely, that Sodom and Gomorrah are evil and will be destroyed. Lot's choice places a branch of Abram's family in danger, but YHWH remains silent.

    The portrayal of Abram's exemplary character continues in the next chapter. When Sodom is attacked in Genesis 14 and Lot is carried off captive by the raiding Mesopotamians, Abram does not hesitate to raise an army to rescue Lot and the other captives. When the king of Sodom offers a reward, Abram turns it down, and instead worships YHWH at the site of Salem, that is, Jerusalem (cf. Ps 76:2). Indeed, Gen 14:18 identifies Melchizedek as the priest of El Elyon at Salem (cf. Psalm 110 in which YHWH informs David that he is a priest after the order of Melchizedek). In addition, Gen 14:20 notes that Abram paid a tithe at Salem, in keeping with later requirements that Israelite men pay a tenth or a tithe of their annual income to support the Temple and monarchy (Lev 27:30-33; Num 18:21-32; Deut 14:22-29; cf. Gen 28:22; 1 Sam 8:15, 17; *m. Ma'aserot* 1:1).[16] In doing so, Abram already exhibits the piety and observance of later generations of Jews who would worship YHWH at the Jerusalem Temple. YHWH, on the other hand, does nothing to protect Lot.

Having portrayed Abram in such generous and idealistic terms, the block of material concerned with the covenant and its ramifications in Gen 15:1—25:6 then returns to the question of YHWH's fidelity in the initial subunit in Gen 15:1-21 by portraying YHWH's offer of the covenant to Abram together with Abram's concerns. Genesis 15 opens with YHWH's repeated promises to Abram, "Fear not Abram, I am a shield to you; your reward shall be very great."[17] At this juncture, the narrator takes the opportunity to point the reader back to the question of Sarah's barrenness. Without a son, all of Abram's wealth, standing, and special relationship with YHWH are meaningless; there is no one to inherit Abram's estate or to carry on after his death. When Abram points this out to YHWH, YHWH reiterates the promises that Abram will become the father of a great nation that will possess the land of Canaan/Israel. YHWH even signs the agreement in the manner of ancient treaties by symbolically passing between the pieces of sacrificed animals, which signifies that one who violates the terms of the treaty will suffer the same fate as the sacrificial animals (cf. Jer 34:18).[18] But by raising the question of the next generation, Abram in fact raises the question of divine fidelity. Thus far, Abram has done all that is asked of him; but YHWH has not yet fulfilled the promises.

Tension in the portrayal of YHWH is reinforced throughout the portrayal of the covenant's ramifications for Sarah, Isaac, and Abraham in Gen 16:1—25:6 until the concluding statements that Isaac would inherit Abraham's estate, although his other sons would be provided with gifts.

This tension is especially highlighted in the narrative subunit concerning Sarah in Gen 16:1—20:18, which begins with the birth of Ishmael in Gen 16:1-16. Sarah continues to remain barren and, ultimately, she

38 exercises the legal right of women in the ancient Near East to provide her
husband with offspring through a maidservant.[19] In this case, the maidservant is Hagar, an Egyptian woman, who bears Ishmael to Abram. For
the reader of the story, the birth of the half-Egyptian Ishmael is an ironic
twist, that is, Will Abram's covenant continue through an Egyptian, the
very people who threatened Abram in Gen 12:10-20 and the people who
would enslave Abram's descendants in Exodus (cf. the Abram's vision of
Israel's enslavement in Gen 15:13-14)?

Although Ishmael is granted his own set of promises from YHWH,
the second episode in the Sarah narratives in Gen 17:1-27 articulates the
covenant between YHWH and Abram, and thereby asserts the place of
Sarah's son as Abraham's heir. The covenant is sealed by circumcision, in
which Abram symbolically signs the agreement by circumcising himself
and his house. His name is changed to Abraham and Sarai's is changed
to Sarah, and YHWH once again promises Abraham that he will have
children through Sarah who will become a great nation and possess the
land of Canaan/Israel forever. Again, Abraham does all that he is asked,
but YHWH makes promises that are not yet fulfilled. By noting Ishmael's
circumcision, the narrative highlights the fact that no son is yet born to
Sarah and that Ishmael—born to an Egyptian mother—remains available
to serve as Abraham's heir.

The Sarah block in Gen 16:1—20:18 reaches its climax in Gen 18:1—
20:18, in which YHWH promises once again a son to Sarah and Abraham
refers to her once again as his sister. The Sodom-Gomorrah narrative in
Gen 18:1—19:38 focuses its attention ever more closely on the character
of YHWH. Although Abraham plays a major role in these chapters, the
narrative is designed to raise questions concerning YHWH's righteousness
and fidelity. The Sodom and Gomorrah narratives raise these questions in
a very pointed manner. After repeating the still unfulfilled promise that
Sarah will bear a son and that Abraham's descendants will become a great
nation, YHWH informs Abraham of the decision to destroy the purportedly wicked cities. Ironically, it is Abraham and not YHWH who raises the
moral question of the destruction of an entire population, "Far be it from
you! Shall the judge of all the earth not do justice?" Abraham ultimately
persuades YHWH not to carry out the destruction if there are ten righteous
people in the cities; perhaps YHWH was testing Abraham to see what his
response to such an atrocity would be.[20] Despite the portrayal of Sodom
as an entirely wicked city in Genesis 19, readers are nevertheless left with a
very uncomfortable feeling concerning YHWH's proposal to destroy entire
cities. What would YHWH have done if Abraham had not spoken up?

The narrative concerning Abraham's sojourn in Philistia in Gen 20:1-18 once again raises the issue of Sarah's status as his sister. Although this narrative is frequently read in isolation from its literary context as a later insertion into the Genesis narrative, its narrative function in relation to both the preceding and following narratives must be clarified. Unlike Gen 12:10-20, there is no indication of threat to Abraham and family at the outset of the narrative, either by famine or by the Philistine monarch Abimelech. It is at this point that readers are granted an opportunity to see YHWH as a character who will potentially protect Sarah and thereby potentially fulfill the promises of posterity made to Abraham. YHWH's character remains ambiguous, however, insofar as YHWH reiterates the promise concerning the birth of a son to Sarah but still does not fulfill it. Some hope for YHWH's character emerges when YHWH intervenes to inform Abimelech that Sarah is actually Abraham's wife, and Abimelech demands to know why Abraham did not tell him the truth in the first place. Abraham answers Abimelech's criticism by stating his fear of the Philistines, but by allowing Abimelech to make his points first, the narrative provides an opportunity for the reader to begin to reconsider Abraham. Nevertheless, the narrative protects Abraham's character by asserting in v. 12 that Sarah is indeed his half-sister and by portraying Abraham as a prophet who intercedes with YHWH on Abimelech's behalf. In sum, Gen 20:1-18 concludes the Sarah block by teasing the reader with the possibility that YHWH might actually emerge as a righteous deity while continuing to portray YHWH as a deity who does not yet fulfill the promises made to Abraham.

The Isaac block in Gen 21:1—23:20 ultimately resolves the question of an heir for Abraham by portraying the birth of Isaac to Sarah. Nevertheless, this material increases the tension surrounding this question by portraying YHWH's demand that Isaac be sacrificed as a "test" of Abraham's fidelity. Although it also briefly introduces the figure of Rebekah, Isaac's bride-to-be, the death of Sarah at the end of the block raises questions concerning YHWH's treatment of Isaac's mother, the key figure in the question of Abraham's heir to the covenant.

Genesis 21:1-33 begins the Isaac block by presenting the birth of Isaac to Sarah and Abraham, purportedly resolving the literary tensions surrounding Sarah's barrenness and YHWH's unfulfilled promises of a son. And yet, questions concerning the character and fidelity of YHWH remain when the reader sees Hagar and Ishmael expelled with divine acquiescence. Although G-d promises that Ishmael, too, will become the father of a great nation, the reader might ask why Hagar and Ishmael must be expelled from Abraham's household and what effect such an expulsion has on Abraham. And YHWH demands even more of Abraham. Having given him the son that had been promised, YHWH tests Abraham in Gen 22:1-19 by demanding that he offer Isaac as a burnt offering on Mt. Moriah, traditionally understood to be the site of the future Temple in Jerusalem (2 Chr 3:1). There is an irony to this test in that Abraham has never disobeyed YHWH throughout the entire narrative sequence beginning in Gen 11:27, but YHWH's integrity is once again subject to question. If Isaac is to die, the covenant potentially comes to an end; even if Sarah bears another son, the morality of Isaac's death is still in question. Although YHWH stops Abraham from sacrificing Isaac, the reader might wonder whether Abraham is tested in this narrative or YHWH.

Indeed, the questions of YHWH's behavior in these narratives extend to the death of Sarah as well. Following the brief notice in Gen 22:20-24 of the birth of children to Abraham's brother Nahor, including Rebekah, the future wife of Isaac, Gen 23:1-20 reports the death and burial of Sarah. Rabbinic tradition notes that Isaac never comes home to Sarah following this incident, and that Sarah dies thinking that her son is dead (*Leviticus Rabbah* 20:2; *Pirke de Rabbi Eliezer* 32). Genesis 22:19 concludes the Akedah narrative by reporting that Abraham returned to Beer Sheba; no mention is made of Isaac, and Sarah dies at Kiriath Arba/Hebron with no mention that she ever saw Isaac again. Although Sarah is not mentioned in Gen 22:1-19, the reader might wonder whether or not Sarah knew the purpose of the journey and whether she died knowing that her son had been spared. Again, the question of YHWH's character in bringing about this "test" in the first place raises questions with regard to YHWH's relationship with Sarah. In the end, YHWH adheres to the promise of a son and heir to Abraham and Sarah, but all parties suffer during the course of YHWH's fulfillment.

The Abraham block in Gen 24:1—25:6 traces the balance of Abraham's life. Genesis 24:1-67 portrays Abraham's efforts to secure Rebekah as a wife for Isaac, and thereby ensure the continuity of the covenant by making sure that his son would have a proper mother for his own children. Genesis 25:1-6 portrays Abraham's marriage to Keturah and the birth of more children, but the narrative specifies that Isaac would be Abraham's heir and that Abraham's other sons, including Ishmael, would only receive gifts from their father during their lifetimes.

The critical examination of Abraham and YHWH is now complete, and the Abraham and Sarah narrative concludes with the summation of Abraham's life in Gen 25:7-11.

Questions of YHWH's Character and Fidelity

Study of the Abraham and Sarah block in Gen 11:27—25:11 demonstrates that YHWH finally emerges as a righteous figure who shows fidelity in relationship with Abraham even if questions might be raised concerning YHWH's character and fidelity. Nevertheless, the narrative is designed to emphasize these questions to the reader by drawing out the presentation of tension in the relationship between YHWH and the first ancestors of Israel by continually placing threats to the promise of posterity to Abraham and Sarah. In this manner, the narrative forces the reader to confront the question of divine fidelity and righteousness, namely, Will YHWH actually grant the promises made to Abraham? Will Sarah remain barren? Will Abraham's and Sarah's descendants be Egyptian? Will Isaac be sacrificed? By creating such literary tension around these questions, the narrative prompts the reader to reflect upon the character of YHWH and the question of theodicy in light of the later experience of exile and restoration throughout the Hebrew Bible and in the historical experience of ancient Judaism.

God's power over evil (allowing suffering to happen)

TWO

Moses and the
Problem of Divine Violence

Moses is the key human protagonist in the pentateuchal narratives concerning Israel's formation as a nation.[1] Born into a Levitical family at the time of Pharaoh's decree to kill the newborn sons of Hebrew slaves, Moses' life was saved by his mother who bundled him up in a basket of reeds, and floated him down the Nile River until he was found by the daughter of Pharaoh and raised in the Egyptian royal court. After discovering his true identity and his G-d, Moses led the people of Israel out of Egyptian bondage, served as the primary human agent through whom YHWH revealed divine Torah to the people, and guided Israel on a forty-year journey—fraught with conflict between YHWH and the people—through the Sinai wilderness to the promised land of Israel. Indeed, Moses is the founding leader of Israel in the pentateuchal narrative.

Because of Moses' foundational role in leading Israel through the Exodus, Sinai, and wilderness wandering—at great personal sacrifice—YHWH's decision to forbid Moses the right to enter the promised land of Israel comes as quite a surprise. According to Deut 34:1-8, YHWH allows the aged Moses the opportunity to gaze upon the promised land of Israel from the summit of Pisgah on Mt. Nebo in the land of Moab, but Moses dies immediately afterwards at the age of one hundred and twenty and is buried by YHWH in an unknown grave in the valley of the land of Moab somewhere in the vicinity of Baal Peor. Numbers 20:12 (see also Num 27:12-14; Deut 4:21-22) reports that the reason for YHWH's decision is the failure by Moses and Aaron to affirm YHWH's sanctity before the people of Israel at the time that YHWH provided the people with water at Meribah, near Kadesh in the wilderness of Zin. The exact nature of Moses' and Aaron's failure to sanctify YHWH has puzzled interpreters since ancient times. Despite the many proposals that have been raised over the course of the centuries, none has succeeded in convincing interpreters of the specific nature of Moses' and Aaron's sin.[2]

Readers are left to wonder why Moses should be treated in this fashion. Indeed, the issue is compounded by the very contentious nature of the relationship between YHWH and Israel throughout the wilderness period.[3] YHWH delivers the people of Israel from Egyptian bondage, but the people complain in Exodus 16–17 that they were better off in Egypt since they lacked food, water, and security in the wilderness. While Moses is away for forty days and forty nights receiving the divine Torah from YHWH at Mt. Sinai in Exodus 32–34, the people become alarmed that they have been abandoned and compel Aaron to construct a golden calf to worship in place of YHWH. When YHWH vows to destroy the people as a result of this action, Moses intercedes with YHWH on their behalf and prompts YHWH to reconsider. Following another round of complaints in Numbers 11 and a challenge to Moses' leadership in Numbers 12, the people once again are ready to rebel in Numbers 13–14 when they hear the reports of the spies that the land of Canaan is occupied by giants. Once again, Moses must intercede on behalf of the people to prevent YHWH from destroying them entirely, although YHWH decrees that the present generation will die in the wilderness without ever entering the promised land of Israel. The apostasy of Israel at Baal Peor in Numbers 25 underscores the problem once again.

Nevertheless, the narrative concerning the apostasy at Baal Peor also points to a crucial dimension of this problem, namely, the role of Phineas ben Eliezer ben Aaron who would act against those responsible for wrongdoing and therefore to expiate the sins or impurity of the people. As a result of his actions at Baal Peor, Phineas was granted a covenant of peace to designate him as the founder of the Zadokite priestly line that would play a constitutive role in mediating the relationship between YHWH and Israel at the Temple of YHWH throughout Israel's subsequent history. Indeed, Phineas's role follows upon the designations of the Levites in Exodus 32 as those dedicated to YHWH and later Aaron and his sons in Numbers 17–18 as those who would bear the sin of the sanctuary. Inasmuch as the wilderness narratives point to conflict and tension in the relationship between YHWH and the people of Israel, the priesthood emerges as the party that is tasked with mediating that relationship and restoring it when it is disrupted. Insofar as Moses is a Levite, his experience must be considered against the background of these tensions and the emergence of the priesthood as well.

This chapter therefore considers YHWH's decision to bar Moses from the promised land of Israel in relation to the traditions of Israel's rebellion against YHWH in the wilderness and the emergence of the priesthood to mediate the relationship between YHWH and Israel. It proceeds by first examining the account of YHWH's decision to bar Moses and Aaron from the promised land of Israel for failing to sanctify YHWH at the waters of Meribah in Numbers 20. It then examines the rebellion texts in Exodus 16–17, the golden calf episode in Exodus 32–34, and the rebellion texts in Numbers 11–12 and 13–14. Finally, it examines the roles of the priests, including Phineas in Numbers 25, Aaron and sons in Numbers 17–18, and the Levites in Exodus 32 in an effort to demonstrate that Moses' experience is emblematic of that of Israel at large and points to an interest in explaining the emergence of the priesthood as the means to mediate the relationship between YHWH and the people of Israel.

The Punishment of Moses and Aaron

The narrative concerning the punishment of Moses and Aaron at the waters of Meribah in Num 20:1-13 is one of the more enigmatic episodes of the Pentateuch.[4] The narrative begins with a notice of Israel's arrival at Kadesh in the wilderness of Zin where Miriam dies and is buried. When the people complain concerning the lack of water at the site, YHWH instructs Moses and Aaron to take the rod, to assemble the people, and to speak to the rock in their presence so that it will yield water. Moses takes the rod as instructed, assembles the people together with Aaron, says to the people, "Listen you rebels, shall we bring forth water for you?" and then strikes the rock twice with the rod to produce the much-needed water. Because of these actions, YHWH accuses Moses and Aaron of failing to trust YHWH enough to affirm divine sanctity before the people of Israel. YHWH therefore decrees that neither Moses nor Aaron shall lead the people into the promised land of Israel. YHWH's decree is reiterated in Num 20:22-29, which relates Aaron's death at Mt. Hor; Num 27:12-23, which relates the appointment of Joshua ben Nun as Moses' successor; Deut 1:37-38, when Moses recounts the people's journey from Egypt to the promised land of Israel; Deut 4:21-22, when Moses exhorts the people to observe YHWH's commands when they enter the land; and Deut 32:48-52, in which YHWH grants Moses permission to view the promised land of Israel before he dies.

Although the texts very clearly state that their failure to sanctify YHWH before the people is the reason for YHWH's decision to punish Moses and Aaron, interpreters have struggled for centuries to determine what acts constitute the failure to sanctify YHWH. Jacob Milgrom's commentary on Numbers provides a summary of three basic explanations.[5] The first focuses on Moses' action in striking the rock, insofar as he struck the rock instead of speaking; or that he chose this rock whereas the people wanted another rock; or that he struck it twice instead of once. The second focuses on Moses' character, as indicated by his blazing temper, his cowardice in fleeing to the sanctuary, or his callousness in mourning for Miriam while the people thirsted for water. The third sort of explanation focuses on Moses' words, insofar as his question to the people was misconstrued as an expression of doubt in YHWH, his question actually did express doubt in YHWH, he called Israel "rebels," or he credited the flow of water to himself and Aaron by stating that "we will bring forth water for you." Milgrom himself argues that the present text reflects later redactional tampering in which Moses' statement is added to the text, whereas the actual sin lay in striking the rock twice rather than speaking to it as instructed by YHWH. Dennis Olson focuses on the theme of Moses' death in the Pentateuch as a signal for the theological importance of the need to pass on YHWH's teachings to the coming generations who will dwell in the promised land of Israel.[6]

To date, none of the proffered explanations for the sin of Moses and Aaron has succeeded fully in persuading interpreters as to the cause for YHWH's decree of punishment, although Moses' action in striking the rock and his statement to the people have attracted the most support. In order to revisit this question and perhaps to provide a solution, we must reexamine Num 20:1-13.[7]

Numbers 20:1-13 is demarcated at the outset in v. 1 by the notice that the people arrived at Kadesh in the wilderness of Zin in the first month of the year. This notice provides the setting for the following events. The notice in v. 14 of Moses' sending messengers to the king of Edom marks a new subunit by shifting the narrative action to another setting, whereas the etiological statement concerning the waters of Meribah in v. 13 marks the conclusion of the present episode. The *waw*-consecutive syntactical structure of Num 20:1-13 points to basic literary division of the unit into two subunits: v. 1 notes the arrival of Israel in the wilderness of Zin and

46   their encampment at Kadesh together with the death and burial of Miriam at Kadesh. The introductory notice concerning the lack of water at
Kadesh, introduced by the conjunctive-*waw* formation, *wělō' hāyâ mayim
lā'ēdâ*, "And there was no water for the community," marks the beginning
of the primary subunit of the text in vv. 2-13, which is concerned with the
incident at Meribah.

Because—with the exception of v. 13 (see below)—the syntactical
structure of vv. 2-13 is governed by *waw*-consecutive verbs, the literary
structure of this text is evident in the shifts of action by the primary characters of the narrative. The first subunit appears in vv. 2-5, in which the
people state their complaints to Moses concerning the lack of water noted
at the outset of the passage. The second subunit appears in vv. 6-8, in
which Moses and Aaron appeal to YHWH at the tent of meeting as a
result of the people's complaints. Here, YHWH instructs them to take the
rod, speak to the rock before the people, and thereby produce water for
them as indicated above. The third subunit appears in vv. 9-11, in which
Moses takes the rod, assembles the people together with Aaron, speaks to
the people as indicated above, and strikes the rock twice, resulting in the
flow of water for the people. The fourth subunit appears in v. 12, in which
YHWH announces the punishment for Moses and Aaron due to their
failure to sanctify YHWH before the people. Verse 13 begins with the pro-
noun phrase, *hēmmâ mê měrîbâ*, "These are the waters of Meribah . . . ,"
which introduces the etiological statement. Verse 13 thereby provides a
summation of the narrative that explains the significance of this episode
in relation to Israel's challenge of YHWH. The diagram on the following
page (chart 2.1) expresses the literary structure of the passage.

The analysis points to several crucial issues. First, YHWH is indeed
sanctified in this narrative, although it is quite clear that Moses and Aaron
are not the cause of YHWH's sanctification. Although some presuppose
that the water flowing from the rock is the reason for YHWH's sanctification, the narrative structure of the passage indicates that YHWH remains
unsanctified by the beginning of v. 12. The water flows, but Moses' actions
leave the question of YHWH's sanctity in doubt. Instead, the literary
structure of the passage suggests that YHWH's condemnation of Moses
and Aaron establishes YHWH's sanctification following the people's
rebellion and the failure of Moses and Aaron to sanctify YHWH before
the people.

Second, Moses' striking the rock does not seem to be the cause of
the problem, even though he struck the rock twice. Many interpreters
note that Moses struck the rock despite the fact that YHWH instructed

---

Chart 2.1
Israel's Rebellion against YHWH at Meribah
Num 20:1-13

I. Itinerary Notice: Arrival at Kadesh, Wilderness of Zin   1
    a. Arrival notice proper   1aα
    b. Specifications   1aβ-b
      1. Settlement at Kadesh   *1aβ*
      2. Death of Miriam   *1bα*
      3. Burial of Miriam   *1bβ*

II. Rebellion against YHWH at Meribah Proper   **2-13**
  A. People's complaint to Moses and Aaron concerning lack of water   2-5
    1. Notice concerning lack of water   *2a*
    2. Complaints expressed   *2b-5*
      a. People assembled   2b
      b. Complaints stated   3-5
  B. YHWH's instructions to Moses and Aaron   6-8
    1. Moses and Aaron appeal to YHWH at tent of meeting   *6a*
    2. YHWH's instruction to Moses and Aaron   *6b-8*
      a. Appearance of YHWH's Presence   6b
      b. Instruction account   7-8
  C. Moses' and Aaron's actions at the rock before Israel   9-11
    1. Moses takes rod as commanded   *9*
    2. Moses and Aaron assemble people at rock   *10a*
    3. Moses' statement to people: Shall we bring forth water?   *10b*
    4. Moses raises hand and strikes the rock twice   *11a*
    5. Result: water flows from rock   *11b*
  D. YHWH's condemnation of Moses and Aaron for failing to sanctify
    YHWH before the people   12
  E. Summation: Etiology concerning the waters of Meribah   13
    1. Identification of waters of Meribah   *13a*
    2. Significance   *13b*
      a. Where people rebelled   13bα
      b. Where YHWH was sanctified   13bβ

---

him and Aaron to speak to the rock instead. Nevertheless, the alternative version of our narrative in Exod 17:1-7 notes YHWH's instructions to strike the rock in the wilderness of Sin to provide water for the people. Moses strikes the rock as YHWH instructed him, the water flows for the people, the place is named Massah and Meribah, and Moses is

48 not condemned. It is not entirely clear that striking the rock should be wrong in Num 20:1-13, but right in Exod 17:1-7. One might rely on the fact that YHWH did not call for such action in Num 20:1-13 whereas YHWH did call for such action in Exod 17:1-7, but such a position suggests an arbitrary portrayal of YHWH and YHWH's commands. Indeed, the reference to Moses' striking the rock twice could even function as a means to acknowledge the first incident at Meribah in Exod 17:1-7 in the present form of the Pentateuch. These considerations call for an examination of Exod 17:1-7 as well.

The second issue then points to the third, namely, that Moses' words to the people before the rock constitutes the cause for YHWH's charge that he and Aaron failed to sanctify YHWH properly. Several aspects of Moses' statement to the people call for consideration. First is his oft-noted question, "Shall *we* bring forth water for you?" which suggests that Moses' failure to sanctify YHWH lies in his attempt to take credit for himself and Aaron instead of ascribing the action to YHWH. Such a contention does not explain Aaron's punishment, unless one employs an argument from silence concerning Aaron's failure to contradict Moses. Second is Moses' characterization of the people as "rebels" (Heb.: *mōrîm*), and the suggestion that he identifies himself with them. Even a superficial perusal of the wilderness rebellion traditions should put this notion to rest, since the people constantly rebel against YHWH, which is to say that the characterization is correct. As for Moses' identification with the people, Moses has twice challenged YHWH's decision to kill off the people and make Moses into a great nation instead during the course of the golden calf incident in Exod 32:9-14 and at the time of the spy incident, in Num 14:15-35, when the people failed to trust YHWH following the spies' reports of giants in the land of Canaan. Indeed, both of these episodes point to a third consideration, that is, both Moses and Aaron are Levitical priests and—contrary to priestly practice—Moses spoke to the people while officiating at a holy assembly. Due to the holy nature of such assembly, priests do not speak to the congregation while officiating before the people since they are in the presence of YHWH. Insofar as the wilderness rebellion traditions are bound up with the vow of the Levites to act on YHWH's behalf during the golden calf episode in Exodus 32–34; the selection of the Levites, with a special focus on Aaron and his sons, as the holy priests of Israel before YHWH in Numbers 17–18 following the rebellion traditions in Numbers 11–16; and Phineas's actions on YHWH's behalf at Baal Peor, examination of each of these narratives will be necessary to clarify the nature of Moses' and Aaron's rebellion in Num 20:1-13.

Massah, Meribah, and Marah

Interpreters frequently read the narrative concerning YHWH's condemnation of Moses and Aaron at Meribah in relation to Exod 17:1-7, which also recounts the drawing of water from the rock at Massah or Meribah.[8] Such efforts make great sense, since the two narratives appear to be variations of the same basic theme. Indeed, an analysis of the formal structure of Exod 17:1-7 points to fundamental similarities with Num 20:1-13.[9]

Exodus 17:1-7 is demarcated by the introductory itinerary formula in v. 1, which states that the people of Israel journeyed from the wilderness of Sin to encamp at a site called Rephidim. Verse 1 also notes the lack of water at Rephidim, which sets the basic theme of the narrative. The concluding etiological notice in v. 7 concerning the naming of the site as Massah, "testing," and Meribah, "rebellion," closes this brief unit. A new unit concerned with Amalek's attack against Israel at Rephidim then follows. The internal structure of the passage is simple enough, insofar as the syntactical structure of the unit is based entirely on *waw*-consecutive narrative formations. Hence, shifts in the narrative action define the basic literary structure of the passage. Verse 1 sets the scene with the notice of Israel's arrival at Rephidim and the lack of water at the site. Verses 2-3 then relate the people's interchange with Moses concerning the lack of water in which the people demand water, Moses' demands to know why they complain against him and test YHWH, and the people's charge that Moses brought them to the wilderness in order to kill them with thirst. Following this impasse, vv. 4-6 relate Moses' appeal to YHWH for assistance in the matter in which he cries out to YHWH, YHWH instructs him to strike the rock (noting that YHWH will be standing by the rock all the while) so that water will flow, and finally Moses' compliance with YHWH's instructions. The etiological statement in v. 7 concludes the narrative by explaining the etiology of the names Massah and Meribah for the site in relation to the question of the people, "Was YHWH in our midst or not?" The formal structure of the narrative may be presented as follows in chart 2.2 on page 50.

The concern with explaining the place names Massah and Meribah marks Exod 17:1-7 and Num 20:1-13 as variations of the same basic tradition concerning Israel's complaints concerning the lack of water in the wilderness and the provision of water by Moses' striking the rock. Two further basic points may be made. First, the narrative indicates no problem in Moses' striking the rock, particularly since YHWH's instructions to Moses emphasize that YHWH will be present before the rock when

Chart 2.2
Etiological Narrative concerning Massah and Meribah
Exod 17:1-7

I. Itinerary Notice: Travel from Sin to Rephidim	**1**
A. Travel notice: travel from Sin at command of YHWH	1a
B. Arrival at Rephidim	1b
1. Arrival notice proper	*1bα*
2. Notation concerning lack of water at Rephidim	*1bβ*
II. People's Confrontation with Moses over Water	**2-3**
A. People's initial complaint: give us water	2a
B. Moses' response: why complain against me and test YHWH?	2b
C. People's renewed complaint: you intend to kill us here	3
III. Moses' Appeal to YHWH	**4-6**
A. Moses' appeal proper	4
B. YHWH's response: instructions to strike rock and provide water	5-6a
C. Moses' compliance with YHWH's instructions	6b
IV. Concluding Etiology concerning Massah and Meribah	**7**

he strikes it. Second, Moses does not speak to the people when they are assembled to witness his striking the rock, and he is not condemned for his action. This might confirm that Moses' words to the people in Num 20:10 is the basis for the charge that he and Aaron failed to sanctify YHWH before the people.

But there are other considerations beyond those presented within Exod 17:1-7 itself. Exodus 17:1-7 (and Num 20:1-13) is but one component of a much larger wilderness rebellion tradition in which the people of Israel repeatedly complain that Moses or YHWH has brought them into the wilderness to die. The immediate literary context of Exod 17:1-7 provides several episodes of such challenge. Following YHWH's miraculous deliverance of the people from the Egyptians at the sea, Exod 15:22-27 recounts Israel's complaints concerning the bitter waters at Marah. After YHWH provides the means for Moses to make the water drinkable, Moses lays out the conditions of the relationship between YHWH and Israel, namely, if the people will observe YHWH's commands, then YHWH will not bring the plagues suffered by the Egyptians upon Israel. Exodus 16:1-36 takes up the problem of the lack of food in the wilderness. When the people complain to Moses that they will die in the wilderness for lack of food, YHWH responds by providing manna and quail to eat. Conditions are nevertheless imposed, that is, Exod 16:4-8 stipulates that the people must observe YHWH's instructions, here identified as the requirement to observe the sanctity of the Sabbath. Exodus 17:8-16 recounts Amalek's attacks against Israel in the wilderness. With divine assistance, the Amalekite attack is defeated. Although Israel does not complain in this narrative, it is clear that the wilderness is a place of threat in which divine assistance will be necessary in order for Israel to survive.

And yet it is also clear that YHWH is the source of the threat against Israel in the wilderness. This is clear from the above-noted narrative in Exod 15:22-27 concerning the waters of Marah in which YHWH stipulates that the people will observe divine instruction or suffer the plagues suffered by Egypt. It is also clear in the narrative concerning the revelation of divine Torah at Mt. Sinai in which the people are warned in Exod 19:3-6 concerning the experience of the Egyptians as Torah is about to be revealed to them that requires them to be a kingdom of priests. The warning is reiterated in Exod 19:9-13, in which the people are commanded to set boundaries between themselves and the holy presence of YHWH upon the mountain; if they cross these boundaries, they are threatened with death. The threat is repeated once again in Exod 19:20-25.

Israel's questions about YHWH's potential threat against them are hardly confined to the wilderness. As the Marah narrative makes clear, YHWH's plagues against the Egyptians might just as easily be applied against Israel. Indeed, Israel's concerns with YHWH, for instance, YHWH's capacity for violence and YHWH's capacity to act on behalf of the people, are rooted in the fundamental concerns of the exodus narrative, which is constructed to demonstrate YHWH's role as the creator and ultimate power in both the natural and human worlds. The exodus narrative is stylized as a conflict between the pharaoh of Egypt, who was believed by the ancient Egyptians to be a god himself, and YHWH, which demonstrates YHWH's power over against that of Pharaoh. YHWH is able to marshal the classical Egyptian skills, such as the practice of snake charming, the elements of creation in the form of the plagues, and the purported Canaanite practice of sacrificing the firstborn to YHWH, as the means to answer Pharaoh's question in Exod 5:2, "Who is YHWH that I should listen to him to let Israel go? I do not know YHWH, and I will not let Israel go." Of course, when Pharaoh rejects Moses' challenge and imposes even harsher conditions on the Hebrew slaves by requiring them to gather their own straw for brick making, the people complain to Moses and Aaron about their lot, and Moses in turn complains to YHWH in Exod 5:6-23.

The problem is compounded by the fact that not only does YHWH put the people at risk in the exodus narrative, YHWH hardens the heart of Pharaoh throughout the narrative to ensure that he will not listen to YHWH and that he will impose even harsher measures upon the Israelites in response to YHWH's actions against him.[10] The hardening of Pharaoh's heart serves YHWH's ultimate purpose to be recognized as creator and ultimate power in the universe. The moral dimensions of YHWH's treatment of Pharaoh and Egypt come into question; Pharaoh and Egypt do not have the capacity to accept YHWH and suffer as a result of YHWH's actions against them. The people of Israel, much like the Pharaoh and the people of Egypt, are ultimately pawns in a drama that is designed to demonstrate YHWH's power and sovereignty to the world. They are delivered from Egyptian bondage, but when they are led into the wilderness, they face the challenges of starvation and attack that call YHWH's purposes and moral character into question, much like the Abraham and Sarah traditions of Genesis.

Interpreters have tended to accept the claim that Israel rebels against YHWH, but YHWH's own actions may be questioned. After all, the narrative concerning Marah in Exod 5:22-27 makes it clear that YHWH puts Israel to the test in the wilderness just as much as Israel puts YHWH to the test. Indeed, the relationship between YHWH and Israel deteriorates even further from the time of Israel's arrival at Sinai on as expressed in the golden calf tradition of Exodus 32–34 and the post-Sinai wilderness traditions of Numbers 3–36.

The Golden Calf Narrative

A key episode concerning the tensions in the relationship between YHWH and Israel in the wilderness is the golden calf narrative in Exodus 32–34.[11] The narrative presupposes Moses' forty-day audience with YHWH on Mt. Sinai in which YHWH instructs him concerning the building of the tabernacle for holy service by the people (Exod 24:15-18; 25–31). It takes up the theme of the wilderness rebellion tradition by relating Israel's concern that Moses had led them into the wilderness only to abandon them. They therefore call upon Aaron to make a god that will go before them in the wilderness. Aaron responds by making the golden calf, which the people then worship as their own god. While still at Sinai, YHWH points out the apostasy to Moses and proposes to destroy the people and make a new nation from Moses. Moses opposes YHWH by pointing out that YHWH has made a vow with the ancestors of Israel to make them into a great nation. Upon returning from Mt. Sinai with the tablets of the covenant in hand, Moses observes the people's apostasy, smashes the tablets to symbolize the broken relationship with YHWH, destroys the golden calf, and calls upon those who were for YHWH to come to him in order to destroy those who had sinned. The Levites respond and kill some three thousand of the people. On the next day, YHWH refuses to go in the midst of the people lest YHWH destroy them. Moses pitches the tent of meeting outside of the Israelite camp to symbolize YHWH's estrangement from the people while speaking with YHWH to determine how to proceed. Moses persuades YHWH to continue to lead the people, views YHWH's presence from the cleft of the rock on Sinai, and inscribes two new tablets with the terms of the covenant between YHWH and Israel. The account of the people's compliance with YHWH's instructions to build the tabernacle then follows in Exodus 35–40.

The formal structure of the golden calf narrative is defined by its episodic character (see chart 2.3).

Chart 2.3	
Account of Israel's Purification	
Exod 32:1–34:35	
I. The First Day	**32:1-29**
A. Aaron constructs golden calf at people's request	32:1-6
B. Moses dissuades YHWH from destroying people	32:7-14
C. Moses unleashes Levites against the people for their apostasy	32:15-29
II. The Second Day	**32:30-34:35**
A. Plague against guilty among the people	32:30-35
B. Moses persuades YHWH to remain among people	33:1-23
C. Moses views YHWH's presence and receives terms of new covenant	34:1-35

A number of key issues emerge from analysis of this narrative. First, the narrative appears between the account in Exodus 25–31 of YHWH's instructions to build the tabernacle, which serves as the predecessor for the Temple as the holy place for worship of YHWH, and the account of the people's compliance with YHWH's instructions in Exodus 35–40. Insofar as YHWH's presence descends upon the tabernacle at the end of

54   chapter 40, the construction of the tabernacle provides part of the means by which YHWH agrees to remain present in the midst of the people. The destruction of those who committed apostasy in the golden calf narrative is therefore crucial to the overall account of the building of the tabernacle, namely, the people had to be purified from moral and cultic impurity before the tabernacle could be built for the presence of YHWH among the people.

Second, the narrative has a number of intertextual affinities with other narratives in the Pentateuch and Former Prophets that are particularly concerned with questions of Israel's covenant relationship with YHWH and the portrayal of the Northern Kingdom of Israel as apostate against YHWH.[12] The most obvious parallel is the account of King Jeroboam ben Nebat's construction of the golden calves for the northern Israelite sanctuaries at Beth El and Dan in the aftermath of the northern revolt against the house of David in 1 Kgs 12:25-33 (see also 1 Kings 13). In addition to the image of the golden calf/calves, narrative parallels include Jeroboam's statement to the people, "Behold your G-d/gods, O Israel, who brought you up from the land of Egypt," in 1 Kgs 12:28, which echoes Aaron's statement to Israel in Exod 32:4, and the identification of Jeroboam's sons, Abijah and Nadab, who respectively died of disease and revolt (see 1 Kgs 14:1-18; 14:20; 15:25-34), and Aaron's sons, Nadab and Abihu, who died for improperly offering incense before YHWH (Lev 10:1-11). A second parallel is Elijah's experience of the presence of YHWH in a cave at Horeb, the alternative name of Sinai in the Pentateuch, following his forty-day flight into the wilderness at a time when the northern king, Ahab, and his Phoenician wife, Jezebel, sought to destroy the prophets of YHWH (1 Kings 19). Whereas Moses saw YHWH's back, Elijah experiences YHWH, not in fire, wind, or earthquake, but in the silent voice of YHWH speaking to him. The third is the parallel between the renewed law code of Exod 34:10-26 and the prior code in Exod 23:10-19 together with the injunction against intermarrying with the Canaanite nations who would lead Israel into idolatry in Deut 7:1-6. Indeed, the renewed covenant law code in Exod 34:10-26 differs from Exod 23:10-19 by emphasizing a prohibition at the outset with language drawn from Deut 7:1-6. Finally, Moses' destruction of the golden calf by burning it, grinding it into dust, strewing the dust on the water, and making the people drink the water in Exod 32:20 echoes King Josiah's destruction of the idolatrous items dedicated to Baal and Asherah, which were ground to dust by the Wadi Kidron in 2 Kgs 23:4-7, and the destruction of the Beth El shrine, which was also burned and ground to dust in 2 Kgs 23:15. Overall, the interrelationship between

Exodus 32–34 and these various texts indicates that Exodus 32–34 is compositionally dependent upon the other narratives insofar as it brings all of their motifs and concerns together into one narrative. It also demonstrates that Exodus 32–34 portrays Israel's sins with the golden calf in the wilderness in relation to the portrayal of the sins of northern Israel. Insofar as the Josianic edition of the Deuteronomistic History employed this motif as a means to interpret theologically the fall of northern Israel as an act of divine punishment by YHWH,[13] it indicates a similar interest in portraying both the disruption and renewal of covenant in Exodus 32–34. In this respect, Exodus 32–34 points to Israel rather than YHWH as the party responsible for disaster.

Third is the role of the Levites in killing off the apostates in Israel and thereby in purifying the people from moral and cultic impurity. As the priestly tribe of Israel, the Levites are tasked with teaching YHWH's expectations concerning what is clean or required of the people and what is impure or forbidden to the people (Lev 10:10-11) and they are responsible for carrying out the ritual action necessary to maintain the relationship between YHWH and the people. When considered from a diachronic historical standpoint, this role is particularly important insofar as tradition maintains that the firstborn sons originally acted as priests before the Levites were designated for this role (see Numbers 3–4, 8, esp. 3:11-13; 3:40-43; 8:13-19; note especially 1 Samuel 1–3, in which Samuel, firstborn son of Hannah and her Ephraimite husband Elkanah, is raised to serve as a priest in the Shiloh sanctuary). It is also important historically since 1 Kgs 12:31 charges that Jeroboam authorized non-Levites to serve as priests in the north; perhaps the Levites represent a later development in Israelite or Judean religiosity. When considered from a synchronic literary standpoint, however, this narrative points to the Levites as those who would ultimately emerge as the caretakers of Israel's sanctity in the pentateuchal narrative. Not only do they purify the people from impurity by eliminating the apostates in the golden calf episode, but they also emerge as the caretakers of the tabernacle or wilderness sanctuary that will be built in Exodus 25–31 and that prefigures the Temple once the people settle into the promised land of Israel. Indeed, Num 3:10 makes it very clear that the sons of Aaron are responsible for observing priestly duties and outsiders who attempt to carry out these functions will be put to death (see also Numbers 18).

Finally, although the people are clearly portrayed as the guilty party in this narrative, YHWH's own moral culpability comes into question. When YHWH proposes to destroy the entire people for their apostasy in Exod 32:9-14, Moses must challenge YHWH and remind YHWH of the oath by which YHWH swore to the ancestors of Israel—Abraham, Isaac, and Israel (also known as Jacob)—that YHWH would make them into a people as numerous as the stars of the heaven and grant them the land of Israel in which to live. Although YHWH was bound by oath to the ancestors of Israel, YHWH was prepared to transgress that oath, and Moses had to step in and stop YHWH from engaging in what would have been an immoral act. Even so, YHWH's own capacity for violence is allowed to run its course in this passage when the Levites are allowed to kill three thousand Israelites of those worshiping the golden calf and YHWH unleashes a plague against Israel that very carefully kills off those who were guilty of apostasy. YHWH is vindicated in the narrative, but not without a challenge to YHWH's moral character. Ultimately, Moses' vision of YHWH's presence in Exod 34:6-7 outlines YHWH's mercy, or capacity to provide blessing, and justice, or capacity to mete out punishment, even to the descendants of the guilty.

From these issues, it is clear that the golden calf narrative in Exodus 32–34 is designed to articulate the need for moral and cultic purity on the part of the people of Israel when appearing before YHWH in the holy sanctuary. It further points to the role that the Levitical priests will assume in educating the people concerning their responsibilities to YHWH and in mediating the relationship between YHWH and Israel through ritual action and purification in the sanctuary. Altogether, it presumes YHWH's righteousness in this case, insofar as the people engage in apostasy in this narrative, although it acknowledges YHWH's dangerous character. But this narrative raises questions concerning divine culpability as well, especially since it depends upon the historical experience of the destruction of northern Israel to make its case. The Northern Kingdom of Israel was destroyed in the late eighth century B.C.E. by the Assyrian Empire, which sought to expand its military and economic power into western Asia. Northern Israel was an obstacle to those plans and quite possibly had broken an alliance with Assyria that originated in the early years of the Jehu dynasty that ruled Israel from 842 B.C.E. Rather than focus on the political, economic, and military causes of northern Israel's downfall, the Former Prophets portray Israel's fall as a result of apostasy against YHWH from the time of King Jeroboam ben Nebat, who began his reign ca. 922 B.C.E. (see esp. 1 Kings 12–13; 2 Kings 17). In putting forward such a portrayal, the Former Prophets engage in a form of theodicy in which YHWH is absolved of any responsibility for the disaster, and Israel itself is blamed for its own demise. Insofar as Exodus 32–34 draws upon this paradigm for portraying Israel as responsible for its own misfortune in the wilderness, it too must be recognized as a form of theodicy that is designed to justify the righteousness of YHWH as the perpetrator of violence over against Israel as the victim of that violence. The roles of the tabernacle or Temple and the Levitical priesthood, then, perpetuate such theodicy. In this manner, the Exodus 32–34 narrative—like the Former Prophets—engages in such self-condemnation and self-critique as a means to negotiate the realities of historical experience, namely, if Israel suffers, Israel and not YHWH is responsible for its own suffering, and the means to remedy that suffering is by renewed and stronger efforts on the part of the people—as mediated by the tabernacle or Temple and the priesthood—to fulfill YHWH's expectations. In such a manner, YHWH agrees to remain present among the people and to formulate the covenant between them once again.

The Book of Numbers

The book of Numbers is easily the most enigmatic portion of the pentateuchal narrative.[14] Although the book of Numbers appears as a coherent block within the present five-book structure of the Pentateuch, analysis of the literary form of the Pentateuch above points to the role of the *toledoth* formula in setting the basic structure of the Pentateuch as a whole and the role of the itinerary formulas in setting the formal structures of both the History of the Twelve Tribes of Israel, that is, "the generations of Jacob," in Gen 37:2—Num 2:34 (which includes the revelation of Torah at Sinai) and the History of Israel under the Guidance of the Levites in Num 3:1—Deut 34:12, that is, "the generations of Aaron and Moses."

Insofar as Num 3:1—Deut 34:12 presents the journey through the wilderness, readers may note its formal literary structure.[15] The unit begins with an account of the sanctification of the people at Sinai under the leadership of the Levites in Num 3:1—10:10, which introduces the following subunits concerning the journey from Sinai to Moab, just across the Jordan River from the promised land of Israel. Numbers 10:11—11:35a recounts the journey from Sinai to Kibroth Hattaavah, where the people rebel for want of food (cf. Exod 15:22—17:7). Numbers 11:35b—12:15 recounts the journey from Kibroth Hattaavah to Hazeroth where Miriam and Aaron challenged Moses' leadership because of his marriage to a Cushite woman. Numbers 12:16—19:22 recounts the journey from Hazeroth to the wilderness of Paran, and accounts of Israel's rebellion following the reports of the spies who scouted the land of Canaan in Numbers 13–14 and the rebellion of Korah, Dathan, Abijam, and On against Moses and its results in Numbers 15–19. Numbers 20:1-21 recounts the journey from Paran to Kadesh in the wilderness of Zin, including the people's complaints about the lack of water and YHWH's condemnation of Moses and Aaron. Numbers 20:22—21:3 recounts the journey from Kadesh in the wilderness of Zin to Mt. Hor where Aaron died. Numbers 21:4-25 recounts the journey from Mt. Hor to Edom and Moab, including the defeat of Sihon and Og. Numbers 22:1—36:13 recounts the arrival in Moab, including the account of Israel's apostasy at Baal Peor. Finally, Deut 1:1—34:12 recounts Moses' last speeches to the people in Moab and his death prior to their crossing the Jordan River to take possession of the promised land of Israel.

Examination of each subunit in Num 3:1—Deut 34:12 concerning the wilderness journey points to instances of rebellion against YHWH or Moses that highlight tensions in the relationship between Israel, Moses, and YHWH. Because Moses stands as the mediator between YHWH and Israel, his position is particularly difficult since he is repeatedly challenged by the people or elements of the Levites and condemned by YHWH. Nevertheless, these narratives point to resolution of these tensions as well, insofar as they portray the development of the role of the Levitical priesthood as the party responsible for negotiating the relationship between YHWH and the people. Because of YHWH's holy nature and YHWH's expectation that the people will be holy as well, the emerging role of the priesthood is to ensure the sanctification of Israel as they prepare to take possession of the promised land of Israel. Such efforts on the part of the priesthood and the people then emerge as a means to contain potential outbreaks of violence by YHWH against the people.

Numbers 3:1—10:10 begins with the *toledoth* formula, "and these are the generations of Aaron and Moses," as introduction to the establishment of Levitical leadership over the people of Israel.[16] It concludes the census of the Levites and the assignment of specific duties pertaining to the holiness of the people for each Levitical clan in Numbers 3–4; laws pertaining to priestly supervision of Israel to ensure the holiness of the people in Numbers 5–6; the preparation of the holy tabernacle by the Levites for the journey through the wilderness in Numbers 7–9; and construction of the silver trumpets that will summon the people to assemble and undertake their journey, here portrayed as a cultic procession with the tribes arrayed around the tabernacle, through the wilderness.

Numbers 10:11—11:35a takes up the first stage of the journey from Sinai to Kibroth Hattaavah, and focuses on the issue of the people's rebellion against YHWH and Moses for lack of food.[17] Having heard the complaints of the people, Moses in turn complains to YHWH, demanding to know why YHWH has mistreated him by laying the entire burden of responsibility on Moses' shoulders. Moses makes it clear that he has no capacity to provide the people with food and states that he would rather die than continue to bear this responsibility. YHWH's efforts to resolve this problem point both to an effort to address the concerns of both the people and Moses and YHWH's own exasperation and frustration with the people and Moses. YHWH calls upon Moses to gather the seventy elders of Israel, apparently the leadership structure of Israel that appears in various narratives depicting premonarchic Israel and that later plays an important role in selecting and supporting the kings of Israel. YHWH places the divine spirit in them and thereby authorizes them to share in the burden of leading the people of Israel. In this respect, the narrative serves an etiological function by pointing to the origins of Israel's key leadership council. The narrative also expresses YHWH's frustration with the people insofar as it portrays YHWH's anger against them, that is, YHWH responds to the people's complaints by declaring that they will have so much meat that it will come out of their nostrils and become loathsome to them. Once the people had eaten the quail that YHWH provided for meat, YHWH's anger then prompts a plague against the people in retribution for their complaints. Clearly, the tensions remain. This episode therefore represents only a first stage in attempting to resolve the tensions between YHWH, Moses, and Israel.

Numbers 11:35b—12:15 takes up the journey from Kibroth Hattaavah to Hazeroth, and focuses on the challenge to Moses' leadership by Miriam and Aaron.[18] Charging that Moses has married a Cushite woman, they contend that Moses cannot exercise exclusive leadership over the community and that YHWH speaks through them as well. Several issues underlie this charge. First, Moses' marriage to a Cushite woman refers to his marriage to Zipporah, the daughter of Jethro (also known as Reuel or Hobab), the priest of Midian. Although "Cushite" is generally understood as a reference to Ethiopia, Hab 3:7 indicates that Cushan is a part of Midian. Miriam and Aaron's objection is apparently based on Moses' marriage to a non-Israelite foreigner. As a Levite, Moses would presumably be required to marry a virgin from the Levites (see Lev 21:14-15), a widow of a priest, or a virgin from Israel (see Ezek 44:22). Because Zipporah's father, Jethro, is a priest who blesses YHWH and offers sacrifice in Exod 18:10-12 and who advises Moses on how to set up Israel's judicial system, later Jewish tradition recognizes Jethro as a convert to Judaism.[19]

60   Whether one can speak meaningfully of conversion to Judaism in these narratives, it is clear that Jethro functions as a priest to YHWH, and that Moses would therefore be entitled to marry Jethro's daughter. Within the narrative, YHWH makes no reference to the status of Zipporah, but simply declares that YHWH speaks to Moses face to face whereas YHWH speaks to other prophets in a dream. Other traditions question whether Moses can see YHWH's face (e.g., Exod 33:20; cf. Num 12:8), but YHWH's answer is basically an authoritative statement that YHWH will authorize whomever YHWH wishes to serve as leader for the people. Miriam is then struck with leprosy and isolated from the people for seven days for daring to speak against Moses. Again, YHWH resorts to violence and an authoritarian response to settle the issue.

    The lengthy account of Israel's journey from Hazeroth to the wilderness of Paran in Num 12:16—19:22 includes two very important rebellion accounts in which Moses must persuade YHWH not to kill the entire nation of Israel as threatened prior to authorizing Aaron and his sons to serve as priests, to bear the guilt of the guilt of the sanctuary on behalf of the people, and thereby to mediate the relationship between YHWH and Israel. The first appears in Numbers 13–14, which relates the people's rebellion after having received reports from the spies sent to Canaan that the land is inhabited by giants.[20] Only Joshua ben Nun of Ephraim and Caleb ben Jephunneh of Judah argued that Israel should proceed to take possession of the land as YHWH promised. Having heard the people's complaint that they would be better off in Egypt, YHWH confronts Moses demanding to know how long this people would continue to rebel against YHWH and show no faith in YHWH's promises. Upon hearing YHWH's threat to destroy the people in the wilderness and to make a new nation from Moses, Moses must take the moral high road and challenge YHWH by pointing out that such action would destroy YHWH's credibility in the eyes of the nations. Moses repeats the formulaic portrayal of YHWH's mercy from Exod 34:6-7 and asks that YHWH pardon the people. YHWH relents on killing the entire people immediately, but declares that the entire generation, with the exception of Joshua and Caleb, will die during the course of forty years of wandering in the wilderness. When the people grieve and propose to attack the land after all, they ignore Moses' advice that it is too late since YHWH is no longer in their midst, and they are soundly defeated by the Amalekites and Canaanites at Hormah. This narrative again portrays YHWH as a threat to the people, but points to the leadership roles of Joshua of Ephraim and Caleb of Judah, leaders of the two major tribal groups that form the foundation of northern Israel and southern Judah once Israel is settled in the land.

Although the spy narrative points to the emergence of tribal leadership in Israel and Judah, the following rebellion by Korah and other priestly elements portrayed in Numbers 15–19 plays a decisive role in pointing to the rise of Aaron and his sons as the high priesthood within Israel.[21] Numbers 15 calls for offering to be made by the people to YHWH upon entering the promised land of Israel. In addition to regular offerings, the chapter specifies offerings in the event of unwitting violation of YHWH's expectations. The seriousness of the matter and potential for divine violence is underlined by the paragraphs that call for the death of a man gathering wood on the Sabbath—and thereby violating YHWH's expectations that the Sabbath be a holy day. The *tzittzit* or fringes on the corners of garments serve as a reminder to observe YHWH's expectations. The rebellion against the authority of Moses and Aaron by Korah, a Levite, and Dathan, Abijam, and On, members of the tribe of Reuben, in Numbers 16–17 likely presupposes historical conflict within the Israelite priesthood that was settled with the emergence of the Aaronide family as the chief priests. The involvement of the Reubenites may well represent reflection on the loss of the Trans-Jordan—where Reuben was located—to the Arameans and Assyrians in the ninth–eighth centuries B.C.E. It is noteworthy that Eleazar ben Aaron is identified as the figure who would remove the holy firepans left behind and hammer them into plating for the altar. Likewise, Aaron took action to check the plague that broke out against the people in the aftermath of Korah's failed attempt to offer incense. The role of Aaron and his sons as chief priests who would bear the guilt of the sanctuary is then made clear in Numbers 18. In essence, the Aaronic priesthood would serve as guardians of the people who would instruct them in holy behavior and thereby avert the outbreak of divine wrath. Numbers 19 addresses this concern by taking up laws of purification from corpse contamination, particularly since death is the antithesis to holiness in priestly thought (cf. Leviticus 21).

YHWH's condemnation of Moses and Aaron at Meribah in Num 20:1-13 is discussed above. Numbers 20:22—21:3 takes up the journey from Zin to Mt. Hor where Aaron dies. The importance of this passage lies in the transfer of priestly authority from Aaron to his son Eleazar.[22] Numbers 21:4-35 recounts the journey from Mt. Hor to Edom.[23] Although this narrative takes up the defeat of Sihon and Og, it likely reflects Israelite hegemony over Edom and Moab in the tenth–ninth centuries B.C.E. Israel's rebellion in the first part of this narrative, however, results in the construction of the copper serpent figure to protect the people from the *seraphim* or fiery serpents that bit them in the wilderness. The copper serpent is to be identified with Nehushtan, a cultic statue removed from the Jerusalem Temple by King Hezekiah in 2 Kgs 18:4 and likely presupposed in Isaiah's vision of YHWH and the Seraphim in Isaiah 6.

Finally, the lengthy account of Israel's arrival and sojourn in Moab in Numbers 22:1—36:13 relates Balaam's blessing, the apostasy at Baal Peor, Joshua's designation as Moses' successor, and various laws and instruction pertaining to Israel's life in the promised land of Israel. Key for the present concern is the narrative concerning the apostasy at Baal Peor in Numbers 25[24] and the designation of Joshua as Moses' successor in Num 27:12-23.[25] Phineas ben Eleazar ben Aaron is credited with turning back YHWH's wrath at Baal Peor and granted a *berit shalom*, covenant of peace, so that he and his descendants may serve as priests to YHWH forever. Once again, the role of the priests as guardians of Israel's sanctity before YHWH comes to expression together with legitimization of Phineas as ancestor of the Aaronide high priestly line. Just as Aaronic succession is defined in Numbers 25, Num 27:12-23 defines Moses' succession by designating Joshua ben Nun as Moses' successor who would lead the people into the promised land of Israel following Moses' death. Whereas Phineas is a priest, Joshua is described as a "man of spirit," like the seventy elders of Numbers 11 who would serve as political leaders of Israel. The following material in Numbers then calls for ritual instruction and preparation for the conquest and distribution of the promised land among the tribes of Israel.

This survey of Numbers indicates that the wilderness rebellion tradition serves as an etiological narrative for the institution of priestly and political leadership in Israel. It is noteworthy that the priestly leadership in particular is instituted to instruct Israel in holy behavior before YHWH and thereby to avert the potential for divine violence against the people.

Divine Violence
and the Wilderness Rebellion Traditions

This survey of the wilderness rebellion traditions points clearly to the capacity for divine violence against Israel as a fundamental issue, but it also charges that Israel or individuals, such as Moses, Aaron, Miriam, Korah, and others, are culpable for failing to observe YHWH's expectations for holy conduct. Again, the makings of a theodicy are evident, that is, YHWH cannot be held responsible for violence or wrongdoing. YHWH's violence is punishment warranted by the actions of the people, meaning, the victim is responsible for its own victimization.

Two facets of this discussion call for attention. First, the wilderness rebellion traditions employ the motif of YHWH's punishment of Israel for its rebellion as a basis to call for institutional leadership of the nations. The Levitical priesthood is particularly important in this regard since it serves as the guardians of Israel against divine violence by teaching the people holy behavior in accordance with YHWH's expectations. Political leadership also emerges in the form of the elders of Israel, which served as a leadership council for Israel in both the premonarchic and monarchic eras, and in the form of Joshua, who serves in a military, political, and quasi-royal function as Moses' successor. The second facet is the potential historical background for some of the wilderness narratives, that is, the rise of northern Israel under Jeroboam ben Nabat and the foundation of sanctuaries at Beth El and Dan in relation to the golden calf episode in Exodus 32–34; the destruction of Korah and his Reubenite supporters in Numbers 16–17, which may reflect the loss of the Trans-Jordanian region where the tribe of Reuben resided in the ninth–eighth centuries B.C.E.; and the defeat of Sihon and Og in Num 21:4–35, which may reflect Israel's subjugation of Edom and Moab in the tenth–ninth centuries B.C.E. The potential historical dimensions of these narratives are crucial insofar as they explain Israel's reverses and victories as acts of YHWH—the reverses come as the result of Israel's wrongdoing and the victories come as the result of YHWH's blessing. In this manner, the pentateuchal narrative points to Israel's merits or lack of merit before YHWH as the means to explain the nation's fortunes and the need for institutional leadership that will ensure the nation's merits.

This, of course, raises the issue with which this chapter began, that is, YHWH's condemnation of Moses. The need for institutional leadership, whether priestly or political, is crucial to understanding Moses' condemnation, namely, even Moses can fail as a leader, particularly given YHWH's high expectations for holy standards within the people of Israel. But even if a leader of Moses' caliber can fail, there is always a mechanism in place to raise a new leader in his place who will act to ensure Israel's future. In this respect, the pentateuchal narrative represents an effort to account for the reverses that Israel suffers in a very hostile world, but it also points to Israel's leaders, both priestly and political, as the means by which Israel will address and overcome those reversals.

THREE

The Question of Theodicy in the Historical Books
Jeroboam, Manasseh, and Josiah

F or much of the twentieth century, modern scholarly research has focused primarily on the diachronic dimensions of the historical books of the Hebrew Bible. In considering the books of the Former Prophets, that is, Joshua, Judges, 1-2 Samuel, and 1-2 Kings, or the Chronicler's history, that is, 1-2 Chronicles and Ezra-Nehemiah, diachronically oriented scholarship has emphasized two concerns of historical research.[1] The first concern is the historical veracity and plausibility of the biblical narrative, generally in relation to archeological research and ancient Near Eastern historical literature—for instance, To what extent do the accounts of Sennacherib's invasion of Judah and siege of Jerusalem in 2 Kings 18–20 and Isaiah 36–39 represent an accurate portrayal of historical events or a legendary rendition of YHWH's actions? The second concern is the compositional history of the historical narratives in an attempt to specify the historical background of the narratives and the concerns that they were intended to address—for instance, To what extent is the composition of the books of Kings the product of successive attempts by a Josianic edition of the Deuteronomistic History (DtrH) to explain the fall of the Northern Kingdom of Israel as a consequence of the apostasy of the northern tribes, and by an exilic edition of the DtrH to explain the Babylonian exile as a consequence of Judah's failures to abide by the divine will? Both concerns are ultimately bound up with an attempt to reconstruct and understand the historical development of the ancient Israelite nation and the literature of the Hebrew Bible.

The Former Prophets have received the lion's share of attention in historical research, especially since scholars have been more inclined to trust the historical reliability of the books of Joshua, Judges, Samuel, and Kings than the priestly history of the Chronicles and Ezra-Nehemiah. The work of Martin Noth is especially influential since he attempted to define the historiographical outlook of the books of the Former Prophets in relation to the theological viewpoint of the book of Deuteronomy.[2] Based on his observations of the theological compatibility of Deuteronomy and the Former Prophets, Noth argued that Joshua, Judges, Samuel, and Kings constitute a coherent historiographical presentation of Israel's history in the land from the time of Joshua through the Babylonian exile defined in relation to the theological principles of Deuteronomy, for instance, adherence to one G-d, worship at one legitimate site chosen by YHWH, a conditional concept of covenant in which Israel's possession of the land is dependent on their observance of YHWH's expectations as defined in Deuteronomy, and so forth. In essence, Noth argued that the DtrH authors reworked older source material to compile a history that was intended to explain the Babylonian exile as a consequence of Israel's failure to abide by YHWH's expectations.[3] Subsequent scholarship noted nuances in the presentation. Among European scholars, Rudolf Smend and Walter Dietrich noted emphases on prophetic themes and concerns with Torah or Law that pointed to three exilic editions of the DtrH, that is, a foundational DtrG edition that laid out the basic history of Israel in the early exilic period, a prophetic DtrP edition that emphasized the role of the prophets in the historical work, and a nomistic DtrN that pointed to concerns with law in articulating Israel's history.[4] American scholars, such as Frank Moore Cross Jr., Richard Nelson, Gary Knoppers, and myself, emphasize preexilic editions of the DtrH that have been updated in relation to the Babylonian exile.[5] Especially noteworthy in this regard is the emphasis on the sins of northern Israel's first king, Jeroboam ben Nebat, to explain the fall of northern Israel to the Assyrian Empire as an act of divine judgment and the identification of King Josiah of Judah as the ideal monarch of the Davidic line who would reunite northern Israel and southern Judah as in the days of David and Solomon. Following this preexilic Josianic edition of the DtrH, the expanded, exilic edition of the DtrH accounts for the failure of King Josiah's program by pointing to King Manasseh of Judah as a monarch whose sins were so great that YHWH determined to destroy Jerusalem and exile the people of Judah despite Josiah's righteousness.

Modern research on the Chronicler has tended to lag behind that of the DtrH because of its concern with priestly and cultic matters and its rewriting of narratives found in the DtrH. Nevertheless, the work of Martin Noth was again decisive in pointing to the historiographical agenda of the Chronicler as a fourth- or third-century B.C.E. work that sought to justify the character and outlook of the postexilic Judean community over against the Samaritans.[6] Research has advanced considerably since the work of Noth, however.[7] Scholars have come to regard 1-2 Chronicles and Ezra-Nehemiah as two separate historiographical works.[8] First and Second Chronicles must be taken far more seriously as a historical source that preserves historical accounts of Rehoboam's fortification of Judah's northern borders with Israel, Hezekiah's construction of Jerusalem's water system, Manasseh's subjugation to Ashurbanipal at the time of the Babylonian revolt, and so forth.[9] First and Second Chronicles, that is, the Chronicler's History or the ChrH, has its own sense of royalist eschatology that looks forward to an ideal Davidic restoration around the Jerusalem Temple, and it explains disaster and suffering, such as the Babylonian exile, as the consequence of wrongdoing by the affected generation, rather than as the cumulative effect of wrongdoing by earlier generations or individuals as in the DtrH.[10] Overall, the Chronicler's account represents a similar attempt, perhaps from the sixth or fifth century B.C.E., to account for exile and the prospects of restoration, but its viewpoint is quite distinct from the DtrH.

Nevertheless, scholarly discussion of diachronic issues in the Bible's historical literature points to an important synchronic dimension of these books, namely, the degree to which they attempt to explain the disasters of the Babylonian exile and the earlier fall of the Northern Kingdom of Israel. Indeed, these explanations are frequently inadequate. Does Jeroboam's apostasy in setting up the golden calves at Beth El and Dan truly explain why the Assyrians invaded and destroyed northern Israel according to the DtrH? Does Manasseh's apostasy truly warrant the destruction of Jerusalem and the Babylonian exile, despite the righteousness of Josiah, long after their deaths in DtrH? Indeed, this explanation comes into question when one reads in the Chronicler's account of Manasseh's repentance upon being dragged in chains to appear before the Assyrian king in Babylon or of Josiah's guilt leading to his own death. Interpreters are beginning to recognize the theological importance of these attempts to explain disaster as expressions of theodicy, that is, G-d is righteous and all-powerful, the disasters of the Babylonian exile or the earlier fall of northern Israel cannot be attributed to divine impotence, neglect, or evil.[11]

Disaster in the Hebrew Bible may then be explained only by human wrongdoing, and the debate among the historical sources becomes one of identifying which human parties are at fault, namely, Jeroboam and the people of northern Israel, Manasseh, Josiah, or the generation of Judeans at the time of Jerusalem's fall. This chapter therefore examines the presentations of Jeroboam, Manasseh, and Josiah in the DtrH and the ChrH in an attempt to discern how the Bible's historical works wrestled with the problem of theodicy in their attempts to come to grips with and explain theologically the disasters of the fall of northern Israel and the Babylonian exile.

Jeroboam and the Fall of the Northern Kingdom

Jeroboam ben Nebat is the first king of the Northern Kingdom of Israel following the revolt of the northern tribes of Israel against King Rehoboam ben Solomon of the ruling house of David. Although he appears in both the DtrH and the ChrH, the Chronicler portrays him only as a sinful and rebellious foil against Kings Rehoboam and Abijah of Judah in 2 Chronicles 10–13. Indeed, Abijah decisively defeats Jeroboam in battle. Jeroboam led the Israelite delegation that revolted against Rehoboam at Shechem in 2 Chronicles 10, and Abijah's speech prior to his battle with Jeroboam in 2 Chronicles 13 notes Jeroboam's rebellion against Solomon and Rehoboam, his construction of the golden calves, and his banishment of the Levitical priests, but he does not bear the responsibility for causing all Israel to sin thereby leading to the destruction of the Northern Kingdom of Israel as he does in the DtrH. Because of its focus on the kings of Judah and the Jerusalem Temple, the ChrH does not even mention the fall of the Northern Kingdom although it does note that King Hezekiah destroyed all the illegitimate high places throughout the lands of Judah, Benjamin, Ephraim, and Manasseh in 2 Chr 31:1 following his celebration of Passover in Jerusalem that included all Israel and Judah in 2 Chronicles 30. The destruction of northern Israel is not an important topic for consideration in the ChrH.

The destruction of northern Israel is, however, a key issue in the DtrH, and King Jeroboam ben Nebat of Israel bears the primary responsibility in the DtrH for leading northern Israel into sin and its ultimate destruction. Jeroboam first appears in 1 Kgs 11:26-40 as one of Solomon's adversaries who arose late in his reign. Jeroboam is an Ephraimite officer of Solomon who is placed in charge of the forced labor of the house of Joseph. He revolts against Solomon when the prophet Ahijah the Shilonite delivers to him a prophetic oracle in which YHWH designates him as king over the ten tribes of northern Israel. As a result of his rebellion against Solomon, Jeroboam flees to Egypt where he is given sanctuary by Pharaoh Shishak and marries the pharaoh's sister. According to 1 Kings 12, Jeroboam returned from Egypt to lead the northern Israelite delegation when it met with Rehoboam at Shechem to accept him as king. Following Rehoboam's ill-considered response to the northern delegation concerning his intention to press them harder than his father, Solomon, had done, the northern tribes revolt against Rehoboam and designate Jeroboam as their king.

Jeroboam's sins begin in 1 Kgs 12:25 when he begins his reign. After taking defensive measures to protect his kingdom against Judah, he reasoned that northern Israel would need sanctuaries of its own to prevent the people from returning to the Jerusalem Temple to worship YHWH where Rehoboam would be able to instigate the people to overthrow him. Jeroboam therefore built sanctuaries at Beth El and Dan and installed golden calves for worship in each, declaring to the people, "Behold your gods, O Israel, who brought you up out of Egypt!" In addition, he appointed priests, not from the priestly tribe of Levi, but from among all the people to preside over worship and declared a festival (Heb.: ḥag), apparently Sukkot, Tabernacles, to be observed on the fifteenth day of the *eighth* month, rather than the fifteenth day of the *seventh* month when Sukkot is traditionally observed. Such actions constituted great sin on Jeroboam's part in the view of the Kings narrative, since Jeroboam compromised the sanctity of holy worship of YHWH in Israel (see esp. 1 Kgs 12:30; 13:33-34). As a result of his sins, an anonymous man of G-d condemned the Beth El altar when Jeroboam presided over an offering in 1 Kgs 13:1-10, and when Jeroboam's wife came to seek aid for her ill son, the prophet Ahijah the Shilonite declared that the house of Jeroboam would be utterly destroyed because of Jeroboam's sins in 1 Kgs 14:1-20. Jeroboam's dynasty is indeed destroyed when Jeroboam's son, Nadab, is overthrown by Baasha in 1 Kgs 15:25-34 after only two years on the throne.

Although Jeroboam's dynasty is relatively short-lived, the DtrH views him as extraordinarily important insofar as he emerges as the paradigm for sinful Israelite leadership throughout the entire history of the Northern Kingdom in the DtrH.[12] Every northern Israelite king from his son Nadab through Hoshea, the last king of northern Israel, is accused of having followed in the sins of Jeroboam thereby leading the entire northern Israelite kingdom into sin against YHWH. Indeed, the DtrH sermon concerning the fall of the Northern Kingdom of Israel in 2 Kings 17 explicitly charges Jeroboam with having led the nation into sin against YHWH and that this sin is ultimately the cause of YHWH's decision to destroy the Northern Kingdom of Israel. The text in 2 Kgs 17:21-23 makes it clear that the people are charged with having followed in the sins of Jeroboam, and that this sin is the cause of northern Israel's exile to Assyria "until this day."

The DtrH charge that Jeroboam—and all Israel and its kings—are ultimately responsible for their own destruction is particularly striking in the aftermath of the modern experience of the Shoah. Theological discussion of the Shoah clearly raises questions concerning some of the standard theological paradigms of sin and guilt in the Bible as well as in the postbiblical traditions of both Judaism and Christianity. Although many historical treatments of Jeroboam and the history of the Northern Kingdom point to its corrupt character as a basis for considering its ultimate demise at the hands of the Assyrian army in the late eighth century B.C.E., it would be wise to consider some very important historical factors in relation to the DtrH portrayal of Jeroboam and the history of northern Israel.

First, Jeroboam's establishment of the sanctuaries at Beth El and Dan is hardly a sinful act in and of itself. As the narrative in 1 Kgs 12:25-33 makes clear, Jeroboam's reasons for establishing these sanctuaries has little to do with any attempt to commit sin; rather, it is part of his attempt to secure his kingdom against the threat of attack from Judah or Judean attempts to instigate revolt when the people of northern Israel return to Jerusalem to worship YHWH. Earlier biblical tradition points to the foundation of both sanctuaries well before the time of Jeroboam, albeit with different evaluations. Genesis 28:10-22 relates the patriarch Jacob's vision of YHWH and the stairway to heaven when he spends the night at Luz while on his journey to Haran to find a wife. When he awakes from the vision, in which YHWH grants him the covenant of Abraham and Isaac and promises him and his descendants the land, Jacob erects a sacred pillar on the site and renames it Beth El, "House of G-d." In essence, Gen 28:10-22 is a sanctuary foundation narrative that portrays Beth El in a very positive light.[13] Other narratives—such as Genesis 35, in which Rachel dies after departing Beth El; Judges 2, which associates the site with weeping; Judges 19–21, which identifies Beth El as the site at which Israel determined to destroy Benjamin; and Amos 7:10-17 and 9:1-10, in which the prophet Amos condemns Beth El—build a somewhat questionable reputation for the site, apparently due to Judean polemics against Beth El.[14] Judges 17–18 relates the foundation of the sanctuary at Dan in relation to an Ephraimite named Micah, who used money that he originally stole from his own mother to build an idol for worship at the site and corrupted a Levite from Bethlehem who served as priest at Dan.[15] The present form of the narrative clearly reflects Judean polemics against the northern tribes and Dan in particular, but the narrative is likely based on a much older tradition that would have related a more positive foundation narrative much like that of Beth El in Gen 28:10-22. Traces of this earlier narrative appear in the notice of the appointment of Jonathan ben Gershom ben Moses as priest at Dan in Judg 18:30. Although the present text modifies the name Moses so that it appears as Manasseh,[16] Dan was apparently once the sanctuary served by the priestly line of Moses in ancient Israel.

Second, Jeroboam's construction of the golden calves hardly constitutes a sin in and of itself. Although Jeroboam's announcement to Israel, "Behold your gods, O Israel, that brought you up out of Egypt," in 1 Kgs 12:28 (see also Aaron's statement to Israel on presenting them with the golden calf in Exod 32:4, 8; cf. Neh 9:18) indicates that the golden calves are to be worshiped as gods, there is no indication that northern Israelite practice would have called for the worship of golden calf images as suggested in this text. Calf and bull images are frequently associated with Baal or El in Canaanite religious practice to depict the god's strength, virility, and fertility, but the gods are not identified as calves or bulls per se. Rather, ancient Near Eastern iconography frequently portrays the gods mounted on such animals, such as the Syrian, Assyrian, or other storm gods on the back of a bull (ANEP 500–501, 531, 534), the Egyptian goddess Kadesh on the back of a lion (ANEP 470–74; cf. 486), or Ishtar of Arbela on the back of a lion (ANEP 522).[17] Such imagery is often associated with YHWH without any indication of apostasy, for instance, 'ăbîr ya'ăqōb, "the bull/mighty one of Jacob," in Gen 49:24; Isa 49:26; 60:16; and Ps 132:2, 5, or 'ăbîr yiśrā'ēl, "the bull/mighty one of Israel," in Isa 1:24. Indeed, the ark of the covenant housed in the Holy of Holies in the Jerusalem Temple is conceived as a throne, seat, or mount over which YHWH is enthroned as indicated in the formula, "YHWH Sebaoth who is enthroned above the cherubim," in 1 Sam 4:4; 2 Sam 6:2; and Isa 66:1. The issue is not one of apostasy. Rather, it is a question of the iconography employed to depict the same god in different state contexts; northern Israel employs bull or calf imagery to portray the mount of YHWH whereas southern Judah employs the ark as YHWH's throne. Ultimately, the matter turns on the question asked by Jeroboam in the Kings narrative, that is, Will the people worship in the Judean sanctuary at Jerusalem or in the northern sanctuaries at Beth El and Dan?

Third, Jeroboam's acceptance of non-Levitical priests would constitute an act of apostasy in Judah where the tribe of Levi defines the priesthood that would serve in the Jerusalem Temple. It is therefore noteworthy that traces of the history of the priesthood appear in biblical narrative to indicate that the Levitical priests were not always recognized as the sole legitimate priesthood in ancient Israel. The narratives in Numbers 3–10 that discuss the organization of Israel around the ark of the covenant and the Levitical priesthood note in several instances that YHWH chose the Levites to serve as priests so that they might replace the firstborn sons of Israel who had formerly served in such roles, for instance, "YHWH spoke to Moses, saying, 'I hereby take the Levites from among the Israelites in place of all the firstborn, the first issue of the womb among the Israelites: the Levites shall be mine. Every firstborn is mine: at the time that I smote every firstborn in the land of Egypt, I consecrated every firstborn in Israel, man and beast, to myself to be mine, YHWH's'" (Num 3:11-13; cf. 3:9-10; 3:40-51; 8:13-19; cf. Exod 22:28-29; 34:19-20). In this respect, it is noteworthy that Samuel, the firstborn son to Hannah and her Ephraimite husband, Elkanah, is dedicated for service as a priest at the Shiloh Temple in 1 Samuel 1–3. It would appear that Jeroboam's decision to accept non-Levitical priests does not constitute a case of apostasy, but instead constitutes an example of early Israelite practice.

Finally, Jeroboam's institution of a festival of Sukkot in the eighth month is not necessarily a case of apostasy, but perhaps an indication of a different system of calendar reckoning. Biblical tradition provides for the observance of a second festival of Passover in Num 9:1-14 and 2 Chronicles 30 that some recognize as remnants of a different system of festival reckoning in ancient Israel. Indeed, differences in calendar reckoning in the second century B.C.E. appear to lie behind the charges of the Qumran sect that the high priest of the Jerusalem Temple traveled to Qumran to persecute the Righteous Teacher on Yom Kippur.[18]

When these factors are taken into consideration, it seems that the charge of Jeroboam's and northern Israel's apostasy is not so much a matter of fact as it is a matter of Judean attempts to polemicize against the Northern Kingdom of Israel for its abandonment of the house of David and the Jerusalem Temple. It is well known that the Assyrian Empire did not decide to attack Israel or any other nation to serve as YHWH's instrument of punishment, even though they may have found such claims to be useful propaganda. Instead, the Assyrian aim was to gain control over the trade routes between Mesopotamia and Egypt and ultimately to gain control over Egypt itself.[19] In this respect, the claim that the Northern

Kingdom of Israel was destroyed for its sins is an attempt to explain theologically the problem of northern Israel's exile. Such a claim avoids the charge that Israel fell due to weakness or moral failing in YHWH; rather, northern Israel fell because of its own wrongdoing, beginning with its first king, Jeroboam ben Nebat. In this respect, the DtrH presentation of Jeroboam constitutes a case of theodicy insofar as it protects the image of YHWH as a potent and moral deity.

Manasseh's Oppression and Repentance

King Manasseh ben Hezekiah of Judah is both the longest-reigning monarch of the Davidic line and one of the most controversial kings of Israel and Judah. Manasseh ascended the throne following the reign of his father, Hezekiah ben Ahaz, at the age of twelve, and ruled Judah for fifty-five years. Although biblical sources maintain that YHWH delivered Hezekiah from the Assyrian invasion of Sennacherib in 701 B.C.E., historical sources indicate that Assyria maintained control of Judah throughout the first half of the seventh century B.C.E., and that Manasseh, whether voluntarily or under threat, submitted to Assyria as a loyal vassal throughout his reign.[20] Both the DtrH in 2 Kgs 21:1-18 and the ChrH in 2 Chr 33:1-20 charge that Manasseh was an oppressive ruler who filled Jerusalem with blood, presumably in suppressing opposition to his reign. But the two accounts differ markedly in that the ChrH maintains that Manasseh repented of his actions and turned back to YHWH (2 Chr 33:10-17), whereas the DtrH includes no account of Manasseh's repentance and maintains that YHWH decided to destroy Jerusalem and deliver the people of Judah into the hands of their enemies because of Manasseh's great sins (2 Kgs 21:10-15; cf. 23:26-27; 24:3-4).

The DtrH charge in 2 Kgs 21:1-18 that YHWH decided to destroy Jerusalem and exile the people is quite controversial when one considers that the entire nation suffered for the sins of one man. The narrative is clear in charging that Manasseh caused the people of Judah to sin as well, but the narrative does not hold the people accountable for the destruction of the city or for their own exile; only Manasseh is to blame. This charge is all the more remarkable when one considers the DtrH portrayal of Jeroboam ben Nebat as an evil monarch who caused Israel to sin, but the DtrH narrative in 2 Kings 17 maintains that the Northern Kingdom was destroyed on account of the sins of its people, led by Jeroboam and all of the other kings of Israel, throughout its history. Neither Jeroboam ben

Nebat nor any other individual bears the responsibility for the destruction of the Northern Kingdom of Israel. The issue is presented as one of collective guilt.

The DtrH portrayal of Manasseh as the individual responsible for the destruction of Jerusalem and Judah is therefore inconsistent with the DtrH portrayal of Israel's downfall due to collective guilt. Jerusalem falls to Babylon first in 597 B.C.E. during the reign of Jehoiachin ben Jehoiakim and again in 587–586 B.C.E. during the reign of Zedekiah ben Josiah, and exiles of the population follow in each case. Because Manasseh's death is dated to 642 B.C.E., this means that the punishment of Jerusalem and Judah for Manasseh's sins is realized some fifty-one to sixty-one years following his death. Although some of the older inhabitants of Jerusalem and Judah might have been alive during the reign of Manasseh, the punishment falls mainly on those who were not even born during his reign, not to mention that those who were alive were likely infants or children. Such a portrayal of punishment hardly meets with standards of moral accountability in which those who commit sins are responsible for their own punishment.

The DtrH portrayal of Manasseh obviously displays considerable tension in the understanding of moral responsibility and the criteria for punishment or suffering in the DtrH narrative. Indeed, such tension appears in the DtrH understanding of covenant as well. Since the work of Noth, interpreters recognize that the DtrH portrayal employs the understanding of the covenant relationship between YHWH and Israel articulated in the book of Deuteronomy in its portrayal and assessment of Israel's and Judah's history. Deuteronomy lays out YHWH's expectations for Israel, and maintains that Israel will dwell securely in the land if it observes YHWH's expectations and that it faces exile from the land if it does not (see esp. Deuteronomy 28–30). The covenant is therefore largely conditional, insofar as national security is based upon observance of divine expectations, although Deut 30:1-10 indicates that YHWH will prompt the people to repent and restore them to the land once that repentance takes place. The significance of the program of religious reform and national restoration undertaken by Manasseh's grandson, King Josiah ben Amon of Judah, as portrayed in 2 Kgs 22:1—23:30 then looms rather large in relation to the portrayal of Manasseh in the DtrH, particularly since Josiah leads the nation in repentance and return to YHWH following the discovery of a book of Torah in the Temple.[21] Because Josiah's reforms correspond to the expectations for Israel laid out in Deuteronomy, most interpreters maintain that this book of Torah must be some form of Deuteronomy. Despite the nation's repentance under Josiah, 2 Kgs 23:26-27; 24:3-4 maintain that YHWH would not relent on the decision to destroy Jerusalem and Judah.

Tension is evident in the DtrH articulation of the Davidic covenant as well. Whereas 2 Sam 7:1-16 maintains that YHWH would ensure that David's descendants would sit on the throne of Israel forever, 1 Kgs 2:4; 8:25-26; and 9:4-8 indicate that the Davidic line would rule forever only if the Davidic kings would observe YHWH's expectations. Although questions persist concerning the portrayal of Jehoiachin ben Jehoiakim, who eats at the table of the Babylonian king in 2 Kgs 25:27-30, it is clear that he remains in exile at the end of the DtrH and does not occupy the throne of Israel.[22]

Because of these tensions, many scholars argue that the present form of the DtrH is a redactional work that was originally designed to point to King Josiah ben Amon as the ideal king of Israel who would lead the nation in returning to YHWH's expectations and reunite the twelve tribes of Israel under Davidic kingship and around the Jerusalem Temple as in the days of David and Solomon.[23] Josiah's unexpected early death at the hands of Pharaoh Necho of Egypt in 609 B.C.E. cut off such ideal expectations, however, and the subsequent fall of Jerusalem and Judah to Babylonia in 587–586 B.C.E. called for an updating of the Josianic DtrH to account for the Babylonian exile. By charging Manasseh with such egregious wrongdoing, the exilic DtrH sought to explain the Babylonian exile as the result of Manasseh's sins, despite Josiah's exemplary character and repentance. Such a diachronic argument concerning the compositional history and development of the DtrH then explains the literary, theological, and moral tension in the work, originally written for a very different purpose than the one it presently serves.

Ancient readers do not share the premises and conclusions of modern redaction-critical work, however, and the present synchronic form of the DtrH undoubtedly prompted discussion and disagreement among the ancients just as it does today. Insofar as the ChrH account of Manasseh's reign appears to be dependent on the DtrH narrative while reworking portions of the narrative to provide a very different portrait of Manasseh, readers must also consider the account of Manasseh's reign in 2 Chr 33:1-20.[24]

The ChrH account of Manasseh's reign in 2 Chr 33:1-20 begins in vv. 1-9, much like the DtrH account in 2 Kgs 21:1-18, with a portrayal of Manasseh's sins, such as his rebuilding of the illicit shrines that Hezekiah

had abolished, the altars for Baal, the asherim, his consignment of his
sons to the fires in the Valley of Ben-Hinnom, and so forth. Verse 9 (cf.
2 Kgs 21:9) concludes the account of Manasseh's sins with a statement
that he led Judah and Jerusalem into greater evil than that practiced by
the nations that YHWH destroyed before Israel's entry into the land. Second Chronicles 33:10-17 differs from the DtrH account with a narrative that recounts Manasseh's repentance. It maintains that YHWH sent
Assyrian officers to bring him before the king of Assyria at Babylon. As
a result of this experience, Manasseh humbled himself before YHWH,
who answered Manasseh's prayer and returned him safely to Jerusalem.
Manasseh then rebuilt Jerusalem, removed the various illicit religious
installations that he had constructed, and worshiped YHWH alone. The
summation of Manasseh's reign in vv. 18-20 reiterates Manasseh's repentance while giving the usual details of major life events, death, burial, and
succession.

Many interpreters argue that the account of Manasseh's repentance is
a literary fiction that was designed to explain Manasseh's unprecedented
reign of fifty-five years, longer than any other monarch of the Davidic
line.[25] In part, this decision is supported by the view of many modern
scholars that the ChrH is a priestly work that is designed to justify priestly
theology, rendering the work historically suspect in relation to the DtrH.
Nevertheless, scholars have increasingly come to recognize the theological viewpoint of the DtrH as a factor in the presentation of events and
that the ChrH often includes reliable historical information lacking in the
DtrH, for instance, Rehoboam's construction of fortresses to protect his
borders in 2 Chr 11:5-12 or Hezekiah's construction of the Siloam water
tunnel as part of a general refortification of Jerusalem in 2 Chr 32:1-8.[26]
Such episodes have led to a reconsideration of the Chronicler's historical
reliability. Although ChrH presents history according to its own theological viewpoint, its historical claims cannot always be dismissed without
critical reflection.

Manasseh's forced journey to Babylon to appear before the Assyrian
king is a case in point. During the course of Manasseh's reign, Shamash
Shum-ukin, king of Babylon and brother of the Assyrian monarch, Ashurbanipal, revolted against the Assyrian Empire. The revolt was put down
and Shamash Shum-ukin was killed in a very bloody campaign during the
years 652–648 B.C.E.[27] As the son of Hezekiah, who had allied with the
Babylonian prince Merodach-baladan to revolt against Assyria in 705–701
B.C.E., Manasseh would be suspected of sympathy with the Babylonian

cause, if not outright support. Indeed, his grandson Josiah later died in 609 B.C.E. in an attempt to support his Babylonian allies against the Assyrians and Egyptians. Given the history of alliance between the house of David and Babylon, it would make eminent sense for Ashurbanipal to suspect Manasseh of disloyalty and to ensure Manasseh's adherence to Assyria by dragging him in chains to Babylon during or after the revolt to make an inquiry and to intimidate him with the potential consequences of disloyalty to the Assyrian crown. Perhaps Manasseh's building activities were done in preparation for a confrontation with Assyria; perhaps they were done on Assyria's behalf. Unfortunately, the question of the motivation for Manasseh's archeologically well-documented building along the Negev trade routes is unknown. Nevertheless, the portrayal of Manasseh's being dragged in chains to Babylon to appear before the Assyrian king has considerable plausibility as a historical event.

The historiographical perspective of the ChrH enters into the picture, however, when it portrays Manasseh's experience as the result of an act by the all-powerful YHWH. ChrH historiography also accounts for Manasseh's repentance since he survives the experience—unlike his grandson Josiah, who is killed by Pharaoh Necho when he attempts to stop the Egyptians from marching north to support the Assyrians at Haran. Manasseh did not die early in life, therefore he does not persist in his earlier sinful acts. He certainly cannot be held accountable for the Babylonian destruction of Jerusalem and the exile of the people some fifty-one to sixty-one years after his death since, in the ChrH viewpoint, those who do wrong suffer the consequences of their actions themselves. According to the ChrH viewpoint as expressed in 2 Chr 36:14, all the officers, priests, and people of the generation that suffered the destruction of Jerusalem and the exile did so because they committed sins and polluted the Temple of YHWH in Jerusalem. The ChrH has a very different evaluation of the destruction of Jerusalem and the exile of Judah that does not permit to charge Manasseh with responsibility for these disasters.

As noted above, the DtrH presentation of King Josiah of Judah is also tied to the presentation of Manasseh, that is, despite his righteousness, Josiah is unable to overturn YHWH's decision to destroy Jerusalem and exile Judah on account of Manasseh's sins, and Josiah instead dies an early death at Megiddo so he will not have to witness the coming disaster. Such a viewpoint is hardly consistent with that of the ChrH, which maintains that people suffer on account of their own wrongdoing. In order to clarify the ChrH viewpoint concerning the early death of King Josiah of Judah, discussion now turns to the ChrH presentation of Josiah's reign.

King Josiah ben Amon is one of the most remarkable monarchs of the entire house of David.[28] Josiah came to the throne of Judah at the age of eight following the assassination of his father, Amon ben Manasseh, by members of the Judean royal court. The motives for the attempted coup are not known, although it is likely that the coup was inspired by the decline of Assyrian power in the mid-seventh century B.C.E. and resentment against Manasseh and Amon for continuing to serve as Assyrian vassals. The revolt was put down by the 'am-hā'āreṣ, "the people of the land," apparently the rural population of Judah that had acted in the past to install kings at times of national threat (see 2 Kgs 11:18, 20; 14:21; 23:30). The kingdom would presumably be governed by royal advisors until the time when the young king would have reached an age of majority.

Josiah's reign is especially well known for his efforts at religious reform and national restoration. Second Chronicles 34:3 notes that Josiah began to seek the G-d of his father David in the eighth year of his reign (632 B.C.E.) and that he began to purge Jerusalem and Judah of illicit shrines, altars, idols, and the like in the twelfth year of his reign (628 B.C.E.). Both 2 Chr 34:8 and 2 Kgs 22:3 note that Josiah initiated a Temple renovation project in the eighteenth year of his reign (622 B.C.E.), which resulted in the discovery of a book of Torah that most interpreters identify with some form of Deuteronomy. The dates of Josiah's first two actions correspond to important events in the decline of the Assyrian Empire, namely, Ashurbanipal, the last major monarch of Assyria, had died by 631 B.C.E., and Nebopolassar, the founder of the Neo-Babylonian Empire, began his revolt against Assyria in 627 B.C.E. This correspondence indicates that Josiah joined the Babylonians, the former allies of his great-grandfather Hezekiah, in preparing to reassert Davidic independence against Assyrian rule.

Both the DtrH and the ChrH agree that the discovery of the book of Torah in the Temple prompted Josiah's repentance for failing to observe YHWH's expectations and that the book then served as the basis for Josiah's program of religious reform and national restoration. The principles of the reform were those of Deuteronomy, namely, worship of YHWH alone, worship at the one cultic site designated by YHWH, rejection of Canaanite or pagan gods, practices, and worship sites, and observance of YHWH's expectations as defined in Deuteronomy. To this end, Josiah purged and rededicated the Jerusalem Temple to the worship of YHWH, destroyed pagan cultic installations in Jerusalem and Judah, destroyed the northern Israelite shrine at Beth El, and led the nation in reaffirming its covenant with YHWH. Josiah is portrayed in the DtrH as the most righteous monarch of the Davidic line, who "did what was pleasing to YHWH and followed all the ways of his ancestor David, and did not deviate to the right or to the left" (2 Kgs 22:2; 2 Chr 34:2), and who is described in superlative terms, "There was no king like him before who turned back to YHWH with all his heart and soul and might, in full accord with the Torah of Moses; nor did any arise after him" (2 Kgs 23:25). Such language is otherwise employed for Joshua (Josh 1:7-8) and the ideal monarch according to the Torah of the King (Deut 17:18-20). Although David is frequently presented as a righteous monarch, his adultery with Bath Sheba and murder of her husband, Uriah (2 Samuel 10–12), disqualifies him as the ideal monarch of the Davidic line (see 1 Kgs 15:5). The ChrH does not employ such laudatory language for Josiah at the conclusion of his reign, but merely makes reference to his faithful deeds in accordance with the Torah of YHWH in 2 Chr 35:26.

Despite the great promise for his program of religious reform and national restoration, Josiah died in 609 B.C.E. at the age of thirty-nine when he was killed by Pharaoh Necho of Egypt at Megiddo. Josiah led his army to Megiddo, apparently in an effort to halt the Egyptian advance to Haran where the Assyrian army was about to make its last stand against the Babylonians and their Medean allies. Pharaoh Necho II of the Saite dynasty was a long-standing ally of Assyria from the early seventh century when the Assyrians installed his grandfather, Necho I, as an Assyrian client based in the city of Sais in the Egyptian delta.[29] Under his father, Pharaoh Psamtek I, Egypt was united and continued to serve as an ally of Egypt, although Psamtek's forays into Mesopotamia in support of Assyria prior to 609 B.C.E. suggest that the Egyptians were no longer vassals to the Assyrians, but enjoyed a parity relationship instead. Josiah acted on behalf of his Babylonian allies to prevent the Egyptians from joining the Assyrians at Haran. Josiah's act cost him his life. The DtrH and ChrH differ on the circumstances of Josiah's death, that is, 2 Kgs 23:29 simply states that Necho put Josiah to death at Megiddo, whereas 2 Chr 35:20-24 describes the battle between the Egyptians and Judeans at Megiddo in which Josiah was killed. With Josiah's death, Josiah's program of religious reform and national restoration was halted as Judah remained under Egyptian control until the Babylonians defeated Egypt at Carchemesh in 605 B.C.E. As a result of its subjugation to Babylon, its former ally, Judah eventually revolted and suffered destruction and exile at the hands of the Babylonians in 598–597, 588–586, and 582 B.C.E.

Josiah's early death and the demise of his program of religious reform and national restoration clearly constituted a major disaster for the kingdom of Judah. Although there are indications that a Josianic DtrH was written to present Josiah as the ideal monarch of the Davidic line who would reunite the twelve tribes of Israel under Davidic rule around the Jerusalem Temple, the present forms of both the DtrH and the ChrH are written to account for the destruction and exile of Jerusalem and Judah, although each differs in its presentation of Josiah's death in relation to the later reality of destruction and exile.

As noted above, the DtrH simply states in 2 Kgs 23:29 that Pharaoh Necho put Josiah to death at Megiddo, thereby avoiding any mention of the battle that is highlighted in the ChrH account of Josiah's death. Although the battle is the most plausible historical scenario for Josiah's demise, the presentation of Josiah's death corresponds to the DtrH understanding that Josiah would die in peace. According to 2 Kgs 22:11-20, Josiah repented upon hearing the words of the book of Torah read to him by his officials and then consulted the prophetess Huldah to determine the will of YHWH concerning the future of the nation. Huldah's response indicates that YHWH had already determined to bring disaster upon the nation for its wrongdoing, but Josiah's repentance had earned him the right to die in peace before such a tragedy would be realized. Within the larger context of the DtrH, Huldah's oracle presupposes YHWH's earlier determination to destroy Jerusalem and Judah as a result of Manasseh's sins. But Huldah's oracle also appears to be constructed on the basis of Elijah's earlier oracle to King Ahab ben Omri of Israel in 1 Kgs 21:27-29. Upon hearing Elijah's condemnation of the house of Omri for its sins, particularly Ahab's role in the murder of Naboth of Jezreel in an effort to acquire his land, Ahab repented for his crimes. As a result of Ahab's repentance, Elijah granted Ahab the right to die so that he would not see the destruction of his entire house. Ahab was then killed in battle against the Arameans at Ramoth Gilead in 1 Kings 22, and his dynasty came to an end out when Jehu, a commander of Israel's army, seized the throne and wiped out the house of Omri in Jezreel and Samaria in 2 Kings 9–10. Insofar as Ahab's sister or daughter, Athaliah, was married to King Joram ben Jehoshaphat of Judah (2 Kgs 8:18; cf. 2 Kgs 8:27), she became the mother of King Ahaziah ben Joram of Judah and thus the ancestress of the subsequent Davidic line. In the presentation of the DtrH, Josiah's demise appears in relation to YHWH's oath to destroy the house of Omri as well as YHWH's oath to destroy and exile Jerusalem and Judah. Josiah did not die in battle against Pharaoh Necho, however, in order to fulfill Huldah's

oracle that he may die in peace. Ultimately, Josiah's death in the DtrH
serves the larger historiographical interest in explaining the destruction
and exile of Jerusalem and Judah. Even Josiah's righteousness was not
enough to save the kingdom following YHWH's vows concerning Omri
and Manasseh.

Although there are certain similarities with DtrH in the ChrH
account Josiah's death, the ChrH narrative in 2 Chr 35:20-26 has been
sufficiently modified to provide a very different assessment of this event.
As noted above, the Chronicler states that Josiah died in battle against
Pharaoh Necho of Egypt at Megiddo, which is a far more historically plausible account for the circumstances of Josiah's death. Given the Chronicler's view that those who sin suffer the consequences of their own sins,
the encounter between Necho and Josiah prior to the battle is especially
noteworthy. When Josiah comes to Megiddo with his army prepared to
stop Necho's advance, Necho tells Josiah that he had no cause for war with
the Judean monarch. Instead, Necho states that his issue is with another
kingdom that is at war with Egypt, and that it is the will of G-d that Necho
hurry to the coming battle. Indeed, Josiah is interfering with G-d's will and
risks destruction if he does not desist. Josiah ignores Necho's advice, and
commences the battle with Necho in which Josiah is killed. The narrative
is careful to note that Necho's words had come from the mouth of G-d,
which entails that Josiah died at Megiddo at the hands of Pharaoh Necho
of Egypt because he defied the will of G-d. The ChrH narrative includes
the account of Huldah's oracle in 2 Chr 34:22-28, with its promise that
Josiah would die in peace before the destruction of Jerusalem because of
his repentance. The ChrH makes no mention of Manasseh as the cause
of the destruction. Huldah's oracle indicates that YHWH will bring the
curses of the book of the Torah found in the Temple renovations on the
heads of the people for their apostasy, and 2 Chr 36:14 makes it clear that
the destruction took place because the officers, priests, and people had
defiled the Jerusalem Temple. Josiah is spared from seeing the destruction
of Jerusalem and Judah as Huldah promised, but his own death is caused
by his refusal to heed the word of G-d as spoken by Pharaoh Necho of
Egypt. In keeping with the Chronicler's perspective, Josiah dies because
of his own wrongdoing. Furthermore, he does not die in peace as Huldah
indicates; instead, he dies in battle.

Both the DtrH and ChrH presentations of King Josiah's reign are
shaped in relation to their respective historiographical perspectives. The
DtrH lauds Josiah as the most righteous monarch of the house of David
and indeed of all Israel, but it must account for his early death and the

demise of Jerusalem and Judah by maintaining that YHWH had determined to destroy Jerusalem and Judah on account of the sins of Manasseh. The account displays considerable literary and theological tension, due primarily to the compositional history of a work that was written initially to point to Josiah's reign as the culmination of Israel's history but that had to be adjusted to account for the death of Josiah and the subsequent destruction and exile. By placing the blame for the disaster on Manasseh alone, the DtrH account leaves open questions as to why an entire nation and later generations had to suffer for the sins of one man. The ChrH account of Josiah's death presents a much more coherent understanding of Josiah's death that may well constitute an attempt to address some of the questions left open in the DtrH. Although the ChrH narrative appears to be based in part on the earlier DtrH narrative, the Chronicler modifies the narrative to place responsibility for Josiah's death on Josiah himself. Although the ChrH narrative includes the Huldah oracle that promises Josiah a peaceful death prior to the destruction of Jerusalem, the ChrH maintains that Josiah defied the word of G-d in confronting Pharaoh Necho of Egypt, and therefore died in battle against Necho as punishment for his transgression.

Differing Views on the Fall of Jerusalem and Exile

Examination of the historical literature concerning Jeroboam, Manasseh, and Josiah in the Former Prophets and the Chronicler's History demonstrates that both the so-called Deuteronomistic History (DtrH) nor the Chronicler's History (ChrH) present the history of Israel and Judah from distinctive historiographical viewpoints. Both are ultimately concerned with explaining the disaster of the fall of Jerusalem and the beginning of the Babylonian exile in 597 and 588–586 B.C.E., but they differ in accounting for the cause of that disaster.

The DtrH presents a comprehensive examination of the history of Israel from Israel's entry into the land of Israel at the time of Joshua through the release of King Jehoiachin ben Jehoiakim from prison during the reign of the Babylonian monarch Evil-Merodach, who reigned 562–560 B.C.E. The DtrH points especially to problems among the northern tribes of Israel, for instance, the tribe of Ephraim frequently attempts to assert itself over the other tribes in the premonarchic period of the Judges, the northern tribes revolt against the house of David following the death of Solomon, and northern Israel's first king, Jeroboam ben

Nebat, leads the nation into apostasy and ultimate destruction some two hundred years later by erecting the golden calves for worship at Beth El and Dan. Northern Israel's destruction serves somewhat as a precedent for that of Jerusalem and Judah, although the DtrH makes it clear that the sins of King Manasseh ben Hezekiah are the cause of the destruction and exile of Jerusalem and Judah. Manasseh's sins are so great that even the righteous Josiah cannot avert the disaster by repenting, and the DtrH attempts to explain this anomaly by creating an analogy between Josiah and Ahab, that is, like Ahab who was granted the right to die before seeing the destruction of his house, Josiah is granted the right to die before seeing the disaster that will befall Jerusalem and Judah. The account of his death at Megiddo is shaped accordingly to serve this concern.

The ChrH presents a far more comprehensive history of Israel from the time of creation through the decree of the Persian king Cyrus the Great, who decreed that the exiled Jews could return to Jerusalem to rebuild the Temple in 539 B.C.E. The Chronicler pays relatively little attention to the Northern Kingdom of Israel, however, due to its interest in the Jerusalem Temple, its priesthood and ritual, and its place at the center of Israel's life and history. The ChrH is highly dependent on the DtrH, insofar as it frequently repeats DtrH narratives nearly verbatim, but it also changes earlier narratives and adds its own distinctive material to produce a history that presents a distinctive historiographical viewpoint. The ChrH maintains that people reap the rewards or punishments of their actions.[30] With respect to the destruction and exile of Jerusalem and Judah, the ChrH states that the officers, priests, and people of Jerusalem had corrupted the Temple in their own time and thus brought the disaster upon themselves as a punishment for their own wrongdoing. The ChrH maintains that Manasseh was not the great sinner portrayed in the DtrH, but a king who repented and returned to YHWH after he was dragged in chains to Babylon to appear before the Assyrian king. Josiah was an exemplary and righteous king, but in attempting to stop Pharaoh Necho at Megiddo, Josiah defied the will of G-d and thereby brought about his own death in battle against the Egyptians as a consequence of that defiance.

Although both the DtrH and ChrH have their own distinctive historiographical perspectives, they agree on one fundamental point, namely, YHWH was not the party responsible for the destruction of Jerusalem and the exile of the people. YHWH was the omnipotent sovereign of the universe who authorized the destruction, but the wrongdoing of human beings was the cause of the disaster. Both the DtrH and ChrH emerge then as examples of theodicy that defend the power and righteousness of

YHWH in the face of disaster and evil. The fall of Jerusalem, the exile of the people, the deaths and suffering of so many were not due to YHWH's impotency, moral fallibility, or lack of attention. Rather, YHWH's power, righteousness, and attention to human affairs bring about the disaster when human beings fail in their obligations to YHWH. Such assertions of divine righteousness and power enabled both the DtrH and the ChrH to prepare an exilic or postexilic reading audience for the projected reconstruction of Jerusalem and Judah in the early Persian period.

FOUR

Isaiah's Question to G–D

The book of Isaiah is perhaps the best known and most influential of the prophetic books in the Hebrew Bible. Isaiah is the most frequently cited prophetic book in the Christian New Testament;[1] indeed, Isaiah's prophecy of the birth of Immanuel to a young woman in Isa 7:14 is cited in Matt 1:23 according to its Septuagint translation as the basis for the Gospel's claim that Jesus was born to a virgin. The New Testament likewise cites other royal oracles in Isaiah, such as Isa 8:23—9:6, or the so-called Servant Songs of Second Isaiah in Isa 42:1-4 to point to an ideal period of eschatological peace that will be realized with the advent of the Messiah (see Matt 4:12-17; 12:17-21). The liturgical reading of the *haftarot* (*haptārôt*) or prophetic readings that accompany the reading of the Torah in Jewish worship services employs passages from Isaiah more than any other prophetic book.[2] Despite its concern with judgment against Israel in the first part of the book, rabbinic tradition in *b. Baba Batra* 14b views Isaiah as a book of comfort, no doubt because of its initial portrayal of world peace in Isa 2:2-4 in which the nations flow to Zion to learn Torah from G-d and the subsequent portrayal of Israel's return to Zion in Isaiah 40–54 and its task to bring divine light and Torah to the nations of the world (Isa 49:6; 51:4-5; cf. 42:1-4).

The book of Isaiah is presented as a single composition that portrays the vision of the late-eighth-century prophet Isaiah ben Amoz in both Jewish and Christian versions of the Bible, but beginning with the medieval Jewish exegete Abraham ibn Ezra (d. 1167), interpreters have

recognized that portions of the book presuppose very different historical settings. Whereas Isaiah 1–39 clearly presupposes the circumstances
of the late eighth century B.C.E. when the Assyrian Empire emerged as a
threat against both Israel and Judah, Isaiah 40–66 presupposes the circumstances of the mid-sixth century B.C.E. toward the end of the Babylonian
exile when King Cyrus of Persia had taken control of Babylon and decreed
that exiled Jews could return to Jerusalem.[3] The question was heavily
debated by scholars during the late eighteenth and nineteenth centuries
until the celebrated 1892 commentary on Isaiah by Bernhard Duhm posited that Isaiah was the product of at least three distinct writers working
in three distinct time periods, namely, the work of Proto-Isaiah in Isaiah
1–39 from the eighth century B.C.E.; the work of Deutero-Isaiah in Isaiah
40–55 from the late sixth century B.C.E.; and the work of Trito-Isaiah in
Isaiah 56–66 from the postexilic period.[4] Although Duhm's hypothesis
was extensively modified throughout the course of subsequent scholarly
discussion, his fundamental view of Isaiah as the product of three major
prophets or prophetic circles dominated twentieth-century scholarship
on the book. Because of the influence of Duhm's work, interpreters frequently treated Isaiah as two or three separate prophetic works.

The extensive discussion of the compositional history of Isaiah
throughout the nineteenth and twentieth centuries pointed to the role
played by editors or redaction in the production of the book, that is,
someone had to collect the various oracles or sayings of Proto-, Deutero-,
and Trito-Isaiah and assemble them according to their various collections
into the present form of the book. Because the redactors of the Isaian
oracles frequently supplemented the words of the prophets with narratives describing the circumstances of the prophet's activities or updated
the prophet's words with additional material that might address the needs
and concerns of later times, interpreters began to recognize the role that
redaction played in shaping the present form of the book and in articulating its message and viewpoint. Such concerns were evident in material from Proto-Isaiah in Isaiah 1–39 that anticipated the circumstances
of the Babylonian exile as portrayed by Deutero-Isaiah in Isaiah 40–55
or the postexilic period as portrayed by Trito-Isaiah in Isaiah 56–66, for
instance, the portrayal of Babylon's downfall in Isaiah 13–14; the so-called
Isaiah Apocalypses in Isaiah 24–27 and Isaiah 34–35; and the Hezekiah
narratives in Isaiah 36–39. The last example was particularly important
because it concluded with Isaiah's announcement that Hezekiah's sons
would be carried off into Babylonian exile, which suggested that perhaps
the first part of the book in Isaiah 1–39 had been edited or composed to

anticipate the second part of the book in Isaiah 40–66.[5] A multitude of studies began to explore the interrelationships between the various components of Isaiah in an effort to define the literary form and perspective of the book of Isaiah as a literary whole.[6]

As a result of this discussion, scholars have come to see the book of Isaiah as a single literary work, whether or not it was the product of a lengthy compositional history, that lays out a vision of YHWH's plans for Jerusalem and the world at large from the time of the Assyrian invasions in the late eighth century through the projected restoration of Jerusalem at the center of creation. The present form of the book comprises two major components in Isaiah 1–33 and 34–66 that lay out Isaiah's exhortation to Jerusalem and Judah to recognize YHWH's worldwide sovereignty.[7] See chart 4.1 on the following page.

This analysis of the structure of Isaiah indicates that the book is designed to articulate a vision of YHWH's sovereignty over all creation centered at Zion. Such a vision is particularly important for a post-Shoah reading of the Bible insofar as it attempts to explain disaster—that is, the Assyrian destruction of northern Israel and invasion of Judah as well as the Babylonian exile of Jerusalem and Judah—as intentionally devised elements of YHWH's plans to reveal divine sovereignty to Jerusalem/Judah and to the world at large. Several problems emerge from such a scenario, namely, (1) YHWH's initial announcement of judgment for Israel and Judah to Isaiah, including the commission to conceal YHWH's plans lest the people repent and thwart the divine purpose; (2) the book's contrasting portrayals of Kings Ahaz and Hezekiah at a time of crisis, which puts forward Hezekiah, whose plans for revolt prompted Assyrian invasion and devastation of Judah, as a model of piety; (3) the book's portrayal the Persian monarch Cyrus as YHWH's Messiah and Temple builder together with the demise of the house of David; and (4) the failure to achieve the ideals articulated at the outset of the book.

Isaiah's Complicity with G-d's Judgment

Although the literary structure of the book of Isaiah indicates an interest in the realization of YHWH's worldwide sovereignty centered at Zion, the book includes extensive material concerning the judgment of Israel, Judah, Jerusalem, and the nations as part of the process by which the world will be prepared for the recognition of YHWH's sovereignty. Such a concern is especially evident in the first part of the book, which discusses

---

Chart 4.1

**The Vision of Isaiah ben Amoz: Prophetic Exhortation
to Jerusalem and Judah to Adhere to YHWH**

Isaiah 1–66

I. Concerning YHWH's Plans to Reveal Worldwide Sovereignty at Zion — 1:1—33:24

  A. Prologue to the book: Introductory parenesis concerning YHWH's plans
    to purify Jerusalem — 1:1-31

  B. Prophetic instruction concerning YHWH's plans to reveal worldwide Sovereignty
    at Zion: Announcement of the Day of YHWH — 2:1—33:24

    1. Prophetic announcement concerning the preparation of Zion for its role
      as the center for YHWH's worldwide sovereignty — *2:1—4:6*

    2. Prophetic instruction concerning the significance of Assyrian judgment
      against Jacob/Israel: restoration of Davidic rule — *5:1—12:6*

    3. Prophetic announcement concerning the preparation of the nations
      for YHWH's worldwide sovereignty — *13:1—27:13*

      a. Announcements concerning the nations — 13:1—23:18

      b. Restoration for Zion/Israel at the center of the nations — 24:1—27:13

    4. Prophetic instruction concerning YHWH's plans for Jerusalem:
      announcement of a royal savior — *28:1—33:24*

**II. Concerning the Realization of YHWH's Plans for Revealing Worldwide
Sovereignty at Zion** — 34:1—66:24

  A. Prophetic instruction concerning the realization of YHWH's sovereignty at Zion — 34:1—54:17

    1. Prophetic instruction concerning YHWH's power to return redeemed exiles to Zion — *34:1—35:10*

    2. Royal narratives concerning YHWH's deliverance of Jerusalem and Hezekiah — *36:1—39:8*

    3. Prophetic instruction that YHWH is maintaining covenant and restoring Zion — *40:1—54:17*

      a. Renewed prophetic commission to announce YHWH's restoration
        of Zion — 40:1-11

      b. Contention: YHWH is master of creation — 40:12-31

      c. Contention: YHWH is master of human events — 41:1—42:13

      d. Contention: YHWH is redeemer of Israel — 42:14—44:23

      e. Contention: YHWH will use Cyrus for the restoration of Zion — 44:24—48:22

      f. Contention: YHWH is restoring Zion — 49:1—54:17

  B. Prophetic exhortation to adhere to YHWH's covenant — 55:1—66:24

    1. Exhortation proper to adhere to YHWH — *55:1-13*

    2. Substantiation: prophetic instruction concerning reconstituted
      people of Israel in Jerusalem — *56:1—66:24*

      a. Prophetic instruction concerning proper observance of YHWH's covenant — 56:1—59:21

      b. Prophetic announcement of restoration for the people — 60:1—62:12

      c. Prophetic instruction concerning the process of restoration for the people — 63:1—66:24

YHWH's judgment during the Assyrian period as the basis for a projected restoration. The use of imagery pertaining to the refining and smelting of metals in Isa 1:21-26, for example, metaphorically portrays the purification of Jerusalem from its sins or impurities as it is prepared for YHWH's purposes to become a righteous city. The agents of YHWH's punishment, including both Assyria and Babylon, will likewise suffer judgment when they fail to recognize YHWH as indicated in Isa 10:5-34 and 13:1—14:23. Concern with judgment is also presupposed throughout the second part of the book, which turns to scenarios of restoration and return to Jerusalem in the aftermath of exile. Isaiah 40:2 states, for example, that Jerusalem will be redeemed now that she has paid double for all of her sins in keeping with ancient Israelite law in Exod 22:6, which calls for a thief to make double restitution. The second part of the book also envisions continued judgment if the process of purification is not complete, as indicated by the imagery of the corpses of those who continue to rebel against YHWH at the end of the book in Isa 66:24.

For the most part, the conceptualization of judgment in the book of Isaiah shares the perspective of much of biblical literature, namely, that human wrongdoing leads to judgment from G-d and thereby explains the experience of evil in the world. Such a perspective is evident in charges that human idolatry and arrogance will lead to judgment on the Day of YHWH as expressed throughout Isa 2:6-22; crimes of social justice, drunkenness, and iniquity prompt YHWH to call for the Assyrian army to execute judgment in Isa 5:7-30; and the refusal to rely on YHWH for the defense of the nation leads to warnings of judgment from the prophet in Isaiah 30–31 when the nation instead turns to Egypt for a defensive alliance. Concern for the failure to recognize YHWH as the true sovereign and judge of the world appears in the second part of the book, which repeatedly mentions that the time has come for the blind and deaf to recognize YHWH's actions in Isa 35:5; 42:18-21; 43:8; and 48:8.[8] Indeed, calls for the recognition of YHWH's role as sovereign creator reinforce the book's exhortations to carry out YHWH's will in Isa 1:10-20 and to recognize in Isa 40:8; 44:6-8; 52:1-6; and 55:11 that Jerusalem's experience of judgment had been part of the divine plan to reveal YHWH's sovereignty to the world all along. Together with the recognition that judgment punishes wrongdoing, restoration accompanies recognition of and adherence to YHWH in the book of Isaiah.

The Isaian model of reward for righteousness and punishment for wrongdoing may certainly come into question in the aftermath of the

Shoah, particularly since the book of Isaiah emphasizes the motif of YHWH's hidden face as an important element in its depiction of evil in Isa 8:17; 45:15; and elsewhere.[9] As Eliezer Berkovits demonstrates in his study of the *hester panim* motif in relation to the Shoah, the hidden face of G-d becomes a means to explain the problem of evil by maintaining that G-d's absence becomes a summons to humankind to assume responsibility as partners with G-d for the care, well-being, and moral order of the world.[10] In this respect, Isaiah is like many other biblical books in that it engages in theodicy in its attempts to defend G-d's righteousness and power in the face of evil by assigning the blame for evil to human wrongdoing, thereby calling on humans to amend their ways.

But the book of Isaiah raises a very different dimension of the problem of theodicy in its depiction of YHWH's role in relation to judgment, namely, YHWH's deliberate efforts to ensure the judgment of human beings by concealing the means by which human beings might recognize YHWH and repent, thereby averting the punishment that YHWH has decreed for them in advance. This issue is particularly evident in Isaiah 6, which relates Isaiah's vision of YHWH in which the prophet is called to speak to the people on YHWH's behalf.[11] The vision takes place in the year of King Uzziah's death (ca. 742 B.C.E.), which places it well before the Syro-Ephraimitic crisis during the reigns of Jotham and Ahaz and the subsequent Assyrian intervention in the region. The prophet describes a scene in which YHWH sits enthroned, with the divine train robe filling the Temple and the seraphim flying about and declaring YHWH's holiness with a well-known liturgical formula: "Holy, holy, holy, is YHWH Sebaoth! His Presence fills all the earth!"

Isaiah's response to this vision is to declare himself impure and unworthy to behold the divine presence in the Temple. In a scene reminiscent of the mouth-purification rituals employed by Mesopotamian oracle diviners, one of the seraphim takes a coal from the Temple altar, touches it to Isaiah's lips, and declares the prophet purified from iniquity for the visionary experience and the task for which he is to be commissioned.[12] Having been purified, Isaiah then hears YHWH's summons: "Whom shall I send? Who will go for us?" Isaiah immediately volunteers: "Here I am! Send me!" YHWH's commission then follows:

Go and say to that people,
"Hear, indeed, but do not understand; See, indeed, but do not grasp."
Dull that people's mind; stop its ears; and seal its eyes—

> Lest, seeing with its eyes and hearing with its ears, it also grasps with
> its mind,
> And repent and save itself.

YHWH's commission to Isaiah is one of the most theologically problematic statements in the book of Isaiah, insofar as YHWH deliberately
commissions Isaiah to hide the truth from the people to ensure that they
will be judged. YHWH's statement recognizes that if the people do indeed
understand that they have transgressed, they will repent, be delivered
from judgment, and prevent YHWH from accomplishing the divine will.
YHWH's commission to Isaiah is, in and of itself, an evil decree that lacks
moral foundation insofar as it denies people the opportunity to repent
and thereby to avoid the judgment that YHWH has in mind for them.

Even more problematic is Isaiah's response to YHWH's decree.
Rather than protest this decree, Isaiah simply asks, "How long, my
L-rd?" Many detect a note of compassion or resignation to the divine will.
Others maintain that Isaiah's oracles, which constantly charge the people
with wrongdoing, demonstrate his refusal to carry out this divine com-
mission. Nevertheless, he does not directly challenge the evil proposed by
YHWH in this narrative. YHWH's response to Isaiah lays out a scenario
of judgment:

> Till towns lie waste without inhabitants and houses without people,
> And the ground lies waste and desolate,
> —For YHWH will banish the population—
> and deserted sites are many in the midst of the land,
> But while a tenth yet remains in it, it shall repent.
> It shall be ravaged like the terebinth and the oak,
> of which stumps are left even when they are felled:
> its stump shall be a holy seed.

Several dimensions of this passage must be noted. One, is the use
of the verb *š'h*, "to destroy," the verbal root that stands at the base of the
Hebrew noun *shoah* (*šōʾâ*) in the phrases, "until towns lie waste [*šāʾû*]," and
"the ground lies waste [*tiššāʾeh*]." The second is the portrayal of the deci-
mation of the people until only one tenth are left. The third is the imagery
of a tree that has been cut down to a stump to portray the ability of the
remaining 10 percent to grow once again in the aftermath of destruction.
The final verses of this passage portray the ultimate restoration of the
people, but the argument is teleological insofar as it portrays an ultimate

restoration to realize the divine plan, but it does not address the suffering of those who do not live to see the restoration.

Isaiah's failure to challenge YHWH's evil decree stands in marked contrast to other biblical figures who challenge YHWH and generally receive what they ask. Abraham demands that YHWH do justice on hearing of YHWH's plan to destroy all of the people of Sodom and Gomorrah in Gen 18:22-32, and YHWH responds that the cities will not be destroyed if righteous people are found in them. Moses twice challenges YHWH's decision to destroy the entire people of Israel in the wilderness in Exod 32:9-14 and Num 14:11-25, and prompts YHWH to abandon plans to destroy the entire people. Job demands that YHWH come and explain what he has done wrong, and YHWH does appear, even if the explanation might be satisfying only to Job. Amos twice asks YHWH to relent concerning a proposed punishment in Amos 7:1-3 and 7:4-6 that Israel could not withstand, and YHWH agrees both times. Although each of these figures succeeds in their demands for justice from YHWH, Isaiah does not stand up to YHWH when YHWH proposes to conceal the truth from the people and thereby to bring judgment upon them. Based on these examples, the reader might wonder what might have happened had Isaiah demanded justice from YHWH. In the end, Isaiah becomes complicit in the evil proposed by YHWH for the people by his failure to act.

The Ahaz and Hezekiah Narratives

The question of evil in relation to YHWH's commission of Isaiah has implications for reading the narratives concerning Isaiah's interaction with Kings Ahaz and Hezekiah of Judah, namely, confrontation with King Ahaz ben Jotham at the time of the 735–732 B.C.E. Syro-Ephraimitic invasion of Judah in Isaiah 7:1—9:6 and King Hezekiah ben Ahaz's repentance during Sennacherib's 701 B.C.E. invasion of Judah in Isaiah 36–39. Although the two narratives relate events separated by over thirty years, interpreters recognize that they are designed to compare and contrast the two kings in very similar situations of threat.[13] Whereas Ahaz rejects Isaiah's advice to rely only on YHWH to defend Jerusalem against threat, and suffers the consequences for his failure to do, Hezekiah turns to YHWH and Isaiah when his revolt against Assyria fails, and saves Jerusalem from destruction.

Isaiah 7:1—9:6 relates Isaiah's confrontation with Ahaz while the king is inspecting the water system that supplies Jerusalem "at the end of the conduit of the Upper Pool, by the road to the Fuller's Field" (Isa 7:3). The reason for Ahaz's inspection is the impending invasion of Judah and siege of Jerusalem by the Syro-Ephraimitic coalition, an alliance between Aram, led by King Rezin, and the Northern Kingdom of Israel, led by King Pekah ben Remaliah, which was gathering allies in preparation for a revolt against the Assyrian Empire. All small states in the region had agreed to join the coalition except for Judah, and the combined armies of Israel and Aram were about to attack Jerusalem to overthrow the Judean king and force Judah into the alliance. Under threat of a siege, Ahaz was inspecting his water system to ascertain whether or not it would supply Jerusalem during a protracted siege. Isaiah brings his son, Shear Yashuv ("a remnant will return"), to meet Ahaz at the Upper Pool and advise him to rely only on YHWH to defend the city rather than to call on Assyria for assistance. The name of Isaiah's son signifies that Jerusalem and Judah will likely suffer casualties against the Syro-Ephraimitic coalition, but a part of the population will survive. Isaiah promises Ahaz that the Syro-Ephraimitic assault will not succeed:

> It shall not succeed, it shall not come to pass.
> For the chief city of Aram is Damascus, and the chief of Damascus
> is Rezin,
> The chief city of Ephraim is Samaria, and the chief of Samaria is the
> son of Remaliah.
> And in another sixty-five years, Ephraim shall be shattered as a
> people.
> If you will not believe, surely you shall not be established.

Essentially, Isaiah relates to Ahaz the basic tenets of Davidic/Zion theology, that is, YHWH will defend the house of David and the city of Jerusalem forever. Ahaz need only trust in this promise to secure the city from the Syro-Ephraimitic attack. When Ahaz declines to follow Isaiah's advice in Isa 7:12 by stating, "I will not ask, and I will not test YHWH," the prophet responds with a series of oracles that continue through Isa 9:6 and lay out a scenario of Assyrian invasion and subjugation of Judah that culminates in promises of a new and righteous king for Jerusalem who will sit on David's throne in justice and peace. 2 Kings 16 indicates that Ahaz turned to the Assyrian Empire for assistance, which resulted in an Assyrian invasion of Aram and Israel that saw the destruction of Damascus and the capitulation and subjugation of Israel to Assyria. Ahaz himself traveled to Damascus to pay a heavy tribute to the Assyrian king Tiglath-pileser III for saving his country and his throne, and Judah remained a tributary of Assyria for the rest of Ahaz's lifetime.

Isaiah 36–39 presents a very similar set of circumstances to those of the Ahaz narrative by relating Hezekiah's revolt against Assyria in 701 B.C.E. and the Assyrian king Sennacherib's invasion of Judah and siege of Jerusalem. The narrative makes it very clear that Hezekiah's revolt, in which he had allied with the Babylonian prince Merodach-baladon and a number of other countries, was a colossal failure. Sennacherib's armies overran the Judean countryside and devastated Judah. When Sennacherib's officer, the Rabshakeh ("Chief Cupbearer"), comes to negotiate the terms of Jerusalem's unconditional surrender, he stands "near the conduit of the Upper Pool, by the road of the Fuller's Field," the very same location where Isaiah met Ahaz during the Syro-Ephraimitic crisis. Upon hearing Sennacherib's terms, which included the exile of the surviving Judean soldiers defending Jerusalem and complete capitulation, Hezekiah went to the Temple, displayed the document with the Assyrian terms of surrender before YHWH, and prayed to YHWH for deliverance from the Assyrians.

YHWH's response came to Hezekiah through the prophet Isaiah. In a lengthy oracle that expresses disdain for the arrogance of the Assyrian king and his armies, YHWH states in Isa 37:34–35 that the Assyrian king will be defeated and that Jerusalem and the Davidic king will be saved:

> He shall not enter this city; he shall not shoot an arrow at it,
> Or advance upon it with a shield, or pile up a siegemound against it.
> He shall go back by the way he came, he shall not enter the city,
>   declares YHWH;
> I will protect and save this city for My sake and for the sake of My
>   servant David.

Following the presentation of this oracle, the narrative relates that YHWH sends the angel of death against the Assyrian army, which kills 185,000 Assyrian troops. This forces Sennacherib to give up the siege and return to Assyria, where he is assassinated by his own sons in the temple of his own god, Nisroch.

Although modern critical scholarship for most of the nineteenth and twentieth centuries has viewed Isaiah 36–39 as the conclusion of Proto-Isaiah, more recent discussion of the formation of the book of Isaiah as a whole has recognized the transitional role played by the Ahaz and Hezekiah narratives within the literary structure of the book.[14] Many note that

Isaiah 36–39 concludes with a retrospective narrative concerning Hezekiah's reception of ambassadors from Merodach-baladon of Babylonia. When Isaiah upbraids Hezekiah for his reliance on Babylon, he declares that Hezekiah's sons will someday be exiled to Babylonia, which indicates that Isaiah 36–39 functions in relation to the rest of the book in Isaiah 40–66 and not only as the conclusion to Proto-Isaiah in Isaiah 1–39. The presentation of Hezekiah's turn to YHWH in a time of invasion and crisis is intended as a deliberate contrast with Ahaz's refusal to rely on YHWH in a similar situation of crisis. The results likewise contrast. Whereas Ahaz's decision led to subjugation to the Assyrians, Hezekiah's decision led to the defeat of the Assyrian army. Indeed, the two narratives accentuate the two-part literary division of the book into Isaiah 1–33 and 34–66. Isaiah 1–33 anticipates a period of judgment and ultimate restoration once the judgment is over. Within this context, the presentation of Ahaz in Isaiah 7:1—9:6 exemplifies the coming judgment and the restoration beyond Ahaz's life. Isaiah 34–66 presupposes that the judgment is over and that the time of restoration is at hand. Within this context, Hezekiah becomes a role model for repentance and reliance on YHWH for the imminent restoration. In sum, the Ahaz and Hezekiah narratives play an important role in establishing the interrelationship between the two parts of the book and in facilitating transition between them.

The Ahaz and Hezekiah narratives not only play an important role in tying the book of Isaiah together but also in articulating a theology that attempts to explain the disaster of Assyrian (and later Babylonian) invasion as an act of YHWH which demonstrates YHWH's protection of Jerusalem and sovereignty over all creation and the nations of the world. Nevertheless, this model presents some rather disturbing elements when read in the aftermath of the Shoah and the questions of divine complicity in evil that the Shoah raises.

First is the presentation of Ahaz in Isa 7:1—9:6. This narrative is generally read in relation to the account of Ahaz's reign in 2 Kings 16, which relates his journey to Damascus to present tribute to Tiglath-pileser III in the aftermath of Assyria's defeat of Israel and Aram. Upon seeing an altar in Damascus, Ahaz orders a copy of the altar built so that it will replace the altar for YHWH that had been in use in the Jerusalem Temple. Most interpreters conclude that such an act demonstrates both Ahaz's submission to Assyria and to the Assyrian gods, thereby reinforcing the view that Ahaz is an apostate king. Such a view influences interpretation of his response to Isaiah's call to trust in YHWH to defend the city of Jerusalem. A close reading of Ahaz's response, however, indicates that he does not defy Isaiah or YHWH at all. His response to Isaiah's call for him to ask a sign from YHWH to prove that YHWH will defend the city is, "I will not ask, and I will not test YHWH." Such a response hardly calls YHWH into question. Instead, it is a very pious statement that indicates Ahaz's refusal to question YHWH's power or commitment to defend Jerusalem. Furthermore, Isaiah's message conveyed through the symbolism of his son's name, Shear Yashuv, "a remnant will return," suggests that Isaiah's proposal entails that many Judeans would die. Ahaz had little reason to accept the promises of a prophet who called for Ahaz to accept great losses among his people as the will of YHWH. His pious response to Isaiah indicates that he had little reason to question YHWH's commitment to defend the city of Jerusalem and the people of Judah from assault. Ahaz, in fact, is no sinner; he acts to defend his people and to trust in his G-d, but he is portrayed as apostate in Isa 7:1—9:6 to demonstrate his inadequacy in relation to his son Hezekiah. Whereas Hezekiah delivers Jerusalem, Ahaz places Judah and Jerusalem in Assyria's debt.

Second is the presentation of Hezekiah in Isaiah 36–39. Hezekiah emerges as the model of piety who turns to YHWH in a time of crisis and thereby delivers Jerusalem from the Assyrian siege. Although the pious Hezekiah has a certain attraction to readers of the book, they must ask at what cost this piety was achieved. The narrative makes it very clear that Hezekiah repented only after Sennacherib's armies had overrun the whole of Judah, leaving Jerusalem as the last Judean stronghold. Indeed, Isa 36:1 informs readers that Sennacherib marched against the cities of Judah and seized them and Isa 36:10 makes it clear that campaign against Judah resulted in the destruction of the land. Readers of Isaiah may only guess at the full scope of destruction, but Sennacherib's account of the siege indicates that he besieged forty-six cities in Judah, which would account for just about every city in Judah, and that he exiled some 200,151 Judeans. Sennacherib devastated Judah, leaving only Jerusalem. Even so, the Assyrian Rabshakeh's claims that he will give Hezekiah two thousand horses because he knows very well that Hezekiah does not have the men to ride them. Hezekiah's piety—and his victory—comes at the price of the destruction of his entire country. It took Judah nearly one hundred years to rebuild the nation in the aftermath of Sennacherib's invasion. Despite the losses, Hezekiah remains on the throne of Judah. According to Isaiah 36–39, it was because YHWH delivered Jerusalem. Most historians maintain, however, that Sennacherib had to leave him on the throne to avoid a protracted siege of Jerusalem so that he could put down Merodach-baladon's revolt in Babylonia. Hezekiah was no longer a threat to Sennacherib, and Babylon had now become a far more urgent matter in the eyes of the Assyrian monarch.

Redefining the Davidic Covenant

YHWH defended Jerusalem and the house of David in Isaiah 36–39, but subsequent material in the book of Isaiah indicates that the house of David did not and would not survive the Babylonian exile. Isaiah's understanding of Jerusalem's and Judah's relationship with YHWH is based on the Davidic/Zion tradition of an eternal covenant in which YHWH will defend the house of David and Jerusalem forever.[15] Ironically, the book of Isaiah ultimately redefines the Davidic covenant as a relationship not between YHWH and the house of David but as a relationship between YHWH and the people of Israel.[16] Such a reconceptualization is clearly undertaken in recognition of the failure of the house of David to regain the throne in Jerusalem in the aftermath of the Babylonian exile and the early-Second-Temple-period restoration. Nevertheless, the redefinition of the Davidic covenant to eliminate the house of David in favor of the people of Israel negates the very foundation of Jerusalem's and Judah's self-understanding of their relationship with YHWH.

The first portion of Isaiah, which presents the oracles and actions of Isaiah ben Amoz during the late-eighth-century period when Assyria constituted a threat to Israel and Judah, clearly affirms the Davidic ideology of YHWH's eternal relationship with the house of David and Jerusalem. The above discussion already points to the role that such an understanding plays in the narrative concerning Isaiah's confrontation with Ahaz at the time of the Syro-Ephraimitic crisis, namely, Isaiah counsels Ahaz to rely on YHWH rather than on his alliance with Assyria to defend himself and the city against attack. When Ahaz purportedly rejects that advice and turns to the Assyrians instead, Isaiah expresses his frustration and withdraws from further interaction with Ahaz to "wait for YHWH, who is hiding His face from the House of Jacob" (Isa 8:17). Isaiah 9:1-6 presents a very well known oracle in which the prophet expresses his expectation that a new monarch of the Davidic line will arise who will trust in YHWH as anticipated in the Davidic covenant tradition and thereby usher in a period of peace, justice, and security for the nation. Most interpreters view Hezekiah as the monarch anticipated in this oracle. The concluding verses in Isa 9:5-6 read:

For a child has been born to us, a son has been given to us.
And authority has settled on his shoulders. He has been named
"The Mighty G-d is planning grace; The Eternal Father, a peaceable
ruler—"
In token of abundant authority and of peace without limit
Upon David's throne and kingdom, that it may be firmly
established
In justice and in equity now and forevermore.
The zeal of YHWH Sebaoth shall bring this to pass.

This oracle expresses the ideals of Davidic covenant theology in which
YHWH will guarantee the security of the Davidic monarch, the Davidic
monarch will look to YHWH for that security, and the result will be peace
and justice for the land.[17]

Indeed, other oracles of Isaiah in the first portion of the book express
similar ideals. Following a lengthy oracle condemning the Assyrian monarch for his threats against Jerusalem and YHWH, Isa 11:1-16 presents an
oracle that employs the imagery of shoots growing out of a tree stump to
express the renewal of the Davidic monarchy following a period of threat
in which the monarch will be reestablished, will rule in wisdom, understanding, and peace, and will restore the land of Israel, including both
Israel and Judah from foreign threats. The passage begins in Isa 11:1 with
the statement:

But a shoot shall grow out of the stump of Jesse, a twig shall sprout
from his stock.
The spirit of YHWH shall alight upon him: A spirit of wisdom and
insight,
A spirit of counsel and valor, a spirit of devotion and reverence for
YHWH.

The ideal portrayal of his reign in Isa 11:5-6 employs motifs reminiscent of the Garden of Eden to express the peaceful nature of his reign:

Justice shall be the girdle of his loins, and faithfulness the girdle of
his waist.
The wolf shall dwell with the lamb, the leopard lie down with the kid;
The calf, the beast of prey, and the fatling together, with a little boy
to herd them.

As a result of the new Davidic monarch's reign, Isa 11:12 indicates that YHWH will restore the exiles of Israel:

> He will hold up a signal to the nations and assemble the banished of Israel,
> and gather the dispersed of Judah from the four corners of the earth.

Similar sentiments are expressed in Isa 32:1, "Behold, a king shall reign in righteousness and ministers shall govern with justice." As indicated above, the narrative concerning YHWH's deliverance of Hezekiah likewise presumes Davidic ideology concerning YHWH's eternal covenant with the house of David.

It is therefore striking that the second part of the book of Isaiah names King Cyrus of Persia as YHWH's Messiah and Temple builder. In Isa 44:28, YHWH declares, "(I) am the same who says of Cyrus, 'He is My shepherd; He shall fulfill all My purposes! He shall say of Jerusalem, "She shall be rebuilt," and to the Temple: "You shall be founded again".'" Likewise, Isa 45:1 introduces YHWH's words of support for Cyrus's rule, "Thus says YHWH to Cyrus, His Anointed One/Messiah [Heb.: *limšîḥô*]." The references to Cyrus accompany YHWH's announcements of divine sovereignty over the nations, which is expressed in relation to the rise of Cyrus of Persia as the new ruler over Babylon in 539 B.C.E. Indeed, Second Isaiah envisions Cyrus as the new ruler, commissioned by YHWH, who will bring the Babylonian exile to an end, enable the return of Jewish exiles to Jerusalem, and facilitate the restoration of the Temple in Jerusalem. YHWH is identified with the rise of the Persian Empire; indeed, the oracles concerning the nations in Isaiah 13–23, which include Babylon, Assyria, Philistia, Moab, Damascus, Egypt, the Wilderness of the Sea, Dumah, Arabia, the Valley of Vision, and Tyre, presuppose Persian hegemony over these nations and thereby identify YHWH with the rise of the Persian Empire in the first part of the book as well.

The second part of the book does not envision the rise of a new Davidic monarch—Cyrus is YHWH's chosen Messiah or king. At the time of Cyrus's designation as the king of Babylon, no Davidic king emerges. This is hardly surprising since Cyrus would also rule Judah as part of the Babylonian domain, and would hardly allow Judah to restore its monarchy and thereby gain independence from Babylonian or Persian rule. Consequently, Isa 55:3-5 redefines the Davidic covenant. Following statements that call for the people of Israel to listen to YHWH and return to

YHWH, vv. 3-5 promise the Davidic covenant not to a Davidic monarch but to the people of Israel as a whole:

> Incline your ear and come to Me; hearken and you shall be revived.
> And I will make with you an everlasting covenant,
> the enduring loyalty promised to David.
> As I made him a leader of peoples, a prince and commander of peoples,
> So you shall summon a nation you did not know, and a nation that did not know you
> Shall come running to you.

The second part of the book of Isaiah envisions the continuity of the eternal covenant between YHWH and the house of David, but the covenant will not be with the house of David per se. Instead, it will be with the people of Israel.

The final chapter of Isaiah takes the issue a step further. Of course, Cyrus cannot remain YHWH's anointed forever. Isaiah 66:1 thereby employs language that points to YHWH as the true sovereign, both of Israel/Judah and of the world at large:

> Thus said YHWH, "The heavens are My throne and the earth is My footstool:
> Where could you build a house for Me, what place could serve as My abode?"

The language of throne and footstool presupposes the conceptualization of the Ark of the Covenant that stood in the Holy of Holies of Solomon's Temple in Jerusalem. The ark was conceived as a representation of the throne of YHWH and included in its iconography two cherubim, winged composite animal and human figures who guarded the ark or the throne of YHWH. The repeated phrase concerning YHWH, "who is enthroned above the cherubim" (1 Sam 4:4; 2 Sam 6:2; 2 Kgs 19:5; Isa 37:16; Pss 80:2; 99:1; 1 Chr 13:6), draws upon this conceptualization of the Ark of the Covenant.

Within the framework of the book of Isaiah, Isa 66:1 then brings the representation and transformation of the Davidic covenant to its full conclusion, namely, the first part of the book envisions an ideal Davidic monarch; the second part of the book names Cyrus of Persia, a non-Davidic foreign king, as YHWH's designated monarch and reassigns the eternal

Davidic covenant to the people of Israel; and finally, YHWH emerges as the true king of Israel when no Davidic king will appear. On the one hand, Isaiah expresses continuity in the Davidic covenant. On the other hand, it expresses the disruption of the Davidic line and covenant; following the Babylonian exile, no Davidic king ever ruled in Jerusalem again. In the aftermath of the Shoah, readers may ask to what degree was YHWH able or willing to show fidelity to an eternal covenant? Is this a case of abrogation of covenant? Or a case of transformation?

The Failure to Recognize YHWH's Sovereignty

The questions concerning the abrogation or transformation of the eternal Davidic covenant also point to important dimensions concerning the realization of YHWH's plans for the recognition of YHWH's worldwide sovereignty in the book of Isaiah. Despite the idealistic portrayal of the nations and Israel streaming to Zion to learn Torah from YHWH in Isa 2:2-4, 5, the concluding chapters of the book indicate that this ideal has not been achieved.

The concluding portion of the book in Isaiah 65–66 continues to anticipate that both Israel/Judah and the nations will respond to YHWH's call. Isaiah 65:17-25, for example, portrays the rejoicing of YHWH's servants when YHWH announces the intention to create a new heavens and new earth. The images of rejoicing in Jerusalem draw on earlier Isaian oracles from the first part of the book.[18] Isaiah 66:10-14, which calls upon the audience of the book to rejoice with Jerusalem at her restoration, reinterprets the earlier statement concerning Jerusalem's subjugation and rape in Isa 8:6 to a portrayal of a restored mother. The Eden-like imagery of Isa 65:25, in which the wolf and the lion graze together and other animals likewise live in peace, draws on the earlier portrayal of the restored Davidic monarch and kingdom in Isa 11:1-9. Finally, the anticipated reaction of the nations in Isa 66:18-21 who would bring exiled Israelites back to Jerusalem and to behold the glory of YHWH likewise draws on earlier portrayals of returning exiles in Isa 11:10-16; 27:12-13; and 35:1-10.[19]

Nevertheless, Isaiah 65–66 expresses a combination of expectation that ideals are yet to be realized and frustration over the failure to do so. Isaiah 65:1 begins with YHWH's statement of anticipation:

> I responded to those who did not ask, I was at hand to those who
> did not seek Me;

I said, "Here I am, here I am," to a nation that did not invoke My
    Name.
I constantly spread out My hands to a disloyal people,
Who walk the way that is not good. Following their own designs;
The people who provoke My anger, who continually, to My very face,
Sacrifice in gardens and burn incense on tiles; who sit inside tombs
And pass the night in secret places; who eat the flesh of swine,
With broth of unclean things in their bowls;
Who say, "Keep your distance! Don't come closer!
For I would render you consecrated."
Such things make My anger rage like fire blazing all day long.
See, this is recorded before Me; I will not stand idly by, but will
    repay,
Deliver their sins into their bosom, and the sins of their fathers
    as well.

As many interpreters have noted, the chapter differentiates between
those who respond to YHWH and those who do not by specifying judgment for the former and rejoicing for the latter. Isaiah 65:13-16 begins in
v. 13 by making such differentiation very clear:

Assuredly, thus said YHWH, G-d, "My servants shall eat, and you
    shall hunger;
My servants shall drink, and you shall thirst;
My servants shall rejoice, and you shall be shamed.
My servants shall shout in gladness, and you shall cry out in
    anguish,
Howling in heartbreak.
You shall leave behind a name by which My chosen ones shall curse;
So may YHWH G-d slay you! But His servants shall be given a dif-
    ferent name.
For whosoever blesses himself in the land shall bless himself by the
    true G-d;
And whoever swears in the land shall swear by the true G-d.
The former troubles shall be forgotten, shall be hidden from My
    eyes."

The book concludes in Isa 66:24 by calling upon those who adhere
to YHWH to observe the corpses of those who would not respond to
YHWH's call:

> "They shall go out and gaze on the corpses of the men who rebelled
>   against Me:
> Their worms shall not die, nor their fire be quenched;
> They shall become a horror to all flesh.
> And new moon after new moon, and Sabbath after Sabbath,
> All flesh shall come to worship Me," said YHWH.

The concluding images of the book are quite striking, because of the manner in which they portray YHWH's failure to achieve the ideals articulated throughout the book. The failure is not that of YHWH; it is the failure of those who choose not to respond to YHWH's call. Although many interpreters join in the book's theological program by claiming that those who suffer do so because they have sinned against YHWH, readers must remember that the book of Isaiah specifies YHWH's plans in Isaiah 6 to blind the people and render them deaf so that they will neither understand nor repent, thereby enabling YHWH's judgment and the recognition of YHWH's sovereignty to take place. The second part of the book announces the time for Israel to open its eyes and ears in order to recognize YHWH's actions in bringing Cyrus to the throne of Babylon and restoring exiled Jews to Jerusalem, but readers will recognize an attempt to explain the problem of evil—in the form of the Babylonian exile—as an effort to claim that the evil was part of the divine plan, which expresses divine power and concern from the very beginning. A post-Shoah reading of this motif raises questions about the portrayal of those who will suffer and die in this chapter. When readers consider the theological agenda laid out in Isaiah 6, how is one to judge those who are to rejoice and those who are to suffer in Isaiah 65–66? Do those who suffer do so because they have in fact rejected YHWH, or has YHWH rejected them? Is their suffering in fact due to their own sins, or does the charge of sin and rejection then become a means to explain the continuing problems faced by Judah in the early-Persian-period restoration? To what extent do the continuing problems of restoration-period Jerusalem and Judah reflect YHWH's failure to restore the former security of the nation under the ruling house of David and to what extent does it demonstrate an accommodation to Jerusalem's and Judah's new reality as a province ruled by the Persian Empire? As for those who rejoice, to what extent does the portrayal of their rejoicing then serve the rhetorical agenda of the book, that is, to convince the reading audience that YHWH is in fact the sovereign of creation and human events and to appeal to that audience to adhere to YHWH now that the time of restoration is at hand?

Isaiah as a Work of Theodicy

A post-Shoah reading of the book of Isaiah highlights the issues of theodicy that underlie and inform the entire book. Isaiah is clearly designed to wrestle with the problems of evil and exile in the world, particularly the Assyrian invasions of Israel and the Babylonian exile of Jerusalem and Judah, in relation to the questions of YHWH's power and righteousness. Despite the prevailing view in the ancient world that the demise of both Israel and Judah would demonstrate YHWH's failure to defend the nations, the book of Isaiah attempts to counter such assertions by portraying such disasters in keeping with the divine will. Evil serves YHWH's purpose in the book of Isaiah to demonstrate that the deity of two minor monarchies is in fact the sovereign creator of the world who brings judgment against YHWH's own people when they fail to recognize YHWH's sovereignty, who commissions nations to carry out that judgment, who in turn brings judgment against those nations when they fail to recognize YHWH as the source of their power, and who ultimately restores the exiled people to Jerusalem, the site that symbolizes YHWH's role in the world. Isaiah is indeed a work of theodicy that attempts to defend YHWH from charges of impotence and immorality.

Yet the book of Isaiah also raises disturbing questions. To what extent does YHWH consign the people of Israel, Judah, and Jerusalem to suffering by rendering them blind and deaf and therefore unable to understand or to repent? To what extent is their suffering explained by their own wrongdoing, even when they are prevented from recognizing that wrongdoing and changing their ways? What might have become of the people had Isaiah done more than simply ask, "How long, my L-rd?" Would YHWH have responded to Isaiah if he had stood up to YHWH to say that what YHWH proposed was inherently evil insofar as it consigned a generation or more of people to death and suffering without the possibility of repentance? Readers have already seen that Abraham and Moses both succeeded in persuading YHWH in similar situations of threat. Subsequent chapters will demonstrate that Amos and Job achieved similar results when they challenged immoral actions on the part of YHWH. Would readers still see corpses at the end of the book of Isaiah? Or might they see the realization of the ideal vision in Isa 2:2-4?

FIVE

Jeremiah's Struggle with His Divine Commission

The book of Jeremiah is unique among the prophetic books insofar as it presents the oracles and activities of the only one of the prophets to live through the Babylonian siege and destruction of Jerusalem. Other prophets may have lived through such catastrophe—for instance, Ezekiel received the news of Jerusalem's fall while living in Babylonian exile and Isaiah lived at the time of Samaria's fall to the Assyrian Empire—but Jeremiah is the only prophetic book to give its readers a glimpse of life in the doomed city and the struggles in which its inhabitants engaged as they faced the onslaught of the Babylonian army. Indeed, Jeremiah tells his readers more about himself, his own thoughts, and his struggles with his divine commission, than any other prophet in the Hebrew Bible. Jeremiah begins his prophetic career in 627 B.C.E. at the outset of the reign of King Josiah, which promises a restoration of Judean independence and a reunification of Judah and Israel under Davidic rule, but he lives to see the tragic death of Josiah in 609 B.C.E. and the twenty-two-year period that ultimately sees the destruction of Jerusalem and Judah in 587 B.C.E. He is a Levitical priest, who knows, teaches, and reflects upon past tradition in relation to the circumstances of his own time. He is a political partisan, who employs his reflection on past traditions to stake out a political position opposed to that of the pro-Egyptian King Jehoiakim ben Josiah that calls for submission to the Babylonian Empire rather than opposition to it. He is a man who suffers when his own brothers or fellow priests seek his life, when he denies himself the joys of marriage and family life because he understands that the catastrophe is coming, when he sees his own nation and people devastated after they failed to heed his advice and fought their former Babylonian allies, when he is arrested for treason for speaking his mind, and when he is forced into Egyptian exile against his will in order to die in a foreign land.

Modern critical scholarship recognizes Jeremiah's engagement with the destruction of Jerusalem and the Babylonian exile, although it has not fully recognized the relevance of Jeremiah for issues posed by the Shoah.[1] Overall, Jeremiah is portrayed as a prophet of judgment, who proclaims the destruction of Jerusalem, Judah, and the Temple as a result of the people's failure to observe YHWH's Torah.[2] In general, Jeremiah's message of judgment is viewed uncritically as the just punishment of a sinful people who are led astray by false prophets who proclaim peace in a time of threat. Scholars who attempt to reconstruct the compositional history of the book generally argue that the earliest material appears in Jeremiah 1–20 or 1–25,[3] which contain the bulk of the poetic oracles of judgment against Jerusalem and Judah. Many likewise argue that the narrative material in Jeremiah 26–45, which also includes oracles of restoration in Jeremiah 30–31 and 32–33, is later material that does not necessarily represent the work of the prophet.[4] Because of the prevailing view that prophets and priests are fundamentally opposed to each other, Jeremiah's laments, which are formulated according to the patterns of cultic poetry that would have been sung by the Temple priests, are often viewed as secondary additions to the text that likewise do not represent the work of Jeremiah himself.[5] Indeed, Jeremiah's priestly identity is often suppressed or overlooked in modern study of the book. Because Jeremiah is clearly a true prophet, his polemics against false prophets are directed against cynical manipulators of public opinion who speak oracles of support for the monarchy, Jerusalem, and the Temple for their own personal gain.[6]

Although attempts to reconstruct the history of Jeremiah's composition are both legitimate and necessary, they tend to obscure important aspects of the interpretation of Jeremiah. First is the literary form of the book, which is hardly structured on the basis of an early collection of oracles in Jeremiah 1–25 that has been supplemented by later additions in Jeremiah 26–52. Rather, the literary pattern of presentation of the words of YHWH that came to Jeremiah throughout his lifetime point to a literary structure that portrays the prophet's reflection on the fate of Jerusalem and Judah leading up to and beyond the Babylonian exile. The literary structure of the book points to such progressive reflection on divine judgment against the city and the prospects for its restoration after the judgment is complete.[7] See chart 5.1 on the following page.

Indeed, such an integrative reading of the literary structure of Jeremiah places Jeremiah's oracles of judgment in conversation with his oracles of restoration; it places Jeremiah's prophetic identity in conversation with his identity as a Levitical priest; and it places Jeremiah's laments in conversation with his oracles of judgment. Altogether, a synchronic reading of Jeremiah reveals the prophet's struggles to reconcile his understanding of past tradition, such as the Torah or Isaiah's message of deliverance for Jerusalem, with the reality of Jerusalem's impending Shoah or destruction for its failure to submit to Babylonian rule. It points to a man who wants no part of YHWH's divine commission, but who is nevertheless compelled to accept his—and Jerusalem's—fate. Examination of a series of texts, including his commission as a prophet in Jeremiah 1; his early oracles concerning Israel and Judah in Jeremiah 2–6; his famous Temple sermon in Jeremiah 7–10; his laments in Jer 11:18-23; 12:1-6; 15:10-21; 17:14-18; 18:18-23; 20:7-13; and 20:14-18; his diatribes against false prophets in Jeremiah 23 and 27–29; and his visions of restoration in Jeremiah 30–31 and 32–33 point to the various dimensions of his struggle with his divine commission to witness and interpret the Shoah of Jerusalem and Judah.

Jeremiah's Commissioning and Visions

Jeremiah 1 presents three important subunits of the larger literary block in Jeremiah 1–6 that are important for defining Jeremiah's perspectives concerning the fall of Jerusalem and the Babylonian exile. They include the superscription of the book in Jer 1:1-3; the account of Jeremiah's commission as a prophet by YHWH in Jer 1:4-10; and the account of the prophet's visionary experiences that convey YHWH's purposes. Altogether, these subunits demonstrate that Jeremiah is a priest in Jerusalem during the last years of the kingdom of Judah and that he struggled with his prophetic commission to interpret the impending calamity that would overtake his nation.

The superscription for the book in Jer 1:1-3 immediately signals Jeremiah's priestly identity with its opening statement, "The words of Jeremiah ben Hilkiah from the priests who were in Anathoth in the land of Benjamin." Although the superscription identifies Jeremiah as a "priest" (*kōhēn*), it qualifies that identification by specifying that he is from the priests at Anathoth. This indicates that he is not a member of the Zadokite

Chart 5.1
The Words of Jeremiah Ben Hilkiah concerning the Restoration of Jerusalem and the Downfall of Babylon

I. Oracles concerning Israel and Judah	1–6
A. Superscription	1:1-3
B. Commissioning of the prophet	1:4-10
C. Signs concerning YHWH's purpose	1:11-19
D. Oracles calling for Israel and Judah to return to YHWH	2–6
II. Account concerning Jeremiah's Temple Sermon	7–10
III. Oracles concerning Rejection of YHWH's Covenant	11–13
IV. Oracles concerning Drought and Marriage	14–17
A. Drought	14–15
B. Marriage	16–17
V. Oracles concerning Shattered Pot/Judgment against Judah	18–20
VI. Oracles concerning Davidic Kingship	21–24
VII. Narratives concerning Jeremiah's Warnings to Submit to Babylon	25–29
VIII. Oracles concerning Restoration of Israel and Judah	30–31
IX. Narrative concerning Field at Anathoth	32–33
X. Narrative concerning YHWH's decision to give Jerusalem to Nebuchadnezzar	34:1-7
XI. Narrative concerning Reneging on Year of Release	34:8-22
XII. Narrative concerning Fall of Jerusalem	35–39
XIII. Narrative concerning Jeremiah's Removal to Egypt	40–43
XIV. Narrative concerning Jeremiah's Oracles in Egypt	44
XV. Narrative concerning Word to Baruch	45
XVI. Oracle concerning Egypt	46:1-12
XVII. Oracle concerning Babylonian Conquest of Egypt	46:13-28
XVIII. Oracle concerning Small Nations	47–49
XIX. Oracle concerning Babylon	50:1—51:58
XX. Narrative concerning Jeremiah's Instructions about Babylon	51:59-64
XXI. Appendix concerning Fall of Jerusalem	52

priestly line, which served in the Temple of YHWH at Jerusalem, but that he was a member of the priestly line of Eli, whose only surviving member Abiathar was expelled from Jerusalem to Anathoth by King Solomon early in the history of the kingdom of Israel (1 Kgs 2:26-27). This means that Jeremiah comes from a priestly line that has no particular sympathy for either the house of David or for the Jerusalem Temple. Abiathar was expelled from Jerusalem by Solomon after having served David loyally throughout his life. Furthermore, he was expelled prior to the construction of the Jerusalem Temple. Subsequent literary blocks in the book of Jeremiah demonstrate the prophet's capacity to critique king and Temple. Jeremiah 21:11—22:30 presents the prophet's condemnation of Kings Jehoiakim and Jehoiachin of Judah, although his statements make his admiration for the righteous King Josiah very clear. Likewise, Jeremiah 7-10 presents the prophet's famous Temple sermon in which he states that the people cannot expect protection from YHWH based on the existence of the Temple alone. In keeping with his perspective as a Levitical priest, he maintains that adherence to YHWH's Torah is the necessary precondition for YHWH's favor and protection. As a priest of the Elide priestly line, Jeremiah would well remember that his own ancestral sanctuary at Shiloh had been destroyed in the premonarchic period (Jer 7:12-15), and that Jerusalem could just as easily suffer the same fate.

The superscription goes on to specify in vv. 2-3 that the word of YHWH came to Jeremiah from the thirteenth year of King Josiah ben Amon of Judah (627 B.C.E.), through the reign of King Jehoiakim ben Josiah, and until the eleventh year of the reign of King Zedekiah ben Josiah in 587–586 B.C.E. when Jerusalem was exiled. The superscription thereby highlights the importance of the destruction of Jerusalem and the Babylonian exile for the book and for the prophet's career. The attentive reader will recognize, however, that the chronological claims of the book are not quite accurate. Jeremiah does not conclude chronologically with the destruction of Jerusalem. Although Jerusalem's fall is portrayed in Jeremiah 35–39 and 52, the narratives in Jeremiah 40–45 portray the subsequent assassination of Gedaliah ben Ahikam ben Shaphan, the Babylonian-appointed governor of Judah, in 582 B.C.E. and Jeremiah's subsequent removal to Egypt against his will where he spends the rest of his life condemning the people of Judah for their rebellion against the will of YHWH. In considering why the superscription would make such a claim, it should be noted that the span of years from the thirteenth year of Josiah to the eleventh year of Zedekiah totals forty years. Although Jeremiah begins his career in the land of Judah in a time of great optimism over

King Josiah's program of religious reform and national restoration at the time of the Assyrian Empire's decline, he ends his life and career as an exile in Egypt. In this manner, Jeremiah's life represents a reversal of that of Moses, likewise a prophet and Levitical priest, who had led his people on a forty-year journey from Egypt to the land of Israel.[8]

The account of the prophet's commission in Jer 1:4-10 indicates Jeremiah's struggle with his prophetic role and YHWH's insistence that he carry it out despite his objections. The passage presents YHWH's statement to Jeremiah in v. 5 to commission him as a prophet:

> Before I created you in the womb, I selected you;
> before you were born, I consecrated you;
> I appointed you a prophet concerning the nations.

Jeremiah resists YHWH's commission to serve as a prophet in v. 6 by stating: "Ah YHWH, G-d! I don't know how to speak, for I am a boy." Jeremiah's objection to his prophetic commission is common; for instance, Moses responds to YHWH's commission to free Israel from Egyptian bondage by stating that he is inadequate to the task. But YHWH's insistence that he go as instructed in v. 7 indicates an order on YHWH's part that the prophet will not be able to refuse:

> Do not say, "I am still a boy,"
> but go wherever I send you, and speak whatever I command you.
> Have no fear of them, for I am with you to deliver you.

Indeed, Jeremiah's objection here presages his lifelong struggle with his prophetic commission in which he must witness and announce YHWH's judgment against the people of Jerusalem and Judah, culminating in their destruction and exile. Although the prophet's message includes the prospect of restoration following the punishment, the content of YHWH's commission to him in v. 10 emphasizes punishment:

> See, I appoint you this day over nations and kingdoms
> to uproot and to pull down, to destroy and to overthrow,
> to build and to plant.

The four verbs of destruction and two verbs of restoration employed in this passage recur as leitmotifs for the prophet's message throughout the book in Jer 12:14-17; 18:5-10; 24:6; 31:28, 40; 42:10; and 45:4.

Finally, the two vision reports in Jer 1:11-19 emphasize both Jeremiah's priestly identity and the motif of impending judgment and destruction. The first vision account in v. 12 presents Jeremiah's observation of a branch of an almond tree, which YHWH interprets as a demonstration that YHWH is "watchful" to bring the divine word to pass. The vision is based on a pun involving the Hebrew noun *maqqēl šāqēd*, "branch of an almond tree," and the verb *šōqēd*, "watchful, watching." The pun is intended to evoke the image of the sprouting rods of Aaron representing the tribe of Levi in Num 17:16-28 to symbolize the selection of Aaron and the tribe of Levi to serve as priests in Israel. The second vision account in vv. 13-19 employs the image of a steaming pot tipped away from the north to depict the enemies from the north, namely, the Babylonians, who will assault Judah to carry out YHWH's judgment against the nation. Once again, the image evokes Jeremiah's status as a priest whose responsibilities include tending to the pots employed for cooking food for the priests and people during the sacrificial worship services conducted at the Temple. Not only does the image convey Jeremiah's priestly identity, it serves as the basis for YHWH to insist that Jeremiah carry out his prophetic role of announcing judgment despite his objections when YHWH commends him in vv. 17-19:

> So you, gird up your loins, arise and speak to them all that I command you.
> Do not break down before them, lest I break you before them.
> I make you this day a fortified city, and an iron pillar,
> and bronze walls against the whole land—
> against Judah's kings and officers and against its priests and citizens.
> They will attack you, but they shall not overcome you;
> For I am with you, declares YHWH, to save you.

YHWH's command includes a threat; Jeremiah has no choice but to comply—or suffer the consequences.

Jeremiah's Oracles against Jerusalem and Judah

Jeremiah's identity as a Levitical priest plays a crucial role in his prophetic announcements concerning the events of his day and his understanding of YHWH's role in those events. As a Levitical priest, Lev 10:10-11 makes it clear that a central facet of Jeremiah's task is to teach the people of Israel and Judah the entire Torah of YHWH concerning the differences between what is sacred and what is impure. The oracles in Jeremiah 2–6, which constitute the largest block of material in Jeremiah 1–6, demonstrate Jeremiah's attempts to carry out his priestly and prophetic role during the early years of Josiah's reforms and in the aftermath of Josiah's death.[9] Indeed, these oracles demonstrate the prophet's capacity to rethink his teachings in relation to the events of his day and to reflect upon earlier tradition in articulating his understanding of divine purpose.

The present form of Jeremiah 2–6 constitutes Jeremiah's lengthy prophetic summons to repentance directed to Judah. Jeremiah points to YHWH's charges of idolatry against Judah and argues that YHWH will bring an unnamed enemy from the north to carry out the divine judgment unless Judah repents and returns to observing YHWH's expectations. Although the present form of this text is directed to Judah, literary tensions and internal references within this block of material indicate that it is a composite text in which an early summons to repent directed to the Northern Kingdom of Israel was later expanded and shifted so that it would address the Southern Kingdom of Judah instead. The poetic material in Jer 2:1—3:5 and 3:14—4:2 appears to be directed exclusively to Israel/Jacob or the Northern Kingdom of Israel. These passages accuse Israel of forsaking YHWH, transferring their allegiance to the foreign gods or Baalim of Egypt, Assyria, and elsewhere. They assert that northern Israel has suffered YHWH's punishment for such actions, and call upon Israel to return to YHWH at Zion:

> Turn back, rebellious children, declares YHWH.
> Since I have espoused you, I will take you,
> one from a town and two from a clan and bring you to Zion.
> And I will give you shepherds after my own heart,
> who will pasture you with knowledge and skill. (Jer 3:14-15)

> If you return O Israel—declares YHWH
> If you return to Me, if you remove your abominations from My presence
> And do not waver, and swear "As YHWH lives"
> In sincerity, justice, and righteousness—
> Nations shall bless themselves by you and praise themselves by you.
> (Jer 4:1-2)

Jeremiah's call for the repentance of northern Israel and its return to YHWH at Zion articulates the basic goals of King Josiah's program of religious reform and national restoration in the late seventh century B.C.E. At the time of the decline of the Assyrian Empire, which had dominated Judah from the late eighth century B.C.E., Josiah apparently sensed that the opportunity was ripe to assert Judean independence, reclaim the territory and population of the former Northern Kingdom of Israel, and thereby restore the ideal Solomonic empire based on the house of David and the Jerusalem Temple. As a prophet whose career began in the thirteenth year of Josiah—that is, 627 B.C.E., at the outset of Josiah's reform program—Jeremiah appears to serve as a mouthpiece for the king's reform and restoration program insofar as he calls for Israel's return to YHWH, Jerusalem, and Josiah.

The sudden and unexpected death of Josiah at the hands of Pharaoh Necho of Egypt at Megiddo in 609 B.C.E. put an abrupt end to Josiah's program. With his death, Judah became a vassal of Egypt and later of Babylonia, which led ultimately to Jerusalem's and Judah's destruction in revolt against Babylon in 588–586 B.C.E. Jeremiah's recognition of the significance of Josiah's death explains the expansion and reformulation of the original summons to repentance directed to Israel into a summons to Jerusalem and Judah in Jeremiah 2–6. Josiah's death indicated that YHWH's plans for punishment were not yet complete and that Jerusalem and Judah would suffer destruction just like Israel had suffered a century before if they did not observe YHWH's will. The additional material in Jer 3:6-13 demonstrates the prophet's reflection on his message from the days of Josiah and his recognition that Judah must be even more guilty than Israel before her. As a result, the additional material in Jer 4:3—6:30 targets Judah as the object of YHWH's wrath and the prophet's summons to repentance:

> Open your hearts to YHWH, remove the thickening of your
>   hearts—
> O men of Judah and inhabitants of Jerusalem—
> Lest My wrath break forth like fire, and burn with none to quench it,
> Because of your wicked acts. (Jer 4:4)

> Set up a signpost: To Zion.
> Take refuge, do not delay!
> For I bring evil from the north, and great disaster. (Jer 4:6)

Jeremiah's reformulation of his message from a summons directed to Israel to one directed to Judah indicates his recognition of the danger now facing Jerusalem and Judah in the aftermath of Josiah's death. But it also represents his reflection as a Levitical priest on past tradition and his attempts to teach that tradition to his people. Jeremiah 2–6 is peppered with language and phraseology reminiscent of the prophet Isaiah ben Amoz of Jerusalem. A century prior to Jeremiah's time, Isaiah had offered a message of judgment against the Northern Kingdom of Israel and deliverance for the Southern Kingdom of Judah based on his understanding of the Davidic/Zion tradition, which asserted YHWH's promise to defend the house of David and the city of Jerusalem forever.[10] Indeed, Isaiah's oracles envisioned a reunification of Israel and Judah and a restoration of Davidic rule over the north in the aftermath of Israel's downfall:

> In that day, the stock of Jesse that has remained standing
> shall become a standard to the peoples—nations shall seek his
>   counsel
> and his abode shall be honored. . .
> He will hold up a signal to the nations and assemble the banished
>   of Israel,
> And gather the dispersed of Judah from the four corners of the
>   earth.
> Then Ephraim's envy shall cease and Judah's harassment shall
>   end;
> Ephraim shall not envy Judah, and Judah shall not harass
>   Ephraim.
> They shall pounce on the back of Philistia to the west,
> And together plunder the peoples of the east;
> Edom and Moab shall be subject to them
> And the children of Ammon shall obey them. (Isa 11:10, 12-14)

Although such an Isaian perspective may well underlie Jeremiah's calls for Israel's return to Jerusalem in Jer 2:1—3:5 and 3:14—4:2, the calls for Judah's repentance together with its potential punishment in Jer 3:6-13 and 4:3—6:30 often quote Isaian oracles as well. For example, Jer 5:15-17 includes Jeremiah's statements that YHWH will bring "a nation from afar" against the house of Israel:

> Lo, I am bringing against you, O House of Israel, a nation from
>   afar—declares YHWH.
> It is an enduring nation, it is an ancient nation;

A nation whose language you do not know—you will not understand what they say.

Their quivers are like a yawning grave—they are all mighty men.

They will devour your harvest and food, they will devour your sons
and daughters,

They will devour your flocks and herds, they will devour your vines
and fig trees.

They will batter down with the sword the fortified towns on which
you rely.

Jeremiah's statement concerning the approach of a foreign enemy
to punish Israel or Judah is strikingly similar to Isaiah's statements
concerning the approach of the Assyrian army to punish Israel in Isa
5:26-29:

He will raise an ensign to a nation afar, whistle to one at the end of
the earth.

There it comes with lightening speed! In its ranks, none is weary or
stumbles,

They never sleep or slumber;

The belts on their waists do not come loose, nor do the thongs of
their sandals break.

Their arrows are sharpened, and all their bows are drawn.

Their horses' hoofs are like flint, the chariot wheels like the whirl-
wind.

Their roaring is like a lion's, they roar like the great beasts;

When they growl and seize a prey, they carry it off and none can
recover it.

Given the interrelationship between the Jeremian and Isaian oracles,
it would appear that Jeremiah draws on the Isaiah tradition to articulate
his summons to Judah. Coming in the aftermath of Josiah's death and
Judah's subjugation to first Egypt and then Babylon, Jeremiah's vision of a
restored and reunited Davidic monarchy had to be altered to one that saw
the possibility of continued judgment against Judah and Jerusalem like
that suffered by Israel and Samaria. For Jeremiah, the older Isaian message of YHWH's protection for the house of David and Jerusalem could
no longer hold sway. Jerusalem and Judah could fall victim to a Mesopotamian conqueror from the north just as Israel had fallen victim to the
Assyrians a century before.

Jeremiah's Seditious Sermon

Jeremiah's recognition of the potential danger to Jerusalem and Judah appears quite clearly in his famed Temple sermon in Jeremiah 7–10.[11] The sermon appears in the form of YHWH's instructions to the prophet to stand in the gate of the Temple and deliver a sermon to the people that challenges the notion that the presence of the Temple represents YHWH's promise of protection and security for Jerusalem. The narrative in Jeremiah 26 concerning Jeremiah's trial for sedition as a result of his declaration that Jerusalem would be destroyed indicates his compliance with YHWH's instructions. Only the intervention of Ahikam ben Shaphan, a highly placed supporter of Jeremiah, saved the prophet from execution.[12] The narrative in Jeremiah 36 concerning King Jehoiakim's disdainful treatment of the scroll of Jeremiah's sermon indicates that Jeremiah was subsequently banned from speaking publicly at the Temple and sought to work around the ban by having the scribe, Baruch ben Neriah, write a scroll of Jeremiah's words and read it in the Temple in place of the prophet. Jehoiakim's order that Jeremiah be arrested upon hearing the scroll indicates the king's response to the prophet's message.

The sermon is controversial because of Jeremiah's contention that the presence of the Jerusalem Temple will not save the city from potential destruction. It is therefore a challenge to the dominant Davidic/Zion covenant theology of the time that posited YHWH's promise of eternal rule for the house of David (2 Samuel 7; 23:1-7; Psalm 110) and security for the city of Jerusalem (Psalms 2; 46; 47; 48). In keeping with classic Deuteronomic theology and literary form, Jeremiah employs the classic form of the Levitical sermon like that employed by Moses throughout the book of Deuteronomy to argue that the people must observe YHWH's expectations in order to ensure their security in the land (see Deuteronomy 28–30).[13] He cites elements of the Ten Commandments (see Deuteronomy 5) to illustrate what such observance entails. To support his argument, he points to the history of his ancestral sanctuary at Shiloh, which was apparently destroyed by the Philistines (see 1 Samuel 4), to contend that Jerusalem could be destroyed as well. Although one might be surprised that a Levitical priest would present such a critique of the Temple, Jeremiah's role as a priest called for instruction in the proper observance of YHWH's will, including the purification of the Temple (see Lev 10:10-11). As a member of the Elide priestly line whose ancestor Abiathar had been dismissed from service in the Jerusalem Temple and banished to Anathoth in the days of Solomon, Jeremiah would have little sympathy for the Jerusalem Temple or reason to accept its conceptualization as the center or source for creation in ancient Judean thought.

By announcing the potential destruction of the Temple and Jerusalem like Shiloh, Jeremiah challenged the very foundations of Judean self-identity and stood trial for sedition against the king and state for his claims (see Jeremiah 26). The narrative concerning the trial illustrates the desperate nature of Jeremiah's situation. Jeremiah's defense is based on his contention that he speaks on behalf of YHWH, and his supporters point to the example of Micah, whose contention that Jerusalem would be plowed like a field (Jer 26:17-19; cf. Mic 3:12) prompted King Hezekiah's repentance and the deliverance of the city. The execution by King Jehoiakim of a prophet named Uriah ben Shemaiah from Kiriath Jearim appears to have sealed Jeremiah's fate until the intervention of Ahikam ben Shaphan, who like his father had once been an officer in King Josiah's court (see 2 Kgs 22:3, 12). Jeremiah's life is saved, although he is banished from Temple service (see Jer 36:1-8).

Although Jeremiah apparently delivered the sermon as instructed, he clearly struggles with his commission from G-d. Many interpreters contend that the Temple sermon narrative appears only in Jer 7:1—8:3, but the introductory word-transmission formula in Jer 7:1[14] and the following formulas concerning YHWH's continuing instructions to Jeremiah in Jer 7:16, 27; 8:4; and 10:11 indicate that the unit extends much farther, apparently through the end of chapter 10. Within the passage, Jeremiah also speaks to YHWH. Following his admonition that Jerusalem and Judah not follow the way of the nations in Jer 10:2-5, the text in Jer 10:6-10, 12-16 presents the prophet's praise of YHWH in typical Levitical fashion. Following YHWH's statement that YHWH will fling away the inhabitants of the land in Jer 10:18, Jeremiah again addresses YHWH in vv. 19-25 to speak about the sickness and wounds that he must bear as a result of the message that he delivers to the people. The culmination of the prophet's address to YHWH in vv. 23-25 calls for YHWH to show mercy to the people, chastise Jeremiah, and judge the nations that devour Jacob:

> I know, O YHWH, that man's road is not his to choose,
> That man, as he walks, cannot direct his own steps.
> Chastise me, O YHWH, but in measure;
> Not in Your wrath, lest You reduce me to naught.
> Pour out your wrath on the nations who have not heeded You,
> Upon the clans that have not invoked Your name.

> For they have devoured Jacob, have devoured and consumed him,
> And have laid desolate his homesteads.

In calling upon YHWH in this manner, Jeremiah displays the sense of pathos at the suffering of the nation that Heschel deems to be characteristic of both YHWH and the prophet in the book of Jeremiah.[15]

Jeremiah's Seven Laments

Jeremiah's struggle with his divine commission continues throughout the so-called laments of Jeremiah in Jer 11:18-23; 12:1-6; 15:10-21; 17:14-18; 18:18-23; 20:7-13; and 20:14-18.[16] Many modern scholars challenge the authenticity of these laments, arguing that their formulation as liturgical poetry presupposes a setting in Temple worship and that priestly identity precludes authorship by a prophet such as Jeremiah. But Jeremiah's priestly identity buttresses arguments that the laments are indeed authentic. As a Levitical priest, one of Jeremiah's duties would have been to sing liturgical psalms as part of the Temple liturgy.[17] In this respect, it is noteworthy that Chronicles identifies the Levitical Temple singers as prophets.

The first lament in Jer 11:18-23 easily builds upon the portrayal of Jeremiah's Temple sermon in Jeremiah 7–10 and 26 by portraying the opposition that was raised against the prophet. Following a prophetic discourse in Jer 11:2-17 concerning Judah's broken covenant with YHWH, v. 14 presents YHWH's instructions to Jeremiah not to intercede on the people's behalf:

> As for you, do not pray for this people, do not raise a cry of prayer
>   on their behalf;
> For I will not listen when they call to Me on account of their
>   disaster.

Having heard and presumably announced YHWH's decree against the people, Jeremiah's first lament in vv. 18-23 emphasizes the prophet's isolation as the people begin to accuse him and plot his demise. Jeremiah portrays himself as a lamb about to be sacrificed in v. 19 when he states:

> For I was like a docile lamb led to the slaughter;
> I did not realize that it was against me they fashioned their plots:

"Let us destroy the tree with its fruit, let us cut him off from the land
of the living.
That his name will be remembered no more!"

Although YHWH reiterates the intention to punish the men of Anathoth who threaten him in vv. 21-23, such an announcement of the demise
of his own hometown associates can hardly come as much comfort to
the prophet. His second lament in Jer 12:1-6 follows immediately with
the prophet's charges that YHWH does nothing to stop the actions of the
wicked or to protect the righteous in vv. 1-2:

You will win, O YHWH, if I make claim against You.
Yet I shall present charges against You:
Why does the way of the wicked prosper? Why are the workers of
treachery at ease?
You have planted them, and they have taken root,
They spread, they even bear fruit.
You are present in their mouths, but far from their thoughts.

Jeremiah continues by stating that YHWH knows that he is righteous,
and demands to know when YHWH will act against those who are evil
and thereby bring the land to ruin.

The struggle is not Jeremiah's alone, as YHWH also laments over the
coming destruction. After stating in Jer 15:1 that even the intercession
of Moses and Samuel would not stop the coming destruction, YHWH
laments over the coming punishment in vv. 5-6:

But who will pity you, O Jerusalem, who will console you?
Who will turn aside to inquire about your welfare?
You cast Me off—declares YHWH—You go ever backward.
So I have stretched out My hand to destroy you;
I cannot relent.

Jeremiah responds by beginning his third lament in Jer 15:10-21 with
a woe statement that mourns the day of his birth:

Woe is me, my mother, that you ever bore me—
A man of conflict and strife with all the land!
I have not lent and I have not borrowed; yet everyone
curses me.

He continues in vv. 17-18 by charging that YHWH is untrustworthy:

I have not sat in the company of revelers and made merry!
I have sat lonely because of Your hand upon me for You have filled
    me with gloom.
Why must my pain be endless, my wound incurable, resistant to
    healing?
You have been to me like a spring that fails, like waters that cannot
    be relied upon.

Jeremiah is commanded by YHWH in Jer 16:1—17:13 not to marry
or have children because they will only suffer due to the guilt and coming
punishment of Judah. Such a command denies the very first command
of Jews in *halakhah*, "Be fruitful and multiply" (Gen 1:28), and thereby
denies the very life that YHWH grants. Jeremiah nevertheless remains
committed to YHWH in his fourth lament in Jer 17:14-18, pleading with
YHWH:

Heal me, O YHWH, and let me be healed; save me, and let me be
    saved;
For You are my glory.

Jeremiah then demands the condemnation of the people after he is
denounced for comparing the people to a pot that is spoiled on the pot-
ter's wheel. In his fifth lament in Jer 18:18-23, he once again demands
righteousness from YHWH:

Listen to me, O YHWH, and take note of what my enemies say!
Should good be repaid with evil? Yet they have dug a pit for me.
Remember how I stood before You to plead on their behalf,
To turn Your anger away from them!

When he is placed in stocks for smashing a pot to symbolize the coming destruction of the people, Jeremiah launches his bitterest tirades in his
sixth and seventh laments in Jer 20:7-13 and 20:14-18 when he compares
YHWH to a rapist who overpowers him and impregnates him with the
divine word that he can no longer hold inside himself:

You enticed me, O YHWH, and I was enticed; You overpowered me
    and You prevailed.

> I have become a constant laughingstock, everyone jeers at me.
> For every time I speak I must cry out, must shout, "Lawlessness and
> rapine!"
> For the word of YHWH causes me constant disgrace and contempt.
> I thought, "I will not mention Him, no more will I speak His
> name"—
> But His word was like a raging fire in my heart, shut up in my bones,
> I could not hold it in, I was helpless.

In an ultimate statement of bitterness and self-denial at his divine commission and betrayal by YHWH, Jeremiah takes on the role of the newborn baby to curse the day of his birth in vv. 14-18:

> Accursed be the day that I was born!
> Let not the day be blessed when my mother bore me! . . .
> Why did I ever issue from the womb, to see misery and woe,
> To spend my days in shame?

Jeremiah against the False Prophets

Jeremiah's laments over his sense of abandonment by YHWH run parallel to his charges of false prophecy in Jeremiah 23 and 27–29.[18] His questions concerning the trustworthiness of YHWH prompt him to question
the trustworthiness of prophecy as well, although his struggles with the
earlier prophetic work of Isaiah cause him to weigh the applicability of
earlier prophetic tradition in relation to his own time. Whereas earlier
prophetic texts in Isaiah spoke of the downfall of northern Israel and
its Assyrian oppressors, the statements concerning Jerusalem's deliverance would have rung hollow to Jeremiah in the face of the threat posed
by Babylonia. For Jeremiah, Isaiah's statements concerning the downfall
of Israel also should be applied to Judah and Jerusalem, that is, Isaiah's
prophecies would only attain their fulfillment with the punishment of
Jerusalem and Judah as well.

Jeremiah's lengthy discourse in Jer 23:9-40 condemns those who would
prophesy falsely in the name of YHWH. Ironically, this discourse follows
Jeremiah's first royal oracle that condemns the "shepherds" or leaders of
the people who have "scattered the sheep" and anticipates the rise of a
righteous Davidic monarch in terms that recall Isaiah's oracle concerning
the rise of a righteous "branch" of David in Isa 11:1-16. The placement of

Jeremiah's discourse concerning false prophets and the fact that Jeremiah's second royal oracle in Jer 33:14-26 actually applies to the city of Jerusalem rather than to the house of David suggests that the prophet may have had in mind Isaian-inspired prophecies concerning the rise of a new Davidic monarch when he condemned false prophecy.

Jeremiah 23:9-40 begins with a brief superscription that directs his comments "to the prophets" without specifying whether he means true or false prophets. His intentions become clearer, however, when he laments over godless prophets and priests who lead the people into darkness, adultery, and evil by prophesying in the name of Baal. Prophets in the Bible frequently condemn their targets by charging them with idolatry or apostasy. Hosea, for example, charges that Israel has become apostate because it is allied with Assyria rather than with Aram, and Ezekiel charges a group of worshipers at the Temple that includes a supporter of Jeremiah with worship of the sun, when in fact they are engaged in the morning worship service for YHWH. It is therefore imperative that the interpreter determine the specific issue on the prophet's mind. Jeremiah states in v. 17 that false prophets state that "all shall be well with you," which many take as an indication that he condemns in principle those prophets who speak of restoration rather than judgment. But Jeremiah himself speaks of restoration in Jeremiah 30–31 and 32–33, so the interpreter must probe the matter more closely. In v. 30, Jeremiah states that YHWH will condemn those prophets who steal YHWH's words from one another to proclaim "the burden [that is, oracle] of YHWH."

Although Jer 23:9-40 does not give readers a full understanding of Jeremiah's concept of false prophecy, the narrative in Jeremiah 27–28 concerning Jeremiah's confrontation with the prophet Hananiah ben Azzur provides some criteria for making a determination. The narrative setting is during the reign of Jehoiakim ben Josiah when the king was consulting with allies to determine how to respond to the Babylonian victory of Egypt at Carchemesh in 605 B.C.E., although it is also related to the reign of King Zedekiah. Jehoiakim had been placed on the throne by Pharaoh Necho of Egypt in place of his younger half-brother, Jehoahaz, who apparently supported his father Josiah's policy of alliance with Babylon. As an Egyptian client, Jehoiakim was now faced with the prospect of abandoning support for his Egyptian patron to submit to the nation that had just defeated Egypt. In an effort to influence the royal decision, Jeremiah, a consistent supporter of the pro-Babylonian faction in Jerusalem, walked about Jerusalem in a yoke to symbolize the need to submit to the Babylonians. Hananiah confronted Jeremiah, broke the yoke from upon his shoulders, and declared that in two years time YHWH would break the yoke of Babylon and that Jerusalem would once again be free. Hananiah's declaration that Jerusalem would be freed from foreign control reiterates Isaiah's Davidic/Zion theology, in which he declared to King Ahaz of Judah that YHWH would protect Jerusalem and the House of David from foreign threats (see Isa 7:1—9:6). It also takes up Isaiah's admonitions against alliance with the Babylonians (see Isaiah 39). By Josiah's time, Jerusalemites would have understood Isaiah's prophecy to be an announcement of security for Jerusalem, especially since the narratives in Isaiah 36–39 depict YHWH's defense of Jerusalem and Hezekiah once Hezekiah turned to YHWH.

Jeremiah, however, lives in a time and situation far removed from that of Isaiah. As a supporter of alliance with Babylonia from the days of King Josiah, Jeremiah calls for submission to Babylon. But his call for a Babylonian alliance also recognizes Judah's changed status in Babylonia's estimation. Josiah had been an ally of Babylon, and died at the hands of Pharaoh Necho of Egypt supporting his Babylonian allies. Jeremiah apparently took Josiah's death as a sign that things had changed. Furthermore, under Jehoiakim, Judah had broken its alliance with Babylonia to ally with Egypt. For Jeremiah, Babylonia posed a threat to Judah now that it had sided with Babylon's chief enemy in the aftermath of the fall of the Assyrian Empire. Jeremiah returns to walk the streets of the city with a yoke of iron so that he might announce that YHWH's decision was firm, that is, Babylon would rule with a yoke of iron and Judah would be compelled to submit. To underscore Jeremiah's point, the narrative concludes with an announcement of Hananiah's death. By challenging a prophet who spoke a message of deliverance for Jerusalem in keeping with the earlier prophecies of Isaiah, Jeremiah demonstrates an interest in reflecting on earlier prophetic tradition and its applicability to the present situation—that is, whereas Isaiah prophesied judgment against Israel and deliverance for Jerusalem, Jeremiah recognized that Jerusalem would potentially suffer as well if it did not recognize the lesson to be derived from the experience of northern Israel. Ironically, the book of Isaiah would expand in the exilic and postexilic periods to account for the Babylonian exile as well.

Indeed, Jeremiah's position concerning Babylonian exile is stated in his letter to the exiles in Jeremiah 29 in which he tells those Judeans exiled to Babylon in 597 B.C.E. to build houses, plant gardens, raise children, and so forth, because they will be in exile for seventy years as an expression of the will of YHWH. Jeremiah's letter was prompted by announcements that prophets among the exiles had apparently spoken a message of deliverance that would soon be realized much like that of Hananiah. Jeremiah instead names those prophets and charges them with deluding the people. He advises the exiles to turn to YHWH and wait; YHWH will first ravage Jerusalem with the Babylonians, and only after the punishment has reached its full course will the exile return. Again, Jeremiah refutes the Isaian-inspired message of deliverance. Jerusalem would suffer before any restoration would begin.

Jeremiah's Understanding of Restoration

Although Jeremiah's message focuses on judgment and exile for Jerusalem and Judah, he also announces restoration as part of his efforts to discern divine intention in relation to the course of events in the ancient world and his struggle to understand earlier Judean tradition in relation to those events.[19] His commission as a prophet in Jer 1:10 includes the two verbs of restoration, to build and to plant, in addition to the four verbs of destruction. In this respect, Jeremiah continues the perspective of Isaiah, but he differs by anticipating a long period of judgment that overtakes Judah as well as Israel before the restoration can be realized. Two passages in particular lay out Jeremiah's understanding of restoration, namely, Jeremiah 30–31 and 32–33.

Jeremiah 30–31 anticipates Israel's return to Jerusalem in terms that reflect Josiah's program of religious reform and national restoration.[20] Although the current form of the passage clearly envisions a restoration of both Israel and Judah following the period of punishment, redaction-critical analysis of this passage demonstrates that it is an expanded form of an underlying set of oracles that depict northern Israel's return to Jerusalem. Whereas the present form of the text presupposes the final editions of the book of Jeremiah from the exilic period or later, the underlying oracles concerning Israel's return to Jerusalem presuppose King Josiah's program of religious reform and national restoration. Both editions of this text employ a teleological perspective in which the projected outcome of a period of punishment is restoration and YHWH's renewed commitment to secure Israel and Judah.

The final form of Jeremiah 30–31 portrays a restoration for Israel and Judah. This intention is made clear in Jer 30:1-4, in which YHWH instructs Jeremiah to write down the divine words spoken to him concerning the restoration of both Israel and Judah. The following sequence of oracles in Jer 30:5—31:40, each of which begins with the formula, "Thus says YHWH," or a variant, then lays out a scenario in which the restoration will be realized. Jeremiah 30:5-11 projects the deliverance of Jacob, that is, Israel, so that Jacob might serve the Davidic king. Jeremiah 30:12-17 promises Zion that those who wanted to devour Zion shall themselves be devoured. Jeremiah 30:18—31:1 promises to restore the relationship between Jacob or Israel and YHWH so that YHWH will be G-d to all the clans of Israel and they shall be YHWH's people. Jeremiah 31:2-6 portrays Israel as a maiden who takes up her timbrels to dance as she returns to YHWH at Zion. Jeremiah 31:7-14 depicts the return from the north of the remnant of Israel to the heights of Zion. Jeremiah 31:15 briefly portrays Rachel, the matriarch of the northern tribes of Ephraim and Manasseh, as she weeps for her children who are gone. Jeremiah 31:16-22 calls for the cessation of weeping as Ephraim or Israel repents and returns to YHWH. Jeremiah 31:23-34 portrays the restoration of Israel and Judah in the land of Judah, particularly in relation to YHWH's new covenant with both. Jeremiah 31:35-36 declares Israel's relationship with YHWH to be eternal. Jeremiah 31:37-40 will be eternal, before it describes the rebuilt city of Jerusalem.

Although the final form of Jeremiah 30–31 portrays the restoration of both Israel and Judah, the core of the oracles that begin with the formula, "Thus says YHWH," depict northern Israel's return and restoration to Zion or Jerusalem. Those elements of the oracular sequence that begin with the formula, "Behold the days are coming," in Jer 30:3-4; 31:27-30, 31-34; and 31:38-40 takes up the restoration of both Israel and Judah/Jerusalem. The reference to Zion in Jer 30:17 is a secondary adjustment of a reference to "prey" (Heb.: ṣēdenû) to "Zion" (Heb.: ṣîyôn), in keeping with the larger concerns of the expanded text. It would appear that a text that originally outlined the return of Israel to Zion/Judah has been expanded to take up the restoration of both Israel and Judah. Such an expansion indicates the prophet's attempt to rethink an earlier oracle that supported King Josiah's reform, particularly his efforts to reunite the former Northern Kingdom of Israel with southern Judah under Davidic rule and thereby to restore the former united kingdom of Solomon. With the realization that judgment would overtake Judah as well, insofar as Babylonia would ultimately invade Judah and destroy Jerusalem, Jeremiah's expanded oracle envisions the ultimate restoration of both Israel and Judah once the punishment is complete.

Jeremiah 32–33 presents a scenario of restoration for Jerusalem and Judah once the period of judgment is complete. Although chapters 32 and 33 are frequently treated as separate texts due to their seemingly different concerns, the introductory word transmission formula in Jer 32:1

and successive word-transmission formulas linked by *waw*-consecutive construction in Jer 32:26; 33:1; 33:19; and 33:23 point to Jeremiah 32–33 as a coherent unit. The unit begins with a portrayal in Jer 32:1-25 of Jeremiah's efforts to redeem family property in Anathoth during a lull in the Babylonian siege of Jerusalem. The prophet has the legal documents written, including "the sealed text and the open one" (v. 14), which is a common means in ancient Judah to provide a public document with the general provisions of the deed and a sealed document that includes the details of the transaction.[21] Jeremiah 32:26-44 then lays out the prophet's understanding of his purchase of land as an act that symbolizes YHWH's intention to restore Judah following the period of punishment; that is, Jeremiah's redemption of land symbolizes YHWH's coming redemption of the land once the war and exile are over. Jeremiah 33:1-18 follows with an oracle sequence that announces YHWH's willingness to explain "wondrous things" and "secrets you have not known" (v. 3). Those secrets project the restoration of Israel and Judah under the rule of a righteous Davidic branch, which includes the restored city of Jerusalem and the line of Levitical priests. Jeremiah 33:19-22 promises that YHWH's covenant with David will never be broken, and Jer 33:23-26 promises that YHWH will never reject the offspring of Jacob and YHWH's servant David.

Redaction-critical analysis once again points to a text that has been expanded in relation to later times and circumstances. Most notably, the reference to "the sealed text and the open one" in Jer 32:14 apparently prompted writers to attempt to discern divine purposes in relation to Judah's restoration following the period of punishment. Jeremiah 33:1-26 attempts to project restoration as the secret that is hidden in the symbolic action of Jeremiah's redemption of land at Anathoth. Although the portrayal of Judah's and Benjamin's restoration in Jer 33:1-13 may well be the work of Jeremiah, the material concerning the righteous Davidic branch in Jer 33:14-26 appears to be much later, particularly since this material is entirely absent in the Septuagint form of Jeremiah. Overall, the scenario laid out in Jer 33:14-26, which is introduced once again by the formula, "Behold, the days are coming," presupposes the circumstances of the early Persian period. As Goldman's analysis of this material demonstrates, the oracles concerning the restoration of a Davidic branch are formulated to refer to the city of Jerusalem, not to a new Davidic monarch.[22] Likewise, the text envisions the restoration of the Levitical priesthood together with the Davidic "branch." According to Jer 33:14-26, the Davidic monarchy is not reestablished, but the city of Jerusalem is restored and the Levitical priesthood emerges as the leadership of Judah

126   under Persian rule. Altogether, this restoration fulfills the eternal promise to Israel's ancestors, Abraham, Isaac, and Jacob in Jer 33:26. As Goldman demonstrates, this scenario is derived from an exegetical reformulation of the monarchic oracle in Jer 23:1-8; statements concerning YHWH's promise concerning the house of David in 1 Kgs 2:4; 8:24-26; and 9:4-6; and Jeremiah's portrayal of YHWH's covenant with Israel and Judah in Jer 31:35-36, 37-40. Unlike the reformulation of Jeremiah 30–31 noted above, the reformulation of Jeremiah 32–33 appears to be the product of a hand much later than that of the prophet himself. The most likely setting for such a reformulation of Jeremiah's material in Jer 32:1—33:13 is the early Persian period when the house of David faltered at the time of the building of the Second Temple and the Temple priesthood rose to fill the void left by the absence of the monarchy.

Jeremiah's Struggles with His Divine Commission

The remaining portions of the book of Jeremiah in chapters 34–52 focus on the fall of the city of Jerusalem to Babylonian forces; the destruction of the city and the exile of much of its surviving population; the assassination of Gedaliah, the Babylonian-appointed governor of Jerusalem; the removal of Jeremiah to Egypt and his activities there; and the oracles against the nations. Nevertheless, the material from Jeremiah analyzed here points to the prophet's struggle with his divine commission from the time of Josiah's reform through the last years of Judah when it becomes increasingly apparent to him that Judah will fall to the Babylonian Empire. Overall, Jeremiah struggles repeatedly with YHWH for forcing him into his role as the prophet who will oversee and interpret YHWH's actions to the people. Moreover, he struggles with past tradition, particularly the work of the prophet Isaiah whose oracles concerning the downfall of Assyria and YHWH's support for the Davidic monarch and the city of Jerusalem were read in relation to Josiah's program of national restoration and reunification in the aftermath of the Assyrian Empire's collapse. In struggling with his divine commission and past tradition, however, Jeremiah ultimately grapples with the challenges posed to Judah by the power of the Babylonian Empire and the reality of Jerusalem's and Judah's impending demise. For a Levitical priest like Jeremiah, such an act could only come at the direction of YHWH, who sought to punish Judah and Jerusalem for failing to observe YHWH's Torah. In order to defend the sanctity, righteousness, and power of YHWH, Jeremiah's only recourse was to argue

that the people—and not YHWH—were responsible for their own fate
and that YHWH would ultimately act to restore Jerusalem, Judah, and
Israel once the period of exile and punishment was over.

SIX

Ezekiel and the Holiness of G–D

E zekiel is the most enigmatic, bizarre, and perplexing book among all of the prophetic literature. The book begins in Ezek 1:1—3:15 with the prophet's inaugural vision of the divine throne chariot, which approaches him from the heavens while he stands by the banks of Chebar Canal in Babylonia, and concludes in Ezekiel 40–48 with Ezekiel's vision of the restored Temple, which matches neither Solomon's Temple nor the Second Temple built in the early Persian period. Both of these images have provoked considerable speculation in later tradition. Ezekiel's vision of the divine throne chariot provided the basis for the development of early merkavah or heikhalot mysticism and its accounts of heavenly journeys by rabbinic mystics who appeared before the divine throne.[1] His vision of the restored Temple was ultimately recognized as a depiction of the so-called Third Temple, which will signal the beginning of the messianic age in rabbinic eschatology.[2] Interpreters both ancient and modern have struggled with the book.[3] R. Hananiah ben Hezekiah burned three hundred barrels of oil working nights to reconcile the halachic differences between Ezekiel and the Torah, ultimately demonstrating that the book of Ezekiel could be included in the Jewish Bible and that the prophet Ezekiel could be considered as a halachic authority on a par with Moses (b. Shabbat 13b; b. Menahot 45a). Modern interpreters have speculated about Ezekiel's mental stability, potential drug use, and misogyny, although his identity as a Zadokite priest, raised to serve in the Jerusalem Temple, does much to explain his unusual visions, actions, concepts, and ideas.[4] Despite his bizarre perspectives, Ezekiel has profoundly influenced modern Judaism as well. Reform Judaism declared its synagogues to be Temples in keeping with the prophet's final vision of the Temple, and modern Israel named its first major city Tel Aviv after Ezekiel's home in Babylonia to symbolize Israel's or Judaism's status and perspectives in the modern world.

Like his colleague Jeremiah of the Elide priestly line, Ezekiel struggles to interpret the destruction of Jerusalem and the Temple of Solomon by the Babylonians in 587/6 B.C.E., although he does so from the standpoint of an exile in Babylonia rather than as a resident of Jerusalem. As a Zadok- ite priest of the Jerusalem Temple, perhaps even as the future high priest, Ezekiel was among the leading figures exiled by the Babylonians from Jerusalem with King Jehoiachin ben Jehoiakim in 597 B.C.E. Ezekiel's inau- gural vision then takes place five years later as he is standing by the banks of the Chebar Canal in Babylonia (see Ezek 1:1-3), and the chronological notices that signal the basic literary structure of the book indicate that his prophetic career extended over the next twenty years, from the fifth year of the exile of King Jehoiachin until the final vision of the Temple in the twenty-fifth year of the exile (see Ezek 40:1). Indeed, the twenty-year chronological sequence for Ezekiel's oracles enables interpreters to under- stand the initial reference to the inaugural vision in "the thirtieth year" (Ezek 1:1) as his age at the time of his inaugural vision. Zadokite priests served from the age of thirty until the age of fifty, and Ezekiel's chronology corresponds to the years that he would have served as an active priest had in remained in Jerusalem for service at the Jerusalem Temple (see Num 4:3, 23, 30, 39, 43, 47). Because he is an exile in a profane land and unable to serve in the Holy Temple, Ezekiel adapts his priestly status and perspec- tives to serve as a prophet in exile who interprets YHWH's holy presence and purpose even in the midst of Babylonia.[5]

Although early critical scholars attempted to strip away priestly ele- ments of the book as the product of later priestly redaction of the works of the prophet Ezekiel,[6] his priestly identity is crucial for understanding his perspectives on exile and restoration.[7] Such influence begins with his inaugural vision, which replicates the visions experienced by the priests as they enter the Holy of Holies of the Jerusalem Temple where the Ark of the Covenant resides to encounter YHWH's Holy Presence (see esp. Leviticus 16) and which employs the model of the seven-day priestly ordination (see Exodus 28–29; Leviticus 8; Numbers 8) to express his ini- tial commission as a prophet and priest who teaches YHWH's Torah (see Lev 10:10-11), and culminates in the restored Temple once the land of Israel and creation at large have been purged of impurity. Like his priestly colleague Jeremiah, Ezekiel also asserts the righteousness of YHWH in a time of evil insofar as he maintains that human beings have corrupted or profaned the Holy Temple and creation at large by failing to live in accordance with YHWH's Torah. Indeed, the literary structure of the book of Ezekiel chronicles the career of the Zadokite priest and visionary prophet who interpreted the Babylonian exile as YHWH's attempt to purge Jerusalem and creation of impurity so that the Holy Temple could be established once again.[8] See chart 6.1.

Chart 6.1 Ezekiel's Visions concerning the Purge and Restoration of Jerusalem	
I. Introduction: Ezekiel's Oracles concerning His Inaugural Vision	1–7
II. Ezekiel's Oracles concerning His Vision of YHWH's Departure from the Jerusalem Temple and Its Significance	8–19
III. Ezekiel's Oracles concerning the Punishment of All Israel	20–23
IV. Symbolic Actions concerning the Destruction of Jerusalem and the Punishment of Neighboring Nations	24–25
V. Oracles concerning Tyre and Its Rulers	26–28
VI. The First Oracle concerning Egypt	29:1-16
VII. The Second Block of Oracles concerning Egypt	29:17—30:19
VIII. The First Oracle concerning Pharaoh	30:20-26
IX. The Second Oracle concerning Pharaoh	31
X. Oracle concerning Pharaoh and Egypt	32:1-16
XI. Final Oracle concerning the Nations and Ezekiel's Role as Watchman	32:17—33:20
XII. Oracles concerning the Restoration of Israel	33:21—39:29
XIII. The Vision of the Restored Temple	40–48

Examination of the materials associated with Ezekiel's inaugural vision in Ezekiel 1–7; his visions concerning the destruction of Jerusalem and the Temple in Ezekiel 8–11; his role as watchman and his concern with the purification of the land in Ezek 32:17—33:20 and 33:21—39:29; and his final vision concerning the restoration of the Temple in Ezekiel 40–48 indicate how his priestly perspectives inform his understanding of YHWH's character and purposes in bringing about the exile as a means

to purge Israel and all creation from impurity and to restore the holiness $\qquad$
of both.

Ezekiel's Inaugural Vision and Symbolic Actions

Ezekiel's inaugural vision of YHWH's throne chariot in Babylonia appears in the first major block of the book in Ezekiel 1–7, which is dated to "the thirtieth year" and specified as "the fifth year of the exile of King Jehoiachin" (Ezek 1:1-3). As noted above, the chronological statements indicate that Ezekiel is thirty years old, the age at which a Zadokite priest is ordained for service in the Temple, and that he is in Babylonian exile in 592 B.C.E., five years after having been exiled with King Jehoiachin of Judah. Ezekiel remains silent for seven days following his vision (see Ezek 3:15), which corresponds to the time that young priests are isolated in the sanctuary or tent of meeting until the ordination is complete (Lev 8:33-35; Exod 29:30, 35-37).[9] Because he is in Babylonian exile rather than in the Jerusalem Temple, Ezekiel's inaugural vision adapts his would-be priestly ordination so that he will speak as a prophet of YHWH to the exiled Jewish community in Babylonia rather than serve at the Temple altar at the completion of his seven-day consecration. Ezekiel's role as prophet thereby develops out of his role as priest, since Exod 29:42 specifies that YHWH will meet and speak with Israel through the priests at the Holy Temple (see also Exod 25:22, which indicates that the Ark with its cherubim is the location for such an encounter). In this manner, Ezekiel serves as a key figure in interpreting YHWH's will and action in relation to the significance of the Babylonian exile and the coming destruction of the Jerusalem Temple.

Ezekiel's inaugural vision is designed to evoke images of the Ark of the Covenant in the Holy of Holies of the Jerusalem Temple and adapt them to the setting of the Babylonian exile. His initial view of the throne chariot occurs as he is standing by the Chebar Canal in Babylonia where he sees a storm wind sweeping in from the north with heavy cloud, flashing fire, a surrounding radiance, a gleam of amber, and four creatures at the center.

The four creatures, later identified in Ezek 10:1-25 (see esp. vv. 15, 20, 22) as cherubim, are based on the four cherubim or winged composite figures that surrounded the Ark of the Covenant in the Jerusalem Temple. Although descriptions of the Ark indicate that it was built with only two cherubim atop its mercy seat (Exod 25:10-22, esp. vv. 19-22), the description of the Holy of Holies of Solomon's Temple indicates that it, too, was built with two cherubim inside, so that the total number of cherubim around the Ark would be four when the Ark was placed inside the Holy of Holies (see 1 Kgs 6:23-28). The function of the cherubim is to serve as guards or escorts for the divine throne, much as cherubim were frequently built on either side of royal thrones in the ancient Near East to serve a similar function.[10] Each is described as having four faces, which expresses the qualities or attributes of YHWH, namely, the ox to symbolize divine strength or power, the lion to symbolize divine sovereignty, the eagle to symbolize divine freedom, and the human to symbolize divine intelligence. Each has a single, rigid leg, calves' hooves, human hands, and four wings. Insofar as the throne chariot moves simultaneously in each of the directions of the four faces of the cherubim, the vision attempts to depict divine movement as movement in four directions at once. Of course, such movement is impossible to conceive in normal spatial terms, but this becomes a means to convey divine movement in this text. The cherubim are described as sparkling with the luster of burnished bronze. Although the cherubim are overlaid with gold in Exod 25:18, Pharaoh Shishak of Egypt reportedly forced King Rehoboam to strip the gold of the Temple during his invasion of Israel and Judah, and Rehoboam was consequently obliged to replace the stripped gold with bronze (see 1 Kgs 14:25-28). The number four also builds upon the symbolism of the Temple altar, which is built with four horns to indicate the four cardinal directions (see Exod 27:1-8, esp. v. 2), insofar as the Temple stands at the center of creation and ensures the stability and order of the created world.[11] Indeed, the iconography of the Temple, the interior of which is inlaid with images of pomegranates, palm trees, lions, cherubim, and so forth, is designed to evoke the Garden of Eden. Ezekiel's designation as "son of Adam" presupposes the role of the high priest as representative of humankind who attempts to enter the Holy of Holies, qua Garden of Eden, each Yom Kippur.[12] The appearance of the divine Ark or throne chariot in Babylonia then expresses YHWH's role as creator as well as master of creation. The visionary appearance of the Ark in Babylonia might also presuppose that the Babylonians had taken it from the Temple to Babylon at the time of Jehoiachin's exile, but this cannot be certain.

The other elements of Ezekiel's initial description of the approaching throne chariot likewise represent images pertaining to the Ark of the Covenant. The approach from the north presupposes the placement of the Ark in the Temple Holy of Holies relative to the city of Jerusalem. The Temple was built on the hill to the north of the City of David, which sloped southward away from the Temple mount. The images of cloud and flashing fire presuppose the imagery of the Temple in operation during the worship services, insofar as the *heikhal*, or main hall, included ten incense altars and ten *menorot* or lampstands, each with seven burning oil lamps, that would produce the imagery of flashing lights in the midst of thick cloud (see 1 Kgs 7:27-50). The gleaming amber at the center presupposes the gold-overlaid Ark that would reflect the light from the *menorot* in the Temple during the worship surface to represent the incorporeal presence of YHWH enthroned above the cherubim (see 1 Sam 4:4; 2 Sam 6:2; 1 Chr 13:6; 1 Kgs 19:15; Isa 37:16; Pss 80:2; 99:1).

An additional feature of the vision is the wheels that accompany the four creatures. The wheels are described as built with a wheel within a wheel. The imagery of the wheels is based on the four gold ring structures built into the Ark to facilitate carrying the ark with poles (see Exod 25:12) or on the wheels of the cart employed to carry the Ark to Jerusalem (2 Sam 6:3). Although many have conceived the wheel within a wheel as a hub or a second wheel placed perpendicularly within the first wheel to enable movement in any direction, the description of the movement of the cherubim in the direction of each of their four faces simultaneously indicates that the wheels within the wheels are also intended for such movement in four directions simultaneously in order to convey the supernatural movement of the divine.

Finally, Ezekiel's attempt to describe the Presence of YHWH employs the imagery of amber, again presupposing the reflective gold overlaying the mercy seat of the Ark where YHWH is enthroned. Although he begins with an attempt to employ the metaphor of human loins to describe the divine presence, the prohibition against portraying YHWH in corporeal terms compels him to shift to images of light, sapphire, gleaming amber, and the rainbow to convey the incorporeal divine presence. Such an image presupposes the visual standpoint of a priest who enters the Holy of Holies of the Temple while the incense burners and *menorot* are in operation.

In the context of this vision, YHWH appears to Ezekiel and offers him a scroll written with lamentations, dirges, and woes that the prophet is to speak to the house of Israel. Ezekiel eats the scroll to ingest the divine message. As a result, he will serve as YHWH's watchman to warn the people of Israel on YHWH's behalf of impending judgment should they commit sins. The watchman role reflects the classic role of the priest, who is to stand as a mediator between YHWH and the people to ensure their purity before YHWH and to communicate YHWH's will (Num 8:13-19; 18:1-32; cf. Num 17:8-15; Psalms 15; 24). Such a role signals Ezekiel's understanding of the Babylonian exile as a purge or purification of the Temple and creation insofar as he would contend that such an act presupposes that the Temple and creation had been profaned by the actions of the people.[13]

Having been commissioned or ordained by YHWH as the priestly/prophetic watchman over the people of Israel, Ezekiel then engages in a series of symbolic actions to illustrate his understanding of the exile as acts of divine punishment for human impurity in Ezekiel 4–7. In the first act, Ezekiel takes a brick which he sets up to symbolize the city of Jerusalem under siege surrounded by siege mounds, battering rams, and so forth. He then lies on his left side for 390 days to symbolize the punishment of Israel and on his right side for forty days to symbolize the punishment of Judah. Although the significance of these years is uncertain, the forty years of Judah's punishment corresponds to the years from the beginning of Josiah's reform in the twelfth year of his reign, that is, 627 B.C.E., until the destruction of Jerusalem and the Temple in 587/6 B.C.E. The 390 years for Israel would then correspond roughly to the time of Israel's history from the reign of King Saul (ca. 1017 B.C.E.?) to the beginning of Josiah's reform.

The second symbolic action calls for Ezekiel to eat limited amounts of food and to drink limited amounts of water to symbolize the rations on which the people of Jerusalem would have been placed during the time of siege. YHWH instructs Ezekiel to cook his meals over human excrement, but relents when Ezekiel protests and allows him instead to use cow excrement. Such an act again symbolizes conditions in the besieged city and the defiling of the holy priest.

A third symbolic action requires Ezekiel to cut off his hair and divide it into three bundles to symbolize the fate of the people in the besieged city of Jerusalem. The first bundle is destroyed in fire to symbolize the destruction of the city. The second bundle is struck with a sword to symbolize those killed in battle. The third bundle is scattered to the wind to symbolize those who will go into exile.

Finally, YHWH commands Ezekiel to prophesy to the hills and land of Israel to communicate the defilement of the land. Such an act again presupposes YHWH's role as creator of the natural world as well as master of human events. It also points to the interrelationship between human action, whether holy or profane action, and the effect it has on the land and all creation. In Ezekiel's priestly perspective, human righteousness preserves the purity or sanctity of the land and human wrongdoing profanes the land.

The Destruction of Jerusalem and the Temple

The question of the purity of the land, Temple, and people underlies the portrayal of Jerusalem's destruction in Ezekiel 8–11. These chapters introduce the long segment in Ezekiel 8–19, dated to the sixth year of Jehoiachin's exile (591 B.C.E.), which portrays the destruction of the city and its significance. Ezekiel's portrayal of the destruction of Jerusalem is central to his understanding of YHWH's actions, namely, the Jerusalem Temple and all creation have been corrupted by idolatry and human impurity, and must be purged to allow for the reestablishment of a new Temple at the center of a renewed Israel and a renewed creation. Altogether, Ezekiel 8–11 portrays the destruction of Jerusalem as a cultic action initiated by YHWH analogous to the scapegoat ritual performed by the high priest at Yom Kippur to symbolize the purging and purification of the people and land of Israel.[14]

The narrative begins in Ezekiel 8 in the sixth year of Jehoiachin's exile (591 B.C.E.) with a portrayal of Ezekiel's visionary journey of the Jerusalem Temple led by an angelic guide. Ezekiel is taken by the hair of his head from his home in Babylonia, where he was sitting with the elders of Judah, to the entrance of the Penimith Gate on the north side of the courtyard of the Jerusalem Temple. Led by his angelic guide, Ezekiel sees "the infuriating image" north of the gate of the altar. Although the text does not specify what this image might be, it is likely a Babylonian victory stele erected in the Temple courtyard where it would be visible to all following the Babylonian subjugation of Jerusalem in 597 B.C.E. Such a stele would likely include images of Marduk or other Babylonian gods and proclaim their and Nebuchadnezzar's victory over YHWH and Judah.[15]

Ezekiel is commanded to dig through the courtyard wall so that he can see the abominations practiced in the Jerusalem Temple. Such an act likely represents the siege tactics of Babylonian sappers who would dig through or under walls to undermine them and enable Babylonian assault troops to enter a walled city. Because the northern walls of Jerusalem were the only ones built on relatively level ground, most conquerors in antiquity attacked Jerusalem at that most vulnerable point. Upon entering the Temple, Ezekiel witnesses the detestable forms of creeping things and beasts and all the fetishes of the house of Israel on the walls of the Temple. The interior walls of the Temple were decorated with pomegranates, palm trees, lions, cherubim, and so forth, to represent the imagery of the Garden of Eden, but in Ezekiel's visionary perspective, such images would have represented Israel's idolatry and corruption of the House of YHWH.

136   His vision of the seventy men with their incense censers, led by Jaazniah ben Shaphan, who state that "YHWH does not see" and that "YHWH has abandoned the land" is indicative of Ezekiel's perspective as a Zadokite priest. Jaazniah ben Shaphan is a member of the ben Shaphan family that provides support to Jeremiah throughout this period.[16] Because Ezekiel is a Zadokite priest who was exiled from the Temple, it is likely that he views a Temple controlled by elements of a secondary priestly line as having been corrupted.

Ezekiel's vision of the women weeping for Tammuz presupposes the worship of a key Babylonian fertility god who is raised from the underworld by Ishtar in the late summer to symbolize the onset of the rains at New Year's and Sukkot in the fall.[17] Although Ezekiel identifies their actions as worship of Tammuz, it is likely that they are engaged in mourning rituals typical of Israel and Judah in the late summer that likewise anticipate the onset of the fall rains. Ezekiel's vision of the twenty-five men with their backs to the Temple worshiping the sun likewise illustrates his perspective, since the men would be engaged in the typical morning service of Temple worship that would have been directed to the east at sunrise. In Ezekiel's perspective of a corrupt and idolatrous Temple, a legitimate act of Judean worship of YHWH becomes an idolatrous act of apostasy.

The visionary portrayal of Jerusalem's destruction begins in Ezekiel 9 with the angelic guide's call for the approach of six men armed with weapons of destruction. Again, they approach from the north, the direction from which ancient Jerusalem is most vulnerable to attack. Among them is a man dressed in white linen, the typical garments of a priest officiating at the Temple altar (Exod 28:39; Lev 6:10), with a writing case at his side to record the sacrifices. As the men approach, the presence of the throne chariot of YHWH with its four cherubim becomes evident as the action proceeds. The six men are commanded to mark the foreheads of all the men who "moan and groan because of all the abominations committed within it," meaning, within the city of Jerusalem. Although many interpreters struggle to discern a moral criterion in the selection of those who are marked for survival, the description of those to be killed in the city, namely, the "graybeard, youth and maiden, women and children," indicates that the *men* of the city are to be spared while the old, the young, the women, and the children are all to be killed regardless of their respective moral standings.[18]

With the execution of those unmarked completed in Ezekiel 10, the throne chariot of YHWH moves from the cherubim to the platform of the House of YHWH. There, YHWH commands the man dressed in white linen to take glowing coals from among the cherubim so that he might ignite the doomed city in an act that resembles the kindling of the sacrificial altar at the Temple. Once the man in white linen fulfilled the command, the cherubs and the throne chariot rise above the city as the Presence of YHWH prepares to depart. Because the imagery of the throne chariot is based on that of the Ark of the Covenant, which symbolizes the throne and presence of YHWH in the Jerusalem Temple, YHWH's departure signifies the final profanation of the site and perhaps even the Babylonians' removal of the Ark from the Temple in 597 B.C.E.

As the throne chariot departs from Jerusalem in Ezekiel 11, YHWH tells Ezekiel that those marked would not be killed in the city as if they were a sacrifice cooked in a pot. Rather, they will be taken to the borders of Israel where some would be killed, apparently representing the Babylonian execution of key Judean figures at Riblah in the aftermath of the city's destruction (see 2 Kgs 25:6-7, 18-21). The remnant of those not killed at the border would be taken into Babylonian exile where they would eventually be gathered, purified with a new heart so that they would observe YHWH's Torah, and returned to the land of Israel to restore and purify it from its abominations. With the vision completed, the throne chariot departs Jerusalem and Ezekiel is returned to his home in Babylonia to tell the exiles what he had seen.

Ezekiel's vision of the destruction of Jerusalem is quite remarkable because of its portrayal of Jerusalem's cultic impurity—even though many of the images are based in fact on normal Judean practice—and because of its use of sacrificial imagery to portray death and destruction in the city. The vision clearly represents Ezekiel's priestly viewpoint, that is, the city must be purged because of its impurity. Such purges are well known throughout Judean history as Temple purges or purifications were carried out by King Hezekiah in 2 Kgs 18:1-8 and 2 Chronicles 29–31; King Josiah in 2 Kgs 23:1-25; and Judah the Maccabee in 1 Macc 4:36-51. Each involves the sacrifice of a *ḥaṭṭaʾat* or "sin offering" (see Leviticus 4–5), which includes seven bulls, seven rams, seven lambs, and seven goats, which symbolizes the purging of the Temple from its corruption or impurity.

Although the analogy of the *ḥaṭṭaʾat* aids in understanding Ezekiel's perspective, it does not fully explain the vision, particularly since the men who moan and groan over the abominations in the city are spared and all others are killed. As noted above, there is no moral differentiation as the men who survive and the old, the young, the women, and the children who are killed are both treated collectively rather than on the basis of their individual moral standings. Because those who survive form the basis of the remnant that will ultimately restore the land of Israel, interpreters must look to the scapegoat offering of Leviticus 16 to understand the significance of Ezekiel's vision. The scapegoat offering calls for the presentation of two goats as ḥaṭṭaʾat offerings at Yom Kippur to symbolize the purification of the nation. One goat is sacrificed as the ḥaṭṭaʾat offering, but the other goat is released into the wilderness after the sins of the nation are symbolically transferred to it by the high priest. Such a model, in which one goat is randomly sacrificed whereas the other goat is randomly released to represent the restoration of the nation, underlies Ezekiel's understanding of Jerusalem's destruction and the fate of its people. Such an act is necessary in Ezekiel's view to purge Jerusalem of its impurity and to prepare for the reestablishment of a new Temple following the completion of the exile and purification of the land of Israel in Ezekiel 40–48. In this manner, Ezekiel interprets the destruction of Jerusalem and the Temple as YHWH's act of purging and purification of the corrupted city and Temple.

Ezekiel's Oracles of Purification and Restoration

The purification of the land of Israel in preparation for the reestablishment of the new Temple appears in Ezek 32:17—33:20, which presents Ezekiel's last oracle concerning Egypt and outlines his role as watchman for Israel, and in Ezek 33:21—39:29, which portrays the restoration of Israel per se, including the gathering of the scattered people, their reunification under a Davidic monarch, and the purification of the land from contamination by the corpses of the dead.[19]

Building on the earlier concerns with portraying the impurity of the land of Israel and of the nations, especially Egypt, in the earlier portions of the book, Ezek 32:17—33:20 presents a very unusual combination of concerns with its focus on the downfall of Egypt in Ezek 32:17-32 and Ezekiel's role as watchman for Israel in Ezek 33:1-20. Most interpreters would maintain that these oracles should be treated separately—and this is correct on diachronic grounds since the two oracles were likely not composed in relation to each other—but the present synchronic configuration of the book places them together with the introductory chronological notice in Ezek 32:17 that they came to Ezekiel in the twelfth year of Jehoiachin's exile. The reason for the combination of such seemingly distinct oracles lies in the portrayal of the dead of Egypt and the descent of its warriors into Sheol. In addition to the Egyptians, the oracle also notes the dead of Assyria, Elam, Meshech, Tubal, Edom, and Sidon to represent the nations at large that have been destroyed by the sword. In priestly thought, death constitutes the ultimate impurity and the portrayal of the corpses of Egypt and the mighty of the nations symbolizes the impurity of all creation—like that of Jerusalem and Judah—that must be purified before the Holy Temple can be rebuilt. Ezekiel's role as watchman then plays an essential role in warning the people of impending danger when YHWH will bring a sword against them due to wickedness. Ezekiel thereby becomes responsible for the well-being of the people, which is his responsibility as a priest of the Jerusalem Temple, and he is therefore charged with purifying the people from wickedness in preparation for the reestablishment of the Temple and creation at culmination of the book.

Ezekiel 33:21—39:29 then lays out a sequence of oracles that portray the purification of the land and people of Israel in preparation for the restoration of the Temple. The introductory chronological notice in Ezek 33:21-22 places these oracles in the twelfth year of Jehoiachin's exile, on the fifth day of the tenth month (that is, 5 Sivan) in 585 B.C.E., some seven months following the fall of Jerusalem. Ezekiel's mouth is opened by YHWH so that he can speak on the day prior to receiving the news of Jerusalem's fall from a fugitive who fled the scene.

The first oracle in the sequence appears in Ezek 33:23-33, which charges that the fall of the city is due to the impurity of the people. It is formulated as a disputation which challenges the people's contention that YHWH grants them the land of Israel because they are so many in comparison to Abraham, who was granted the land by YHWH even though he was only one man.[20] Ezekiel claims that the people have defiled themselves with blood and with fetishes and cannot therefore expect to possess the holy land of Israel. Instead, YHWH will turn the land into a waste picked over by animals and subject to pestilence as part of the process by which the land will be purified. Ezekiel's charges are a classic case of blaming the victims for their own suffering. Such charges provide him with the means to explain the catastrophe that overtook Jerusalem and Judah while defending the holiness and integrity of YHWH in the face of overwhelming evil.

The second oracle appears in Ezek 34:1-31, which portrays YHWH's punishment of the leaders of the nation whom Ezekiel charges with having led the people astray. The oracle employs the metaphor of shepherds leading their sheep to depict the negligence of Israel's leaders in seeing to the welfare of their flocks. The metaphorical portrayal of kings and other leaders as shepherds is widespread throughout Israel/Judah and the ancient Near Eastern world at large. Having portrayed the neglect of the shepherds resulting the scattering of the flock and its victimization by wild animals, Ezekiel maintains that YHWH will require a reckoning of the shepherds. Whereas YHWH will rescue the flock, the shepherds will be dismissed. The oracle then portrays YHWH's establishment of a new Davidic "shepherd" to tend to or rule the people. The oracle includes no further details concerning the nature of this change, although subsequent portrayals of the new Davidic monarch portray him as a figure who rules over a reunited Israel, acknowledges YHWH at the Temple, and serves under the guidance of the priests (see Ezek 37:24-27; 45:17; 46:1-8, 16-18). In this manner, Ezekiel depicts YHWH's purge of Israel's leadership.

The third oracle in Ezek 35:1—36:15 portrays the punishment of Edom and the restoration of Israel. Edom is targeted here because its eponymous ancestor Esau is Jacob's fraternal twin who attempted to kill him for taking the right of the firstborn and their father's blessing in Genesis 25–35 and because Edom apparently cooperated with the Babylonians in destroying the Jerusalem and the Temple (see Obadiah 11–14; Ps 137:7-9).[21] Because of Edom's hatred of Israel and aspirations to rule over its land, YHWH turns Edom into a desolation in Ezek 35:1-15 and restores Israel in deliberate contrast to Edom in Ezek 36:1-15.

The fourth oracle in Ezek 36:16—37:14 focuses on the purification and restoration of Israel. Most interpreters would treat Ezek 36:16-38, which portrays YHWH's decision to restore Israel for the sake of YHWH's holy name, and Ezek 37:1-14, which portrays the prophet's vision of the valley of dry bones as two separate oracles, but the introductory YHWH word-transmission formula in Ezek 36:16 binds the two oracles together. Indeed, both take up the question of Israel's purification and restoration from a priestly standpoint. Ezekiel 36:16-38 emphasizes YHWH's decision to purify or sanctify Israel and restore it from exile by cleansing them with water and by placing a new heart and spirit within the people. Such an act presupposes the priestly ritual of washing or immersion in the Miqveh as an act of purification before serving at the altar of the Holy Temple (e.g., Lev 15:7, 11-12). Following the priestly perspective, such an act also entails observance of YHWH's Torah as a means to remove iniquity. Because such impurity constitutes profanation of the divine name in priestly thought, YHWH's actions are portrayed as an effort to ensure the sanctity of the divine name. Ezekiel's vision of the restoration of the dry bones also conveys an image of the purification of the land. Again, death is the ultimate impurity in priestly thought and a land covered with corpses is rendered impure. The restoration of the dead bones or corpses to life then symbolizes the purification of the land from corpse contamination. Insofar as the oracle identifies the bones as those of the whole house of Israel, the oracle portrays the restoration of the whole nation.

The fifth oracle in Ezek 37:15-28 portrays the reunification of Israel and Judah under the rule of the Davidic king.[22] The reunification is portrayed as the joining of the stick of Joseph and the stick of Judah. Joseph is the father of Ephraim and Manasseh, the two primary tribes of the Northern Kingdom of Israel. Because of the emphasis on reunification of north and south under the rule of a Davidic king, it is likely that this oracle was composed in relation to Josiah's program of national restoration and religious reform. If Ezekiel was thirty years old in 592 B.C.E., he would have been born in 622 B.C.E. at the outset of Josiah's reforms in the twelfth year of Josiah's reign (see 2 Chr 34:3). The oracle now appears as a projection of Israel's reunification and restoration in the aftermath of the Babylonian exile.

The sixth and concluding oracle of the sequence appears in Ezek 38:1—39:29 in the prophet's portrayal of YHWH's defeat of Gog from Magog. The identity of Gog from Magog is uncertain, although his association with Meshech, Tubal, Gomer, and Togarmah—all nations identified with ancient kingdoms in Asia Minor—suggests that Gog might be identified with the seventh-century monarch, Gyges of Lydia, in Asia Minor. The historical identity of Gog pales in comparison to the significance of his image and function in the book. Gog is the leader of a host of nations that threaten Jerusalem or Zion. Just as earlier nations would be destroyed when they stepped on the land of Israel to threaten it (e.g., Isa 14:24-27), so YHWH would defend the land from attack by Gog's hordes. In addition to the motif of Gog's defeat by YHWH, a key element in the presentation of Ezekiel 38–39 is the role that corpses of Gog's army play in defiling the land of Israel and the need to purify the land from corpse contamination by the bodies of the enemy soldiers. The seven-month process is portrayed as a purging of the land, first by the fires that were lit and fueled by the discarded weapons and equipment of Gog's army, and second by the sacrificial feast in which the birds and beasts from creation will come to devour the corpses. Such a purification is designed to reveal to the house of Israel that YHWH is G-d. Although many interpreters view Ezekiel 38–39 as a proto-apocalyptic text that must be separated from its current context in the book of Ezekiel and read separately, the motif of purification of the land from the corpses of those who threatened it is an essential motif

142 in preparing for the restoration of the Temple at the center of Jerusalem, Israel, and creation, following the purge from iniquity that is portrayed throughout the book. The oracle culminates with YHWH's declarations that YHWH will take back the people in love and that all Israel and the nations will know that YHWH is G-d. Interestingly, Ezek 39:23-24, 29 attempts to explain that YHWH hid the divine face from Israel, resulting in their punishment and exile, as a result of Israel's iniquity. Again, such a contention is an example of theodicy in which YHWH's reputation is protected in the face of evil by asserting instead that the victims were responsible for their own suffering.

Ezekiel's Temple Vision

With the land and people of Israel purged of impurity, Ezekiel 40–48 then proceeds to describe the restoration of the Holy Temple at the center of Jerusalem, a reunited Israel, and a restored creation. The Zadokite priest Ezekiel maintains that the need for the restored and purified Temple and all creation explains YHWH's decision to bring about the destruction of Solomon's Temple and the Babylonian exile.

Rabbinic tradition notes that the book of Ezekiel presents many problems due to its many differences from Mosaic Torah, particularly in relation to its description of the restored Temple. According to Talmudic tradition (b. Shabbat 13b; b. Menahot 45a), R. Hananiah ben Hezekiah burned three hundred barrels of oil working nights to reconcile the differences between Ezekiel and the Torah so that the book of Ezekiel might be accepted as sacred scripture within the Jewish Bible. Unfortunately, the details of R. Hananiah's work have been lost, although the Talmudic discussions preserve a few of the details, for instance, (1) Ezekiel 43:12 designates the entire Temple as "the Holy of Holies," whereas Exod 26:33 identifies only the Devir or the inner chamber of the Temple where the Ark is placed as "the Holy of Holies"; (2) Ezekiel 43:16 states the Temple altar will measure twelve by twelve cubits, whereas Exod 27:1-8 states that it will measure five by five by three cubits; (3) Ezekiel 43:17 includes a ramp or steps for the altar, whereas Exod 20:23 expresses forbids such a feature; (4) Ezekiel 43:22 calls for the use of a goat as a ḥaṭṭa'at or "sin offering," whereas Exod 29:37 and Lev 8:14-15 call for one bull (but cf. Lev 4:22-26; Num 28:11-15, which allow goats under certain conditions); (5) Ezekiel 44:31 states that priests may not eat anything that died (apart from ritual slaughter) or that was torn by beasts, whereas Lev 5:7-10 allows birds killed by twisting the neck to be used for sin and whole burnt offerings; and (6) Ezek 45:20 calls for atonement in the Temple on the seventh day of the first month on behalf of one who sins in error, but no such purging is known in the Torah. On a more general note, Ezekiel 18 calls for a doctrine of individual (or more correctly, the individual generation) punishment, whereas Exod 20:5-6 and 34:7 call for punishment that extends to the third and fourth generations.

Rabbi Hananiah reportedly reconciled the differences so that Ezekiel could be recognized as a halachic innovator like Moses. He apparently also left some issues to be decided in the future by the prophet Elijah, who will return at the time of the messianic age to settle halachic issues in Jewish thought. It is partly on this basis that medieval Jewish Bible commentators, such as Rashi (R. Solomon ben Isaac, 1040–1105 c.e.) and Radaq (R. David Kimḥi, 1160–1235 c.e.) declared that Ezekiel's vision of the restored Temple must be recognized as "the future Temple" or the third Temple," that is, the Temple that would be established in the messianic age according to Jewish tradition.

Ezekiel's vision in Ezekiel 40–48 is dated to the twenty-fifth year of the exile, that is, 572 b.c.e., which would correspond to his fiftieth year when he would have retired from active service as a priest at the Jerusalem Temple.[23] The specification at "the beginning of the year, the tenth day of the month" indicates that the vision is set at the time of Yom Kippur, which occurs on the tenth day of Tishri following Rosh HaShanah on the first day of Tishri. The vision therefore corresponds to the vision of YHWH to be experienced by the high priest upon entering the Holy of Holies of the Jerusalem Temple according to Lev 16:1-5 (cf. Exod 25:22). Ezekiel is brought to the land of Israel and set on a mountain with the city (Jerusalem) set to the south. An angelic guide, described as a man who shone like copper with a linen cord and a measuring rod in his hand, then takes Ezekiel on a tour of the Temple.

The first element of the vision is the Temple structure itself in Ezek 40:5—42:14. Ezekiel begins with the walls, gates, and courtyards of the Temple complex in Ezek 40:5-47. The Temple complex is enclosed by an outer wall with the main entry gate located on the eastern wall and secondary entry gates located on the northern and southern walls. Each gate is built with a threshold, three recesses, and an inner vestibule, much like the Solomonic gates built into ancient Israelite city walls during the tenth to eighth centuries b.c.e. The outer wall encloses the paved outer court with thirty chambers used by the Levites for dwellings, cooking, storage, and so forth (see Jer 35:2-4; Neh 13:4-14). Each

144   gate faces a corresponding gate that provides access into the inner court of the Temple. The inner court of the Temple includes chambers for use by the Zadokite priests, and it encloses an area that includes the Temple itself, the altar, and the areas and tables where the offerings are to be washed and slaughtered prior to sacrifice at the altar. The Temple structure itself appears in Ezek 40:48—41:26. It is built according to the standard three-room pattern of Solomon's Temple and other Israelite, Canaanite, and Syrian examples, including the 'ûlām, "portico," which serves as an entry hall; the hêkāl, "great hall," which includes the table or altar that stands before YHWH; and the qōdeš, "shrine," which is the enclosure that would have once contained the Ark of the Covenant and now symbolizes the holy presence of YHWH in the Temple.[24] The three stories of chambers that enclose the Temple on the north and south sides of the structure appear in Ezek 42:1-14. The Temple complex opens to the east so that the rising sun will progressively illuminate the complex and the interior of the Temple at morning services.

With the vision of the Temple and its courts completed, Ezek 43:1-12 describes the return of the divine throne chariot, representing the Presence of YHWH, to the Temple. YHWH's statements upon entering the Temple emphasize the need for Israel's holiness so as not to defile the holy Name of YHWH. The Temple is to stand at the center of Israel and serve as the source of knowledge concerning YHWH's holiness that the people are to observe to sanctify the divine name and all creation.

Ezekiel 43:13—46:24 then describes the various structures associated with the Temple and the rituals that express the holiness of YHWH's presence. Ezekiel 43:13-27 describes the altar and associated regulations concerning the offerings made to YHWH during Temple worship. The altar is a four-level stepped structure surrounded by a trench, which is placed at "the bosom of the earth" (v. 14; Hebrew, ḥêq hāʾāreṣ, "the trench in the ground") to signify its role as the center of all creation.[25] Ezekiel 44:1—46:24 includes a series of regulations concerning the Temple, including regulations concerning the sanctity of the Zadokite priests, who alone may enter the Temple to serve before YHWH (Ezek 44:1-31); the allotments of living space in the Temple and offerings from the people on the holidays and other holy occasions to support the priests (Ezek 45:1-25); and regulations concerning the role of the prince who governs the people Israel on behalf of YHWH (Ezek 46:1-24).

The concluding segment of Ezekiel's vision in Ezekiel 47—48 emphasizes the role of the Temple at the center of a restored creation and a restored twelve tribes of Israel. Ezekiel 47 relates the gushing of water from underneath the platform of the Temple to the east along the south wall of the Temple so that it will water the region of the Dead Sea and the Arabah and turn these traditionally dry and dead areas into thriving regions filled with water, fish, plants, and trees for food. An expanded land of Israel then will become the home of the restored twelve tribes of Israel, arrayed from north to south, with the Temple at the center and a sacred city inhabited by the priests, Levites, Israel, and the prince. The tribes of Dan, Asher, Naphtali, Manasseh, Ephraim, Reuben, and Judah are arrayed in equal allotments to the north, and the tribes of Benjamin, Simeon, Issachar, Zebulun, and Gad are arrayed to the south. At the end of the book, Ezekiel therefore proclaims that the name of the city is "YHWH is there" to signify the restoration of YHWH's holy presence.

Ezekiel and the Problem of Evil

The book of Ezekiel reflects the prophet's efforts to grapple with the problem of evil in his time, specifically the evil of the destruction of the Temple and the city of Jerusalem as well as the exile of the people of Judah to Babylonia. As a priest, he employs a perspective that emphasizes the holy character of YHWH and the holy character of YHWH's creation. In an effort to defend the sanctity, righteousness, and power of YHWH, Ezekiel therefore contends that the people—and not YHWH—were ultimately responsible for the disaster of destruction and exile. Ezekiel holds that the people of Israel had failed to observe YHWH's requirements for holiness and that they, the Temple, and all creation had become contaminated with the impurity of their actions. Ezekiel contends that YHWH was compelled to purge the Temple, the nations, and creation of its impurity in order to restore the holy character of each. Ezekiel therefore describes a restored Temple and a restored Israel at the center of a restored creation to signify the outcome of YHWH's efforts to purge the world of its impurity or corruption and to reestablish the sanctity of creation.

Ezekiel's portrayal of the purging of the Temple, Israel, and creation clearly employs a teleological model of moral action in which the end result is intended to achieve the ideal good and welfare of all involved. Unlike Abraham, Moses, Jeremiah, and others, Ezekiel never challenges the sanctity, power, or moral character of YHWH, and always attempts to justify YHWH's actions by accusing the people of wrongdoing in order to protect YHWH. Although such a position may have been necessary to ensure continued adherence to YHWH in exile and beyond, modern

146   readers in the aftermath of the Shoah will recognize the inadequacy of such a model, insofar as it argues that those who suffered must have been themselves responsible for their own suffering.

SEVEN

The Twelve Prophets and the Question of Shoah

The Twelve Prophets constitute a somewhat enigmatic example of prophetic literature in the Jewish and Christian Bibles because they form one book of twelve individual prophetic compositions. In Jewish tradition, the Twelve Prophets or the *Tĕrê ʿĀśār* (Aramaic for "the Twelve") are counted as the fourth book of the Latter Prophets (Isaiah, Jeremiah, Ezekiel, Twelve Prophets), although the individual compositions are noted. Thus, the Babylonian Talmud calls for scribes to write manuscripts of the Book of the Twelve Prophets with four blank lines separating it from both the preceding and following books in the canonical order of the *Tanakh* or the Jewish version of the Bible in keeping with standard practice for the presentation of individual biblical books (*b. Baba Batra* 13b). But the Talmud also stipulates that each of the Twelve Prophets be separated by three blank lines within the whole to point to their discrete characters as individual prophetic compositions. In Christian tradition, the Twelve Minor Prophets, so designated because of their relatively small size in comparison to the Major Prophets (Isaiah, Jeremiah, Ezekiel, Daniel), are counted as twelve prophetic books in the Old Testament, although they are typically grouped together and designated as the *Dōdekaprophēton* (Greek for "the Twelve Prophets"). The order of the Twelve Prophets varies in each tradition as well. The standard order of the Twelve Prophets in the *Tanakh* is Hosea, Joel, Amos, Obadiah, Jonah, Micah, Nahum, Habakkuk, Zephaniah, Haggai, Zechariah, and Malachi. The standard order of the Christian *Dōdekaprophēton* was originally based on the Septuagint order, that is, Hosea, Amos, Micah, Joel, Obadiah, Jonah, Nahum, Habakkuk, Zephaniah, Haggai, Zechariah, and Malachi. Other orders are also known at Qumran and in Christian tradition.[1]

Whether conceived as one book or twelve, the Twelve Prophets are an important resource for understanding the Bible's engagement with issues posed by the Shoah. Each of the individual books of the Twelve deals in one way or another with issues posed by the destruction or the threat of destruction and exile against Jerusalem, Judah, or the Northern Kingdom of Israel or by the restoration of any or all of these entities in the aftermath of their respective destructions and exiles. Although at least two orders for the book of the Twelve Prophets appear in Jewish and Christian canonical orders of the Bible, the arrangements of books in each of the two principle orders displays a concerted effort to read the *Tĕrê ʿĀśār* or the *Dōdekaprophēton* in relation to the Shoahs that faced ancient Israel and Judah, namely, the destruction and exile of the Northern Kingdom of Israel in 722/1 B.C.E. and the destruction and exile of Jerusalem and Judah in 587/6 B.C.E., as well as the efforts at restoration in the aftermath of these events.[2] In all cases, ancient Israelites and Judeans faced the same basic issues that modern religious thinkers face in the aftermath of the Shoah, namely, the question of evil, the righteousness and power of G-d, and the role of human beings in engaging these issues.

Interpreters paid very little attention to the order of the books of the Twelve Prophets or to the significance of the Twelve Prophets as a single book until recent years.[3] The reason for such neglect was that scholars throughout the nineteenth and twentieth centuries were especially interested in reconstructing the words and deeds of the prophets in relation to the historical circumstances and concerns in which the respective prophets lived and spoke. The order of the Twelve Prophets was the product of later redactors and arrangers, who had little to do with the original prophets per se other than to arrange the twelve compositions into their current order. For the most part, interpreters presupposed that the order of the Twelve Prophets was based on their chronological order.

Greater attention to the interpretative significance of the redaction of biblical literature and the various versions in which it appears, however, has prompted scholars to reconsider the significance of the order—or more properly, the orders—of the books now found in the Twelve Prophets. As noted above, there are two primary orders of the books of the Twelve represented in the Hebrew Masoretic and the Greek Septuagint forms of the Twelve Prophets that suggest some reflection and hermeneutical intent in the respective arrangements. Furthermore, examination of the individual compositions contained with each order of the Twelve Prophets demonstrates that neither is organized according to a chronological order. Hosea is the first book in both orders, but historical scholarship demonstrates that Amos was the earlier of the two, insofar as Amos's book is set in the mid-eighth century whereas Hosea's book is set in the latter part of the eighth century. Likewise, traditional views of Joel, Obadiah, and Jonah would place each of these prophets in the ninth or early eighth centuries, well before either Amos or Hosea. Thus, Joel 4 refers to King Jehoshaphat's defeat of a coalition of Moabites and Ammonites in 2 Chronicles 20, which would place Joel in the ninth century. Obadiah is identified with the officer of King Ahab who hid the prophets of YHWH and aided Elijah during the ninth century B.C.E. (see 1 Kings 19). Jonah ben Amittai is identified with the prophet who spoke of the restoration of Israel's territories by King Jeroboam ben Joash of Israel in 2 Kgs 14:25, which would place Jonah in the early eighth century. Although historical critical scholarship demonstrates that each of these prophetic books was written at a time long after these purported settings, traditional readings of each would have placed them in the earlier settings. Likewise, Zephaniah appears after Nahum and Habakkuk in both forms of the Twelve Prophets, although Zephaniah is dated to the early reign of Josiah, Nahum is dated to the late reign of Josiah in 612 B.C.E. when Nineveh fell, and Habakkuk is dated to the period following Josiah's death in 609 B.C.E. when the Babylonians took control of Judah. Finally, questions continue to abound about Malachi, whose name means "my messenger," sparking doubts as to whether Malachi can be viewed as a proper name or simply a reference to YHWH's angel or messenger. Traditional readers tend to identify Malachi with YHWH's messenger announced in Exod 22:20, 23 and with the prophet Elijah mentioned in Mal 3:22-24, which would place Malachi in an earlier historical period (b. Megillah 17a; b. Baba Batra 15a; Targum Jonathan to Mal 1:1).

Because a chronological principle fails to explain the order the Twelve Prophets in either the Masoretic or the Septuagint orders of the book, other principles must be considered. It is noteworthy, therefore, that both orders begin with the prophet Hosea, who speaks metaphorically about the potential divorce between Hosea and his wife, Gomer, as a model for breaking the covenant relationship between YHWH and "his" "bride," Israel, and Malachi, who quotes YHWH's statement, "I detest divorce," in Mal 2:16, that metaphorically expresses YHWH's commitment to maintain the relationship with Israel in the larger context of the book.[4] The differences in order within the MT and LXX versions of the book are also noteworthy. The LXX order of the Twelve Prophets begins with Hosea, Amos, and Micah, the three prophets who are placed in the mid- to latter eighth century B.C.E. at the time that the Assyrian Empire destroyed the northern kingdom of Israel and subjugated Jerusalem and the Southern Kingdom of Judah. Concern with the demise of the northern kingdom—and its implications for understanding the potential fate of Jerusalem and Judah as well—appears in all three of these books. It is striking, therefore, that these books are followed by Joel, which is concerned with the threat posed to Jerusalem by the nations; Obadiah, Jonah, and Nahum, which are each concerned with nations, such as Edom and Assyria; and Habakkuk, Zephaniah, Haggai, Zechariah, and Malachi, which return to concern with Jerusalem's judgment and restoration to conclude the book. Such an arrangement suggests that the compilers or composers of the Book of the Twelve arranged the individual prophets in an order that would facilitate reflection on the fate of northern Israel as an example or paradigm for Jerusalem and southern Judah.

The MT order of the Twelve Prophets places Joel, with its concerns for YHWH's defense of Jerusalem against foreign invaders, immediately after Hosea, which takes up the question of northern Israel's potential judgment, but envisions Israel and Judah reunited under a Davidic king in Hosea 3. Although Amos is also largely concerned with judgment against northern Israel, it concludes by envisioning the restoration of "the fallen booth of David" to reunite and rule Israel in Amos 9:11-15. Obadiah, with its concern for Edom's threat to Jerusalem, and Jonah, with its concern for YHWH's mercy to the Ninevites, then precedes Micah, which once again takes up concerns with northern Israel but combines them with Jerusalem and Judah and lays out a scenario in which a new Davidic monarch will defeat the nations that threaten Zion. Nahum celebrates the downfall of Nineveh, which destroyed northern Israel and threatened Jerusalem; Habakkuk anticipates the defeat of the Babylonians that threaten Jerusalem; and Zephaniah calls for the repentance of the people of Jerusalem and Judah before calamity strikes and envisions the restoration of Bat Zion, that is, the daughter of Zion who metaphorically personifies Jerusalem. Haggai, Zechariah, and Malachi all deal with issues pertaining to the restoration of Jerusalem and the Temple. The order of books in the MT version of the Twelve Prophets indicates a concern with reflection on the city of Jerusalem throughout, including both the threat of judgment and the restoration of the city and Temple in the aftermath of that judgment.

Both versions of the Twelve Prophets demonstrate a concern with reflection on the problem of evil, here expressed as judgment against northern Israel and Jerusalem and Judah. Although each version varies in its concerns, either northern Israel as an example for Jerusalem and Judah or Jerusalem as the focus throughout, both employ a judgmental and teleological perspective in portraying their respective concerns. Both constitute a form of theodicy insofar as they respectively contend that the people are responsible for their own judgment or victimization, and both employ a teleological perspective that envisions YHWH's acts of restoration as a means to resolve the judgment portrayed throughout the book.

Each of the Twelve Prophets also engages the problem of Shoah in ancient Israel and Jerusalem/Judah from its own unique perspective. As a means to illustrate individual perspectives, examples from Hosea, Jonah, Nahum, Habakkuk, and Malachi follow.

Hosea

The book of Hosea is frequently read as an example of the prophet's righteous condemnation of a sinful Israel and YHWH's gracious willingness to take the people of Israel back in love just as Hosea ultimately accepts his unfaithful wife, Gomer.[5] And yet a reading of the book raises disturbing questions about the book's characterization of Gomer and Israel as sinful, when neither has the opportunity to speak on her/their own behalf when their husbands Hosea and YHWH charge them with infidelity.

The superscription in Hos 1:1 places the prophet Hosea ben Beeri in the reigns of the eighth-century monarchs, Uzziah (783–742 B.C.E.), Jotham (742–735 B.C.E.), Ahaz (735–715 B.C.E.), and Hezekiah (715–687/6 B.C.E.) of Judah and Jeroboam ben Joash (786–746 B.C.E.) of Israel. Israelite kings following Jeroboam ben Joash are not listed. Jeroboam's son, Zechariah, who ruled only for six months in 746 B.C.E., was assassinated in a coup against the ruling house of Jehu, which was allied with Assyria since the days of the dynasty's founder, Jehu (842–815 B.C.E.). Following Zechariah's assassination, the Israelite throne changed hands repeatedly as competing factions calling for alliance with Assyria or Aram competed with each other for control of the throne by assassinating the current incumbent and seizing power. Of the six Israelite monarchs during this period, four were assassinated, namely, Zechariah (746 B.C.E., pro-Assyrian), Shallum (745 B.C.E., pro-Aramean), Pekahiah ben Menahem (738–737 B.C.E., pro-Assyrian), and Pekah (737–732 B.C.E., pro-Aramean), one died of natural causes (Menahem, 745–738 B.C.E., pro-Assyrian), and another, Hoshea (732–724 B.C.E.), was removed from power by Assyria at the time of Israel's revolt. As a result of the instability of the Israelite throne and its own interests in expansion, the Assyrian Empire began to pressure Aram and Israel beginning in 745 B.C.E. during the reign of Tiglath-pileser III. By 724 B.C.E., Israel revolted against Assyria, and it was destroyed in 722/1 B.C.E. by Kings Shalmaneser V and Sargon II.

Hosea must be read against this historical background. Following the superscription, the book begins in Hos 1:2—2:2 with a third-person narrative concerning YHWH's commands to Hosea to marry "a wife of whoredom" and to beget "children of whoredom" with her in a symbolic action that will symbolize Israel's straying from following YHWH. The narrative proceeds by portraying the births of three children who are symbolically named to illustrate this message. The first child, a boy, is named Jezreel to symbolize YHWH's punishment of the House of Jehu, which came to power in a coup against the ruling house of Omri that took place at the city of Jezreel (see 2 Kings 9–10). The second child, a daughter, is named Lo-Ruhamah, a term that means "no mercy," to symbolize YHWH's refusal to show Israel mercy for its purported sins. The third child, another son, is named Lo-Ammi, a term that means "not my people," to symbolize YHWH's dissolution of the relationship with Israel. The following core of the book in Hosea 2:3—14:9 presents a series of the prophet's speeches to Israel in which he appeals to his children for their mother's return to him (Hos 2:3—3:5); presents YHWH's basic charge that Israel has abandoned YHWH (Hos 4:1-19); specifies YHWH's charges against Israel (Hos 5:1—14:1); and appeals for Israel's return to YHWH (Hos 14:2-9). An exhortation concerning YHWH's righteousness concludes the book in Hos 14:10.

Interpreters by and large accept the claims of the book that Israel has abandoned YHWH and that such abandonment must be considered as a form of idolatry, since Israel, like Gomer, pursues other lovers in place of her G-d or husband, YHWH or Hosea, in keeping with the common Israelite tradition that portrays YHWH's relationship with Israel as a marriage relationship between husband and wife.[6] The charges of idolatry are especially reinforced in Hos 4:1-19 by charges that Israel's leaders, that is, the priests and the prophets, have failed to teach Israel true knowledge of YHWH. They are further reinforced by charges that the kings of Israel have led the people astray (e.g., Hos 13:9-11). Many interpreters gush over YHWH's graciousness and love for Israel in standing ready to accept Israel's return, just as Hosea stands ready to remarry his wayward bride in Hos 3:1-5.[7]

But several dimensions of the book of Hosea demand critical reflection. First is the charge of idolatry. The issue of idolatry and Israel's pursuit of other gods certainly looms large throughout the book of Hosea, but closer examination reveals that the charges of idolatry are bound up with Israel's relationship with Assyria and Egypt. Hosea 12:2, for example, highlights Israel's relationship with the Assyrian Empire by stating that "now they (Israel) make a covenant with Assyria, how oil is carried to Egypt," which refers to a treaty between Assyria and Israel that would allow trade in (olive) oil to be conducted with Egypt. Such a reference presupposes Israel's strategic location on the trade routes through the Jezreel Valley and the Mediterranean coastal plain that make trade possible between Egypt and Africa on the one hand and Assyria and Mesopotamia on the other hand.[8] Hosea elliptically alludes to Israel's subjugation to Assyria in such a relationship in Hos 11:5, "They return to the land of Egypt, and Assyria is their king," which also highlights a reversal of the exodus tradition that stands at the foundation of Israel's identity as a nation. Indeed, historical records confirm that the great peace enjoyed during the reign of Jeroboam ben Joash, who presided over a kingdom like that of Solomon extending from Lebo-Hamath in northern Aram to the Sea of the Arabah or the Red Sea south of Judah (see 2 Kgs 14:23), as a result of a suzerain-vassal treaty relationship between the suzerain Assyria and the vassal Israel from the early days of the house of Jehu. King Jehu himself, the founder of the dynasty, is pictured kneeling in submission at the feet of the Assyrian king Shalmaneser III on the so-called "Black Obelisk," which proclaims Shalmaneser's triumphs in western Asia.[9] Likewise, Jehu's grandson and Jeroboam's father, Joash ben Jehoahaz, is listed among the tributaries of the Assyrian king Adad Nirari III.[10] The house of Jehu secured Israel from the attacks by the Arameans that plagued Israel throughout the reign of the Omride dynasty by submitting to Assyrian protection, thereby threatening Aram with invasion by Assyria along the Assyrian/Aramean border should Aram ever threaten Assyria's client, Israel. For his part, Hosea opposes this relationship as a betrayal of YHWH.

The second issue pertains to the reasons for Hosea's opposition to Israel's relationship with Assyria. Hosea is hardly an isolationist who decries treaties between Israel and foreign nations in principle. There are reasons underlying his opposition to the treaty with Assyria in particular. For one, the treaty with Assyria puts Israel in a position to facilitate trade with Egypt, Israel's oppressor in the exodus tradition. Such a relationship thereby betrays Israel's fundamental identity as a nation that was freed from Egyptian bondage by YHWH. Hosea recalls this

154 event in Hos 12:10, 14 when he refers to YHWH's leading Israel from Egypt to the land of Israel by means of a prophet. Although the prophet remains unnamed, the reference obviously refers to Moses. But Hosea 12 also refers to other elements of Israel's national identity and story,[11] particularly to Jacob, the eponymous ancestor of Israel (see Genesis 25–35). Hosea portrays several key events in Jacob's life, namely, Jacob's struggle with his brother (Esau) in the womb (v. 4; cf. Gen 25:19-26); Jacob's struggle with the angel (v. 5; cf. Gen 32:23-33); Jacob's encounter with YHWH at Beth El (v. 5; cf. Gen 28:10-23); Jacob's treaty with Laban, his father-in-law and the eponymous ancestor of Aram, at Gilead/Gilgal in which the two men settled their differences and their boundaries so that they might live in peace (v. 12; cf. Genesis 31); and Jacob's sojourn in Aram so that he might marry his beloved Rachel (and Leah as well; v. 13; cf. Genesis 29–31). By rehearsing Jacob's—and therefore Israel's—history, Hosea reminds his audience of Israel's close relationship with Aram, from where Israel's ancestors had come, and thereby calls upon Israel to break its relationship with Assyria so that it might resume a relationship with Aram. This was precisely the issue that divided Israel and prompted the assassinations and struggles for control of the throne during the years 746–724 B.C.E. Although Hosea does not call explicitly for the assassination of Jehu or pro-Assyrian monarchs, he is aligned with those who do.

The third issue is a hermeneutical stance that emerges from the above-noted historical background, namely, neither Gomer nor Israel ever speak in the book of Hosea. Francis Landy, in his innovative commentary on Hosea, notes this very pointedly when he observes how difficult Gomer's marriage to Hosea must have been, particularly when he sits, brooding and writing, while he excoriates her as an example of Israel's infidelity.[12] Gomer never speaks, and never has the opportunity to present her view of the relationship in which she might defend herself or challenge her husband's portrayal of her as a harlot. Readers do not know if Hosea's charges are true, or if he has somehow maligned his wife and children. Readers must bear in mind that it is not unusual for a philandering husband to accuse his wife of adultery to cover his own infidelity or neglect. Indeed, this issue is pertinent for considering YHWH's relationship with Israel, particularly since YHWH, as the G-d of the nation Israel, was responsible for ensuring Israel's security. In the face of overwhelming Assyrian power, however, YHWH's failure to protect Israel produces a charge of Israel's infidelity to YHWH. Such a charge protects YHWH's reputation, power, and righteousness in the face of charges that YHWH was unwilling, unable, or negligent in seeing to the protection of the nation. Of course, we will never know if Gomer was a harlot or not, but the uncritical acceptance of this charge on the part of interpreters has resulted in interpretation of the book that accepts Hosea's portrayal of her infidelity and thereby charges that the victims of evil, whether Gomer or Israel, are responsible for their own suffering.[13] In the aftermath of the Shoah, the uncritical acceptance of such a charge is unconscionable.

Jonah

The book of Jonah, concerning the prophet who was swallowed by a great fish, presents one of the best-known narratives in both Jewish and Christian biblical tradition. Jonah functions as the *haftarah* or prophetic reading for Yom Kippur afternoon in Jewish tradition, where it serves as a basis for reflection on divine mercy and justice as "the day of atonement" moves toward its close. The so-called sign of Jonah in Matt 12:38-42 and Luke 11:30-32 presupposes that Jonah's three days and nights in the belly of the fish presages the three days that Jesus is in the earth between crucifixion and resurrection.

Modern scholarship emphasizes the literary character of the work and its late compositional setting in the exilic or postexilic periods.[14] Although Jonah ben Amittai is mentioned in 2 Kgs 14:25 as a prophet who announced the reign of King Jeroboam ben Joash of Israel over a kingdom, much like that of Solomon, that extended from Lebo Hamath to the Sea of the Arabah, the motif of the great fish that swallows Jonah for three days marks the book as a work of fiction designed to reflect upon Jonah's experience. Interpreters note the literary artistry of the book, particularly its two-part structure in which Jonah is commissioned by YHWH to speak a message of divine judgment to the Ninevites, first in Jon 1:1-2 and again in Jon 3:1-2.

The first part of the narrative in Jonah 1–2 then relates Jonah's attempt to escape his divine commission by booking passage on a ship of Tarshish. When the ship is threatened by a storm, the pagan passengers worship YHWH in an attempt to save themselves. When the sleeping Jonah is awakened and discerns that he is the cause of the threat to the ship, the sailors initially refuse his request to throw him into the ocean, but relent and throw him overboard when they find that he could not escape. Once in the sea, Jonah is swallowed by a great fish for three days where he prays to YHWH and ultimately accedes to YHWH's will. Although modern interpreters debate whether or not the psalm of Jonah is original to the narrative, it plays a key role in the development of the plot insofar as it demonstrates YHWH's power, Jonah's own repentance, and YHWH's mercy on Jonah.[15]

The second part of the narrative in Jonah 3–4 relates YHWH's repeated command to Jonah to prophesy judgment against Nineveh. Jonah obeys YHWH's command, enters the great city, and speaks his message of judgment. Rather than seeing the judgment realized, Jonah sees the people of Nineveh, from the king on down to even the animals of the city, repent upon hearing the prophetic word. When YHWH renounces the punishment of Nineveh, Jonah becomes angered, charging that YHWH had reversed the divine decree and stating his preference for death rather than life as a result. After YHWH provides Jonah with a ricinus plant for shade from the blazing sun and then sends a worm to kill it, Jonah declares once again his preference for death. This provides the opportunity for YHWH to observe that Jonah cares so much for a plant that he did not grow and that YHWH should therefore care for an entire city of 120,000 and their animals.

Many interpreters view Jonah's initial attempt to escape from his divine commission to prophesy to Nineveh and his later anger at YHWH for forgiving the Ninevites after he had proclaimed judgment against them as signs of his petulance and refusal to accept that YHWH should show mercy to Gentiles.[16] Such an interpretation draws upon and indeed advances anti-semitic stereotypes from throughout classical and Christian history of Jews as misanthropes who hate their Gentile counterparts and seek their destruction. Furthermore, it overlooks a number of key elements of this narrative that point to a very different underlying interest in the question of theodicy together with that of YHWH's justice and mercy.

The first issue is Jonah's historical identity as an early eighth-century prophet who foresaw the reign of Jeroboam ben Joash over a reunited and secure kingdom of Israel. Interpreters are correct to reject the historical character of this narrative, but the use of the figure of Jonah ben Amittai from 2 Kgs 14:25 points to a concern with the issue of true and false prophecy and with the purpose of prophetic announcements of judgment per se. Jeroboam foresees Jeroboam's kingdom in 2 Kgs 14:25 and therefore may be considered as a true prophet in Deuteronomic theology insofar as Deut 18:15-22 defines a true prophet as one whose prophetic announcements come true. Many interpreters charge that Jonah's anger against YHWH stems from YHWH's reversal of judgment against Nineveh, which turns Jonah into a false prophet, but such a charge overlooks the significance of

Nineveh in Israel's history and Jonah's presumed knowledge of that role as a true prophet of YHWH. Nineveh is the capital of the Assyrian Empire, which will ultimately destroy the kingdom of Israel by the latter part of the eighth century B.C.E. Although Jonah's anger in the narrative stems from YHWH's reversal of judgment, both the fictive Jonah and the Judean reading audience will know of Nineveh's role in Israel's destruction. By saving the Ninevites in Jonah's time, YHWH saves the very city that will be responsible for Israel's destruction some twenty-four years after the death of Jeroboam ben Joash. At this point, a question of theodicy looms, namely, Why does YHWH save the Ninevites when they will become the agents of Israel's destruction?

The question of theodicy and YHWH's role in ensuring the destruction of northern Israel by saving Nineveh then informs the second major issue, YHWH's justice and mercy. The question is not one of YHWH's mercy to the Gentiles as some maintain; rather, it is the ontological interplay between YHWH's justice and mercy. Although many would maintain that YHWH's ultimate or teleological intent to restore both Israel and Judah in biblical prophecy points to YHWH's mercy (see, e.g., Isaiah 11; Jeremiah 30–31; Ezekiel 37; 47–48; Hosea 3; Amos 9; Micah 4–5; Zechariah 14), such a view does not justify the suffering of the generation that experiences the Assyrian invasion or those that remain in exile or under foreign rule until the restoration takes place. Israelites in the future will suffer as a result of YHWH's decision. In this respect, YHWH's decision to forgive the Ninevites following their repentance then comes into focus, that is, because they repent, YHWH shows them mercy after having threatened them with punishment. Such a view presupposes that the prophetic proclamation of judgment is not a final proclamation; rather, it is designed to have an impact on its audience, to prompt that audience to reconsider its actions, repent, and adopt the course of action asked of it by YHWH and the prophet who represents YHWH.

The rhetorical function of prophecy then points to the third issue, namely, What impact is the book of Jonah designed to have on its own audience of exilic or postexilic Jewish readers following the experience of exile?[17] Indeed, Jonah then emerges as an exhortation to its audience to repent and return to YHWH when the threat of judgment looms. This perspective applies as well to later Christian readers of the book. Jonah is not intended to condemn Jonah or Jews for failing to accept divine mercy toward Nineveh or Gentiles in general; it is intended to exhort its readers to see themselves in the position of the Ninevites as portrayed in the book and to adopt their course of action by turning to YHWH in times

158   of crisis in the hope of receiving divine mercy. Although such a position raises once again the question of victims who are blamed for their own victimization, it emphasizes that the book of Jonah is not to be read as a condemnation of Jonah but as an exhortation to him as well as to the Ninevites. Indeed, the final question of the book spoken to Jonah by YHWH, "And should I not care about Nineveh?" applies to Jonah and the readers of the book just as much as it applies to the fictive Ninevites portrayed therein. YHWH is hardly off the hook for the ultimate destruction of northern Israel, but Jonah does emphasize the role of human responsibility in defining a relationship with YHWH.

Nahum

The book of Nahum is one of the most maligned books in all of the prophetic literature. Because Nahum celebrates the destruction of the city of Nineveh by a combined force of Babylonians and Medes in 612 B.C.E., many interpreters decry Nahum as an inherently violent book that demonstrates Judean hostility to foreign nations.[18] But such a view of Nahum misses a fundamental point: Nineveh was the capital city of the Assyrian Empire, which had destroyed the Northern Kingdom of Israel in 722/1 B.C.E. and subjugated the Southern Kingdom of Judah from the late eighth century B.C.E. through the mid-seventh century B.C.E. when declining Assyrian power forced the empire to loosen its grip on the small states of western Asia. Assyria had imposed its will on Judah through the use of military force to suppress Judean independence, particularly during Sennacherib's invasion of Judah and siege of Jerusalem in 701 B.C.E. and through the imposition of heavy tribute and demands for service to the Assyrian state. The account of the reign of King Manasseh ben Hezekiah of Judah in 2 Kgs 21:1-18, who is charged with shedding so much innocent blood in Jerusalem, illustrates the heavy price paid by a monarch who himself suppresses dissent against the Assyrians to ensure that his country will not be invaded once again. When Nineveh fell in 612 B.C.E., it constituted the fall of Judah's oppressor and marked the point near the end of the reign of King Josiah of Judah (640–609 B.C.E.) when full liberation of Judah could be fully realized. Such an event would be akin to the downfall of Nazi Germany at the end of World War II. Nahum is hardly a book about vengeance as many contend; it is a book about liberation from oppression.

    The book of Nahum is concerned with much more than the simple downfall of the oppressor. Because of Judah's suffering under Assyrian rule for over a century, many in Judah would contend that YHWH had somehow failed in the fundamental divine task of defending the nation from foreign assault (see 2 Samuel 7; Isaiah 36–37; Psalms 2; 46; 47; 48). Close study of the literary structure, language, and ideas expressed in the book of Nahum demonstrates that it is organized to present a defense of YHWH's power, willingness to act, and righteousness in the face of a century of Judean suffering under Assyrian rule.[19] Overall, the book of Nahum contends that the downfall of Nineveh signals YHWH's power, righteousness, and commitment to the welfare, independence, and security of Jerusalem and Judah.

The superscription of the book in Nah 1:1 defines it simply as "a pronouncement [*maśśā'*] on Nineveh: the book of the vision of Nahum the Elqoshite." Although the superscription provides no hard historical information, the concern with the downfall of Nineveh places the book in relation to the year of Nineveh's destruction in 612 B.C.E.

The body of the book in Nah 1:2—3:19 appears as the *maśśā'* or "(prophetic) pronouncement" proper, which presents a refutation of the popular contention that the long period of Assyrian oppression had demonstrated YHWH's impotence in the face of Assyrian power. The *maśśā'* contends instead that YHWH was responsible for bringing down the Assyrian oppressor. The argument proceeds in the three major subunits of the *maśśā'*.

The first subunit is Nah 1:2-10, which is formulated as an address to Judah chastising the nation for its low estimate of YHWH's powers and intentions. The subunit begins in vv. 2-8 with a partial acrostic hymn that celebrates and asserts YHWH's power to defend those who hope in YHWH against enemies who would threaten and destroy them. The following v. 9 is frequently mistranslated as a rhetorical question that indicts those who plot against YHWH, namely, "Why do you plot against YHWH" (NRSV). Such a translation misconstrues the Hebrew *'el*, "unto," as Hebrew *'al*, "upon, against," based on the assumption that YHWH's question is directed to Judah's enemies.[20] Taking the Hebrew, *'el*, into consideration, however, the question should read, "What do you reckon unto YHWH?" or more idiomatically, "What do you think about YHWH?" It is directed not to Judah's enemies, but to Judeans themselves, and begins the challenge of the popular belief that YHWH had failed to protect the people.

The second subunit is Nah 1:11—2:1, which is formulated as an address to Judah asserting that the downfall of Nineveh is an act of YHWH, which in turn supports the contentions that YHWH is powerful and that YHWH acts on behalf of the nation. Again, problems in translating a key verse have prompted confusion and misunderstanding concerning the interpretation of this passage. Verse 11 is frequently taken as an accusation leveled against the wicked in Judah who are identified with the demon figure Belial, specifically, "From you one has gone out who plots evil against YHWH, who counsels wickedness." But such an interpretation is based on a failure to observe the significance of the second person singular address forms in the verse and a failure to recognize that the personification of the Belial figure as a demon akin to Satan is a later development of the Greco-Roman period.[21] In the late monarchic period, Belial (Heb.: *běliyâ'al*) is simply a term that conveys "worthlessness, uselessness, foolishness," based on the combination of the Hebrew terms, *běli*, "without," and, *yâ'al*, "profit." The second-person feminine singular address forms match with those employed for Judah in Nah 2:1 and presupposes the common personification of cities and nations as women. The question then conveys Nahum's challenge to his Judean audience once again, "From you has come forth evil/wrong thinking about YHWH, worthless counsel," that is, which function as the charge, "You have been wrong about YHWH." The prophet's presentation of YHWH's promises to defend Jerusalem/Judah and to bring down the Assyrian oppressor then round out the subunit.

The final subunit in Nah 2:2—3:19 then constitutes a lengthy address to Nineveh and to the Assyrian king asserting that the downfall of Nineveh is an act of YHWH.

Altogether, the book of Nahum is formulated to celebrate the downfall of an oppressor comparable to the downfall of Nazi Germany or Imperial Japan in World War II; it is not an expression of Judean hatred against Gentiles or a glorification of violence.

Habakkuk

The book of Habakkuk is especially well known for its expressions of fundamental principles of halachic observance in Jewish tradition and of faith in Christian tradition. Habakkuk 2:4 is a particularly important text in this regard. Rabbi Simlai declares that it is a summation of the 613 *halakhot* or rabbinic laws in *b. Makkot* 23b–24a, and Paul cites Hab 2:4 as an example of his doctrine of justification by faith in Rom 1:17 and Gal 3:11.

But Habakkuk also raises key questions concerning divine justice and the capacity and will of YHWH to protect Judah from foreign invasion. The so-called dialogue between Habakkuk and YHWH in Habakkuk 1–2 presents the prophet's questions to YHWH concerning the subjugation of Judah by the Neo-Babylonian Empire in the early seventh century B.C.E. When Habakkuk pleads that YHWH must stop the Babylonians from threatening the nation, YHWH responds claiming to be the party responsible for bringing the Babylonians in the first place. In answer to Habakkuk's continued questions concerning such an act, YHWH employs a teleological argument to respond that ultimately the oppressor will fall. The psalm of Habakkuk in Habakkuk 3 then portrays YHWH's defeat of enemies that threaten the nation.

Modern critical scholarship focuses on the historical background of the book of Habakkuk, and correctly identifies the Babylonian defeat of Egypt at Carchemesh in 605 B.C.E. and its subsequent subjugation of Judah as the historical setting of the book.[22] But modern critical interpretation of Habakkuk misses crucial aspects of the prophet's perspective by attempting to read the book of Habakkuk as an indictment of Judah by YHWH for its sins. The issue centers on the identification of the "wicked" in the book of Habakkuk. Interpreters demonstrate a great deal of confusion on this issue by identifying the wicked first with Judeans who reject YHWH's justice or Torah in Hab 1:2-4 and then with the Babylonians who swallow the righteous in Hab 1:12-17. Such a reading is inconsistent, particularly since the text offers no clear signal that the referents of the term *rāšā'*, "wicked," have shifted within the book. Identification of the wicked with the Babylonians throughout the book provides a consistent reading that points to the prophet's concern with the question of theodicy in the wake of the Babylonian subjugation of Judah in 605 B.C.E. The issue is especially important because Judah had been an ally of the Babylonians since the reign of Hezekiah in the late eighth century B.C.E. Indeed, Hezekiah's great-grandson, Josiah, died acting on behalf of his Babylonian allies in an attempt to block the Egyptians from assisting Babylon's Assyrian enemies in 609 B.C.E. But when the Babylonians took control of Judah in 605 B.C.E., they found Jehoiakim, a pro-Egyptian son of Josiah on the throne, and treated Judah as a potentially hostile vassal rather than as a valued ally that had assisted them during their rise to power.

The formal structure of Habakkuk provides a basis for understanding its concerns with the question of theodicy in relation to Babylonia's subjugation of Judah.[23] The superscriptions of the book in Hab 1:1 and 3:1 point to a basic two-part structure in which "the *maśśā'* or (prophetic) pronouncement which Habakkuk the prophet saw" appears in Habakkuk 1–2 and "the *tĕpillâ* or prayer of Habakkuk the prophet concerning *šigyōnôt* or supplications/lamentations" appears in Habakkuk 3.

Following the superscription in Hab 1:1, the *maśśā'* or (prophetic) pronouncement proper in Hab 1:2—2:20 presents a dialogue between Habakkuk and YHWH concerning the rising threat of the Babylonians against Judah. Habakkuk's initial complaint to YHWH in Hab 1:2-4 calls upon YHWH to act against the wicked who surround the righteous so that justice or order in the world is perverted. YHWH's response to Habakkuk in Hab 1:5-11 includes the surprising disclosure that YHWH is the party responsible for bringing the *kaśdîm*, "Chaldeans," a term employed for the Neo-Babylonian Empire founded by Nebopolassar in 627 B.C.E. and later ruled by his son Nebuchadnezzar beginning in 605 B.C.E. YHWH never defines the reason for bringing the Babylonians, but simply describes their appearance as evidence of a great work that is being done among the nations and refers to their fearsome and impious character. Habakkuk's rejoinder to YHWH in Hab 1:12-17 expresses the prophet's astonishment that YHWH would be responsible for such a travesty in the world and would stand by idly while the wicked devour the righteous. Habakkuk stands watch to wait for YHWH's answer in Hab 2:1-19. YHWH's answer emphasizes that the arrogant oppressors will ultimately fall as a result of his greed and gluttony in swallowing up that which does not belong to him. A series of woe oracles in vv. 6b-20 then illustrates the coming downfall of the wicked oppressor. Again, no reason for the appearance of the oppressor emerges other than YHWH's great deeds.

The prayer of Habakkuk in Habakkuk 3 constitutes Habakkuk's petition that YHWH act against the oppressor together with a portrayal of YHWH's anticipated action against the enemy. Following the superscription in Hab 3:1, the prayer proper appears in Hab 3:2-19a. The prophet's petition that YHWH make known YHWH's legendary power to act appears in v. 2. A theophanic portrayal of YHWH's action, including a report of YHWH's approach in vv. 3-7 and an address to YHWH in vv. 8-15 relates YHWH's projected defeat of the enemy. An expression of the prophet's confidence in YHWH appears in vv. 16-19a. Finally, instructions to the choirmaster in v. 19b close out the psalm with an indication that it was to be performed as part of a liturgical ritual.

Such a portrayal hardly expresses the prophet's condemnation of Judah for sins against YHWH. Indeed, YHWH emerges in the book of Habakkuk as a potentially culpable figure, who brings a threat against Judah without any explanation other than an interest in pointing to great deeds among the nations. In the end, the book of Habakkuk emerges as the prophet's plea to YHWH to end the threat leveled against Judah by the Babylonians, who would ultimately destroy Jerusalem and Judah in the early sixth century B.C.E. Just as early warnings concerning Hitler's aims at world domination and the extermination of Jews, Gypsies, homosexuals, and Slavs produced no substantive action on the part of the Roosevelt administration and other allied governments during World War II, so Habakkuk's pleas to remove the Babylonian threat, although heard by YHWH, likewise resulted in no substantive action on YHWH's part.

Malachi

The book of Malachi is a very enigmatic composition that has provoked tremendous difficulties among interpreters both ancient and modern.[24] One of the most enduring problems of the book is the question as to whether Malachi is indeed the name of a prophet whose work appears in the book or a simple designation of YHWH's angel or messenger as "my messenger." Indeed, this question is raised already in the Babylonian Talmud (see *b. Megillah* 17a; *b. Baba Batra* 15a; *Targum Jonathan* to Mal 1:1), although the question is left unresolved. Because of uncertainty over this question and because the superscription of the book in Mal 1:1 labels it as "a *maśśā'* or (prophetic) pronouncement of the word of YHWH to Israel by the hand of Malachi/my messenger," interpreters have speculated that the book may constitute a segment of Zechariah, insofar as both Zechariah 9–11 and 12–14 are labeled respectively as "*maśśā'*, (prophetic) pronouncement" like Malachi. The book is best known for its opposition to divorce, based on YHWH's statement, "I hate divorce," in Mal 2:16 and for its concluding anticipation of the return of the prophet Elijah in Mal 3:22-24.

Critical scholarship has focused especially on defining the literary form of the book and its historical setting and perspective. Interpreters correctly identify the five disputation speeches that provide the basis for the formal structure of the book.[25] A disputation speech is designed to refute a prevailing belief held by the audience to which the speech is directed and to argue on behalf of another perspective conveyed within the speech.[26] Because the disputations point to a situation in which the Temple has been rebuilt but the people are not providing adequate support, interpreters correctly identify the period following the reconstruction of the Temple during the years 520–515 B.C.E. and prior to the respective careers of Nehemiah, beginning in 445 B.C.E., and of Ezra, beginning in

397 B.C.E., who initiated a series of reforms that reorganized the Jerusalem-based Jewish community around the Temple and ensured its support in the early Persian period. The disputation speeches of Malachi point to many of the problems that the reforms of Nehemiah and Ezra addressed.

Modern interpreters tend to emphasize the sinfulness of the postexilic Jewish community in failing to support the Temple,[27] but such an emphasis overlooks the substantive questions raised in the early-Persian-period Jewish community of Jerusalem. The building of the Temple was supposed to signal a time of renewal in Judah, including the restoration of Zerubbabel as the new Davidic king, as well as recognition of YHWH among all the nations of the world according to the books of Haggai and Zechariah. But such restoration, recognition, and well-being were not forthcoming in the aftermath of the building of the Temple. Zerubbabel, the grandson of King Jehoiachin ben Jehoiakim of Judah and therefore a member of the royal Davidic line, disappears from history with no apparent explanation. Judah continued to be a backwater—indeed, the city of Jerusalem remained unprotected until Nehemiah rebuilt the walls of the city in his first official acts as the newly appointed governor of the Persian province or satrap of Yehud—and the Temple did not fulfill its role in signaling YHWH's worldwide sovereignty.

The questions posed by the Jewish community that Malachi is designed to answer hardly constitute examples of sinfulness. They are legitimate questions that arise in the aftermath of exile, Temple building, and unrealized expectations articulated by earlier prophets. Following the superscription for the book in Mal 1:1, the first disputation speech in Mal 1:2-5 attempts to refute the charge that YHWH no longer loves the people of Judah by pointing to the example of Edom, which was slowly being swallowed up by incursions of Arab tribal groups, such as the Qedarites and Nabateans, in the sixth to third centuries B.C.E. Because Judah was not suffering destruction like the Edomites, YHWH must still love Judah. The second disputation in Mal 1:6—2:16 is designed to counter the assertion that the priests and people have properly sanctified YHWH's holy name by charging that neglect of Temple ritual and support and the prevalence of intermarriage between Jewish men and Gentile/pagan women has eroded the holy character of the community. The third disputation in Mal 2:17—3:5 employs a teleological perspective by asserting that divine justice will be done on the coming Day of YHWH when YHWH's messenger comes to inaugurate divine action. The image of YHWH's messenger draws upon Exod 23:20, 23, which portray the role of YHWH's messenger or angel in leading the people into the promised land. The perspective of the people is particularly important here because of their charge, "All who do evil are good in the sight of YHWH," and their question, "Where is the G-d of justice?" expressed in Mal 2:14-16. Such a perspective points to the sense of failed expectations on the part of the population. The fourth disputation in Mal 3:6-12 counters the people's assertions that they are offering sufficient support for the Temple by charging instead that they are defrauding the Temple by offering inadequate tithes of their income in harvest and flock due to support the Temple and its priesthood. The fifth disputation in Mal 3:13-21 again employs a teleological perspective to assert that YHWH's justice will be realized on the Day of YHWH when the wicked will be judged. Again, the perspectives of the people are expressed in their own assertions and questions that "It is useless to serve G-d. What has been gained by keeping His charge and walking in abject awe of YHWH of Hosts?" Rather than expressing sinfulness on the part of the people, their statements express frustration at YHWH's failure to act as promised in Haggai and Malachi. The book then closes in Mal 3:22-24 with YHWH's charge to be mindful of Mosaic Torah and promise to send the prophet Elijah on the Day of YHWH to reconcile differences in the community and to save it from judgment.

When viewed from the standpoint of the people's own perspective, the book of Malachi must be judged not as an indictment of Judah for its sins, but as part of a dialogue that was taking place in the early-Persian-period Jewish community of Jerusalem and Judah. YHWH had promised to act on behalf of the people in the books of Haggai and Malachi (and indeed, Habakkuk as well), but such action had not yet been realized. Malachi attempts to provide answers to those questions in a time of crisis. Ironically, those answers ultimately do come in the form of Nehemiah and Ezra. As officials appointed by the Persian government, Nehemiah and Ezra reorganize the Persian-period Judean community as a holy community centered in Jerusalem and based on adherence to YHWH through worship at the Jerusalem Temple and observance of YHWH's expectations through YHWH's Torah.

The Book of the Twelve and the Shoah

This examination of the Book of the Twelve Prophets points to some important dimensions for reading the book, both as a whole and as individual components, in relation to issues posed by the modern experience of the Shoah. The Book of the Twelve is organized to address issues posed by

Israel's and Judah's own experience of Shoah, insofar as the book arranges its constituent books to examine the significance of the destruction of northern Israel and the destruction of Jerusalem and Judah. Individual components likewise raise issues. Hosea/YHWH charge Gomer/Israel with infidelity when neither has the opportunity to speak for herself or to raise questions about YHWH's failure to provide and protect. Jonah objects to YHWH's deliverance of Nineveh knowing that someday, Nineveh will destroy the nation Israel. Nahum celebrates the downfall of Nineveh, the oppressor who destroyed Israel. Habakkuk questions YHWH's purpose in bringing a new oppressor in the form of the Babylonian Empire, and never receives an adequate answer. Malachi attempts to refute some very important concerns about YHWH's efficacy in the early Persian period. Every one of these books raises issues concerning YHWH's power, righteousness, and willingness to act in relation to the experience of Shoah in the ancient world. Indeed, these are the same questions posed about G-d in relation to the modern experience of Shoah.

EIGHT

Complaints to G–D in Psalms and Lamentations

The Voice of the Victims

T he books of Psalms and Lamentations are generally recognized as examples of cultic poetry employed in the liturgy of the Jerusalem Temple and perhaps other Israelite or Judean sanctuaries and worship settings.[1] The book of Psalms is frequently described as the hymnbook of the Jerusalem Temple, and the book of Lamentations is recognized as a dirge form that is designed to mourn for the loss of the Jerusalem Temple in 587/6 B.C.E. Scholarly interpretation has focused especially on analyzing the functions of cultic poetry in relation to the social and institutional settings of Israelite or Judean worship, with a special emphasis on defining the different types or genres of cultic poetry and the purposes each genre served within the settings of Israelite and Judean worship. As scholarly research on the Psalms and Lamentations has advanced during the course of the twentieth and early twenty-first centuries, interpreters have come to recognize the importance of the overarching forms and formal structures of the books of Psalms and Lamentations as well, since the collection, presentation, and reading of cultic poetry in the respective books has the potential to reveal much concerning the conceptualization of Israelite and Judean worship and the means by which it is carried out.

Although much past research has focused on the descriptive study of cultic poetry, its presuppositions, and its functions, an important and emerging dimension in contemporary study is the recognition of the dialogical character of the Psalms and Lamentations.[2] The Israelite and Judean liturgies and the cultic poetry that functions within them provide one of the opportunities for the ancients to address YHWH with their praise as well as with their questions, concerns, and fears. Worship and liturgy presuppose the gathering of people before YHWH, generally at a cultic site, to express themselves to YHWH. The Israelite and Judean priesthoods play crucial roles in these encounters insofar as they serve as intermediaries between YHWH and the people, that is, they represent YHWH to the people and the people to YHWH. In such a situation, the priesthood plays a key role in establishing appropriate and effective communication between YHWH and the people. On the one hand, they communicate the holiness and sovereignty of YHWH as a basis for the people's worship, and on the other, they communicate the people's concerns to praise, thank, and glorify YHWH as G-d of Israel/Judah and creation and to address YHWH with their concerns for national or personal security in the face of human enemies or natural calamities and to ensure the moral order and stability of their nation and homes.

Modern research has tended to emphasize the communication of YHWH's holiness and sovereignty to the people. Thus, the portrayals of YHWH as king of Zion and creation and as protector of Israel and the Davidic monarchy have played important roles in research, particularly in relation to the psalms of praise and thanksgiving.[3] But interpreters increasingly recognize that the people's communication to YHWH has a dimension that has received less recognition, namely, the people ask YHWH for a response to their complaints concerning impending threats and dangers. The process of communication between YHWH and the people in the Psalms and Lamentations is not limited to a simple address of the one to the other; it presupposes an ongoing dialogue in which Israel's or Judah's response to YHWH calls for observance of YHWH's expectations, in the form of holy action, observance of YHWH's commands, and so forth, but YHWH's response to Israel calls for something as well, protection from enemies; relief from drought, famine, suffering, death, and the like; and restoration of what has been destroyed, such as the Temple, the city of Jerusalem, and the nation itself. A further dimension of this issue is the recognition that YHWH does not always respond to the complaint or the request of the petitioners in the Psalms, either immediately or at all. A large number of psalms complain that YHWH is hiding the divine face and that YHWH continues to do so despite prior appeals for divine intervention.[4] Theologically, such an observation entails that YHWH does not always respond to appeals to redress evil in the world. One can only imagine the appeals addressed to YHWH at the Temple during the Babylonian siege of Jerusalem. Those appeals were

not answered with anything other than the final assault of the Babylonian army and the exile of many of those who survived the last stand on
the Temple mount in 587/6 B.C.E. Furthermore, Balentine's study of the
motif of the hidden face of G-d in the Psalms and elsewhere in the Bible
challenges the common perception that human suffering is the result of
punishment for human sin, that is, study of the hidden face of G-d motif
in the Psalms indicates that those who suffer are not always guilty of some
sin, and still no answer from YHWH is forthcoming.[5] This left the ancient
Judeans and Israelites with the question, What does it mean when YHWH
does not respond to appeals for protection at such a time of crisis and
potential death and destruction? That ancient Judeans did not break off
the dialogue with YHWH is evident in the fact that we have a book of
Psalms and a book of Lamentations today, not to mention the entirety of
the Bible and the traditions that grow out it.

A further dimension of the dialogical character of Psalms is the recognition that the dialogue is not limited only to antiquity. Certainly, the
Babylonian exile plays a key—albeit not exclusive—role in relation to the
questions posed to YHWH in the books of Psalms and Lamentations. Both
books would have been read and understood in relation to the Roman
destruction of the Second Temple in 70 C.E. and the brutal Roman suppression of the Bar Kochba revolt in 132–135 C.E. Subsequent disasters in
Jewish tradition would be included as well, such as the 1492 expulsion of
the Jewish community from Spain by King Ferdinand and Queen Isabella
or the 1648 Chmielnitzki massacres of Jews in Poland and the Ukraine. All
of these disasters are associated with Tisha b'Av, the ninth day of the Jewish
month of Av, the traditional day of mourning in Judaism, which is identified as the date of the destructions of the First and Second Temples as well
as other disasters such as those here named.[6] Lamentations is read as part
of the Tisha b'Av liturgy, and the Psalms—even though they are not always
associated with specific days in Jewish tradition—have a timeless character that enables them to express the concerns, fears, and frustrations of
people in times of crisis, whether those crises take place in antiquity or in
modern times. Indeed, David Blumenthal demonstrates the importance
of reading the Psalms in relation to the modern experience of the Shoah
or to the timeless experience of a child abused by a parent.[7] In considering
the Psalms in relation to the Shoah, Blumenthal asks the reader to consider G-d as an abusive parent, and argues that the victims of such abuse
must learn somehow to forgive the abusive parent. Forgiveness in this case
functions not to absolve the guilt of the abuser but to enable the victim
somehow to let go of anger, to restore the relationship with the abuser in

170   the aftermath of abuse, and to thereby enable the abused victim to heal and to go on with life despite the abuse suffered in the first place. He then provides resources for the reading of Psalms 128, 44, 109, and 27 in relation to traditional Jewish sources, sources concerned with parental abuse of children, and sources concerned with the Shoah, to demonstrate the relevance of the modern reading of Psalms as a means for contemporary human beings to come to grips with the problems posed by the modern experience of the Shoah.

In order to develop the dialogical character of the Psalms and Lamentations in antiquity and in the aftermath of the Shoah, the following sections will provide an overview of the book of Psalms, a close analysis of the psalms of complaint as elements in a dialog, sometimes unanswered, between human beings and G-d, and finally an analysis of the book of Lamentations, again as an expression of human dialogue with G-d in the aftermath of Shoah.

Structure and Genre in the Psalms

Although modern study of the book of Psalms has tended to focus on the individual psalm types and their functions, the macrostructure of the book of Psalms displays an intentional arrangement of five collections or components within the overall structure of the book.[8] Each of the five components of Psalms concludes with a doxology or formulaic expression of praise of YHWH, namely, *bārûk yhwh . . .* , "Blessed is YHWH . . . ," in the case of the first four doxologies and *hallĕlû-yah*, "Hallelujah," in the fifth. The five collections within Psalms and their concluding doxologies include Psalms 1–41 (Ps 41:14); Psalms 42–72 (Ps 72:18-20); Psalms 73–89 (Ps 89:53); Psalms 90–106 (Ps 106:48); and Psalms 107–150 (Ps 150:1-6).

Interpreters have faced tremendous difficulties in attempting to explain the significance of this five-book arrangement. Rabbinic tradition maintains that the five-part structure of Psalms deliberately correlates with the five-part structure of the Torah (*Midrash Psalms* 1:2), and reduces the number of Psalms to 147 so that they will correlate with the 147 *sĕdārîm* or sections of the Torah that would have been read on each Sabbath in the triennial lectionary cycle employed in antiquity (*b. Ber.* 9b-10a).[9] The rabbinic viewpoint presupposes that Psalms 1 and 2 have been combined into one psalm, and possibly Psalms 114 and 115 and Psalms 117 and 118 as well. Many modern scholars observe that Psalms 1 and 2

together function as an introduction to the book of Psalms, insofar as the
initial concerns with Torah and righteousness in Psalm 1 and YHWH's
father-son relationship with the Davidic king in Psalm 2 set basic themes
of the book as a whole. Likewise, the Hallelujah psalm in Psalm 150
appears to serve as a conclusion to the book of Psalms as a whole as well
as to the fifth collection within the book. Unfortunately, clear evidence for
a correlation of the five Psalms collections with the books of the Torah or
the individual psalms with the individual sections of the Torah read in the
triennial cycle is lacking thus far. Although readers may note a potential
correlation with the five-part macrostructure of Lamentations or the five
mĕgillôt or scrolls (Song of Songs; Ruth; Lamentations; Qoheleth; Esther)
read on Jewish festivals, clear evidence for such a contention is once again
lacking.

No explanation for the five-part structure of Psalms has yet gained
full acceptance. Textual versions must also be considered, insofar as the
Septuagint adds an additional Psalm 151 and the Syriac *Peshitta* adds
additional Psalms 151–155, which might have functioned to fill out the
numbers of psalms required to correlate with Torah readings in the ancient
triennial cycle. Other proposals have been suggestive, but have likewise
failed to convince. Gerald H. Wilson argues that the current sequence
of five collections in the Psalms presupposes a concern with explaining
the demise of Davidic kingship by pointing ultimately to YHWH's sovereignty.[10] James Crenshaw and others note a progressive movement from
lament in the first collection to praise in the fifth.[11] Unfortunately, the
underlying conceptualization of the five-part macrostructure of the book
of Psalms remains elusive, although it does seem to correlate with the
five-part structures of the Torah, the book of Lamentations, and the five
mĕgillôt. Such a correlation suggests a liturgical function or organization
that is now lost to us.

Although the portrayals of ancient Israelite or Judean liturgies are
limited, the few examples that do exist suggest that the Psalms were
employed individually rather than in relation to collections. The account
of David's bringing the Ark to Jerusalem in 1 Chronicles 16 portrays a liturgy that employs elements from Psalms 96, 105, and 106, although readers may note that each appears in the fourth subdivision of the Psalms.
The portrayal of the liturgy that accompanied the laying of the foundation
stone for the Second Temple in Ezra 3:10-13 notes that the priests and
the Levites were singing hymns of praise for YHWH, citing the refrain,
"For He is good, His steadfast love for Israel is eternal" (v. 11), which
appears as a standard phrase in Pss 106:1; 107:1; 118:1, 29; and 136:1. This

172   phrase also appears in the account of the psalms sung in praise of YHWH
by the Levitical singers at Solomon's dedication of the First Temple in
2 Chr 5:13, immediately prior to Solomon's dedication speech, and again
in 2 Chr 7:3, immediately following Solomon's speech when the sacrificial
fires were lit. Second Chronicles 7:6 indicates that the Levitical singers
continued to praise YHWH with this refrain throughout the dedication
service. Second Chronicles 29:26-30 simply indicates that the Levitical
singers performed at Hezekiah's dedication of the Temple as the people
bowed and prostrated themselves. There is no indication that collections
like those found within the book of Psalms played a role in the ancient
Judean liturgy. Psalms appear to be performed individually in relation to
liturgical events at the Jerusalem Temple.

In part because psalms appear to function individually in the liturgies
presented in the Bible, modern critical research on the Psalms has tended
to focus on individual types or genres of psalms. Interpreters have identified a number of basic psalm genres that stand behind the individual
psalms.[12] Each type has its own typical and distinct ideal structure and
function that inform the unique form, function, and composition of each
psalm. Multiple genres may appear within individual psalms to serve the
unique purposes for which it was composed and for which it functions.
Typical structural elements of genres may also be lacking in individual
psalms for similar reasons.

The fundamental genre of cultic poetry in the book of Psalms is the
hymn of praise, which appears in Psalms 8, 19, 29, 33, 47, 65, 66, 78, 93, 95–
100, 103–106, 111, 113, 114, 117, 134, 135, 136, and 145–150. The hymn
of praise is based on a very simple two-part structure, which includes
(1) the call to praise, in which the people are summoned to assemble in
the Temple to praise YHWH, and (2) the basis or reasons for the praise,
which include YHWH's might, sovereignty, and mercy in delivering the
people or the king from threat by enemies or other afflictions and in
ensuring the order of creation.

The most numerous type of cultic poetry in the book of Psalms is
the *lament* or *complaint*, which constitutes approximately one third of the
Psalter. The high representation of this genre is likely because the fear of
threats of any type is a major motivating factor in liturgical addresses to
the divine. The laments or complaints appear as community laments, in
which the nation as a whole addresses YHWH at a time of national threat
or crisis, and as individual laments, in which an individual addresses
YHWH in a time of need. Community laments appear in Psalms 12, 44,
60, 74, 79, 80, 83, 85, 90, 94, 108, 123, 129, and 137. Individual laments

or complaints appear in Psalms 3–7, 9–10, 13, 14, 17, 22, 25, 26, 28, 31, 35, 36, 38, 39, 40, 41, 42–43, 51, 52, 53, 54–59, 61, 64, 69, 70, 71, 77, 86, 88, 102, 109, 120, 130, and 140–143. Typical elements of the lament or complaint genre include (1) the address to YHWH, in which YHWH is invoked; (2) the complaint proper, which lays out the situation of crisis that has prompted the nation or the individual to appeal to YHWH; (3) the request for help from YHWH to resolve or alleviate the crisis; (4) the affirmation of trust in YHWH that confirms the nation's or the individual's confidence in G-d; and (5) a vow to praise YHWH once the crisis has passed.

The *thanksgiving psalm* genre appears in Psalms 18, 30, 32, 34, 40, 66, 92, 116, 118, and 138. The thanksgiving psalms are designed to express thanks to YHWH for deliverance from some threat or crisis, and they appear to presuppose liturgical processions in the Temple (Ps 118:19-29) or a thank offering (Ps 66:13-15; 116:12-19). Typical elements of the thanksgiving psalm include (1) an invitation to give thanks to YHWH, often employing a form of the Hebrew verb, *ydh*, that is, *hôdû lyhwh*, "Give thanks to YHWH"; (2) an account of the crisis and YHWH's actions of deliverance or relief; (3) praises of YHWH for having acted; (4) offertory formulae to accompany the presentation of a thanksgiving sacrifice; (5) blessings for the participants in the ceremony; and (6) an exhortation to trust in YHWH.

The so-called *royal psalms* appear in Psalms 2, 18, 20, 21, 45, 72, 89, 101, 110, 132, and 144. They were very likely composed during the monarchic period to address some event in the life of the king. Such royal events might include the king's coronation, wedding, victory in battle, deliverance from enemies, and so forth. They are a particularly controversial genre because they lack any typical structure and are identified instead by their concern with the monarch. They frequently display elements of complaint, thanksgiving, and hymns, which suggests that they are not a genre per se, but thematically defined psalms that employ various generic elements to serve their respective purposes.

The *songs of Zion* appear in Psalms 46, 48, 76, 84, 87, and 122. The Zion songs have no typical formal structure or elements, but are instead identified by their celebration of YHWH's choice of Zion as the site for the Temple or divine presence in the world. Many of the Zion psalms presuppose a liturgical procession, which suggests that they were composed to function as part of celebration of YHWH's sovereignty in the world.

Wisdom and Torah psalms appear in Psalms 1, 19, 37, 49, 73, 112, 119, 127, 128, and 133. The wisdom and Torah psalms appear to be designed for meditation or reflection on issues pertaining to G-d, worship, study of Torah, and life in the world. They have no set structure or elements, but once again appear to be defined on thematic grounds. Consequently, their identification as discrete genres is questionable.

Various liturgical psalms appear in Psalms 15, 24, 50, 68, 81, 82, 95, 115, and 132. Many presuppose antiphonal dialogue associated with liturgical action, but their identities as distinct genres are often questionable. Entrance liturgies, which express the ideal qualities of one who would enter the Temple, appear in Psalms 15 and 24. Psalm 50 takes up covenant renewal. Psalms 68, 91, 118, and 132 take up liturgical processions. Psalm 81 anticipates repentance by the people, and Psalm 82 calls for judgment against the foreign gods for failing to do justice.

Altogether, the various psalm genres provide the opportunity for ancient Judean and Israelite worshipers to address YHWH in the institutional context of the Temple liturgy. Such an address presupposes dialogue between the people and YHWH in which the people praise or thank YHWH for some act of beneficence or lament or complain to YHWH in a time of need. Clearly, the psalms of praise or of thanksgiving can easily function in relation to actions or events that would be perceived as a divine response to a lament or complaint, but interpreters must ask, What happens when no divine response is forthcoming? In the context of a dialogue that is presumed to exist in a liturgical setting, silence then functions as a form of response that challenges worshipers who are left to address the crises themselves.

Psalms of Lament and the Divine Response

Individual examples of the psalms of lament or complaint point to a dialogue between the people and YHWH that presupposes divine response to human appeals, but nevertheless can or does go unanswered. Selected examples of individual psalms provide an overview of the range of possibilities in divine-human dialogue and the issues that arise from that dialogue or from its absence.

Psalm 7 is a typical example of the individual psalm of complaint in which the psalmist appeals to YHWH for relief from unspecified pursuers and enemies.[13] The superscription in Psalm 7:1 identifies it as "a *shiggaion* (*šiggāyôn*) of David, which he sang to YHWH concerning the affairs of the Benjaminite Cush." The term *shiggaion* refers to a type of lamentation as indicated by the Akkadian cognate *šegu*, which refers to a song of lament.[14] The reference to the Benjaminite Cush finds no exact correspondence in biblical literature. Attempts have been made to relate the name to Saul ben Kish of the tribe of Benjamin who so frequently pursued David (1 Samuel 24, 26).[15] A closer match appears in 1 Samuel 18–19 in which a Cushite plays an important role in bringing David the news concerning his defeat of Absalom's revolt as well as the death of his son. Nevertheless, there is no indication that the Cushite is Benjaminite, although the revolt was initially centered in the region of Benjamin from which David was forced to flee by Absalom's forces. The setting may be contrived or otherwise unknown, but it recalls the sense of fear and threat expressed throughout the psalm.

The formal structure of the psalm then includes the basic elements that typically appear in the psalms of complaint, although they appear within the context of the two major components of the psalm defined by their respective modes of address.

The first major portion of the psalm appears in vv. 2-8, which constitute a second-person address by the psalmist to YHWH to ask for divine support in a time of threat. The subunits of this segment are identified by the initial addresses to YHWH in vv. 2, 4, and 7. Verses 2-3 constitute the initial invocation and appeal to YHWH for deliverance from pursuers, which includes the metaphorical portrayal of the psalmist devoured by lions to highlight the desperate nature of the situation. Nevertheless, the psalmist expresses confidence in YHWH's protection and capacity to respond. Verses 4-6 present the psalmist's confession of innocence in which the psalmist, much like Job, both asserts righteousness before YHWH and allows that punishment is justified if in fact the psalmist has done wrong. Verses 7-8 then contain the appeal for YHWH's actions to rise up and defeat the enemy in an act that highlights divine justice and sovereignty. Such emphases subtly highlight an appeal to YHWH's reputation as a powerful, just, and sovereign G-d.

The second portion of the psalm in vv. 9-10 appears to be a transitional section in which the psalmist combines second-person appeals to YHWH with third-person statements concerning YHWH's anticipated righteous actions against the enemy. The psalmist speaks in first person throughout, but the second-person address forms once again petition YHWH to act and anticipate that YHWH will do so. The characterization of YHWH's righteousness again provides motivation for YHWH to act.

Finally, the third major segment of the psalm in vv. 11-18 appears as a first-person speech by the psalmist who lauds YHWH and thereby expresses confidence in YHWH's willingness and ability to act. Verses

11-12 refer to YHWH simply as G-d, and emphasize divine protection and vindication of the righteous, again subtly identifying the psalmist as such. Verses 13-17 then portray YHWH's actions against those who are evil should they decide to oppose YHWH. When the evil ones fall into a trap of their own making, just retribution is achieved. The psalm then concludes in v. 18 with the psalmist's oath to thank and praise YHWH, characterized as righteous and most high.

Throughout Psalm 7, the psalmist's righteousness, YHWH's righteousness and power, and YHWH's response to the psalmist's appeal is presumed.

Psalm 94 takes the dialogue with YHWH in a time of crisis a step further than Psalm 7 insofar as Psalm 94 again appeals to YHWH in a time of crisis but very pointedly questions YHWH rhetorically in a manner that subtly challenges YHWH's lack of response.[16] Psalm 94 lacks a superscription and no liturgical or literary setting is specified. Instead, it turns directly to the appeal to YHWH for deliverance from foes before turning to addresses to both the congregation and YHWH once again. The psalmist speaks on behalf of both the nation as a whole and of himself, so that the psalm combines elements of the communal and individual psalm of complaint. The formal structure of the psalm includes the psalmist's initial address to YHWH in vv. 1-7; an address to a group of people rhetorically characterized as brutish and foolish people in vv. 8-11; and a third section in vv. 12-23 that combines address to YHWH with address to the congregation in the Temple. Altogether, the psalm is designed to convince YHWH to act in a time of crisis and, more importantly, to convince the congregation that YHWH will act.

The first major component of Psalm 94 appears in vv. 1-7, in which the psalmist addresses YHWH directly with appeals to appear and act against the enemies that threaten the people. The initial address characterizes YHWH as a G-d of retribution, which indicates a situation in which some wrongful act is already presupposed. The appeal to YHWH to "appear" presupposes divine absence in a time of crisis, and the following appeal to "rise up" against the foes is a standard form of appeal in the psalms. The rhetorical questions in vv. 3-4 then reinforce the initial appeals for YHWH's actions by pointing to the consequences of YHWH's absence and inaction and thereby subtly questions why YHWH has not yet appeared. The question, "How long shall the wicked exult?" points to an intolerable situation of injustice prevalent in the world, particularly given YHWH's reputation for justice. The situation of intolerable injustice is reinforced by the portrayal of the wicked speaking insolently and vaunting themselves over the people and ultimately over YHWH. The portrayal of their brutal acts against YHWH's own people highlights the suffering of the widows, strangers, and orphans, the stereotypical weak parties in ancient Israelite society who need divine protection. The section culminates in v. 7 with the charge that the wicked believe that YHWH neither sees nor understands what is happening, which challenges YHWH's power and wisdom.

The second component in vv. 8-11 then addresses a group identified as brutish and foolish. Such a portrayal is a typical wisdom device that is designed to motivate an audience to accept a speaker's position by not being included among the fools. In this case, the psalmist appeals to the people to understand that YHWH does indeed hear and see and that YHWH will indeed act against the situation of threat and injustice described in the first section. Again, rhetorical questions are employed by the psalmist to make the point, culminating in the claim that YHWH indeed knows the plans of human beings and that they are indeed futile. In this manner, the psalmist attempts to build confidence in the audience by convincing them that YHWH will act.

The final segment in vv. 12-23 then combines address to YHWH with address to the people in an effort to tie the first two segments of the psalm together in a portrayal of YHWH's coming annihilation of the enemy. This segment proceeds in three subsections in vv. 12-15, 16-19, and 20-23, each of which begins with an address to YHWH or with a rhetorical question followed by assertions of YHWH's actions, righteousness, and power. The first subsection appears in vv. 12-15, introduced by the felicitation, "Happy is the man whom you discipline, O YHWH," which aids in portraying suffering as an intentional element of divine discipline and education. Such sentiments transition to an assertion that YHWH will not forsake the people and that divine justice will prevail. The second subsection appears in vv. 16-19, which begins with the rhetorical questions, addressed generally to both YHWH and the congregation, asking, Who will take the part of the psalmist against the wicked? These questions are followed by assertions that YHWH is the psalmist's help and that YHWH's faithfulness and assurance will see the psalmist through the crisis. The final subsection in vv. 20-23 begins with a rhetorical question addressed to YHWH demanding to know if the seat of injustice is YHWH's partner, which suggests that YHWH tolerates injustice and thereby motivates YHWH to act. The following statements reiterate the threatening actions of the wicked, but culminate once again in assertions that YHWH is a shelter for the people and that YHWH will annihilate the foe.

Overall, Psalm 94 presupposes an increased sense of threat and crisis insofar as the psalmist does not simply appeal for YHWH's aid, but poses rhetorical questions to YHWH that suggestion delay, inaction, or injustice on YHWH's part. Such suggestions function as a means to motivate YHWH to act and to convince the liturgical audience that YHWH will do so.

Psalm 22 presents a different situation from that of Psalms 7 and 94 in which the psalmists appeal to YHWH for an answer.[17] The psalm thereby raises the prospect that YHWH has abandoned the psalmist by failing to answer thus far, either in prior petitions or in the present, and thus highlights the psalmist's increasing desperation. The superscription in Ps 22:1 notes an instruction to the director, presumably of the musicians and singers who will perform the psalm, identifies it both as "a deer of the morning ['ayyelet haššahar]" and as "a song [mizmôr] of David." The reference to "a deer of the morning" likely refers to a type of psalm that is unknown to us, although it might suggest a role in the morning liturgy.

The formal structure of the psalm itself again includes the typical elements of the lament or complaint genre, although it is organized into two major subunits that express the psalmist's appeal to YHWH in vv. 2-22 and the psalmist's address to others, presumably the Temple congregation in vv. 23-31.

The psalmist's appeal to YHWH in vv. 2-22 is stylized as an alternating second-person addresses to G-d and first-person statements concerning the psalmist's desperate situation. The initial invocation to G-d appears in vv. 2-3, marked by addresses to "my G-d" in each verse, in which the psalmist both calls upon G-d and demands to know why G-d has not answered. Verses 4-6 directly address G-d with the introductory statement, "And you are holy," to begin a recitation of the basis on which the ancestors of Israel trusted in G-d. Of course, such a portrayal is designed to call for response insofar as it subtly raises questions about the basis for the psalmist's trust when G-d does not respond. Verses 7-9 employ the introductory statement, "And I am a worm and not a human being," to highlight the psalmist's desperation and low state. The section includes a statement by the psalmist's oppressors who tell him to rely on G-d for deliverance, again to provide motivation for divine response. Verses 10-11 return to direct address to G-d, specifically, "But you drew me from the womb," to highlight the past in which G-d protected the psalmist from birth, again supplying motivation for divine response. Verses 12-19 turn to the primary appeal of the psalm, beginning with the statement, "Do not be far from me, for trouble approaches." The section provides a detailed description of that trouble, employing metaphors of bulls, lions, dogs, and so forth, that devour the bones of the psalmist. The appeal appears once again in vv. 20-22 with an emphatic statement, "And you, O YHWH, do not be far, my strength, hasten to my aid," followed by renewed metaphorical appeals for deliverance the dogs, lions, and horns of wild oxen.

The second major subunit of the psalm in vv. 23-31 begins in v. 23 with a second-person address to YHWH in which the psalmist states the intention to praise YHWH. The language then shifts to third-person descriptions of YHWH to an unspecified audience, presumably worshipers in the Temple. These verses are constituted as a hymn of praise in an effort to evoke response from YHWH who has remained silent thus far. The call to praise appears in v. 24, and is directed to those who fear YHWH. The basis for praise appears in v. 25 by highlighting YHWH's past refusal to hide the divine face from those in need. The emphasis on YHWH's past willingness to listen again attempts to evoke response in the present. Elaboration on the basic hymn of praise then follows in vv. 26-31. The psalmist emphasizes that praise is motivated by YHWH's reputation and calls for sustenance for those in need and worship of YHWH throughout the nations because of recognition of YHWH's acts of deliverance. The segment concludes with a reference to how future generations will offer praise to YHWH, thereby recapping the initial statement of the psalmist's willingness to do so in v. 23. Again, the appeal to YHWH's reputation is designed to motivate YHWH to respond at a time when no response has been forthcoming.

Although Psalm 22 presupposes a situation of desperation in which YHWH has not responded, the psalm is designed to motivate that response by appealing to YHWH on the basis of past actions and reputation throughout the world. Despite the lack of response thus far, the psalm presumes that ultimately YHWH will respond.

Psalm 83 reflects an even greater situation of desperation and frustration from the preceding psalms by charging YHWH with silence in the face of enemies who threaten the nations.[18] Such a charge presupposes that the people have already appealed, that YHWH has had ample opportunity to act, and yet YHWH remains silent. The superscription of the psalm in v. 1 identifies it as "A song, a psalm of Asaph." The terms *šîr*, "song," and *mizmôr*, "psalm," are general terms for cultic poetry. Asaph identifies one of the families of Levitical singers commissioned to perform in the Temple (2 Chronicles 25). Psalm 83 is the last of the psalms of Asaph in Psalms 73–83. The psalm itself is a communal psalm of lament or complaint. It comprises two major subunits, including an appeal in

180   vv. 2-9 for G-d not to be silent in the face of enemies and an appeal in
vv. 10-19 for G-d to act against the present enemies in keeping with
divine acts of past deliverance. The address to G-d and not to YHWH has
prompted many interpreters to suggest that this psalm, as one of the 'lhym
psalms, may have had northern origins.

The first subunit in vv. 2-9 emphasizes G-d's silence in the face of enemies who threaten the nation. The subunit begins with appeals to G-d in v.
2, "do not be silent," do not hold aloof," "do not be quiet," all of which function as accusations of divine negligence or absence in the face of threat.
The initial appeals to G-d are reinforced by extensive descriptions of the
enemies' actions that threaten the nation, emphasizing the people's relationship to G-d and the fact that these enemies ultimately challenge G-d.
Ironically, the nations listed suggest a historical setting of threats against
the Northern Kingdom of Israel in the eighth century B.C.E. The mention
of Trans-Jordanian kingdoms, such as Moab, Ammon, and Edom together
with various tribal groups, the Philistines and Tyre, and finally Assyria,
suggest the collapse of support for northern Israel prior to its destruction
by Assyria in 722/1 B.C.E. When the psalm is read and performed in a
Judean context, the memory of northern Israel's destruction raises questions of divine silence in the face of catastrophe much as many interpreters
raise the question of divine silence in relation to the modern Shoah.

The second major section of Psalm 83 appears in vv. 10-19, which
calls upon G-d to deal with enemies much as G-d defeated enemies in the
past. The section begins with references to G-d's defeat of Midian, including their generals Oreb and Zeeb and their kings Zebah and Zalmuna in
the time of Gideon (Judges 6–8) and the defeat of Sisera and Jabin at the
Wadi Kishon in the time of Deborah (Judges 4–5). Such appeals to Israelite traditions concerning the foundation of the nation in the land during the time of the Judges is designed to restore confidence in G-d in the
aftermath of northern Israel's destruction and thereby becomes a means
by which ancient Israel—or more properly, perhaps, Judah—attempted to
answer questions about divine silence and inaction in relation to a Shoah
in antiquity.

Finally, Psalm 44 brings the liturgical dialogue to full expression in
a time of threat with charges of continuing divine rejection and disgrace
of Israel despite the people's fidelity to their covenant.[19] Although the
address to YHWH demonstrates the psalmist's confidence that dialogue
with YHWH is still possible and potentially efficacious, the psalm raises
very pointed questions about YHWH's willingness to respond and act in
accordance with divine fidelity to the covenant.

The psalm begins with a superscription in Ps 44:1, which instructs the musical director that it is a *maśkîl*, a term of uncertain meaning that perhaps relates to the psalm's performance, and identifies it a one of the psalms of Korah. Korah refers to a priestly family that served both as Temple singers (2 Chr 20:19), gatekeepers (1 Chr 9:19; 26:1, 19), and bakers (1 Chr 9:31). The psalm is a communal psalm of complaint. Following the superscription, its formal structure includes four major subunits in vv. 2-9, 10-17, 18-23, and 24-27, each of which constitutes an address to G-d. As one of the *'lhym* psalms, many interpreters maintain that it is originally a northern psalm that was transmitted to southern Judean circles.

The first major address in vv. 2-9 begins with a statement by the psalmist asserting how the people have heard of G-d's reputation for great deeds on behalf of the people from antiquity. It focuses especially on G-d's role in defending the people from attack by enemies, and emphasizes that past victories over enemies were not won by the people's efforts, but by G-d's. As part of its litany of great acts by G-d, the first subunit announces that G-d is king and that the people glory in G-d's name.

The second major address in vv. 10-17 then turns to the major issue at hand with direct and lengthy sequence of charges that G-d has rejected and disgraced the people, that G-d does not go out with the armies, that G-d scatters the people among the nations, that G-d has sold out the people, and so forth. The subunit concludes with statements of the psalmist's disgrace and shame having been taunted by vengeful enemies.

The third major address in vv. 18-23 states that all these misfortunes have come about, but nevertheless the people have been true to G-d and their covenant with G-d. Such a contention cuts to the heart of the issue of theodicy, much like Job, as the people believe themselves to be righteous but nevertheless suffer. The segment emphasizes that if the people had indeed turned to a foreign god, G-d would know. Such a statement serves as proof of the assertion of righteousness and a prelude to the charge that the people are dying on behalf of G-d with no relief apparent. Such a statement is particularly apt in relation to both ancient and modern experiences of Shoah.

Finally, the fourth major address in vv. 24-27 calls once again for G-d to arise to deliver the people. Rhetorical questions charge that G-d is asleep, hiding the divine face, and ignoring the distress of the people who lie in the dust. Such charges point to the failure of G-d to live up to the covenant with the people. Indeed, the last statement of the psalm demands that G-d arise to redeem the people for the sake of G-d's fidelity to the covenant.

Psalm 44 therefore expresses the frustration of the people who see themselves as maintaining fidelity to G-d when G-d does not reciprocate or respond. Although some might attempt to charge the victims with sinfulness in making this assertion, such a charge unjustifiably condemns the victims of a crime. In this case, G-d's fidelity comes into question when righteous people suffer for want of divine support. But one point stands out, namely, the people do not give up on G-d but continue to address G-d to demand relief from their suffering.

The Five Dirges of Lamentations

The book of Lamentations is one of the five *mĕgillôt* or scrolls that are read as part of the liturgy for major Jewish festivals.[20] Lamentations is read on the Jewish observance of Tisha b'Av or the Ninth of Av, the traditional day of mourning in the Jewish calendar, which commemorates the fall of both Solomon's and the Second Temple as well as other catastrophes in Jewish history, such as the expulsion of Jews from Spain in 1492 by King Ferdinand and Queen Isabella and the Chimielnitzki massacres in Poland and the Ukraine in 1648. In Christian Bibles, Lamentations is placed together with the book of Jeremiah because of the tradition in both Christianity and Judaism that Jeremiah was the author of Lamentations (cf. 2 Chr 35:25; b. Baba Batra 15a).

Lamentations employs the *dirge* or *qinah* (Hebrew, *qînâ*) genre, which typically appears in literature of mourning.[21] The dirge is characterized by a metrical 3/2 pattern in which each bi-colon includes three heavy beats in the first half followed by two heavy beats in the second. Such a metrical pattern likely accompanies a limping dance or processional march that would be employed at times of mourning, particularly in liturgical contexts in which the fertility god would be mourned in anticipation of his return from the underworld to the world of the living at the onset of the rainy season (see 1 Kings 18). Although ancient Judah and Israel would not have venerated such a pagan deity, the dirge would have played a role in mourning rituals during the weeks prior to Rosh HaShanah and Sukkot, which marked the onset of the rainy season. Lamentations 1–4 also employs the acrostic form, an artistic device in which each stanza begins with a successive letter of the Hebrew alphabet. The dirges in Lamentations 1, 2, and 4 each begin with the exclamation, *ĕkâ*, "alas!" "how!" which frequently gives expression to mourning or alarm (see 2 Kgs 6:15; Isa 1:21; Jer 48:17; cf. 2 Sam 1:19; Jer 2:21; 9:18; Mic 2:4; Qoh 2:16).

Lamentations itself would have originated in mourning rituals for the loss of Solomon's Temple in 587/6 B.C.E insofar as it appears to be based in part on the experience of those who were in the city of Jerusalem at the time of the Babylonian siege and destruction. Mourning rituals for the loss of the Temple appear in biblical literature. Jeremiah 41:5 indicates that eighty men came to Jerusalem from Samaria or Shechem with their beards shaved to mourn for the loss of the Temple immediately prior to the assassination of the Babylonian governor of Judah, Gedaliah ben Ahikam ben Shaphan, in 582 B.C.E. Zechariah 7:5 also mentions fast days and laments for the loss of the Jerusalem Temple (cf. Zech 8:19). The writings of Second Isaiah appear to presuppose Lamentations. Lamentations 4:15 is cited in Isa 52:11; the Bat Zion or Daughter Zion figure is prominent in both; and the depiction of Zion's comforter in Isa 40:1; 49:13; 51:19; 51:12; and 54:11 appears to presuppose Lamentations 1. Lamentations also resembles the Sumerian laments over fallen cities, such as Ur, Nippur, Eridu, Uruk, Sumer, and so forth from the Isin-Larsa period (1950–1700 B.C.E.), which were designed to function as apologia for the foundation of new ruling dynasties and capital cities in times of political transition. Indeed, Tod Linafelt argues that Lamentations is a form of survival literature.[22] Lamentations does not intend to explain suffering in the traditional sense of the literature of theodicy. Instead, Lamentations gives voice to suffering and mourning for the loss of the Temple and thereby lays the groundwork for future restoration of the Temple and the people of Jerusalem and Judah.

The macrostructure of Lamentations includes five dirges, each of which constitutes a chapter of the book. The first four are stylized as acrostics. Each dirge emphasizes a particular character, including the city of Jerusalem personified as the woman Bat Zion or Daughter Zion in Lamentations 1 and 2; an anonymous man, perhaps based on a royal or priestly figure who speaks on behalf of the community in Lamentations 3; and the community itself in Lamentations 4 and 5. The five dirges take the reader or the liturgy through the expression of mourning and suffering from the standpoint of the personified city of Jerusalem, through the expression of the city's representative, and finally through the people who constitute the community of the Temple or city per se to culminate in appeals for restoration.

Lamentations 1 is a communal dirge over the suffering of the city of Jerusalem, which focuses on the plight of Jerusalem and appeals to YHWH for relief.[23] It begins with the typical opening cry, *ʾêkâ*, "alas!" "how!" to introduce the pattern of mourning for the depiction of the lonely and

184   lost city. Following the opening cry, the dirge comprises two major subunits. The first subunit in vv. 1-11a is a description of Jerusalem's misery
in which the narrator portrays Jerusalem as Bat Zion, Daughter Zion, a
desolate woman or widow who weeps over the exile of her children, the
people of Judah, and the downfall of the city of Jerusalem. Verses 5 and 8
refer to her transgressions and sins that brought about the disaster. Verse
9b appeals to YHWH to see her misery, presumably so that YHWH may
take action to deliver her, and v. 10b reminds YHWH directly how the foreign nations have invaded the Temple that YHWH had expressly denied.
The second subunit in vv. 11b-22 portrays Jerusalem's own lament. The
first segment in vv. 11b-16 constitutes Bat Zion's first-person address to
YHWH in the laments to YHWH and to passers-by concerning her current condition. She appeals for YHWH to act against her enemies in v.
11b, and in v. 14 she refers to her offenses that have caused YHWH to
punish her so. The second segment in v. 17 describes how Zion spreads
out her hands in mourning while YHWH summons enemies against
Jacob. The third segment in vv. 18-22 returns to Bat Zion's first-person
address to YHWH in which she acknowledges her guilt in vv. 18, 20, and
22, but appeals to YHWH in vv. 20 and 22 to punish the enemies who
have brought her suffering about.

The dirge in Lamentations 2 gives expression to communal mourning
by reversing the typical portrayal of YHWH's actions on behalf of Israel
to portray YHWH instead as the cause of Jerusalem's suffering.[24] Again,
the dirge begins with the typical *ĕkâ*, "alas!" "how!" in v. 1. The dirge proceeds in four subunits. The first in vv. 1-10 begins with a third-person
description of YHWH's actions against Jerusalem, again portrayed as the
young woman, Bat Zion. Such a portrayal highlight Jerusalem's suffering
as a victim of war, particularly since women in the ancient world were the
survivors of war—the men having been killed by the attacking forces—
leaving the women defenseless at the mercy of the invaders. Here YHWH
becomes the enemy, rejecting the altar and the sanctuary and handing
over the city to the attackers as Bat Zion and the women of Jerusalem sit
in silence on the ground in dejection and mourning. The poet employs a
first-person perspective in the second subunit in vv. 11-16 to lament over
the destruction of the city in a second-person address to Bat Zion that
expresses pathos and identification with her suffering. The narrator then
turns to a third-person affirmation of YHWH's actions followed by calls
to Bat Zion to mourn in the third subunit in vv. 17-19, emphasizing how
YHWH accomplished purposes decided upon long ago (cf. Deut 28:15-
68, which expresses curses if Israel fails to observe YHWH's instructions).

The last subunit in vv. 20-22 is a direct address by Bat Zion to YHWH in which she accuses YHWH of having brought about her destruction and suffering and illustrates her accusations with depictions of women forced to eat their own babies, priests and prophets lying dead in the Temple, and dead old and young people lying about the city.

Lamentations 3 again expresses a communal dirge, but this time emphasizes the role of an anonymous man in giving expression to mourning.[25] Although some argue that the man may be based on a royal, Zion, or even a christologically influenced figure,[26] a priest would make a more likely representative of the people in their address to YHWH, particularly since Lam 4:20 refers to the capture of YHWH's anointed. Lamentations 3 lacks the introductory *ĕkâ*, "alas!" "how!" and proceeds instead to a four-part address that culminates in appeals for YHWH's assistance. The first subunit in vv. 1-20 is a first-person complaint uttered by the man, who identifies himself as one who has suffered affliction. He speaks of YHWH throughout in the third person as he describes in detail the suffering that he has endured at YHWH's hand. The second subunit in vv. 21-39 is once again a first-person expression by the man who expresses confidence in YHWH's righteousness and mercy. The man emphasizes his hope in YHWH's willingness to maintain *ḥesed*, "fidelity," to the relationship with Jerusalem. He acknowledges the sins of the city, but in keeping with Pentateuchal notions of covenant in Deuteronomy 28–30, trusts in YHWH's forgiveness of those who turn to YHWH. The third subunit in vv. 40-48 therefore calls for the people to repent and subtly calls for YHWH's forgiveness by reminding YHWH that no forgiveness has yet been forthcoming. Verses 49-66 then conclude with a petition for help from YHWH, who has seen the atrocities and now act to punish the culprits and deliver the city.

Lamentations 4 is a community dirge in which the people as a whole give expression to their suffering.[27] Again, the introductory *ĕkâ*, "alas!" "how!" opens the dirge, which then proceeds in four subunits. The first subunit is a descriptive lament of the people over their suffering, although the first-person perspective of the subunit suggests that the anonymous man of Lamentations 3 may still be the speaker. Verses 11-16 describe YHWH's anger against the people in third-person language that does not identify speaker or addressee, but emphasizes the sins of the prophets and the priests as the cause of the city's downfall and suffering. A communal lament in vv. 17-20 in first-person plural form expresses the people's suffering and hope in deliverance as well as the chase of the pursuers who ultimately captured the king. The dirge concludes in vv. 21-22 with appeals for Edom's punishment, for sins that likely include complicity in Jerusalem's destruction (cf. Obadiah; Psalm 137).

Finally, the last dirge in Lamentations 5 again constitutes a community complaint in which the people appeal to YHWH to take the people back.[28] Lamentations 5 lacks the introductory *ĕkâ*, "alas!" "how!" and instead presents a first-person plural appeal for YHWH to remember the people, see their current suffering, and accept their return to YHWH. The final appeal for restoration emphasizes the permanence of YHWH's sovereignty in the world and recalls the days of the past when the relationship was first constituted.

Although many contend that Lamentations cannot be compared to the Sumerian lament literature due to the lack of a king, the appeals for restoration in the aftermath of catastrophe are instructive.[29] Lamentations does not necessarily call for the restoration of an Israelite or Judean king or dynasty, in part because it points to YHWH as king and in part because the Jerusalem Temple would express divine sovereignty. But the call for restoration of the people and their relationship with YHWH entails the restoration of both city and Temple rather than a transition to a new dynasty and capital city as in the Sumerian model. Like Sumerian and later Mesopotamian mourning rituals that call for the restoration of Dumuzi or Tammuz in anticipation of the rainy season, Lamentations gives expression to suffering, but it does so in anticipation of future reconstruction. Both are necessary to give identity and coherence to a devastated people. Based in part on the anticipatory liturgical functions of dirges that look forward to the rainy season, Lamentations thereby provides an important foundation for reconstruction and restoration in the aftermath of Jerusalem's destruction. Lamentations thereby continues dialogue with YHWH—much like the complaint psalms in relation to disaster—and thereby provides a model for continuing the relationship between YHWH and the nation.

Dialogue with YHWH

The preceding examination of the psalms—particularly the psalms of complaint or lament—and the book of Lamentations demonstrates a liturgical means by which dialogue with YHWH is carried out in ancient Judah and Israel even in the face of disaster. By addressing YHWH with laments, complaints, and dirges concerning the suffering of the people due to famine, disease, enemies, and even the reality of the destruction of Jerusalem and the Temple, Psalms and Lamentations both presuppose that YHWH will respond to the appeals and concerns laid out in this literature and therefore that the nation's dialogue with YHWH will continue despite the reverses suffered by the people. They give expression to repentance when necessary, but they are also not hesitant to accuse YHWH of abandonment, neglect, and even deliberate wrongdoing when evidence of the people's transgressions is not evidence. Such a dialogue points to a robust relationship between YHWH and the people in which both parties express themselves, forcefully and deliberately, when either perceives wrongdoing on the part of the other. Nevertheless, neither YHWH nor the people abandon the dialog, but instead look for the means to ensure its continuity.

NINE

Divine Hiddenness and Human Initiative in the Wisdom Literature

Because of the overwhelming interest in historical narrative and prophetic literature during the nineteenth and twentieth centuries, the wisdom literature of the Hebrew Bible is frequently overlooked or deemphasized in modern biblical theology.[1] Many interpreters view wisdom as a relatively late phenomenon in ancient Israelite and Judean literature and thought that is largely derived from Greek philosophy and that has little to do with interpreting the major events of divine judgment and salvation in Israel's and Judah's experience. Because wisdom employs principles of empirical observation and rational evaluation of the world by human beings, wisdom is generally not considered on a par with divine revelation of Torah at Mt. Sinai or of divine purpose and guidance in the history of Israel and Judah. Because wisdom is concerned especially with the natural world of creation and the human world of social interaction, it is frequently viewed with suspicion as a quasi-pagan type of literature and knowledge rooted in the fertility religions of the ancient Near East.

Wisdom literature does not merit such dismissive treatment in the field of biblical theology.[2] Wisdom literature is hardly a late phenomenon, insofar as it is rooted in the wisdom instruction of ancient Egypt and Mesopotamia. It is fundamentally concerned with observing and interpreting both the world of creation and the world of human interaction as an arena for observing revelation of the divine that set the worlds of creation and human life in order and endowed them with divine principles of stability, life, and moral order. As a result, the observation and evaluation of nature and human beings as expressed in wisdom literature functions alongside portrayals of revelation by divine word or decree. Wisdom literature ultimately functions as a primary means for raising questions concerning the fundamental order—or lack thereof—in the world in which ancient Israelites and Judeans lived and for drawing conclusions about that world. Such questions and conclusions pertain to the fundamental stability or chaos of the natural world of creation, the political and moral actions of human beings, and even the righteousness and power of G-d. Thus, the wisdom literature of the Hebrew Bible provides the ontological and epistemological basis for interpreting the worlds of nature, human beings, and the divine.

Because of the experience of the twentieth century, which included two world wars, the threats of nuclear and environmental annihilation, and the recognition that purportedly advanced human societies were capable of carrying out genocide in the form of the Shoah and other assaults on relatively powerless human communities, biblical theologians have turned increasingly to the wisdom literature in their efforts to understand questions concerning moral order in the world. Works such as Proverbs posit a moral order and stability in the world that includes its interrelated natural, human, and divine dimensions. Other works, such as Job, raise very pointed questions about the presumed moral order and stability of the world by pointing out that even the righteous suffer without adequate cause and that wisdom concerning the world is often beyond the capacity of human beings to understand. Qoheleth muses over the reality of death and the transitory existence of human beings in the world in an effort to come to grips with the ultimate futility of human existence. The Song of Songs points to the creative capacities of human beings through sexuality and sensuality to create relationship and knowledge and ultimately to serve as partners with G-d and with each other in the world of creation. Wisdom also has influence on other types of literature, including didactic narratives concerning historical events and human interaction, law and legal instruction concerning life in human society, cultic poetry that is addressed both to G-d and to human worshipers, prophetic literature with its attempts to discern and interpret both divine and human action in the world, and apocalyptic literature in its attempts to look beyond this world for understanding of the principles and motivations that influence this world.

Indeed, the wisdom literature is fundamentally concerned with both examining the world and charting a course for human beings to live in

190   that world based upon the knowledge gained through critical examination of that world and involvement in it. The wisdom books of the
Hebrew Bible clearly presuppose royal patronage, insofar as kings such
as Solomon and Hezekiah are so frequently identified as the authors or
patrons of the wisdom books, including Proverbs, Qoheleth, and Song of
Songs. Such patronage points to royal support for the writing of wisdom
literature and the means by which such literature has its influence on
Israelite and Judean society, perhaps through the support of teachers and
schools that employ such literature in the teaching of children among
the royalty, the priesthood, and other leadership classes.[3] Nevertheless,
wisdom literature appears to be rooted in the fundamental concerns of
the family, specifically parents who instruct their children in the means
by which to understand and make their way in the world. The wisdom
literature often points to parents, kings, priests, and G-d as respected
and wise authority figures to whom the young must look for instruction
and understanding. Nevertheless, in its quest for knowledge, wisdom
literature is not afraid to challenge these authorities—including both
human beings and G-d—when they are perceived to stray from their
ideal norms.

Proverbs

The book of Proverbs constitutes the foundational expression of wisdom
in the Hebrew Bible.[4] Although the key superscriptions of the book in
Prov 1:1; 10:1; and 25:1 ascribe it to King Solomon ben David of Israel
and Judah, interpreters generally recognize Proverbs as a later composition that grew in stages over the course of time. The royal court was
likely a major patron of the wisdom tradition, insofar as wisdom literature appears designed to train young men for public leadership in royal,
priestly, administrative, and perhaps other roles. The basic literary unit
of the book is the *māšāl*, "proverb, parable," a short, often parallel or contrasting couplet that presents a maxim or didactic saying designed to
impart some generally universal teaching concerning the world and life
therein based on practical experience.[5] The teaching may be based on
some metaphor, allegory, or simile that establishes a relationship between
phenomena in the natural world and practices, events, or behavior in the
human world to make its point. Proverbs calls upon its readers to observe
the world in order to discern its principles of order as the basis for a successful and productive life in that world.

Most analyses of Proverbs focus on its diachronic dimensions, particularly how its various collections of individual proverbs emerged and were collected together in the present form of the book. The first major collection of the book appears in Proverbs 1–9, introduced by the superscription in Prov 1:1, "The proverbs of Solomon son of David, king of Israel." Most interpreters consider this a late collection that employs the principle stated in Prov 1:7, "The fear of YHWH is the beginning of knowledge," to serve as an introduction to the older collections that follow. The second collection in Prov 10:1—22:16, introduced by the superscription in Prov 10:1, "The proverbs of Solomon," is usually viewed as the oldest collection in the book due to its relatively simple style. Most critical interpreters argue that Prov 22:17—24:22 constitutes a discrete collection in the book due to its introductory call to attention in Prov 10:17, "Incline your ear and hear the words of the wise, that you may set your heart on my knowledge," and the parallels of this section with the well-known thirteenth- to twelfth-century B.C.E. Egyptian wisdom composition, the *Instruction of Amenemopet*.[6] A short superscription in Prov 24:23, "These too are from the wise," marks a short collection in Prov 23:23-34. A fifth collection in Proverbs 25–29 is generally considered to be later due to its superscription in Prov 25:1 that identifies the collection as "The proverbs of Solomon which the men of Hezekiah, King of Judah, transmitted." Two further collections, generally considered as later appendices to the book, appear in Proverbs 30 as "The words of Agur son of Jakeh, the oracle pronounced by the man of Ithiel, to Ithiel and Ucal" (30:1), and in Proverbs 31 as "The words of Lemuel, King of Massa, by which his mother instructed him" (31:1). Agur and Lemuel are clearly celebrated wisdom figures and perhaps also kings, although nothing is otherwise known about them.

The synchronic literary structure of the book of Proverbs generally follows the collections identified above, although the lack of a superscription in Prov 22:17 requires that Prov 22:17—24:22 be treated as part of a larger collection together with Prov 10:1—22:16. Likewise, the introductory conjunction *gam*, "too, also," in Prov 24:23 and 25:1 requires that both Prov 24:23-34 and 25:1—29:27 be treated as subunits of the larger unit in Prov 10:1—29:27. The result is a four-part superstructure for the book in which each component of the proverbs of Solomon and the other sages presents a distinctive collection of materials that articulates the basic teachings of the book to observe the world and learn from those observations in order to lead a successful and well-ordered life in accordance with the will of YHWH. The literary structure of the book appears in chart 9.1 on the following page.[7]

Chart 9.1 The Proverbs of Solomon Son of David, King of Israel Proverbs 1–31	
I. The Proverbs of Solomon Son of David, King of Israel, Proper	1–9
II. The Proverbs of Solomon	10–29
A. The proverbs of Solomon proper	10:1—24:22
B. The words of the sages	24:23-34
C. The proverbs of Solomon that the men of Hezekiah transmitted	25:1—29:27
III. The Words of Agur the Son of Jakeh	30
IV. The Words of Lemuel, King of Massa	31

Although the macrostructure of Proverbs presents a relatively simple sequence of collections, closer analysis of each subunit in relation to that macrostructure reveals the hermeneutical perspectives and didactic functions of the book that posits a stable, discernable, and moral world order laid out by YHWH, the creator of heaven and earth.

The first major subunit of the book in Proverbs 1–9 lays out the hermeneutical premises by which the rest of the book is to be read. It begins with the above-mentioned superscription, which introduces both the book as a whole and Proverbs 1–9 by virtue of its placement at the head of the book and the collection in Prov 1:1. Following the superscription, the unit proceeds with a prologue in Prov 1:2-7, which identifies the basic purposes and perspectives of the book—namely, it is intended to impart wisdom, discipline, righteousness, and so forth, in an effort to teach the reader that "the fear of YHWH is the beginning of knowledge."

The following materials in Prov 1:8—9:18 comprise eleven lectures on various topics formulated as speeches by a father to a son, each of which typically includes (1) a call to attention; (2) a lesson on the topic at hand; and (3) a conclusion that states the general principle of the lesson, and four interludes that metaphorically portray wisdom as a woman who imparts her teachings as basic principles in the world of creation.[8] The first lecture in Prov 1:18-19 admonishes the son to avoid sinners who engage in violence and robbery. The first interlude in Prov 1:20-33 portrays Lady Wisdom's condemnation of those who are evil and her promise of security to those who listen to her. The second lecture in Prov 2:1-22 exhorts the son to allow the fear of YHWH guide him on the proper path of wisdom. Lecture three in Prov 3:1-12 calls upon the son to honor YHWH as the basis for wisdom. Interlude two in Prov 3:13-20 portrays the man who finds Lady Wisdom as happy, and most importantly states a basic premise of the book, namely, "YHWH founded the earth by wisdom," in vv. 19-20. Lecture four in Prov 3:21-35 calls upon the son to act with integrity toward others. Lecture five in Prov 4:1-9 calls upon the son to acquire wisdom from the father as a guide for life. Lecture six in Prov 4:10-19 contrasts the path of wisdom with that of wickedness. Lecture seven in Prov 4:20-27 calls upon the son to employ honest speech in dealings with others. Lecture eight in Prov 5:1-23 calls upon the son to adhere to his own wife and to avoid other women. Lecture nine in Prov 6:1-19 is sometime treated as an interlude because it differs from the typical lecture form, but it nevertheless employs four epigrams to provide examples of righteous and wicked behavior and their respective results and consequences. Lecture ten in Prov 6:20-35 warns the son against adultery with another man's wife. Lecture eleven in Prov 7:1-27 warns against accepting the overtures of a seductive woman who would lead him from his wife. Interlude three in Prov 8:1-36 again personifies wisdom as a woman whom YHWH created and consulted at the outset of creation so that she would set the basic principles by which the world functions. Finally, interlude four in Prov 9:1-18 calls on readers to accept the banquet invitation of Lady Wisdom and not that of the stupid woman. In doing so, it reiterates the principle, "The fear of YHWH is the beginning of knowledge"

The main block of material in the book appears in Proverbs 10–29, initially identified in Prov 10:1 as "The proverbs of Solomon," with its three subunits in Prov 10:1—24:22; the words of the wise in Prov 24:23-34; and the proverbs of Solomon transmitted by the men of Hezekiah in Proverbs 25–29. Proverbs 10:1—24:22 constitutes the largest collection of the classical proverb style in the book, which it employs to address a range of topics for proper behavior in the world, that is, contrasts between the rewards and punishment of the righteous and the wicked; proper and honest speech versus deceit; the contrasting rewards and consequences of a disciplined and industrious life versus laziness, sloth, and stupidity; proper control of anger and the use of forethought rather than impulse in dealings with others; loyalty and faithfulness to G-d, king, and others in all of one's dealings; honesty in all affairs; the need to seek out and heed wise advice; sobriety and moderation versus drunkenness and gluttony; respect for parents; proper behavior before the king; avoidance of envy; and others. The principle of the fear of YHWH is also articulated throughout this subunit. The second, brief subunit concerning the words of the wise in Prov 24:23-34 calls for honesty in jurisprudence and diligence rather than laziness. The third subunit in Proverbs 25–29 emphasizes the role and responsibility of the king in discerning wisdom in order to provide guidance in the world. This subunit has a very distinctive style that employs short comparisons, especially with events and features of the natural world, and imperative instruction to convey its basic teachings. This section emphasizes the need for proper speech to persuade others, prudent interaction with neighbors, feeding the hungry, righteous action, avoidance of dullards and self-aggrandizement, the need to discern dishonest speech, avoidance of jealousy, fidelity to friends throughout generations, diligence in work, avoidance of greed, trust in YHWH, avoidance of harlots, discipline for sons, and other teachings.

The third collection in Proverbs 30 is identified as "The words of Agur son of Jakkeh," although the reference to Massa is frequently taken as a tribal name on analogy to the mention of Lemuel as king of Massa in Prov 31:1.[9] Here, Massa appears to function as the Hebrew term *maśśā'*, "pronouncement, saying," which refers to the teachings spoken by this otherwise unknown sage. The brief instruction begins with a discourse in which Agur dismisses his own wisdom and ascribes all knowledge to G-d. He asks little for himself, but does request that lies be kept far from him and that he not be given riches. His teachings emphasize threats to society, such as the debilitating effects of need and poverty, the unapologetic actions of an adulteress, the upending of social order when those who are low or stupid replace those who are high or in positions of authority. Models for emulation include the ants, who despite their small size are wise, well prepared, and organized, and spiders, who are small but found in royal palaces. He looks to animals such as the lion and the greyhound as models for the king who must act to avoid strife.

The final collection in Proverbs 31 presents the words of Lemuel, king of Massa, with which his mother instructed him. The collection appears as the mother's instruction to the son. She counsels him not to waste his strength with women and wine, and instead to strive for righteous rule that looks to the welfare of the poor and needy. The bulk of the collection is the hymn concerning the capable wife, whose wisdom, industry, charity, and righteousness ensures the standing of her husband and the welfare of her family.

Altogether, Proverbs envisions a secure, stable, and moral world order that is readily discerned and understood by those who wisely observe the world and draw conclusions as to how to act in relation to the natural order of the created world. Fear of YHWH, hard work, a temperate appetite, respect for parents and other forms of authority, and loyalty to wife and friends are rewarded with success and security in life. Wisdom, personified as a woman who was the first creation by YHWH, is embedded in creation itself and thereby functions as the basic principles by which the world and all in it operate.

Job

The book of Job constitutes the antithesis to Proverbs insofar as it portrays YHWH's willingness to subject an exemplary and righteous man to arbitrary suffering and the deaths of his children for reasons that are never made known to him.[10] The book opens with a portrayal of Job as an ideal righteous man who, in keeping with the teachings of Proverbs, "feared G-d and shunned evil" (Job 1:1). Following the portrayal of Job's exemplary righteousness, the scene shifts to a conversation between G-d and the Satan figure in heaven in which G-d allows Satan to afflict Job in order to determine whether or not suffering would prompt Job to abandon his righteous ways. Job's property is lost, his ten children perish, and he is afflicted with sores. When his wife calls upon him to curse G-d and die, Job responds "Shall I receive good from G-d and not evil?" and continues in his refusal to sin against G-d. Job's three friends, Eliphaz the Temanite, Bildad the Shuhite, and Zophar the Naamathite, come to comfort him, which leads to an extensive dialogue in which Job and his friends examine the questions of human suffering, human wrongdoing and righteousness, and divine righteousness or capriciousness in causing humans to suffer. Throughout the narrative, Job demands a hearing from G-d to learn the reasons for his suffering while the three friends argue that he must have sinned in some manner to prompt such suffering. A fourth figure, Elihu, enters the debate to summarize elements of the discussion and to contend that Job should accept his suffering as divine discipline. The book concludes with G-d's appearance and confrontation of Job. G-d declares that Job was right to question G-d and that his friends were wrong in their understanding of human sin and divine righteousness. G-d heeds Job's solicitation to spare the lives of his friends, restores Job's property and health, and gives Job ten new children to replace those who were lost. Afterwards, Job lives happily ever after.

Modern critical scholarship has focused especially on the diachronic questions of the historical setting of the book and the history of

196   its composition.[11] Although the setting of the book appears to be in an early pre-Israelite period, most interpreters agree that the linguistic features of the narrative framework of Job and the book's concern with the problem of evil indicate that the final form of Job was written at some point from the mid-sixth century B.C.E. through the mid-fourth century B.C.E., to coincide with the period from the Babylonian exile through the end of Persian rule prior to the time of Alexander the Great. Most interpreters argue that the narrative framework of the book in Job 1:1—3:1 and 42:7-14 is a later addition to the poetic core of the book that appears in the speeches of Job and his three friends in Job 3:2—31:40 and G-d's speeches in Job 38:1—42:6. Other elements, such as the wisdom poem in Job 28 and the speeches of Elihu in Job 32–37, are likewise considered as later additions to the book.

Although scholars have always recognized that the question of theodicy is the central issue of the book, the late date of Job, its character as a wisdom text, and the overriding theological concern of the twentieth century with G-d's righteous acts in history have relegated Job to secondary importance in modern discussion of biblical theology. Throughout much of the twentieth century, biblical theologians have accepted the principles of divine righteousness and human sinfulness. The Babylonian exile was viewed as justified punishment for Judah's sins in keeping with the portrayals of the historical and prophetic books of the Hebrew Bible. Job might raise an interesting theological question, but such questioning of G-d could only be viewed as a concession to human intellect that was graciously allowed by an all-righteous and loving G-d.[12]

The modern experience of the Shoah played an instrumental role in changing such views, particularly as theologians and ethicists began to recognize the problem of charging the victims of the Shoah, particularly the 1,500,000 children who were executed by Germany and its supporters, with moral responsibility for their own suffering and deaths. Ironically, Shoah theologians such as Martin Buber, Elie Wiesel, and Emil Fackenheim were key figures in changing the terms of the debate; biblical theologians who were so heavily influenced by historical concerns were slow to recognize the importance of the theological challenge of the Shoah. But Buber's question, whether the Job of the gas chambers could continue to praise G-d's goodness and mercy, pointed to the fundamental moral problem of the book.[13] Wiesel's portrayal of a Job who gives up hope in G-d or in the future, and Fackenheim's questions concerning the meaning of Job's restoration for his ten dead children have prompted biblical theologians to recognize that Job's questions pose some of the most important theological issues of contemporary biblical interpretation.[14] Indeed, G-d never explains to Job why he suffered, but instead challenges Job's right to question the creator of the universe before ultimately affirming that right. Can we in fact continue to accept the principle of divine righteousness and human sin as articulated throughout the Pentateuch, the historical narratives, and the prophetic books? G-d's ultimate affirmation of Job's questions does in fact point to our need and obligation to raise such questions even if the answers are not forthcoming.

Indeed, a synchronic post-Shoah literary and theological reading of the book of Job indicates that the book calls upon its readers to engage the very questions that Job poses concerning divine righteousness and human suffering. Perhaps Job has a compositional history, but the compositional history does not address the key theological issue of the book. The diachronic models so frequently employed in modern critical readings of Job address important questions concerning the compositional history and setting of the book, but they frequently leave the impression of a book that has been reduced to its constituent pieces.

A synchronic reading of the book provides the basis for an integrated reading of the book and the presentation of its theological concerns. The book of Job is presented as a narrative account of the dialogue between Job and three sets of dialogue partners, including his three friends (Eliphaz, Bildad, and Zophar), Elihu, and G-d, concerning the questions of the meaning and purpose of human suffering, divine righteousness, and human accountability. The introductory narrative in Job 1:1—2:13 sets the basic issues and identifies the basic characters of the following dialogue by pointing to the absurdity of Job's punishment, that is, a demonstrably righteous and ideal man who is afflicted because the Satan figure challenges G-d's contentions concerning Job's righteousness and integrity. The introduction in fact goes to great lengths to demonstrate that an exemplary righteous man will suffer punishment—not because he has done wrong but because of the possibility that he might do wrong, and because such wrong is defined in this instance by the possibility that he might question G-d's right to afflict him when he has not sinned. There is no sin in Job, only the possibility that he might sin by questioning suffering or punishment that has no apparent cause. Indeed, human experience in principle reflects such a premise, namely, human suffering without moral cause.

The balance of the book then presents three stages in the dialog, that is, the report of the dialogue between Job and his three friends in Job 3:1—31:40, which begins with a narrative introduction in Job 3:1, "Afterwards,

Job opened his mouth and he cursed his day [that is, 'the day of his birth'],"
and it concludes with the statement in Job 31:40 that "The words of Job
are completed"; the report of the speeches of Elihu in Job 32:1—37:24; and
the report of YHWH's response to Job in Job 38:1—41:26 together with
Job's reply to YHWH in Job 42:1-6. The report of Job's dialogue with his
friends begins in Job 3:1-26 with Job's cursing his birth and demanding to
know why G-d gives life to humans only to make them suffer. Cycles of
dialogue then follow in which each of the friends speak and Job responds
in turn in Job 4:1—7:21 (Eliphaz); Job 8:1—10:22 (Bildad); Job 11:1—
14:22 (Zophar); Job 15:1—17:16 (Eliphaz again); Job 18:1—19:29 (Bildad
again); Job 20:1—21:34 (Zophar again); Job 22:1—24:25 (Eliphaz a third
time); Job 25:1—26:14 (Bildad a third time); and concluding speeches by
Job in Job 27:1—28:28 and Job 29:1—31:40. The formal literary structure
of Job is outlined in chart 9.2 on the following page.[15]

A number of key features of the book emerge from a synchronic analysis of Job's formal literary structure and the presentation of its concerns.
First is the narrative dialogue format, which provides the opportunity for
the characters to examine the fundamental questions of the book, namely,
Why do the righteous suffer?[16] Does G-d indeed protect the righteous?
Is a human being capable of questioning G-d? Is it sinful for a human to
question G-d? Is it futile for a human to question G-d? Is suffering the lot
of human beings because humans must ultimately die? Can humans correct G-d? Can humans challenge G-d's power?

Clear answers are not provided for these questions, but the book raises
them, not only for the characters to debate but for the readers of the book
to debate as well. Throughout the dialogue Job maintains his innocence,
so far as he knows, but he also articulates his willingness to accept that G-
d may make known to him the cause of his suffering. If he is sinful, he is
willing to accept the punishment, and he always accepts the right of G-d
to judge. The speeches of Elihu and the final encounter with G-d reiterate
these principles. But again, neither Elihu's nor G-d's speeches ever provide
the answers to Job's questions concerning the reasons for his suffering.
They merely affirm G-d's right to decide. In this respect, the book of Job
accepts that there is moral order in the universe, even if it is difficult or
even impossible to discern.

Indeed, G-d's speech also affirms Job's right to question G-d on the
matter. A key element in the discussion are the two brief references to
Proverbs teaching that the fear of YHWH is the beginning of knowledge
(Prov 1:7, 9). As noted above, Job 1:1 portrays Job as a righteous man
who "feared YHWH and shunned evil." Likewise, Job 28:28 reiterates

---

Chart 9.2

The Account of Job's Debate with His Friends and with G-d concerning Divine Righteousness and Human Suffering

Job 1:1—42:17

I. Introductory Account of Job's Suffering without Moral Cause at the Hands of G-d	1:1—2:13
II. Account of Job's Dialogue with his three friends: Eliphaz, Bildad, and Zophar	3:1—31:40
A. Job's initial speech: curse day of birth and question suffering	3:1-26
B. Eliphaz's statement and Job's response conc. whether the righteous are punished	4:1—7:21
C. Bildad's statement and Job's response concerning G-d's protection of the righteous	8:1—10:22
D. Zophar's statement and Job's response concerning whether Job is able to question G-d's understanding	11:1—14:22
E. Eliphaz's second speech and Job's response concerning Job's sinfulness in questioning G-d	15:1—17:16
F. Bildad's second speech and Job's response conc. The futility of Job's questioning of G-d	18:1—19:29
G. Zophar's second speech and Job's response conc. whether suffering is the lot of human beings	20:1—21:34
H. Eliphaz's third speech and Job's response conc. whether humans can correct G-d	22:1—24:25
I. Bildad's third speech and Job's response concerning whether humans can challenge G-d's power	25:1—26:14
J. Job's speech conc. the hidden nature of wisdom	27:1—28:28
K. Job's concluding speech asking for a hearing from G-d	29:1—31:40
III. Account of Elihu's Four Discourses to Job concerning His Need to Submit to G-d's judgment	32:1—37:24
IV. Account of G-d's Debate with Job concerning the Futility of Job's Challenge and His Righteousness in Making It	38:1—42:6
V. Narrative Resolution: Job Restored	42:7-17

---

that "fear of YHWH is the beginning of wisdom and turning from evil is understanding." Unlike Proverbs, which portrays wisdom as readily accessible to the human who both fears G-d and employs the intellect to discern divine wisdom in the world, Job 28 portrays wisdom as hidden to humans, difficult to discern, and known only to G-d. Just as Job's friends and G-d debate with him in the book, so the book of Job debates with the book of Proverbs in the context of the Bible. Rather than condemn Job and the readers of the book for asking such questions, the book of Job is designed to elicit and affirm such questions, even if the answers are not easily forthcoming.

The literary form of the book of Job provides a model for human beings to examine and debate the crucial theological questions raised therein. In light of G-d's response to Job affirming his right to pose such questions, Job's questions indeed become a human obligation, particularly since human beings are purportedly distinguished for their capacity to discern what is good versus what is evil.

Qoheleth

The book of Qoheleth is well known for its theological skepticism, particularly because it examines the reality of human mortality and concludes that, because all humans must ultimately come to the grave, human existence is ultimately futile and that life is best lived and enjoyed when it is available without worry about what is to come beyond the grave.[17] The superscription of the book in Qoh 1:1 identifies the work as "The words of Qohelet son of David, King in Jerusalem." The Hebrew term *qōhelet* is not a proper name. Instead, it is a feminine participle that refers to "one who gathers" or "one who assembles" a group, presumably as an audience for the discourses presented in the book or perhaps for some other instructional, liturgical, or public occasion. The LXX employs the term *ekklēsiastēs*, Ecclesiastes, which conveys the same meaning in Greek. The reason for the feminine form of the Hebrew term is uncertain, but later Jewish and Christian traditions identify Qoheleth as Solomon, due to the references to "the son of David" and "king in Jerusalem." Rabbinic tradition considers Qoheleth to be a presentation of Solomon's reflections on life in his old age. The book is one of the five *mĕgillôt* in the Jewish Bible, and is read as part of the liturgy for the festival of Sukkot, "Tabernacles, Booths." Sukkot commemorates the conclusion of the fruit harvest and the onset of the rainy season in Israel together with the period of wilderness wandering following the exodus from Egypt. The word *sukkot*, "booths," refers both to the temporary dwellings that Israelites lived in while out in the fields during the concluding harvest as well as the temporary dwellings of the wilderness. Because Qoheleth reflects on the transitory nature of life, it is associated with the festival named for the transitory life that Israel led at the concluding harvest and in the wilderness.

Modern critical scholarship has raised important diachronic issues. Qoheleth is identified as an example of the royal testament or royal autobiography, a typical Egyptian and Mesopotamian wisdom genre, in which a king or other royal figure presents a discourse or a set of discourses that summarize his reflections on his life as a legacy or testament to be passed on to his descendants, heirs, or successors.[18] Most scholars date the book to the Persian period in the sixth to fourth centuries B.C.E. or perhaps to the Hellenistic period in the fourth through second centuries B.C.E.[19] Some also argue that that later editing and additions appear within the book, for instance, Qoh 12:9-14, although the question of Qoheleth's compositional history has not been as important an issue as it is in relation to other biblical books.

Key issues in modern research on Qoheleth have been the identification of its formal literary structure and the articulation of its arguments and ideas. Scholars are divided concerning the literary structure of the book, which provides few clues concerning its organization.[20] Many follow variations of an initial proposal by Addison Wright, who points to the role of formulaic language, particularly catchphrases, such as "vanity and a striving after wind," that mark eight subunits in Qoh 1:12—6:9; "not find out/who can find out," which marks four subunits in Qoh 6:10—8:17; and "do not know/no knowledge" that mark six subunits in Qoh 9:1—11:6.[21] Other features of the book include the superscription in Qoh 1:1; the motto in Qoh 1:2 and again in Qoh 12:8; an introductory reflection on human labor in Qoh 1:3-11; a concluding discourse concerning youth and old age in Qoh 11:7—12:7; and an epilogue in Qoh 12:9-14. The formal literary structure appears in chart 9.3 on the following page.[22]

The formal structure of Qoheleth points to several important dimensions of the teachings conveyed in the book. First, the two variations of the motto of the book, "'vanity of vanities,' said Qoheleth, '(vanity of vanities,) all is vanity,'" appear at both the beginning of the presentation of Qoheleth's discourses in Qoh 1:2 and immediately following the conclusion of his discourses in Qoh 12:8. The motto expresses Qoheleth's basic conclusion concerning the futility of human endeavor given the ultimate reality of death and therefore the existential context in which human life and effort must exist. The discourses themselves in Qoh 1:3—12:7 present a detailed examination of life that illustrates the motto of the book as well as Qoheleth's conclusions and instructions about how to live life in light of this reality. As interpreters universally acknowledge, Qoheleth calls upon its readers to seize the opportunity to live and enjoy life to its fullest. Qoholeth also calls upon readers to do so responsibly with an eye to justice and avoidance of that which is wrong or counterproductive, because life, particularly youth, is fleeting and old age comes upon one all to quickly in the passage of time. Based upon the presentation of Qoheleth's discourse, the epilogue calls upon readers to emulate Qoheleth's pursuit of wisdom

---

Chart 9.3

The Royal Testament of Qoheleth:

Discourses on the Meaning of Human Existence

Qoh 1:1—12:14

I. Superscription: Words of Qoheleth ben David, King in Jerusalem　　1:1

II. Presentation of Qoheleth's discourses　　1:2—12:14

　A. Motto: Vanity of vanities　　1:2

　B. Qoheleth's discourses　　1:3—12:7

　　1. Introductory reflection on the futility of human labor　　*1:3-11*

　　2. Examination of life　　*1:12—6:9*

　　　a. Qoheleth's situation and task　1:12-18

　　　b. Reflection on pleasure　2:1-11

　　　c. Reflection on wisdom and folly　2:12-17

　　　d. Reflection on human labor　2:18-26

　　　e. Reflections on labor and time　3:1—4:6

　　　f. Reflection concerning "two"　4:7-16

　　　g. Summary instruction and reflection　4:17—6:9

　　3. Conclusions concerning life　　*6:10—11:6*

　　　a. Introduction concerning divine causality and human impotence　6:10-12

　　　b. Inability of humans to find out what is good　7:1—8:17

　　　　i. Instruction to enjoy the good　7:1-14

　　　　ii. Instruction concerning illusive nature of right and wrong　7:15-24

　　　　iii. Instruction concerning women　7:25-29

　　　　iv. Instruction concerning the wise man　8:1-17

　　　c. Inability of humans to know wisdom　9:1—11:6

　　　　i. Introductory reflection on human inability to know wisdom　9:1-6

　　　　ii. Instruction concerning enjoyment of life　9:7-10

　　　　iii. Instruction concerning the unknown fate of all humans　9:11-12

　　　　iv. Instruction concerning examples of unknown fate　9:13—10:15

　　　　v. Instruction concerning human need to live active and assertive life　10:16—11:6

　　　d. Concluding reflection concerning youth and old age: seize the opportunity

　　　　to live　11:7—12:7

　C. Concluding motto: Vanity of vanities　　12:8

　D. Epilogues　　12:9-14

　　1. Emulate Qoheleth's pursuit of wisdom　　*12:9-11*

　　2. Fear G-d　　*12:12-14*

---

despite the ultimate futility of life and to fear G-d while doing so. Such conclusions are in keeping with the teachings of both Proverbs and Job.

Qoheleth's examination of the futility of human life in the face of death clearly presents some important universal insights concerning the human opportunity and obligation to engage life and the world in which we live. The experience of the Shoah, however, accentuates these teachings, both for those who would find themselves the victims of Shoah and for those who find themselves as the witnesses of Shoah or of potential Shoah. Qoheleth's teachings concerning the transitory nature of life and the uncertainty resulting from the chances that life and security might end at any time point to realized and continued threats to morality and stability exist in our world. Of course, the Shoah perpetrated by Nazi Germany and its European supporters in World War II points to the past realization of such threat and the Shoah against Israel and Jews in general proposed by Islamic extremists, such as Hamas, Hizbollah, al-Qaeda, and the governments of Iran and Syria, points to the potential realization of such a threat once again in the contemporary world. Qoheleth's call for human beings to live with integrity in the world then becomes a call to ensure that threats to human life and morality posed by past and potential Shoahs must never be ignored.

The Song of Songs

The Song of Songs is the most controversial book in the entire Hebrew Bible because of its graphic portrayals of sensuality and sexuality in the relationship between the female and male lovers who star as the main characters throughout the book.[23] Both Jewish and Christian traditions read the book allegorically. Jewish tradition includes it as one of the five měgillôt to be read at the festival of Passover, so that the relationship between the two lovers symbolizes the relationship between YHWH and Israel at the time of the exodus from Egypt. Despite controversy concerning the inclusion of Song of Songs in the Jewish Bible, perhaps because of its mystical associations, Rabbi Akiba declares it to be "the holy of holies" of Jewish scripture, employing the terminology used to describe the inner sanctum of the Temple of Jerusalem (*m. Yad.* 3:5). Early Christian canon lists, such as those of Bryennios or Melito, group it together with the other works attributed to Solomon, namely, Proverbs, Ecclesiastes, and the Wisdom of Solomon, so that Song of Songs is considered as a wisdom book that portrays the relationship between Christ and the church.[24] Indeed, allegory, metaphor, and simile are typical devices in biblical wisdom literature.

The superscription of the book in Song 1:1 ascribes the Song of Songs to King Solomon based on his own reputation as a lover of women, having some seven hundred wives and three hundred concubines (1 Kgs

11:1-3) and his reputation for wisdom and the composition of songs (1 Kgs 5:9-14). Linguistic features of the book point to the Persian period or possibly the Hellenistic period as the time for the composition of the Song of Songs. The Hebrew term *pardēs*, "garden" (Song 4:13), is a Persian loan word used to describe the gardens of royal palaces, and the Hebrew term *'appiryôn*, "sedan, palanquin" (Song 3:9), is derived from a Greek loan word, *phorein*, with the same meaning. Despite the relatively late date of its composition, elements and motifs of the Song of Songs may be traced back to distant antiquity. Many scholars point to the Egyptian love poetry of the fourteenth to twelfth centuries B.C.E. as a model for the Song of Songs, particularly due to the appearance of the *wasf* form, an artistic device that metaphorically describes the physical form of the body of the lover (for instance, Song 4:1-8; 5:10-16).[25] Others point to the Sumerian love poetry concerning Inanna and Dumuzi or others that was employed in the ritual celebration of sacred marriage at the time of the Sumerian new year.[26] The metaphorical portrayal of YHWH and Israel as lovers is also well known in Israelite and Judean traditions, such as Jeremiah 2; Hosea 1–3; Zephaniah 3:14-20; Isaiah 49–54; and Ezekiel 16, in which YHWH is portrayed as husband and Israel or Bat Zion/Jerusalem as wife. Such portrayals may have played a role in Israelite liturgy as indicated by the portrayal of the dancing maidens at the Shiloh Temple who are taken as brides by the men of Benjamin at the festival of Sukkot (Judg 21:19-24).

Interpreters have both delighted in and struggled with the Song of Songs. Indeed, more commentaries have been written on Song of Songs than on any other biblical book. The use of allegory, metaphor, and simile to portray the relationship between the lovers both enables interpreters to range widely in their attempts to ascribe meaning to the text and frustrates them in their attempts to discern historical setting and interpretation. Song of Songs extensively employs images of sexuality and sensuality from the human and the natural world. Images of fruit, flowers, plants, animals of various types, and so forth convey beauty, aroma, strength, ardor, and emotion as the two lovers approach each other, lose track of each other, and consummate their relationship during the course of the book.

Interpretation of the literary form of the book has proved to be especially difficult, although a recent study by Trible takes account of the roles of the major characters of the book and their relation to the dramatic presentation of the text to discern a literary structure of five major

movements.[27] The primary characters are of course the female and male
lovers, but Trible points to the voices of a group of women identified as
"the daughters of Jerusalem" who appear in four formulaic variations of
the phrase, "I adjure you, O Daughters of Jerusalem," that mark the conclusions of four major episodes in the dramatic presentation of the text
in Song 2:7; 3:5; 5:8; and 8:4. Following the superscription in Song 1:1,
which identifies the work as "the Song of Songs which is Solomon's," the
body of the book in Song 1:2—8:14 presents a sequence of five movements in the dramatic or narrative action of the Song that describe five
successive episodes as the lovers approach each other and consummate
their love. The first movement in Song 1:2—2:7 portrays the woman's
expression of her desire for her lover as she anticipates their meeting.
The second episode in Song 2:8—3:5 then portrays the approach of the
male lover as a gazelle or stag bounding over the mountains together
with the woman's search throughout the city to find him. The third episode in Song 3:6—5:8 employs the *waṣf* form to describe the physical
charms of both the woman and the man, but when the woman opens to
the man, he is gone. The man's disappearance provides the opportunity
for the woman to express her distress at the loss of her lover, which likewise introduces an element of dramatic tension in the presentation. The
fourth movement in Song 5:9—8:4 again employs the *waṣf* to describe
the two lovers as they are ultimately reunited. The fifth and concluding
movement in Song 8:5-14 relates the consummation of the relationship
and opines that love is stronger than death and that passion is as mighty
as Sheol. The formal structure of the Song of Songs may be portrayed as
follows in chart 9.4.

Chart 9.4
Allegorical Dramatization of Relationship between Two Lovers
Song 1:1—8:14

I. Superscription: Solomon's Song of Songs	1:1
II. Dramatization Proper in Five Movements	1:2—8:14
A. Woman expresses desire for her male lover	1:2—2:7
B. Approach of the male lover	2:8—3:5
C. Loss of the male lover	3:6—5:8
D. Reunion of the two lovers	5:9—8:4
E. Consummation	8:5-14

The formal dramatic structure of the Song of Songs conveys its basic thesis, namely, that the love expressed by the two lovers overcomes death. Although the Song clearly understands this thesis as a means to celebrate love, sensuality, and passion among human beings in the world, it takes on a particular importance when read in the aftermath of the Shoah. Quite strikingly, G-d is absent in the Song of Songs. As allegorical interpretation of the Song has posited, G-d may well stand hidden behind the text—some interpreters have argued that the Hebrew term *šalhebetyâ*, "blazing flame," points to the hidden presence of G-d in the Song insofar as the last syllable of the Hebrew term constitutes an abbreviated form of the divine name.[28] Nevertheless, this element simply conveys the intensity of the flame, and G-d is never expressly mentioned in the encounter between the two very human lovers. Perhaps G-d is to be found in the intimacy of their passion, but interpreters must take the absence or hiddenness of G-d seriously in theological interpretation of the Song.

The absence or hidden nature of G-d in the Song of Songs allows the human characters of the Song full play as actors and powers in creation. The drama celebrates their sexuality, which in biblical tradition is a function of knowledge or wisdom like that gained by Eve in the Garden of Eden (Genesis 3). Although Eve and Adam are condemned by G-d for their acquisition like G-d of the knowledge of good and evil, their newly gained sexuality enables them to create a new relationship with each other as well as new life that stems from that relationship.[29] Ultimately, their sexuality enables them to stand as creators on a par with G-d. The celebration of human sexuality in the Song of Songs thus ultimately points to the roles of human beings as creators and agents of action in the world of creation.

Such a role is particularly striking in the aftermath of the Shoah, particularly in light of the absence or hiddenness of G-d expressed in the text. The question of divine absence or impotence is key in relation to the Shoah, but the question of human responsibility to act in the world is also key. Although Song of Songs clearly celebrates human love in relation to divine hiddenness, the question of threat must also be considered, that is, To what extent does Song of Songs call upon human beings to use their capacities to act and to create in the world to overcome the threats or realities of death or evil in general? Song of Songs points directly to that responsibility, namely, human beings cannot always wait for G-d to act in the world. Although other books of the Bible point to divine action to over come evil, Song of Songs points to the role of human action. In the absence of G-d, human beings must act as creators like G-d to create relationship, to create life, and to overcome death, evil, and the absence of G-d in the world of creation when the threat or reality of Shoah manifests itself.

Wisdom Literature's Call to Human Beings

The wisdom literature of the Hebrew Bible points to some very important dimensions that are relevant to the concern with Shoah in both the ancient and the contemporary worlds. Wisdom literature presupposes that there is order in creation, both natural and moral, that ultimately stems from G-d and that human beings must come to understand in order to live with integrity in the world of creation.[30] Although Proverbs expresses this order and posits that human beings may easily discern order in creation and learn to live according to its principles, other books point to the difficulties posed by the hiddenness of wisdom and the divine in a world that so frequently manifests the threats and realities of evil, chaos, and Shoah. Job charges that G-d may allow humans to suffer without moral cause and posits that wisdom is difficult—if not impossible—for anyone but G-d to know. Although the book ultimately affirms G-d's righteousness, it challenges the premises of Proverbs by raising disturbing questions concerning the limited capacities of human beings to understand the world in which we live and the lack of explanation forthcoming from G-d. The book of Qoheleth likewise posits the hidden nature of wisdom in the world and the difficulties inherent in human attempts to understand the ultimate meaning of a life that must necessarily end in death. Nevertheless, Qoheleth points to the human responsibility to create meaning in life despite the difficulties in doing so. Song of Songs, often misunderstood because of its celebration of human sexuality, likewise posits the absent or hidden nature of G-d in the world and calls for human beings to employ their powers, roles, and responsibilities as creators on a par with G-d to undertake action in the world that will overcome the threats and realities of death, evil, and Shoah. Ultimately, the wisdom literature of the Hebrew Bible calls upon human beings to act, that is, to discern wisdom and order in the world and to act on that knowledge, however limited it might be, to ensure a stable and productive order in creation and life in the world.

TEN

Lessons from the Didactic Narratives of the Writings

The narrative books of the Writings in the *Tanakh*, including Ruth, Esther, Daniel, Ezra-Nehemiah, and 1-2 Chronicles, frequently suffer relative neglect in biblical theology when compared to the narratives of the Pentateuch, the Former Prophets, and the Latter Prophets.[1] Such neglect is due in part to the relatively late dates of these narratives, their association with priestly and ritual concerns, and questions concerning their historical veracity and moral or theological worldviews. First and Second Chronicles is generally treated as a secondary historical account of questionable reliability that has been derived from 1-2 Samuel and 1-2 Kings to serve priestly interests in the postexilic period. Ezra-Nehemiah is a difficult narrative, due in part to its literary inconsistency, which portrays the establishment of a postexilic priestly theocracy antithetical to prophetic values, that defined Judaism as an exclusive ethnic group hostile to Gentiles, and constituted Judaism as a religion devoted exclusively to "Law." Ruth is often read as a narrative opposed to the ethnically exclusive viewpoint of Ezra-Nehemiah, insofar as it portrays Ruth, the Moabite widow of a Jewish husband, as a model for inclusion in the postexilic Jewish community. Esther is frequently read as a morally problematic book that promotes Jewish hostility to Gentiles, insofar as it celebrates the execution of Haman's extended family. Daniel is read as an apocalyptic book that points to an era well beyond its narrative present in the Babylonian period when G-d will intervene in human history to bring salvation and resurrection to the righteous of the world.

Although historical questions have frequently played an important role in prompting interpreters to devalue or dismiss the narratives of the Writings, more recent scholarly engagement with the literary and didactic characters of these narratives has prompted interpreters to reconsider their importance, not as witnesses—whether reliable or not—to Israel's history, but as literature that is designed to impart important lessons concerning the character and actions of G-d; the role, identity, and responsibility of human beings in the world; and the nature of Jewish religious life and national identity in an era in which Judah is dominated by foreign powers.[2] Indeed, such perspectives apply to the narrative literature of the Torah and the Former and Latter Prophets as well, insofar as interpreters have come to recognize the role of historiographical and theological viewpoints in shaping the presentations of these books. The Torah does not simply chronicle the history of Israel from creation to the entry into the land of Canaan; it lays out a theological view of history that presents YHWH's efforts to create Israel as a holy people in the world through the revelation of divine Torah and the establishment of the tabernacle as the model for the later Temple that will stand at the center of Israel's life in the land. The Former Prophets do not simply recount Israel's history in the land, but attempt to explain the problem of the Babylonian exile and the prior destruction of the Northern Kingdom of Israel as a consequence of the people's failure to observe divine Torah—not as any failing on YHWH's part to protect the people from enemies. The Latter Prophets do not simply recount their respective prophets' careers, but likewise reflect on the question of exile, each from their particular theological viewpoint, by pointing to human wrongdoing and divine plans to restore Israel once the period of punishment has concluded.

Each of these narratives raises important issues when considered in relation to the experience of Shoah in both the ancient and modern worlds, although they vary considerably in their perspectives. As demonstrated above in chapter 4, 1-2 Chronicles reflects on the questions of divine and human responsibility in relation to the problem of exile just as intently as the Former Prophets or the Deuteronomistic History, although its perspectives and conclusions differ markedly from the earlier work. The interpretation of Ezra-Nehemiah has been unduly influenced by theological anti-semitism insofar as Ezra's and Nehemiah's reforms are improperly characterized as hostile to Gentiles and legalistic, when in fact they are intended as the means to restore the social and religious life of Judaism in the aftermath of exile and in keeping with prior Jewish tradition, including both the Torah and the Prophets. Ruth is not antithetical to Ezra-Nehemiah, which never denies the place of Gentiles who become a part of the Jewish people, but points to adherence to Jewish values and conversion to Judaism as the means by which Gentiles may become part of the Jewish community. Esther takes up the question of a Gentile government that attempts to exterminate the Jewish people under its rule and the human role to stop such action when G-d is conspicuously absent. Daniel likewise takes up the question of divine absence at a time of threat against the Jewish people by a Gentile government, and points to a period of future divine intervention on behalf of those devoted to G-d who take action to oppose the attempted destruction of Jews. All are ultimately concerned with questions of survival and restoration in relation to threats realized or anticipated against the life of the Jewish people.

Because 1–2 Chronicles has already been treated in chapter 4 above, discussion will begin with Ezra-Nehemiah, which so frequently serves as the basis for problems in reading the didactic narrative books of the Writings.

Ezra-Nehemiah

Ezra-Nehemiah is an especially difficult narrative due to its literary inconsistency, particularly its combination of autobiographical material depicting both Ezra and Nehemiah with third-person accounts of events in the period, its combination of Hebrew and Aramaic sources, its capacity to telescope events, and its problems in presenting the chronology of events portrayed in the book.[3] Modern critical research on Ezra-Nehemiah recognizes that the two books actually form a single narrative, but the literary tensions within that narrative point clearly to a complicated history of composition in which several earlier narratives—including Nehemiah's memoirs, Ezra's memoirs, and third-person accounts of the reconstruction of the Temple and the efforts of Ezra and Nehemiah to restore Jerusalem as the center of Jewish life and worship—have been brought together and edited to produce the present form of the narrative.[4] Although many early scholars argued that Ezra-Nehemiah and 1-2 Chronicles were written by the same authors, recent scholarship has come to view them as independent literary works.

A major issue in this discussion is the relative chronology of the figures Ezra and Nehemiah. Although the narrative portrays Ezra's arrival in Jerusalem during the seventh year of King Artaxerxes of Persia (465–424 B.C.E.), that is, in 458 B.C.E. (Ezra 7:1), and Nehemiah's arrival in the twentieth year of Artaxerxes, that is, in 445 B.C.E. (Neh 2:1, 11), the narrative suggests that Nehemiah arrived long before Ezra. Some interpreters argue that Ezra's arrival should be dated to the seventh year of Artaxerxes II (404–358 B.C.E., that is, in 397 B.C.E.).[5] Although objections have been raised against such a chronology, particularly since the narrative makes no historical distinction in the portrayal of King Artaxerxes, such a hypothesis would allow for Ezra's arrival in Jerusalem and appearance together with Nehemiah at the reading of Torah in Nehemiah 8–10 near the end of Nehemiah's life. In such a scenario, Ezra would serve as a successor to Nehemiah, although Ezra's status as a priest and Nehemiah's status as governor would suggest some modification or change in emphasis in the administrative structure of Persian-ruled Judah.

Synchronic literary research on Ezra-Nehemiah has made some strides despite continued problems in diachronic research on the book. A recent literary study by Tamara Cohn Eskenazi emphasizes that Ezra-Nehemiah is organized at the synchronic level to portray the efforts of the early-Persian-period Jewish community to observe divine Torah.[6] Although there are variations in the details of specific analyses of the literary structure of Ezra-Nehemiah, most interpreters point to four or five basic building blocks in the narrative, namely, the account of the building of the Second Temple in Jerusalem from the time of King Cyrus of Persia through the reign of Darius I in Ezra 1–6; a partially autobiographical account of Ezra's return to Jerusalem and his efforts to organize the Jewish community in Jerusalem around the new Temple in Ezra 7–10; Nehemiah's memoirs concerning his return to Jerusalem and his efforts to secure the city of Jerusalem and to organize its social and religious life in Nehemiah 1–7; and the account of the combined efforts of Ezra and Nehemiah to implement religious reforms in Jerusalem in Nehemiah 8–13. Some argue, however, that the account of the reading of the Torah to the people in Nehemiah 8–10 and the efforts at reform in Nehemiah 11–13 should be read as separate subunits within the larger narrative.[7] Although this analysis differs somewhat from that offered by Cohn Eskenazi, it does support her contention that the narrative is organized to portray the attempts of the Persian-period Judean community to live in accordance with divine Torah.

Because of the portrayal of Ezra's efforts to institute divine Torah as the basis for Jewish life in the early Second Temple period, many modern interpreters contend that Ezra must be recognized as "the father of Judaism," insofar as Judaism is distinguished as a religion based on Torah as book in contrast to the preexilic Israelite religion that was based on the

Temple ritual and prophetic activities associated with the Israelite monarchies.[8] Indeed, rabbinic tradition portrays Ezra as a second Moses, insofar as it contends that Ezra could have served as G-d's agent for revealing the Torah to Israel had Moses not preceded him (*t. Sanh.* 4:4).[9]

Nevertheless, the view that Ezra marks the origins of Judaism must be rejected, insofar as it serves a larger anti-Jewish polemic that seeks to distinguish Israelite religion and the prophets from later (or early) Judaism and to identify early Christianity as the true Israel and people of G-d. Although Torah emerges as an important feature of Judaism in this period, either as the currently known Five Books of Moses or in some earlier form, Judaism originated as the Temple-based religion of the Davidic kingdom of Judah during the monarchic period, and it continued as a Temple-based religion through 70 C.E. when the Second Temple was destroyed by the Romans.[10] The Hebrew term *tōrâ* means "instruction," and it appears throughout biblical literature as a term that especially indicates divine instruction by the Temple priesthood. The term *tōrâ* only comes to refer to the Five Books of Moses at some point during the Second Temple period when they achieved their current form. In the context of the Temple-based religion of monarchic-period Judah, the teaching of divine *tōrâ* in some form or another was the basic task of the Temple priesthood (cf. Lev 10:10-11), as indicated by the charges of various monarchic-period prophets that the Temple priests had not performed this task adequately (e.g., Amos 2:6-16; Hosea 4; Isa 1:10-17; Jeremiah 7; etc.). Although rabbinic Judaism emphasizes the observance of divine Torah in the aftermath of the destruction of the Second Temple and the subsequent exile of the Jewish people from the land of Israel, rabbinic observance of Torah anticipates the reconstruction of the Temple and the need to maintain the sanctity of the Jewish people as a kingdom of priests. Observance of Torah in rabbinic Judaism would then metaphorically construct the Temple in the lives of the people even in exile until such time as the Temple itself would be reestablished in Jerusalem. Ezra's efforts to promote observance of Torah hardly mark the beginning of a new religion of Judaism. Instead, his efforts mark the emergence of a new stage in the development of Judaism from monarchic times on.

An especially important issue in post-Shoah biblical interpretation is the charge found so frequently in scholarly and popular literature on Ezra-Nehemiah that Ezra was an exclusionary legalist whose expulsion of the foreign wives and children of many of the Jewish men of Jerusalem was intended to create Judaism as an ethnically based religion that was inherently hostile to Gentiles (see Ezra 9–10; Nehemiah 13).[11] Such a charge ultimately implies a form of Jewish racism against Gentiles, and echoes the charges made against Jews from ancient Egypt and the Greco-Roman period through modern times. Insofar as Second Isaiah calls for Jews to serve as a light to the nations and to bring divine Torah to the Gentiles, Ezra's actions are sometimes portrayed as an effort to reverse the prophetic element of universalism in Israelite religion. Indeed, the portrayal of Ruth as a Moabite woman willing and eager to embrace Judaism and Trito-Isaiah's call for foreigners (and eunuchs) to be included in the divine covenant in Isa 56:1-8 are frequently identified as texts written to oppose Ezra's exclusionary policies.

A recent study by Klaus Koch, a German Protestant Old Testament scholar, attempts to discredit the charges that Ezra's reforms were antithetical to prophetic teachings.[12] Koch does accept the principle that Ezra's reforms mark the beginnings of Judaism as a Torah-based religion, but he attempts to demonstrate the continuity between Ezra's reforms and the prophetic traditions of earlier periods, particularly Isaiah, which plays such an important role in the Gospel accounts of the life and significance of Jesus and in Christian understandings of divine efforts to reach out to Gentiles. Although the portrayal of Ezra indicates a figure who attempted to shape his program in accordance with the teachings of the Torah, Koch attempts to counter the view that Ezra was a strict legalist by pointing to his dependence on prophetic traditions and his attempts to construct his return to Jerusalem and his reforms as fulfillment of prophetic tradition. Koch argues that Ezra's return to Jerusalem was stylized as a partial fulfillment of divine historical purpose in the form of eschatological prophetic expectations for the reestablishment of a Holy Temple-based Jewish community in Jerusalem (see, e.g., Isa 4:2-6; Ezekiel 40–48). He argues that although the account of Ezra's return begins with a focus on Torah in Ezra 7:10, which indicates his dedication to the study of Torah, the larger literary context in Ezra 7:11-20 indicates Ezra's larger purpose to return the Temple vessels to Jerusalem and to restore effective and permanent worship of YHWH in the Jerusalem Temple.

Koch also notes that Ezra's processional return to Jerusalem is stylized as a "second exodus" in keeping with the portrayal in Second Isaiah of the return of the Babylonian exiles as an exodus from Babylon to Jerusalem like that of the original exodus when Jews returned to the land of Israel from Egyptian bondage. Indeed, the construction of Ezra's return as a second exodus is indicated by his efforts to depart Babylon on the first day of the first month (Ezra 7:9) in keeping with the departure from Egypt

214   on the first day of the first month (Exod 12:2; Num 33:3) and by Ezra's refusal to leave for Jerusalem until he was joined by the Levites who would conduct worship in Jerusalem and maintain the sanctity of the returning procession as they did at the time of the exodus from Egypt (Ezra 8:15-20; cf. Num 10:13-36). Upon arrival in Jerusalem, Ezra imitates the activities of Joshua and Israel at the time of the exodus from Egypt by separating the people from other nations by forbidding intermarriage with Gentiles (Ezra 9:1; cf. Deut 7:1-6; Joshua 1–12) and by observing the festival of Sukkot or Tabernacles (Neh 8:17, which refers to Joshua's observance of Sukkot). In such manner, Ezra attempted to restore the "holy seed" of Israel (Ezra 9:2), much as Isaiah called for the restoration of the "holy seed" of Israel in the aftermath of divine punishment (Isa 6:12-13).

Although Koch is correct to point to Ezra's concerns to shape the return to Jerusalem as an eschatologically oriented fulfillment of divine purpose and particularly of prophetic tradition in the form of a new exodus from Babylon, critics continue to point to Ezra's ban on intermarriage as a particularly sore point and indication of hostility to foreigners contrary to the teachings of Isaiah, Ruth, and other elements of biblical tradition. But such a view overlooks an important dimension of Ezra's program, namely, he does not deny the presence of foreigners who adhere to YHWH's Torah, but instead targets foreign wives who continue to practice the pagan religious traditions of their own nations and teach their children, born to Jewish fathers, to do so as well (see, e.g., Neh 13:23-30). The reliance of Ezra's program on Deut 7:1-6, which forbids Israel to intermarry with the Canaanite nations, is well known. The rationale for such a ban is the recognition that such intermarriage would prompt Israel to worship the pagan gods of these nations and therefore to abandon YHWH. And yet it is striking that Deuteronomy is filled with references to the need to accept the *gērîm*, "resident aliens," among the people of Israel so long as they observe the requirement of YHWH while living in the land (e.g., Deut 1:16; 5:14; 10:18, 19; 14:29; 16:11, 14; 24:19, 20, 21; see also Exod 12:19, 48, 49; 22:20; 23:9; Lev 16:29; 24:16, 22; Num 9:14; 15:14; etc.). Indeed, rabbinic tradition later employs the term *gēr*, "resident alien," to refer to converts to Judaism. With regard to foreign wives, Deut 21:10-14 specifies the process by which a foreign woman captured in war might be married to an Israelite man and thereby become a part of Israel.

These considerations may well explain Ezra's actions. He does not call for the expulsion of foreign men. Foreign men who had become a part of Israel in the time of Ezra and Nehemiah would have been considered as *gĕrîm*, who would observe YHWH's requirements and thereby be considered as an early form of convert to Judaism. There would be no need to expel them because they would have acted in keeping with the expectations laid out for *gĕrîm* in the Torah. Given Deuteronomy's consideration of the means by which a foreign woman might become a part of Israel in Deut 21:10-14, the case of women would follow a similar pattern. Nehemiah 13:23-31 indicates that the reforms targeted women who maintained the languages and traditions of their home nations and did not become a part of the Jewish people. The Ezra-Nehemiah narrative does not mention foreign women who observed YHWH's commandments. Nevertheless, Ruth would serve as an example of the possibility of conversion to Judaism in this period, but readers must note that she swears to accept the G-d of Israel as her own and not to continue in her Moabite religious practice (see Ruth 1:16-17). Trito-Isaiah in Isa 56:1-8 likewise lays out the conditions for a eunuch or a foreigner who become a part of the covenant between YHWH and Israel, that is, to observe the Shabbat, hold fast to the covenant with all of its expectations, and to do righteousness and refrain from doing evil. The issue in this literature is not simply the acceptance of foreigners among the people of Israel; the foreigners who would become a part of Israel are expected to identify with Israel and to observe divine expectations.

The portrayal of Ezra's reforms does not stand in tension with Ruth or Trito-Isaiah on these points. Although the evidence is not decisive, interpreters must reckon with the reality of converts to Judaism in the time of Ezra and the absence of any indication that he took action against them. Instead, Ezra acts to protect his people against those who would promote apostasy and abandonment of Jewish identity.

Ruth

The book of Ruth presents the story of Ruth, a Moabite widow of a Judean husband during the time of the Judges, who followed her mother-in-law, Naomi, back to Beth Lehem in the land of Judah. Ruth declares her desire to become a part of Israel, and ultimately marries Boaz, a Judean kinsman of her late husband. Ruth stands as a model of a righteous convert to Judaism. Indeed, the book of Ruth is one of the five *mĕgillōt*, and it is read as part of the liturgy for the festival of Shavuot or Weeks. Shavuot celebrates the revelation of Torah at Mt. Sinai as well as the conclusion of the grain harvest. Because of its focus on the acceptance of Torah, Shavuot

216   has come to be identified as a festival that also celebrates conversion to Judaism. Ruth's conversion to Judaism therefore makes the book of Ruth a particularly appropriate reading for Shavuot.[13]

Although the book of Ruth presents itself as a historical account of the experiences of Ruth and her mother-in-law, Naomi, during the period of the Judges, modern critical interpretation has correctly recognized the generic character of Ruth as a novella.[14] As such, the book of Ruth is a didactic narrative that is designed to make a point or teach a lesson. Most recognize that lesson as an attempt to present the Moabite widow Ruth, who ultimately becomes the ancestor of the royal house of David, as an ideal convert to Judaism. The literary structure of the narrative is relatively straightforward and proceeds on an episodic basis that includes four basic subunits.[15] The first subunit in Ruth 1:1-22 relates the return of Naomi and Ruth to Judah following the deaths of their husbands in Moab. Included in this subunit is Ruth's emphatic statement in Ruth 1:16-17 that she will become a part of Naomi's people, accept her G-d, and live out her life with Naomi until the time of her death. Ruth's statement constitutes her intention to become a part of Israel and thereby to convert to Judaism. The second subunit in Ruth 2:1-23 relates Ruth's initial encounter with Boaz while gleaning in his fields in a manner typical of the poor. The third subunit in Ruth 3:1-18 portrays the developing relationship between Ruth and Boaz in which Ruth spends the night with Boaz. The final subunit in Ruth 4:1-22 recounts the marriage of Ruth and Boaz and the birth of their son, Obed, who in turn fathered Jesse, and who in turn fathered David. The narrative in Ruth 4:11-12 emphasizes the acceptance of Ruth by the people of Beth Lehem. The conclusion of the narrative indicates that Ruth's conversion and her parentage of the Davidic line are key concerns of the book.

Although modern interpreters recognize that Ruth's conversion and her acceptance are key elements of the narrative, the underlying reasons for such a narrative concern are problematic. Many interpreters recognize that Ruth is intertextually dependent on Genesis 38, which relates Tamar's successful attempt to produce a son by her father-in-law, Judah, following the deaths of his three half-Canaanite sons to whom she was successively married.[16] Although the narrative does not say so, many presume Tamar to be a Canaanite and contend that Genesis 38 is concerned in part with the acceptance of foreign women in Judah.[17] Such a conclusion is unwarranted, however; although Ruth is intertextually related to Genesis 38, the deaths of Judah's sons, born to his Canaanite wife, point to an interest in establishing an Israelite/Judean line for Judah, much as the narratives in

Genesis 12; 20; 26; and 34 point to a concern with the potential roles of foreigners such as Egyptians, Philistines, and Canaanites as ancestors of the people of Israel. It is more likely that Tamar ensures that Judah's line is not Canaanite. Ruth reworks the basic motifs of the Tamar narrative and the ambiguity of Tamar's status to state unequivocally that Ruth is a foreigner and to affirm both her conversion to Judaism and her acceptance in Judah.

The emphasis on Ruth's status as a Moabite convert to Judaism is evident in its textual interrelationship to texts concerned with banning the acceptance of Moabites and Ammonites as a part of Israel, including Deut 23:4-7, which justifies the ban by pointing to their hostility to Israel during the wilderness period, and Ezra 9–10 and Nehemiah 13, which relate Ezra's rejection of foreign women in the postexilic Jewish community. Other relevant texts include Deut 7:1-6, which bans intermarriage with the Canaanite nations; Num 25:1-9, which relates Israel's apostasy with Moabite and Midianite women at Baal Peor; and Isa 56:1-8, which allows foreigners to become a part of Israel if they will observe the covenant, most notably Shabbat. Many interpreters argue that Ruth was written to counter the hostility to foreigners expressed in these texts, contending instead that Israel should accept foreigners in keeping with the teachings of Deutero-Isaiah, who calls for Israel to be a light to the nations.[18] Of course, such a contention is in keeping with Christianity's own sense of mission, which calls for active proselytizing among all the nations of the world to bring them to Christ. Standing in the background of this contention is the charge that Jews are hostile to foreigners, which originated in the Greco-Roman world, particularly in Egypt, when Jews declined to abandon their distinctive traditions and observances to assimilate into the larger Gentile world.[19] Such charges were characteristic of Christian Europe from late antiquity, the Middle Ages, and well into modern times, when they served as a basis for church or governmental laws restricting Jewish religious, economic, and social activities (including intermarriage between Christians and Jews and the conversion of Christians to Judaism), and ultimately fueled the European anti-semitism that culminated in the modern experience of the Shoah.[20]

It is not certain that the book of Ruth was written deliberately to challenge the positions of Deuteronomy or Ezra-Nehemiah. Nevertheless, the inclusion of Ruth in the Jewish Bible together with Deuteronomy and Ezra-Nehemiah indicates that an intertextual dialogue must take place between these books whether or not they were written with such dialogue in mind. And yet an important element of such an intertextual dialogue is frequently absent in the arguments of those who contend that Ruth challenges the purportedly exclusionary policies of Deuteronomy and Ezra-Nehemiah, namely, Ruth's unequivocal acceptance of YHWH as her G-d and her willingness to become a full member of the people of Judah (or Israel). As noted in the discussion of Ezra-Nehemiah above, the foreign women expelled by Ezra and Nehemiah continued to adhere to their own languages and traditions; they did not accept the G-d of Israel nor did they become a part of Israel. Ezra-Nehemiah makes it clear that their continued adherence to their native traditions rendered them as a threat to Jewish identity and integrity as indicated in Deut 7:1-6. Deuteronomy makes it clear that foreigners or *gērîm* are permitted to live in Israel as long as they abide by YHWH's expectations. Likewise, Isa 56:1-8 makes it clear that foreigners and eunuchs who would join YHWH are expected to abide by the terms of the covenant, particularly observance of Shabbat. When read intertextually, Ruth does challenge the absolute ban on accepting Moabites (and presumably Ammonites) as a part of Israel, but it does so on the condition that they abide by YHWH's expectations. Isaiah 56:1-8 takes a similar position; foreigners must observe YHWH's covenant, beginning with the observance of Shabbat. Ruth does not challenge the position of Ezra-Nehemiah, however, which also points to the failure of the foreign women to abide by YHWH's expectations as the reason for their dismissal from the Jewish community. In this regard, both Deut 7:1-6 and Num 25:1-9 point to the apostasy, whether realized or potential, of the foreign women in question.

Three fundamental points emerge from consideration of Ruth. First, the biblical books, much like later rabbinic Judaism, engage in dialogue with each other and often arrive at different conclusions from each other. In the intertextual dialogue between Ruth and Deuteronomy, the position of the book of Ruth ultimately overrode the position of Deuteronomy on the question of Moabite conversion to Judaism. Second, the basic criterion for the acceptance of converts into the Jewish community is the commitment to abide by the expectations of the covenant in Judaism. Gentiles who continue to adhere to their earlier or native religious traditions are not acceptable as converts to Judaism. Ruth declares her willingness to accept the G-d of Israel and to become a member of the house of Israel. Third, the Jewish community itself, based on its understanding of divine expectations, determines whether or not a potential convert is acceptable. Non-Jews do not have the right to make that decision on behalf of Judaism. The people of Beth Lehem affirmed Ruth's decision to become a part of Judah (or Israel).

The book of Esther is one of the five *mĕgillôt* of the Jewish *Tanakh*; it is read on the festival of Purim to celebrate the deliverance of the Jewish people from annihilation by the Persian Empire during the reign of King Ahasuerus or Xerxes I (486–465 B.C.E.). The book relates how Esther, a beautiful Jewish woman, was selected by Ahasuerus to be his bride, how Esther's uncle Mordecai saved the king from a plot to overthrow the monarchy, how the evil Persian government minister Haman plotted to destroy the entire Jewish people because of his jealousy of Mordecai, and how Esther revealed Haman's plot to Ahasuerus, how Haman and his entire family were executed, and how the festival of Purim was instituted to celebrate the deliverance. The book of Esther is included among the Historical Books of the Christian Old Testament because it is cast as a narrative historical work.[21]

Esther has always been treated as a particularly controversial book in both Jewish and Christian tradition, particularly because it never mentions G-d.[22] Other grounds for controversy in Jewish tradition include Esther's intermarriage with a Gentile monarch, the general absence of traditional Jewish observance, and the role of the Jewish community in the slaughter of some seventy-five thousand members of Haman's family. Rabbinic tradition notes some disagreement concerning the status of the book as sacred scripture, insofar as Rab Judah questioned whether the book does not defile the hands, that is, whether it is not sacred, but ultimately stated that it is indeed sacred, although it was composed to be recited orally rather than read silently as a written text (*b. Meg* 7a). Levi ben Samuel and R. Huna ben Hiyya likewise questioned the status of the book, but were reproved by Rab Judah (*b. Sanh* 100a). Medieval Jewish exegetes went to great efforts to demonstrate divine action in the book of Esther, and modern interpreters continue to point to problems in the historical presentation of the book, for instance, a Jewish woman could never have become queen of Persia, Ahasuerus was not the drunken fool portrayed in the book, and no record of Esther's predecessor Vashti, who was dismissed by Ahasuerus when she refused to show her beauty to Ahasuerus's drunken cronies, has ever been preserved. Because of its association with Purim and the general frivolity of the day, modern interpreters tend to recognize Esther's literary character as a novella that is designed to entertain rather than as a historical work that is designed to record and to reflect upon historical events.

Esther suffers from similar concerns in Christian tradition. The Septuagint version of the book, which was composed by Hellenistic Jews but served as the early form of the book in Christian scripture, reworked the narrative to include mention of G-d. Such revision was apparently due to discomfort at the omission of G-d in the Hebrew version. Many early church fathers, such as Melito of Sardis, Athanasius, Gregory of Nazianzus, Theodore of Mopsuestia, and others, denied the canonical status of the book, and Martin Luther expressed his hostility to the book due to its Judaizing character and heathen perverseness. Modern Christian interpreters have also noted the quasi-historical character of the book of Esther, and many recoil at the slaughter of Haman's family, often contending that such an act represents the hostility of the Jewish people against Gentiles. More recently, Christian interpreters attack the supposed nationalism of the book as a means also to attack modern Zionism and the modern state of Israel. Others simply ignore the book or pass over it lightly in treatments of the theology of the Old Testament.

Nevertheless, Esther remains a part of the sacred canons of both Judaism and Christianity and it demands serious theological interpretation as such. Indeed, the modern experience of the Shoah points to the theological importance of a book that depicts divine absence at a time that the Jewish people is threatened with extermination by the government of one of the most advanced and powerful nations of the time. Esther is written to make a point, namely, human beings must act to defeat evil in the world when G-d fails to do so. Such responsibility for human action applies to everyone and anyone, no matter how unlikely a candidate one might be, such as a relatively unreligious and assimilated young woman who rises to prominence by means of a beauty pageant or her equally unreligious and assimilated uncle and manager/confidant. There are no great religious or military heroines or heroes in Esther, like Deborah or King David, only ordinary people who find themselves by happenstance to be in a position to act against gross injustice.

The literary character of Esther as a novella, with its development of plot, characterization, and its exaggeration and hyperbole in the portrayal of events, plays an important role in enabling the book to convey its teachings.[23] Interpreters generally recognize its episodic narrative structure, that is, it develops a plot that emphasizes the setting of the scene, the introduction and preparation of the major characters of the drama, the introduction of the narrative conflict or tension in the form of Haman's plot to destroy the entire Jewish people, and the resolution of the narrative tension when Esther exposes Haman's plot and Ahasuerus acts against Haman and his supporters.[24] The exaggerated portrayal of events plays a key role in building the narrative tension and the resolution of the novella. Ahasuerus appears as a drunken fool throughout the narrative, which contradicts the image of the powerful monarch of the leading empire of the time. His drunkenness and foolishness prompts him to dismiss his wife, Vashti, when she refuses his request to show her beauty to his equally drunken friends at a banquet. Vashti's dismissal provides the basis by which Esther, a beautiful young Jewish woman, becomes Ahasuerus's wife and queen of Persia by an unlikely national beauty contest, which runs counter to the Persian royal practice of marrying only within a select group of Persian noble families. Chance plays a role as well when Esther's uncle, Mordecai, overhears a plot against the king and thwarts it by reporting the matter to the authorities. When Mordecai is honored for his loyalty to the crown, the evil minister Haman plots to kill the entire Jewish people due to his envy of Mordecai's honor. When Haman's plan is approved by the king without any serious discussion of such an act, Esther invites both Ahasuerus and Haman to a banquet at which Haman's accidental fall onto Esther's couch convinces the king that Haman has attempted to assault his wife and aids in convincing him to act against the man who would kill Esther and her entire people. When Haman and his son are executed by order of the king, he also authorizes the Jewish people to attack and kill Haman's entire family, numbering some seventy-five thousand persons. The plot itself is seemingly incredible, although the modern experience of the Shoah has demonstrated that such a scenario is not as incredible as perhaps Esther's authors and readers might have imagined it to be.

Key to Esther's role in this narrative is Mordecai's statement to her in Esth 4:13-14 when she is reluctant to act, "Do not imagine that you of all the Jews, will escape with your life by being in the king's palace. On the contrary, if you keep silent in this crisis, relief and deliverance will come to the Jews from another quarter, while you and your father's house will perish. And who knows, perhaps you have attained to royal position for just such a crisis." As an assimilated Jewish woman, Esther is an unlikely heroine, but she is in a position to act and therefore has the responsibility to do so.

The identity of the primary protagonists in the narrative, Esther, Mordecai, and Haman, is also key to the narrative's didactic purposes, insofar as they are constructed to reprise the failure of King Saul, the first king of Israel, to obey G-d's instruction through the prophet Samuel to kill the Amalekite king, Agag, and thereby to destroy an implacable enemy of Israel who would rise again and again in attempts to destroy the entire Jewish people (1 Samuel 15). As a result of his failure, Saul lost his right to serve as king of Israel and later died as a suicide in 1 Samuel 31 as his people were defeated by the Philistines. On introducing Mordecai, Esth 2:5 identifies him as "the son of Jair son of Shimei son of Kish a Benjaminite," which recalls the identity of King Saul son of Kish of the tribe of Benjamin in 1 Sam 9:1-2. As Mordecai's niece, Esther would share his ancestry and identification with King Saul. On introducing Haman to the narrative, Esth 3:1 identifies him as the son of Hammedatha the Agagite, which of course reprises the character of Agag the Amalekite king from 1 Samuel 15. Exodus 17:8-15 and Deut 25:17-19 identify the Amalekites as a people who are cursed because they attacked Israel from the rear in the wilderness when they were faint and weary. Later Jewish tradition identifies Amalek as the quintessential enemy who will stop at nothing to destroy Israel and which must itself be destroyed before it succeeds in Israel's destruction. By identifying Mordecai and Esther with Saul and Haman with Agag in this manner, the book of Esther places its protagonists in the same positions occupied by Saul and Agag in 1 Samuel 15. But this time there is a different result, that is, Mordecai and Esther take action against Haman and his plot and in doing so save the entire Jewish people from annihilation by a powerful Gentile government.

Finally, the absence of G-d in the narrative is also a key element. As is so often the case in the Shoah and other atrocities or disasters in human experience, the presence of G-d is difficult or impossible to discern. On such occasions, human beings must take the responsibility to act in the face of evil. Divine absence hardly portends divine judgment; rather, it functions as a call for humans to act as responsible partners with G-d in creation.

Although Esther is so frequently overlooked or maligned, no other book in the Bible so fully addresses the theological issues posed by the modern experience of the Shoah.

Daniel

The book of Daniel is the only apocalyptic book to appear in the Hebrew Bible. As such, Daniel is generally considered to be a book that points beyond the concerns of this world to the realm of the divine. The commonly accepted definition of apocalyptic literature by John Collins well expresses this view, "'Apocalypse' is a genre of revelatory literature with a narrative framework, in which a revelation is mediated by an otherworldly being to a human recipient, disclosing a transcendent reality which is both temporal, insofar as it envisages eschatological salvation, and spatial insofar as it involves another, supernatural world."[25] In general, modern interpreters tend to view apocalyptic literature as the product of visionary circles derived from prophecy and wisdom and opposed to the priesthood. In projecting visions of a fixed future in which the righteous will be vindicated and the wicked punished, the largely powerless apocalyptic groups deal with the cognitive dissonance prompted by the failure of their expectations to be realized by positing ultimate triumph through the intervention in human affairs.[26] Ultimately, modern scholarly views of apocalyptic literature contend that G-d, while absent in the present of the apocalyptic writers, will ultimately act to uphold righteousness in the world.

In the case of Daniel, such a scenario involves the downfall of the evil empire that oppressed the righteous in antiquity. When read in the historical context in which the book of Daniel was written, such a scenario looks forward to the downfall of the Seleucid Syrian Empire, led by Antiochus IV Epiphanes (ca. 176–163 B.C.E.), against whom Judah revolted in 167 B.C.E. under the leadership of the Hasmonean priestly family. Although both Antiochus and the Hasmonean leader, Judah the Maccabee, died during the course of the war, Judah ultimately won its freedom from Antiochus's successors under the leadership of Judah's brothers, Jonathan and, later, Simon, in 142 B.C.E. When read in relation to later historical contexts, either in Jewish or Christian tradition, the book of Daniel anticipates the divinely instigated downfall of evil oppressors, such as Rome, Islam, and others, or even the downfall of evil itself.

Such a portrayal of the book of Daniel certainly serves the interests of a post-Shoah reading of the Bible insofar as the anticipated downfall of the evil oppressive empire would include Nazi Germany when the book is read with twentieth-century concerns in mind. Nevertheless, two major aspects of the contemporary critical reading of the book require reconsideration in light of issues posed by the Shoah.

First is the modern critical reading of the book as a composite work that includes the court tales of Daniel 1–6 and the visions of Daniel 7–12. Most scholars correctly recognize the difference in form between the two major sections and posit separate origins for each.[27] Insofar as the court tales portray Daniel and his colleagues as Jews who maintain Jewish faith and practice while in the employ of the Babylonian Empire, interpreters view the court tales as fourth- or third-century compositions that address efforts to maintain Jewish identity under Gentile rule. The visions of Daniel 7–12 portray the ultimate downfall of the oppressor, the restoration of

224   the Temple, and the resurrection of those among the righteous who died resisting the empire. Again, interpreters correctly recognize that the accurate portrayal of historical events from the conflict between the Ptolemaic and Seleucid Empires during the third century and into the beginning of the second century B.C.E. through the outbreak of the Jewish revolt against Seleucid Syria in 167 B.C.E. and the inaccurate portrayal of events from that point on points to the period 167–164 B.C.E. as the time of the composition of the visions. The visions anticipate the capture and restoration of the Jerusalem Temple in December 164 B.C.E. by Judah the Maccabee and his followers.

Although the court tales and the visions may have distinct origins, they are designed to be read in relation to each other in the present form of the book.[28] The court tales are written in third-person narrative form and the vision reports in first-person narrative form with Daniel as the narrator, but the third-person literary framework established in Dan 7:1 and 10:1 points to a redactional effort to rework the two sections of the book so that they might be read as one continuous narrative. Furthermore, although the court tales portray Daniel and his friends as faithful Jews who maintain their identity in the Babylonian court and do not challenge the Babylonian Empire, the portrayal of the Babylonian king and empire is designed to evoke images of Antiochus IV and a critique of his actions against Jews and Judaism. Thus, the portrayal in Daniel 1 of the efforts by Daniel and his friends to maintain Jewish identity by the observance of kosher dietary laws challenges Antiochus's attempts to proscribe Jewish practice. The portrayal in Daniel 2 of Daniel's successful efforts to interpret Nebuchadnezzar's dream of the downfall of the colossus figure ultimately points to the downfall of the Seleucid and Ptolemaic Empires, symbolized by the mixed clay and iron feet of the colossus. The portrayal in Daniel 3 of the deliverance of Daniel's three friends in the fiery furnace following their refusal to worship Nebuchadnezzar's idol recalls Antiochus's efforts to demand the worship of the idol of Zeus placed in the Jerusalem Temple. The portrayal in Daniel 4 of Nebuchadnezzar's madness recalls charges by classical pundits that Antiochus Epiphanes, that is, Antiochus the manifest god, should be called Antiochus Epimanes, that is, Antiochus the mad. The portrayal in Daniel 5 of Daniel's interpretation of the writing on the wall at Belshazzar's feast in which the Babylonian monarch served wine in vessels plundered from the Temple recalls Antiochus's plunder of the Temple treasury to finance his war against Ptolemaic Egypt. The portrayal in Daniel 6 of Daniel's deliverance in the lion's den, where he had been imprisoned for continuing to worship G-d in defiance of Nebuchadnezzar's decree, again recalls Antiochus's attempts to proscribe Jewish worship. In sum, each of the court tales calls upon Jews to maintain Jewish identity in the face of persecution by the Gentile Empire in anticipation of the divine deliverance laid out in the visions of Daniel 7–12. In their present form, the court tales call for Jewish resistance against the efforts of Antiochus IV to suppress Jewish religious identity and national autonomy.

Second is the widely accepted view that the book of Daniel in particular and apocalyptic literature in general is the product of visionary circles that are marginalized by and opposed to the Temple priesthood.[29] The identity of such visionaries is disputed, although an otherwise unknown group portrayed as faithful to G-d and identified as the Hasideans in the book of Daniel is frequently considered as a likely candidate. Such a view is influenced by the visionary and predictive character of the book and apocalyptic literature at large insofar as such perspectives are believed to derive from prophecy, which so frequently articulates criticism of the Temple and its priesthood. It is also derived from Wellhausenian perspectives in which prophetic models are pitted against the hierocratic models of the Roman Catholic Church or rabbinic Judaism to demonstrate the ultimate triumph and righteousness of Protestant Christianity over its (allegedly) ritually and nomistically oriented rivals.

And yet such a view ultimately displaces the identity of the oppressor from the Seleucid Syrian Empire—or other such oppressors like Rome or Islam—to the Temple priests and even the Temple itself. Of course, the Temple priests and the Temple constitute the institutional leadership of Second-Temple-period Judaism so that Jews or Judaism emerges as the oppressor of those faithful to G-d. Such a scenario is quite striking when one considers that the revolt against the Seleucid Empire was led by the Hasmonean priestly family and that one of its first goals and accomplishments was the liberation of the Jerusalem Temple and its purification so that it could once again serve as the holy center of Judaism, Jewish worship, and Jewish national identity.

Indeed, more recent studies of apocalyptic literature point to its use of priestly language, concepts, and imagery.[30] The Jerusalem Temple was conceived in ancient Judaism as the cosmic center of all creation in which divine presence was manifested in the world.[31] The Temple was therefore the locus of the mythological traditions of creation of the world by YHWH and YHWH's actions in the world in relation to Israel and the nations of the world at large. Daniel's throne vision, in which One Ancient of Days passes judgment on the kingdoms that would oppress the righteous, evokes the image of the Holy of Holies in the Jerusalem Temple where the Ark of the Covenant had once resided as the divine throne symbolizing YHWH's presence and sovereignty in the world. Within the context of the book of Daniel, the throne vision in Daniel 7 then provides the context for the mythological images that follow, namely, the conflict between the ram and the goat in Daniel 8, which symbolizes the conflict of the Persian and Greek Empires, the projection in Daniel 9 of Jerusalem's restoration based on a reinterpretation of Jeremiah's prophecy of seventy years, and the portrayal of the war between the king of the south and the king of the north in Daniel 10–12 that will ultimately lead to the restoration of Jerusalem and the resurrection of its dead. Interpreters frequently overlook the fact that many of the prophetic visionaries are priests, that visionary experience in the ancient world is associated with temple sites, and that the high priest of the Jerusalem Temple is expected to have a visionary experience of G-d when he enters the Holy of Holies once each year at Yom Kippur (see Leviticus 16).

In sum, such a priestly context for the visions of Daniel suggests that the Hasideans for whom the book is written would be the Hasmoneans priests and their supporters who fought to capture and restore the Temple in 167–164 B.C.E. When the court tales of Daniel 1–6 and the vision reports of Daniel 7–12 are read together, the book of Daniel emerges as a book that is designed to support the Hasmonean revolt against the Seleucid Empire of Antiochus IV. Although the book portrays G-d as the ultimate guarantor of the Seleucid downfall, Jews, led by the Hasmonean priesthood, are called upon to take action, both to maintain Jewish identity in the face of oppression and to resist the oppressor. The book of Daniel portrays visions of the world of heaven, but it is ultimately concerned with events in the human world.

Defending Jewish Life, Practice, and Identity

Consideration of the didactic literature of the *Ketuvim* or Writings of the Hebrew Bible points to some very important dimensions of biblical interpretation and theology in the aftermath of the Shoah. For one, biblical interpretation has been employed as an important tool in continued attempts to denigrate Jewish practice and identity. Reconsideration of Ezra-Nehemiah demonstrates that these books do not represent Jewish hostility to the Gentile world as many modern interpreters charge, but attempts to constitute Jewish identity and practice under the new circumstances of rule by the Persian Empire. The book of Ruth does not represent suppressed resistance to the xenophobic, mysogynistic, and reactionary policies of Ezra and Nehemiah, but instead portrays the means by which the Moabite woman Ruth anticipated the practice of conversion to Judaism. The book of Esther is not a vengeful and antireligious book that celebrates the massacre of Gentiles, but it is a serious reflection on the issue of the absence of G-d at a time of mortal threat to the Jewish people by a foreign empire. The book of Daniel is not simply an otherworldly apocalyptic work that envisions ultimate triumph over a wicked priesthood, but a work that endorses a revolt led by Jewish priests against an empire that threatens Jewish practice and identity. Fundamentally, readers of the didactic narrative literature of the Hebrew Bible learn the importance of Jewish life, practice, and identity, and the imperative to assert and defend all three when living in a Gentile world.

What Have We Learned?

Areading of the Hebrew Bible in the aftermath of the Shoah points to a number of troubling theological issues. Fundamentally, our reading demonstrates the problematic character of G-d as a figure whose righteousness, power, fidelity, and engagement in the world of creation and human events continue to come into question throughout the Hebrew Bible. Biblical literature charges the people of Israel and Judah with moral failings that result in their punishment, whereas both nations looked to YHWH as creator of the universe and the protector of their respective monarchies for defense against nations that sought to subjugate and destroy them. All too frequently, YHWH fails to live up to the promise to ensure the security of either Israel or Judah and the people are then blamed for their own victimization when the enemy prevails.

Although biblical literature frequently presumes divine righteousness and charges Israel and Judah with moral wrongdoing, it is also clear that the literature of the Hebrew Bible is by no means in agreement on this issue. Various books, such as Job and Esther, directly challenge such an understanding of G-d and Israel/Judah, and others raise questions or provide the opportunity to reflect on the issue. Indeed, the varying positions and portrayals of this issue among the writings of the Hebrew Bible suggest that they are frequently in debate with each other on the questions of divine righteousness, power, presence, and fidelity on the one hand and human accountability on the other in the face of evil.

The foundational narrative traditions concerning the history of Israel and Judah clearly take up the problem of accountability for evil on the part of either G-d or human beings. The Pentateuchal traditions present the opportunity for readers to reflect on divine fidelity in the Abraham and Sarah traditions by raising questions concerning G-d's willingness and ability to provide Sarah with a son so that the covenant may continue and by raising questions concerning G-d's willingness to destroy all the people of Sodom and Gomorrah and to demand Isaac, the firstborn son of Sarah and Abraham, as a sacrifice. The Pentateuchal narrative also presents conflict between Moses and G-d throughout the wilderness period that culminates in the divine decision to forbid Moses' entry into the promised land because of his failure to sanctify G-d at Meribah. In both cases, human protagonists, namely, Abraham and Moses, are compelled to confront YHWH over immoral decisions to destroy entire cities or nations without regard for the righteous who might be among them or the promises made to ancestors of Israel. The Former Prophets attempt to explain the fall of the Northern Kingdom of Israel to Assyria in 722/1 B.C.E. and Jerusalem and Judah to Babylon in 587/6 B.C.E., not as the result of the divine failure to protect the nations that depended on YHWH for their very existence but by instead charging that their kings, most notably King Jeroboam ben Nebat of Israel and King Manasseh ben Hezekiah of Judah, had sinned and thereby played key roles in prompting YHWH to destroy both Israel and Judah. No confrontations of YHWH like those of the Pentateuch take place in the Former Prophets, but Judah suffers for the sins of one man some fifty to sixty years after his lifetime. Such a portrayal of history stands in contrast with the Chronicler who charges instead that neither king bore responsibility for the downfall of their respective kingdoms—indeed, Manasseh repented—but that the generation alive at the time of the destruction had sinned and therefore had to bear responsibility. The contrasting viewpoints of the DtrH and ChrH writers point to a debate that took place among the historical writers of the Hebrew Bible concerning the question of moral accountability for the destruction of Israel and Judah.

Similar questions arise among the Latter Prophets of the Hebrew Bible. Each of the prophetic books of the Hebrew Bible, namely, Isaiah, Jeremiah, Ezekiel, and the Book of the Twelve Prophets, focuses in one manner or another with the question of moral accountability for the destruction and exile of Israel by the Assyrians in 722/1 B.C.E. and of Judah by the Babylonians in 587/6 B.C.E. All agree in exonerating YHWH for these disasters and instead point to the people of Israel and Judah themselves as the parties responsible for their own respective victimizations. Nevertheless,

230   each of the prophetic books raises some rather disturbing questions. The book of Isaiah portrays Jerusalem's judgment and restoration as an act of YHWH and charges that the Davidic kings, Ahaz and Hezekiah, bear responsibility for the Assyrian assaults brought by YHWH against Judah due to their failures to believe in YHWH's claims of fidelity to covenant and promises to protect Jerusalem and the house of David. Nevertheless, Isaiah's vision of YHWH in Isaiah 6 posits YHWH's commands that the people be rendered blind, deaf, and unknowing by the prophet so that they cannot repent and be saved from the judgment. Likewise, the book posits the end of the ruling house of David by positing that the Persian king Cyrus will be YHWH's anointed to whom Israel must submit.

The book of Jeremiah presents the destruction of Jerusalem and exile as the result of the people's failure to observe YHWH's Torah, and the prophet himself emerges as an unwilling participant in the divine drama of punishment. Indeed, Jeremiah metaphorically portrays himself as a woman who was raped by YHWH to give birth to a prophetic word that he does not want and yet cannot hold in. Ezekiel portrays Jerusalem's destruction as an act of purging or purification on YHWH's part, in which the fate of the city's population is metaphorically portrayed as the scapegoat offering of Yom Kippur, in which the men are marked for exile like the goat sent to the wilderness whereas the old, the young, the women, and the children, are killed much like the goat sacrificed for the sin offering.

The Book of the Twelve reflects on the question of YHWH's justice in relation to destruction. Hosea metaphorically portrays Israel as an adulterous woman who cuckolded her husband YHWH as a means to justify judgment against her, but such a move sidesteps the moral question of YHWH's failure to protect his people/bride. Jonah ben Ammitai, a northern Israelite prophet from the time of Jeroboam ben Joash, is forced to watch as YHWH allows Nineveh to survive following repentance so that it might someday destroy his native Israel. Nahum is condemned by modern interpreters as vindictive for his celebration of Nineveh's downfall, despite the fact that Nineveh is the capitol of the Assyrian Empire that destroyed the kingdom of Israel. Habakkuk turns to YHWH for help at the time of the Babylonian subjugation of Judah, only to learn that YHWH was the one who brought the Babylonians in the first place. Malachi reflects a debate in Persian-period Judah as to when YHWH might act to fulfill promises of restoration.

The third major section of the Hebrew Bible, the *Ketuvim* or Writings, is perhaps the most underutilized and misunderstood segment of the Bible, in part because its books so frequently challenge the dominant paradigm of reward for righteousness and punishment for wickedness found in the Torah, the Former Prophets, and the Latter Prophets. We have already seen how the Chronicler challenges the historical portrayal of the Former Prophets with regard to accountability for destruction and exile. The Psalms are frequently read as liturgical expressions of piety, but it is noteworthy how frequently they raise questions to YHWH. The lament is the most frequently encountered genre of cultic poetry in the Psalms, which represents the dialogue of worshipers with YHWH who demand to know why YHWH does not respond in times of crisis. Lamentations follows suit with explicit reference to the fall of Jerusalem.

The Wisdom literature likewise engages in debate concerning YHWH's engagement and righteousness. Whereas Proverbs maintains that wisdom is based in the fear of YHWH and that such wisdom is easily learned by studying the world of creation and human life, Job maintains that YHWH may be quite arbitrary in treating human beings and that wisdom is so well hidden in the world as to be nearly unattainable. At the end of the book, YHWH condemns Job's friends who defended YHWH's righteousness and declared that Job was right to raise questions. Qoheleth for his part declares the futility of human life while nevertheless calling upon his readers to engage in that life despite its futility. The Song of Songs posits a scenario in which YHWH never appears and presents the human actors of the book as those who create relationships and meaning in the world in which we live.

The didactic narratives of the Writings have frequently been misinterpreted, often with anti-semitic overtones. Ezra-Nehemiah is widely dismissed as a bigoted and reactionary work insofar as Ezra demands the expulsion of foreign wives, but his move is directed against those women who did not convert to Judaism and instead maintained their pagan religious traditions. Ruth is frequently read as a protest against the policies of Ezra, but she emerges as the model of the righteous convert to Judaism. Esther is frequently read as a book that promotes Jewish hatred of Gentiles, but it presents Esther as the unlikely heroine who must act at a time when a Gentile government undertakes an effort to destroy the Jewish people, an obvious analogy to the Nazi attempt to exterminate Judaism. Finally, Daniel does not portray an otherworldly apocalyptic scenario of salvation, but instead calls on Jews to maintain their identity in an effort to resist and defeat a foreign empire that sought to subjugate Judah and proscribe the practice of Judaism.

Altogether, our reading points, on the one hand, to serious debate in the Hebrew Bible concerning the righteousness, fidelity, power, and

232   engagement of G-d and, on the other hand, the moral accountability and responsibilities of human beings in relation to questions of evil, particularly the destruction and exile of Israel or Judah. Indeed, brief surveys of early Christianity and rabbinic Judaism indicate that these issues were addressed in later times as well based on each tradition's respective reading of the Hebrew Bible and their attempts to come to some understanding of the issues.

The Christian Gospels and the Character of G-d

A popular stereotype is that the New Testament portrays a G-d of love whereas the Old Testament portrays a violent and vengeful G-d. The willingness of Jesus to sacrifice himself for the sins of humanity in the New Testament is frequently taken as a manifestation of divine empathy and compassion for human suffering in which G-d sacrifices the son for the sake of humankind whereas the Old Testament penchant for judgment against sinners emerges as a manifestation of divine wrath and judgment. Although such a portrayal may seem theologically attractive, closer examination of the Gospel traditions suggests that it is quite a superficial understanding, insofar as the Gospel portrayals of Jesus' life and death are built upon the presumption of the destruction of the Jerusalem Temple and the suffering of the Jewish people at the hands of the Romans during the first revolt against Rome in 66–74 C.E. Because the epistles of Paul predate the destruction of Jerusalem, we will focus only on the Gospels. Some of the other epistles may date to the period following the destruction of Jerusalem, but there are questions concerning their composition. Insofar as the book of Revelation anticipates the downfall of Rome, it too need not be considered here.

The Gospel of Mark is generally considered to be the earliest of the Gospels insofar as it appears to have been written shortly following the destruction of the Jerusalem Temple in 70 C.E.[1] Mark is frequently understood to present an apocalyptic scenario insofar as it portrays the coming "Son of man" as a messianic figure who will appear following a period of persecution and turmoil to send out the angels to "gather his elect from the four winds, from the ends of the earth to the ends of heaven" (Mark 13:27). Although some have suggested that the period of turmoil envisioned by Mark may be identified with the Roman emperor Nero's persecution of Christians in 64 C.E., Jesus' statement in Mark 13:2 concerning the Temple, "Not one stone will be left here upon another; all will be thrown down," indicates that the Gospel understands that Jesus' life and significance is portrayed in relation to the destruction of the Temple and Jerusalem by the Romans in 70 C.E. The destruction of the Jerusalem Temple and the defeat of Judea by the Romans in 66–74 C.E. is generally recognized as an event analogous to the Babylonian destruction of the Temple and the exile of Judah in 587/6 B.C.E. and together these events are often portrayed in relation to the Shoah by post-Shoah theologians such as Ignaz Maybaum, Richard Rubenstein, Emil Fackenheim, Eliezer Berkovits, and others. Although the Gospel of Mark clearly understands the life, death, and resurrection of Jesus as an act of divine grace, it just as clearly gains its significance in relation to one of the greatest religious and national tragedies suffered by the Jewish people in history. In this respect, Mark's portrayal of divine compassion in Christ emerges as another example of theodicy, that is, an attempt to defend G-d against charges of neglect, impotence, unrighteousness, and infidelity, insofar as G-d failed to defend Jerusalem and Judea against the onslaught of an imperial oppressor. In short, Mark portrays an occasion of divine failure to protect Jews and Judaism from an oppressor as an occasion of divine compassion and grace so that the issue becomes one of divine suffering on the cross rather than human suffering by the Roman sword and crosses since this was the fate of those who resisted Rome. Mark thereby identifies G-d with Roman imperial oppression of Judea and its suppression of Jewish independence.

Analogous observations may be made in relation to the Gospels of Matthew and Luke, both of which were written ca. 85 C.E. following the destruction of the Jerusalem Temple and the composition of the Gospel of Mark. Matthew is well known as a Gospel directed to Jewish readers insofar as it attempts to portray Christ as the fulfillment of Jewish scripture.[2] The portrayal of Jesus' genealogy in Matt 1:1-17, for example, is designed to establish Jesus as a descendant of Abraham and the house of David. The account of his birth to the virgin Mary is designed to demonstrate fulfillment of Isa 7:14, which in the Greek Septuagint portrays the birth of Emanuel to a virgin. Although the agenda to portray Jesus as the Christ who fulfills Jewish scripture is evident throughout the Gospel, Matthew is also notorious for its efforts to charge Jews with responsibility for the crucifixion of Christ. Matthew 27 portrays the efforts of the Roman procurator, Pontius Pilate, to release Jesus and spare him from crucifixion, but the Jews of the time are insistent that Jesus be put to death despite Pilate's efforts to show mercy. The infamous statement, "May his blood be on us and our children," in Matt 27:25 then provides the basis for the charge of deicide against the Jews on the part of the church for centuries to follow. Such a charge is striking when one considers that Pontius Pilate was the only Roman procurator in Judea removed from office for excessive cruelty. Furthermore, the timing of Jesus' trial before the high priest Caiaphas, the priests, and the council at Passover is also questionable (see Matt 26:17-68), insofar as the priests and the council (Sanhedrin) would not compromise the sanctity of a Jewish holiday by meeting at such a time to pass judgment on anyone. The portrayal of Pilate in Matthew contrasts sharply with the historical portrayal of the man and his motives. Matthew's portrayal of Jesus' trial and of Pilate suggests an effort on the part of the Gospel writer to exonerate the Romans and charge the Jews instead with responsibility for the death of Christ. Not only does Matthew portray the life and death of Jesus as an act of divine mercy on behalf of the Jews, but it also portrays his crucifixion as an act of Jewish betrayal of that very mercy. When read against the background of the destruction of Jerusalem by the Romans, such an account serves as an example of theodicy that attempts to defend G-d against charges of abandonment and infidelity in the face of Roman oppression by charging Jews with infidelity and abandonment of G-d. In sum, Matthew blames the Jews, the victims of Roman imperialism, for their own victimization.

Luke, or, more properly, Luke-Acts, takes a somewhat different approach.[3] Luke-Acts is addressed to a Gentile audience insofar as it attempts to persuade Gentile readers that Jesus manifests divine mercy in relation to all humankind, both Jewish and Gentile. Luke is well known for its use of Hellenistic literary technique—for instance, the initial dedication to Theophilus—to appeal to the aesthetic tastes of its Greco-Roman audience. Once again, the backdrop of the destruction of Jerusalem and the Temple is of paramount importance for understanding the account of Jesus' life and crucifixion and the spread of the early church from Jerusalem to Rome. Overall, the narrative portrays the movement of divine spirit from Jerusalem to Rome. Such a portrayal has an important theological message, particularly in the aftermath of the Roman destruction of Jerusalem, that is, the manifestation of divine grace has moved from Jerusalem, the former center for the worship of G-d by Jews, to Rome, the center of the Gentile or Greco-Roman world. Such a portrayal acknowledges and affirms the destruction of Jerusalem as an act of G-d's mercy insofar at it portends the salvation of all humankind. Once again, G-d is defended from charges of infidelity, unrighteousness, absence, and impotence in relation to the destruction of Jerusalem. The destruction of Jerusalem instead emerges as an act of divine grace to bring about the

salvation of all humankind. As in Matthew, Jews failed to grasp the significance of such a divine act of mercy and compassion and therefore suffer
the consequences for failing to realize that the center of the world—and
divine activity in that world—has now shifted to Rome. Like Matthew,
Luke-Acts identifies divine purpose with the imperial oppressor of Judaism and thereby blames the victim for its victimization.

Finally, the Gospel of John serves an agenda to portray Jews as culpable for their own victimization by the Romans insofar as they fail to
recognize Christ.[4] John is generally considered the latest of the Gospels,
having been written from the mid-80s through the 90s C.E. It is also distinct both theologically and historically. The prologue of the Gospel in
John 1:1-18 identifies Christ as the *Logos* or the epistemological basis
for the created world, which thereby supplants both Greco-Roman and
Jewish epistemological models for understanding the world of creation.
John is also the most historically reliable of the Gospels insofar as it very
carefully avoids the defilement of Passover by portraying Jesus' trial and
execution immediately prior to Passover (see John 18:28—19:42). Nevertheless, the charges of Jewish betrayal of Jesus remain, and elsewhere, the
Gospel of John portrays Jesus as charging that the Jews who do not believe
in him are the sons of the devil (John 8:31-59, esp. vv. 44-45). Once again
in the aftermath of the Roman destruction of Jerusalem, the Gospel of
John defends divine righteousness and charges Jews with unbelief, that
is, once again the victims are charged with responsibility for their own
victimization.

In sum, the Gospel tradition of the New Testament enters into the
debate concerning the character of G-d in relation to the destruction of
Jerusalem and the Temple, that is, the Shoah of the first century C.E. In all
cases, the Gospels choose to defend G-d's righteousness, power, mercy,
and engagement by portraying divine self-sacrifice and compassion in
relation to the crucifixion of Jesus. Thus, the Gospel tradition posits an
element of divine vulnerability by pointing to the crucifixion of Christ.
Early Christian tradition attempts to account for this vulnerability by
developing the doctrine of the Trinity in which the Father serves as the
immutable presence of the infinite, omnipotent, and omniscient G-d,
the Son serves as the vulnerable and empathetic aspect of G-d that suffers for the sins of humanity, and the Spirit serves as the active presence
of G-d in the finite world. The task of human beings is to respond with
faith in G-d to such an act of self-sacrifice. Nevertheless, that portrayal of
divine vulnerability comes with a price. Together with the portrayal of the
crucifixion, the Gospels instead charge the Jews, the victims of Roman

236   imperialism, with failure to recognize and accept G-d's grace. Once again, the victims of Roman oppression are charged with responsibility for their own victimization.

Rabbinic Literature and Divine Responsibility for Evil

Rabbinic literature occupies an especially importance place in discussion of reading the Bible after the Shoah because it builds upon the literature of the Hebrew Bible and because it is written in the aftermath of the failure of the Zealot revolt and the destruction of the Jerusalem Temple in 66–74 C.E., the failure of the diaspora revolt against Rome in 114–117 C.E., and the failure of the Bar Kochba revolt against Rome in 132–135 C.E.[5] The failure of the three revolts ensured that Jews would be regarded with suspicion and treated as enemies of the state throughout the Roman Empire, and the horrendous casualties inflicted by the Roman army during the Bar Kochba revolt and the postwar proscription of the practice of Judaism in Judea ensured the end of Judaism as a meaningful presence in the land of Judea from the second century C.E. until modern times. Indeed, the Roman persecution of Judaism was so far-reaching after the Bar Kochba revolt that the name of Jerusalem was changed to Aelia Capitolina and the name of the land of Israel was changed to Palestine in an effort to eradicate any memory or vestiges of Jewish presence in the land of Israel. By the time the Mishnah, the first written work of rabbinic literature, was composed in ca. 200 C.E., the centers of Jewish life had shifted to Galilee, which continued to suffer under Roman rule, and Babylonia, which was ruled by the Persian Sassanian dynasty. Rabbinic literature displays a keen awareness of divine judgment and displacement from the land of Israel, and calls for the sanctification of Jewish life in accordance with the divine teachings of Torah in order to restore the destroyed Temple in Jerusalem together with Jewish life in the land of Israel at the center of creation.

In general, the rabbinic call for holy life in accordance with divine Torah presupposes the classical defense of divine righteousness, power, engagement, and fidelity that we have seen in many of the writings of the Hebrew Bible, together with the claim that human beings suffered because of their own moral failings. Again, such a view charges the victim with responsibility for its own victimization. Because G-d is all-powerful and just in rabbinic traditions, human beings bear a special measure of responsibility because they possess free will, the capacity to do what is right or what is wrong. Thus, the classical rabbinic example of the heretic, R. Elisha ben Abuyah, a previously revered sage and contemporary of R. Akiba from the time of the Bar Kochba revolt, is forever known as Aḥer, Hebrew for "another person," following his apostasy from Judaism.[6] Rabbinic literature provides a number of explanations for his apostasy, such as, Greek books of poetry would fall from his lap when he would rise from his seat in the Yeshiva lecture hall (*b. Hagigah* 15b; he was reading pagan literature), or he proclaimed "there are two powers in heaven" when he saw the angel Metatron sitting on the divine throne as he entered the divine throne room to appear before G-d (*b. Hagigah* 15a; he followed Gnosticism, which posits multiple gods). Perhaps the most telling traditions about his apostasy are those that report his lack of faith in the justice of Torah observance. In one case, Elisha ben Abuyah witnessed a man who survived after violating the command in Deut 22:7 to allow a mother bird to go free when taking her young, whereas a man who observed this command died as a result (*Deuteronomy Rabbah* 7:4). In another, he saw the tongue of R. Judah Nahtum in the mouth of a dog following his execution by the Romans and proclaimed, "the mouth that uttered pearls licks the dust" (see *y. Hagigah* 2:1, 15b; *b. Kiddushin* 39c).

Nevertheless, rabbinic literature is able to raise critical questions concerning the issue of theodicy in large measure due to its keen awareness of suffering and subjugation to foreign rule as well as to its decentralized understanding of rabbinic authority and leadership. Although G-d's power and sanctity are absolute in the rabbinic understanding, the sages were able to posit that human beings could engage G-d in conversation or debate. The Babylonian Talmud (*b. Baba Metzia* 59b) relates a story in which R. Eliezer called on heaven for support in debate with his colleagues over a point of Jewish law. Although G-d sided with R. Eliezer on the matter, his colleagues nevertheless disagreed pointing to the maxim derived from Exod 23:22, "by a majority you are to decide." G-d's response to being outvoted was to laugh and state, "My children have defeated me." Humans have free will and both the capacity and the responsibility to sanctify the world, even though G-d remains the supreme power, displaying both mercy and justice.

Rabbinic mystical literature likewise posits divine power and righteousness, but it also opens the way for debate on the matter.[7] The *Heikhalot Rabbati*, a work of merkavah mysticism from the third to sixth centuries C.E. that describes the rabbinic ascent to heaven to appear before the throne of G-d raises the question of theodicy.[8] Throughout the work, the principle of *m. Hagigah* 2:1, that only a sage who knows his own

238 knowledge may engage in the exposition of selected Torah and Haftarah passages, is associated with mysticism. Thus, *Heikhalot Rabbati* posits that such a person will know Torah thoroughly and engage in the liturgical worship of G-d, since G-d is found or manifested in the study of Torah and in prayer. The *Heikhalot Rabbati* therefore emphasizes the singing of liturgical hymns and knowledge of the secret names of the angels who guard the gates of the seven levels of heaven. It also demands intricate knowledge of Torah, by employing the finer points of a halachic argument concerning the ritual purity of the mystic, R. Nehunyah ben ha-Qanah, who must be recalled from heaven to answer questions posed during the description of his ascent. When R. Nehunyah appears before the throne of G-d, he asks why G-d allowed the Temple to be destroyed and the martyrs slain by the Romans. G-d's response upholds the value of Torah study insofar as G-d claims that the Jewish people want to study Torah, but G-d also acknowledges the possibility of divine error by carrying out such a harsh decree.[9]

Later Kabbalistic tradition goes so far as to posit evil as part of the divine personality. Thus, the Sefer ha-Zohar, a mystical commentary on the Torah written ca. 1280 C.E. by the Spanish Kabbalistic teacher Moses ben Shemtov de Leon, posits ten *sefirot* (*sĕpîrôt*) or emanations of the infinite G-d that are manifested in the world of creation, including in the personality of all human beings.[10] Among the moral *sefirot*, the emanation or quality of *ḥesed* or mercy is balanced by *geburah* (*gĕbûrâ*), "power" (for judgment). The human task is to balance the capacity for mercy with the capacity for power or evil in order to manifest the presence of the divine in the world. The sixteenth-century Kabbalistic teacher, R. Isaac Luria of Safed, likewise posits evil as an integral part of the divine personality, insofar as G-d's mercy in creating the world also releases divine evil when G-d is no longer infinite as the result of creating a finite world that was distinct from G-d.[11] Because the act of creation resulted in the shattering of the infinite divine presence, Luria posits that the task of humankind is to gather and restore the shattered pieces of the divine presence through acts of Torah designed to resanctify the world by restoring the holy divine presence. In rabbinic mystical tradition, G-d manifests evil and G-d is vulnerable. Human beings must therefore take responsibility for ensuring the sanctity and integrity of the world of creation.

In sum, rabbinic tradition holds to models of divine power, righteousness, fidelity, and engagement, although it also raises questions about such a model by positing the possibility of divine error or even evil. Human beings remain responsible for their own fates and for the sanctity of the world of creation, insofar as humans possess free will so that they may act as partners with G-d in sanctifying the world of creation. In this respect, the victims still bear responsibility for their own victimization, although they also have the capacity to influence the well-being and integrity of G-d. Such divine vulnerability heightens the responsibility and power of human beings for the welfare of the world and even of G-d.

Divine Absence and Human Choice

Although biblical literature frequently portrays G-d as righteous, all-powerful, trustworthy, and engaged in the human world, such a view is frequently contested both in relation to the modern experience of the Shoah and among the biblical books themselves. Indeed, our brief examination of postbiblical New Testament and rabbinic tradition indicates that this issue was an important concern in both early Christianity and rabbinic Judaism as well. Both traditions ultimately developed models of divine empathy and vulnerability to account for the realities of suffering in the aftermath of the Roman suppression of Judaism during the first and second centuries C.E., but they also opted to charge human beings with responsibility for the judgment inflicted on them, that is, the victims of oppression were charged with responsibility for their own victimization.

Although divine power, righteousness, fidelity, and engagement in the world are clearly the ideals of the Hebrew Bible—and early Christianity and rabbinic Judaism as well—the modern experience of the Shoah and our examination of biblical literature demonstrates that the realization of such an ideal is questionable. G-d does not always respond in times of crisis, and we are therefore frequently left on our own to face the challenges of evil in the world, whether such evil comes in the form of the Shoah or even at the personal level of death, suffering, abuse, and so forth. And yet we have also observed that the Hebrew Bible frequently posits that human beings must take responsibility for establishing holiness and righteousness in the world, even when the threat to holiness or righteousness comes from G-d. Surely, our readings of Abraham's confrontation with G-d over Sodom and Gomorrah, Moses' confrontations with G-d in the wilderness, Job's questioning of G-d's purpose in inflicting suffering, the psalmists' crying out to G-d in distress, Esther's actions to defend her people at a time of divine absence, and other examples point to such responsibility and capacity on the part of human beings. Such action on the part of human beings presupposes neither justification nor disparagement of

G-d. Like the child of an abusive parent, we must act in the aftermath of the Shoah because such action is necessary for us to rebuild and continue our lives and our roles as partners with G-d in the world of creation.

The example of Eve in the Garden of Eden provides an especially important model for us to emulate. Eve is frequently charged with sin for disobeying G-d's command not to eat of the tree of knowledge in the garden (Gen 2:15-16), and her action then becomes part of the basis for doctrine of original sin. Nevertheless, we must observe that G-d's command to Adam was given prior to the creation of Eve in Gen 2:18-24. When Eve encountered the snake in the garden in Genesis 3, a plain reading of the Genesis narrative indicates that she did not receive the command directly from G-d. Her statement to the snake in Gen 3:2-3, "We may eat of the fruit of the other trees in the garden; it is only about fruit of the tree in the middle of the garden that G-d said, 'You shall not eat of it or touch it, lest you die,'" suggests that she did not have full understanding of G-d's command, whether through confusion on her part or through miscommunication of G-d's command to her. Both Jewish and Christian tradition go to great efforts to demonstrate that she did know the command in one way or another, but such a conclusion is not evident in the plain meaning of the Genesis narrative. When Eve encountered the snake in the garden, she had been—so to speak—"born yesterday," that is, she did not possess full knowledge of the situation to make an informed decision as to how to proceed in the face of the snake's claims. Indeed, many exegetes have observed that the snake was partially right—she would not die (immediately) if she would eat the fruit and she would become like G-d knowing good and evil. Eve was faced with a competing truth claim to her understanding of G-d's command, and she was left to employ her own powers of reasoning and observation to make her choice. She made her choice based on an incomplete understanding of the situation. Unfortunately, she made the wrong choice and suffered the consequences for having done so. G-d did not appear to her prior to her choice to instruct her in proper conduct; G-d only appeared afterwards to punish her (and Adam) for her (wrong) choice. Prior to Eve's choice, G-d was absent—at least as far as Eve was concerned—and Adam did nothing to help.

In the aftermath of the Shoah, we human beings find ourselves in a situation like that of Eve. We have suffered as a result of divine absence, and we must now make choices for the future even though we do not possess full knowledge of our situation. Will G-d act in the world with power, righteousness, and fidelity? Or will G-d continue to be absent? To a degree, the question of divine engagement or absence is irrelevant. The key question for us is, How will we approach the future? Will we continue to uphold the ideals learned from G-d of power, righteousness, fidelity, and engagement in our own lives? Or will we abandon those ideals because we perceive G-d to have abandoned us? Do we recognize that perhaps G-d needs us just as much as we need G-d? We are, after all, created as partners with G-d, and our task is to assist G-d in the completion and sanctification of the world of creation. Like Eve—and countless other examples in the history of human existence—we may err in carrying out such a task, but we must nevertheless accept our own responsibility to complete and sanctify the world of creation in which we live. As Rabbi Tarphon states in the Mishnah, "You are not obligated to complete the work, but neither are you free to desist from it" (*m. Abot* 2:16).

Introduction: The Shoah and Biblical Theology

1. For discussion of the problems presented by the term *Holocaust*, see Zev Garber and Bruce Zuckerman, "Why Do We Call the Holocaust 'The Holocaust?' An Inquiry into the Psychology of Labels," *Modern Judaism* 9 (1989): 197–211, reprinted in Zev Garber, *Shoah: The Paradigmatic Genocide. Essays in Exegesis and Eisegesis* (Studies in the Shoah 8; Lanham, Md.: University Press of America, 1994), 51–67. The term *holocaust* refers to the *ʿōlâ*, "whole burnt offering" of the Temple service (Leviticus 1), which functions as part of the means by which the relationship between ancient Judaism and YHWH was maintained. Unlike Holocaust, the Hebrew term *shoah* (*šôʾâ*), "destruction," implies no redemptive or positive purpose for the murder of six million Jews in World War II.

2. For historical discussion of the Shoah, see especially Lucy S. Dawidowicz, *The War Against the Jews, 1933–1945* (New York: Holt, Rinehart and Winston; Philadelphia: Jewish Publication Society, 1975); Yehuda Bauer, *A History of the Holocaust* (New York: F. Watts, 1982); Martin Gilbert, *The Holocaust: A History of the Jews of Europe during the Second World War* (New York: Holt, Rinehart, and Winston, 1985).

3. For discussion of the history of anti-semitism, see especially Shmuel Almog, ed., *Antisemitism Through the Ages* (Oxford: Pergamon Press, 1988).

4. For discussion of the Shoah in relation to the church and Christian theology, see especially Clark M. Williamson, *A Guest in the House of Israel: Post-Holocaust Church Theology* (Louisville: Westminster John Knox, 1993); Stephen R. Haynes, *Prospects for a Post-Holocaust Theology* (Atlanta: Scholars Press, 1991).

5. For the history of Christian anti-semitism, see the very readable account by James Carroll, *Constantine's Sword: The Church and the Jews* (Boston and New

244   York: Houghton Mifflin, 2001); cf. Daniel Jonah Goldhagen, *A Moral Reckoning: The Role of the Catholic Church in the Holocaust and its Unfulfilled Duty of Repair* (New York: Knopf, 2002).

6. See Jules Isaac, *The Teaching of Contempt: Christian Roots of Anti-Semitism* (New York: Holt, Rinehart, and Winston, 1964); Rosemary Radford Ruether, *Faith and Fratricide: The Theological Roots of Anti-Semitism* (Eugene, Ore.: Wipf and Stock, 1997).

7. For surveys and studies of theological discussion of the Shoah in Jewish thought, see especially Steven T. Katz, *Post-Holocaust Dialogues: Critical Studies in Modern Jewish Thought* (New York and London: New York University Press, 1985); Dan Cohn-Sherbok, *Holocaust Theology* (London: Lamp Press, 1989); Zachary Braiterman, *(G-d) After Auschwitz: Tradition and Change in Post-Holocaust Jewish Thought* (Princeton: Princeton University Press, 1998); Michael L. Morgan, *Beyond Auschwitz: Post-Holocaust Jewish Thought in America* (Oxford and New York: Oxford University Press, 2001). For discussion of the Shoah in Christian thought, see Williamson, *A Guest in the House of Israel*; Haynes, *Prospects for a Post-Holocaust Theology*; Alice L. Eckardt and A. Roy Eckardt, *Long Night's Journey into Day: A Revised Retrospective on the Holocaust* (Detroit: Wayne State University Press, 1988); Charlotte Klein, *Anti-Judaism in Christian Theology* (Minneapolis: Fortress Press, 1978); Franklin Littell, *The Crucifixion of the Jews: The Failure of Christians to Understand the Jewish Experience* (Macon, Ga.: Mercer University Press, 1986).

8. Note, however, that Barth continued to view Judaism from a classical Christian supersessionist perspective despite his calls for the end of Jewish suffering (see Williamson, *A Guest*, 119–22). Bonhoeffer viewed Jews as cursed and called for their conversion early in his career, and did not entirely move away from this position in later life (see Stephen R. Haynes, *The Bonhoeffer Legacy: Post-Holocaust Perspectives* [Minneapolis: Fortress Press, 2006]).

9. For discussion of the Arab expulsions of Jews in relation to the creation of modern Israel, see Norman A. Stillman, *Jews of Arab Lands in Modern Times* (Philadelphia: Jewish Publication Society, 2003), 141–76; Bernard Lewis, *The Jews of Islam* (Princeton: Princeton University Press, 1984), 154–91; Howard M. Sachar, *A History of Israel from the Rise of Zionism to Our Time* (New York: Knopf, 2003), 396–403; Martin Gilbert, *Israel: A History* (New York: William Morrow, 1998), 250–78.

10. See Abraham Joshua Heschel, *Man Is Not Alone: A Philosophy of Religion* (Philadelphia: Jewish Publication Society, 1951); *G-d in Search of Man: A Philosophy of Judaism* (New York: Meridian and Jewish Publication Society, 1955); *The Prophets* (Philadelphia: Jewish Publication Society, 1962); *Die Prophetie* (Krakow: Nakladem Polskiej Akademji Umiejetnosci, 1936). For a bibliographical study of Heschel's early life, see Edward K. Kaplan and Samuel H. Dresner, *Abraham Joshua Heschel: Prophetic Witness* (New Haven: Yale University Press, 1998).

11. Leo Baeck, *This People Israel: The Meaning of Jewish Existence* (New York: Holt, Rinehart, and Winston, 1965).

12. Martin Buber, *I and Thou* (New York: Scribner's, 1970).

13. Martin Buber, *The Eclipse of G-d: Studies in the Relation between Religion and Philosophy* (New York: Harper & Row, 1952).

14. Ignaz Maybaum, *The Face of G-d After Auschwitz* (Amsterdam: Polak and Van Glennep, 1965).

15. Irving Greenberg, "Cloud of Smoke, Pillar of Fire," in *Auschwitz: Beginning of a New Era?* (New York: KTAV, 1977), 23.

16. Richard L. Rubenstein, *After Auschwitz: Radical Theology and Contemporary Judaism* (Indianapolis: Bobbs-Merrill, 1966).

17. Ibid., 223.

18. Emil L. Fackenheim, *G-d's Presence in History: Jewish Affirmations and Philosophical Reflections* (New York: New York University Press, 1970).

19. Eliezer Berkovits, *Faith after the Holocaust* (New York: KTAV, 1973).

20. Elie Wiesel, *Night* (New York: Random House, 1973).

21. Elie Wiesel, *Dawn* (New York: Hill and Wang, 1961).

22. Elie Wiesel, *The Accident* (New York: Hill and Wang, 1962).

23. Elie Wiesel, *The Trial of G-d* (New York: Random House, 1977).

24. Arthur A. Cohen, *The Tremendum: A Theological Interpretation of the Holocaust* (New York: Crossroad, 1981).

25. Rudolf Otto, *The Idea of the Holy: An Inquiry into the Non-Rational Factor in the Idea of the Divine and its Relation to the Rational* (London: Oxford University Press, 1970).

26. David R. Blumenthal, *Facing the Abusing G-d: A Theology of Protest* (Louisville: Westminster John Knox, 1993).

27. For current overviews concerning the field of Old Testament theology, see John H. Hayes and Frederick Prussner, *Old Testament Theology: Its History and Its Development* (Atlanta: John Knox, 1985); Gerhard Hasel, *Old Testament Theology: Basic Issues in the Current Debate* (Grand Rapids: Eerdmans, 1991); Leo G. Perdue, *The Collapse of History: Reconstructing Old Testament Theology* (OBT; Minneapolis: Fortress Press, 1994); idem, *Reconstructing Old Testament Theology: After the Collapse of History* (OBT; Minneapolis: Fortress Press, 2005). For discussion of the field of Jewish biblical theology, see Marvin A. Sweeney, "The Emerging Field of Jewish Biblical Theology," *Academic Approaches to Teaching Jewish Studies*, ed. Z. Garber (Lanham, Md.: University Press of America, 2000), 84–105; idem, "Reconceiving the Paradigms of Old Testament Theology in the Post-Shoah Period," *Biblical Interpretation* 6 (1998): 142–61.

28. Walter Eichrodt, *Theology of the Old Testament*, 2 vols. (OTL; Philadelphia: Westminster, 1961–1967).

29. Ibid., 1:26.

30. Gerhard von Rad, *Old Testament Theology*, 2 vols. (New York: Harper & Row, 1962–1965).

31. For discussion of Esther, see my "Absence of G-d and Human Responsibility in the Book of Esther," in *Reading the Hebrew Bible for a New Millennium: Form, Concept, and Theological Perspective, Volume 2: Exegetical and Theological Studies,* ed., W. Kim et al. (Harrisburg: Trinity Press International, 2000), 264–75.

32. See n. 6 above.

33. See n. 6 above; Rosemary Radford Ruether and Herman J. Ruether, *The Wrath of Jonah: The Crisis of Religious Nationalism in the Israeli-Palestinian Conflict* (New York: Harper & Row, 1989). For more credible portrayals of modern Israeli history, see the volumes by Sachar and Gilbert cited in n. 9 above and Benny Morris, *Righteous Victims: A History of the Zionist-Arab Conflict, 1881–2001* (New York: Vintage, 2001).

34. See n. 4 above.

35. Katharina von Kellenbach, *Anti-Judaism in Feminist Religious Writings* (Atlanta: Scholars Press, 1994).

36. Tania Oldenhage, *Parables for Our Time: Rereading New Testament Scholarship after the Holocaust* (New York: Oxford University Press, 2002).

37. Jon Levenson, *Creation and the Persistence of Evil: The Jewish Drama of Divine Omnipotence* (New York: Harper & Row, 1988).

38. Jon Levenson, "Why Jews Are Not Interested in Biblical Theology," in *The Hebrew Bible, the Old Testament, and Historical Criticism: Jews and Christians in Biblical Studies* (Louisville: Westminster John Knox, 1993), 33–61, 165–70, originally published in J. Neusner, et al,, eds., *Judaic Perspectives on Ancient Israel* (Philadelphia: Fortress Press, 1987), 281–307.

39. Emil Fackenheim, *The Jewish Bible after the Holocaust: A Rereading* (Bloomington: Indiana University Press, 1990).

40. Walter Brueggemann, *Theology of the Old Testament: Testimony, Dispute, Advocacy* (Minneapolis: Fortress Press, 1997).

41. Ibid., 328.

42. Ibid., 329.

43. Rolf Rendtorff, *Theologie des Alten Testaments. Eine kanonischer Entwurf* (Neukirchen-Vluyn: Neukirchener, 1999-2001); ET, *The Canonical Hebrew Bible: A Theology of the Old Testament* (Leiden: Deo, 2005).

44. Tod Linafelt, ed., *Strange Fire: Reading the Bible after the Holocaust* (New York: New York University Press; Sheffield: Sheffield Academic Press, 2000). A companion volume on the New Testament has now appeared, Tod Linafelt, ed., *A Shadow of Glory: Reading the New Testament after the Holocaust* (New York and London: Routledge, 2002).

45. Katheryn Pfisterer Darr, "Ezekiel," in *The New Interpreter's Bible* (hereafter *NIB*), ed. L. Keck, et al. (Nashville: Abingdon, 2001), 6:1073–607; Kathleen M. O'Connor, "Lamentations," in *NIB*, 6:1011–072.

46. James L. Crenshaw, *Defending G-d: Biblical Responses to the Problem of Evil* (New York: Oxford University Press, 2005).

1. Abraham and the Problem of Divine Fidelity

1. For discussion of the history of research on the Pentateuch, see Ernest Nicholson, *The Pentateuch in the Twentieth Century: The Legacy of Julius Wellhausen*

(Oxford: Oxford University Press, 1998); A. De Pury and T. Römer, "Le pentateuch en question. Position du problème et brève histoire de la recherché," in *Le Pentateuch en Question*, ed. A. De Pury and T. Römer (Geneva: Labor et Fides, 1989), 9–80; Joseph Blenkinsopp, *The Pentateuch: An Introduction to the First Five Books of the Bible* (Garden City, N.Y.: Doubleday, 1992); R. Norman Whybray, *Introduction to the Pentateuch* (Grand Rapids: Eerdmans, 1995); Antony F. Campbell and Mark A. O'Brien, *Sources of the Pentateuch: Texts, Introductions, Annotations* (Minneapolis: Fortress Press, 1993), esp. 1–20. For orientations to the discussion of Genesis, see Ronald Hendel, "Genesis, Book of," *ABD* 2:933–41; John J. Scullion, "Genesis, The Narrative of," *ABD* 2:941–62; David M. Carr, *Reading the Fractures of Genesis: Historical and Literary Approaches* (Louisville: Westminster John Knox, 1996), 3–40.

2. See esp. the introduction to Gunkel's commentary, Hermann Gunkel, *Genesis*, trans. M. Biddle (Macon, Ga.: Mercer University Press, 1997), vii–lxxxvi.

3. E.g., John Van Seters, *Abraham in History and Tradition* (New Haven: Yale University Press, 1975); H. H. Schmid, *Der sogenannte J-hwist: Beobachtungen und Fragen zur Pentateuchforschung* (Zürich: Theologischer Verlag, 1976).

4. See Rolf Rendtorff, *The Problem of the Process of Transmission in the Pentateuch*, trans. J. J. Scullion (JSOTSup 89; Sheffield: JSOT Press, 1990); Erhard Blum, *Die Komposition des Vätergeshchichte* (WMANT 57; Neukirchen-Vluyn: Neukirchener Verlag, 1984); Suzanne Boorer, *The Promise of the Land as Oath: A Key to the Formation of the Pentateuch* (BZAW 205; Berlin and New York: Walter de Gruyter, 1992).

5. For methodological studies, see Robert Alter, *The Art of Biblical Narrative* (New York: Basic, 1981); Meir Sternberg, *The Poetics of Biblical Narrative: Ideological Literature and the Drama of Reading* (Bloomington: Indiana University Press, 1985).

6. For redaction-critical analysis, see esp. George W. Coats, *Genesis, with an Introduction to Narrative Literature* (FOTL 1; Grand Rapids: Eerdmans, 1983); Carr, *Reading the Fractures*; for synchronic analysis, see esp. D. J. Clines, *The Theme of the Pentateuch* (JSOTSup 10; Sheffield: JSOT Press, 1982); cf. R. N. Whybray, *The Making of the Pentateuch: A Methodological Study* (JSOTSup 53; Sheffield: JSOT Press, 1987).

7. See W. Lee Humphreys, *The Character of G-d in the Book of Genesis: A Narrative Appraisal* (Louisville: Westminster John Knox, 2001); cf. Tammi J. Schneider, *Sarah: Mother of Nations* (New York: Continuum, 2004).

8. "The Priestly Work," Frank Moore Cross Jr., *Canaanite Myth and Hebrew Epic* (Cambridge, Mass.: Harvard University Press, 1973), 293–325.

9. See now Moshe Weinfeld, "Deuteronomy, Book of," *ABD* 2:168–83; idem, *Deuteronomy* (AB 5; Garden City, N.Y.: Doubleday, 1991), 1–122; Marvin A. Sweeney, *King Josiah of Judah: The Lost Messiah of Israel* (New York: Oxford University Press, 2001), 137–69.

10. I am indebted to Matthew Thomas, Ph.D. student in Hebrew Bible at Claremont Graduate University, who pointed out the significance of Num 3:1 (see

his Claremont dissertation, *These Are the Generations: Identity, Promise, and the Toledoth Formulae* [Ph.D. dissertation; Claremont Graduate University, 2006]); see also Sven Tengström, *Die Toledotformel und die literarische Struktur der priesterlichen Erweiterungsschicht im Pentateuch* (ConBibOT 17; Uppsala: Gleerup, 1981), 54–59.

11. For discussion of the promise of land to the patriarchs, see Claus Westermann, *The Promises to the Fathers: Studies on the Patriarchal Narratives* (Philadelphia: Fortress Press, 1980); see also Harry M. Orlinsky, "The Biblical Concept of the Land of Israel: Cornerstone of the Covenant Between G-d and Israel," *The Land of Israel: Jewish Perspectives*, ed. L. Hoffman (Notre Dame: University of Notre Dame Press, 1986), 27–64.

12. Cf. Schneider, *Sarah*, 33.

13. Cf. Fokkelien Van Dijk-Hemmes, "Sarai's Exile: A Gender-Motivated Reading of Genesis 12:10-13:2," *A Feminist Companion to Genesis 2*, ed. A. Brenner (Sheffield: Sheffield Academic Press, 1997), 222–34. One of the more despicable interpretations of Abram's act holds that he sold Sarah for profit, but such an interpretation draws upon anti-semitic characterizations of Jews as greedy and lacking any values except in profits.

14. See Nahum Sarna, *Understanding Genesis: The Heritage of Biblical Israel* (New York: Schocken, 1970), 102–03; Ephraim A. Speiser, *Genesis* (AB 1; Garden City, N.Y.: Doubleday, 1964), 91–94.

15. See Genesis 16, which relates the birth of Abram's son, Ishmael, to Sarah's Egyptian handmaiden, Hagar. Note also that the Abraham/Sarah narratives ultimately pass the covenant on to Isaac and not to the Egyptian-born Ishmael. This stands in contrast to the birth of Joseph's two sons, Manasseh and Ephraim, to his Egyptian wife, Asenath, in Gen 41:50-52. Both sons are eventually adopted by Jacob in Genesis 48. Nevertheless, it is striking that Abraham, who is often identified in relation to Judean interests (see Ronald E. Clements, *Abraham and David* [SBT 2/5; London: SCM, 1967]), avoids passing his inheritance on to Egyptian-born offspring, whereas Joseph, the ancestor of the major tribes of the northern kingdom of Israel, does not.

16. See Moshe Weinfeld, "Tithe," *Encyclopaedia Judaica* 15:1156–62.

17. For detailed discussion of Genesis 15, see my essay, "Form Criticism," in *To Each Its Own Meaning: Biblical Criticisms and Their Application*, ed. S. L. McKenzie and S. R. Haynes (Louisville: Westminster John Knox, 1999), 58–89.

18. For discussion of sacrifices in relation to ancient Near Eastern treaties, see Moshe Weinfeld, "The Covenant of Grant in the OT and in the Ancient Near East," *JAOS* 90 (1970): 184–203.

19. Sarna, *Understanding Genesis*, 127–29; Speiser, *Genesis*, 119–21.

20. See my essay, "Isaiah and Theodicy after the Shoah," in *Strange Fire: Reading the Bible after the Holocaust*, ed. T. Linafelt (Sheffield: Sheffield Academic Press, 2000), 208–19, which raises similar questions in relation to Isaiah's vision of YHWH in Isaiah 6.

2. Moses and the Problem of Divine Violence

1. For discussion of Moses, see D. M. Beegle, "Moses," *ABD* 4:909–18; George W. Coats, *Moses: Heroic Man, Man of G-d* (JSOTSup 57; Sheffield: Sheffield Academic Press, 1988).

2. For an overview of discussion concerning the death of Moses, see Jacob Milgrom, *Numbers* (JPS Torah Commentary; Philadelphia and New York: Jewish Publication Society, 1990), 448–56.

3. For discussion of the wilderness murmuring or rebellion traditions, see esp. George W. Coats, *Rebellion in the Wilderness: The Murmuring Motif in the Wilderness Traditions of the Old Testament* (Nashville: Abingdon, 1968); cf. Volkmar Fritz, *Israel in der Wüste. Traditionsgeschichtliche Untersuchung der Wüstenüberlieferung des J-hwisten* (Marburg: N. G. Elwert, 1970); Dennis T. Olson, *The Death of the Old and the Birth of the New: The Framework of Numbers and the Pentateuch* (BJS 71; Chico, Calif.: Scholars Press, 1985); Won W. Lee, *Punishment and Forgiveness in Israel's Migratory Campaign* (Grand Rapids: Eerdmans, 2003).

4. For discussion of Num 20:1-13, see Milgrom, *Numbers*, 163–67; Baruch A. Levine, *Numbers 1–20* (AB 4; Garden City, N.Y.: Doubleday, 1993), 483–91; Rolf P. Knierim and George W. Coats, *Numbers* (FOTL 4; Grand Rapids: Eerdmans, 2005), 225–29; Coats, *Rebellion in the Wilderness*, 71–82.

5. Milgrom, *Numbers*, 448–56.

6. Dennis T. Olson, *Deuteronomy and the Death of Moses: A Theological Reading* (OBT; Minneapolis: Fortress Press, 1994), esp. 17–22.

7. For discussion of the formal structure of this passage, see also Knierim and Coats, *Numbers*, 225–28; Lee, *Punishment and Forgiveness*, 152–54.

8. For discussion of Exod 17:1-7, see Nahum Sarna, *Exodus* (JPS Torah Commentary; Philadelphia and New York: Jewish Publication Society, 1991), 93–94; Brevard S. Childs, *The Book of Exodus: A Critical, Theological Commentary* (OTL; Philadelphia: Westminster, 1974), 305–09; George W. Coats, *Exodus 1–18* (FOTL 2A; Grand Rapids: Eerdmans, 1999), 54–60; idem, *Rebellion in the Wilderness*, 53–71; William H. Propp, *Exodus 1–18* (AB 2; Garden City, N.Y.: Doubleday, 1999), 601–13; Umberto Cassuto, *A Commentary on the Book of Exodus* (Jerusalem: Magnes, 1967), 89–91.

9. For discussion of the formal structure of Exod 17:1-7, see also Coats, *Exodus 1–18*, 54–60.

10. For discussion of the hardening of Pharaoh's heart, see esp. Childs, *The Book of Exodus*, 170–75; Cassuto, *Exodus*, 55–57.

11. For discussion of Exodus 32–34, see Sarna, *Exodus*, 202–22; Childs, *The Book of Exodus*, 553–624; Coats, *Rebellion in the Wilderness*, 184–91; Cassuto, *Exodus*, 407–51; Marvin A. Sweeney, "The Wilderness Traditions of the Pentateuch: A Reassessment of their Function and Intent in Relation to Exodus 32–34," *Society of Biblical Literature 1989 Seminar Papers*, ed. David J. Lull (Atlanta: Scholars Press, 1989), 291–99.

12. For detailed discussion, see Sweeney, "The Wilderness Traditions," 291–99.

13. For discussion of the Josianic edition of the Deuteronomistic History, see Marvin A. Sweeney, *King Josiah of Judah: The Lost Messiah of Israel* (New York: Oxford University Press, 2001), 21–177.

14. For discussion of Numbers, see Milgrom, *Numbers*; Levine, *Numbers 1–20*; idem, *Numbers 21–36* (AB 4A; Garden City, N.Y.: Doubleday, 2000); Knierim and Coats, *Numbers*; Olson, *The Death of the Old*; Lee, *Punishment and Forgiveness*.

15. Cf. Knierim and Coats, *Numbers*, 9–26; Lee, *Punishment and Forgiveness*, 73–119; Olson, *The Death of the Old*, 31–125.

16. For discussion of the structural role of Num 3:1 within the book of Numbers, see Matthew A. Thomas, *These Are the Generations: Identity, Promise, and the Toledot Formula* (Ph.D. dissertation; Claremont Graduate University, 2006).

17. See Milgrom, *Numbers*, 76–93; Levine, *Numbers 1–20*, 303–28; Knierim and Coats, *Numbers*, 148–78; Lee, *Punishment and Forgiveness*, 123–29.

18. See Milgrom, *Numbers*, 93–99; Levine, *Numbers 1–20*, 328–33; Knierim and Coats, *Numbers*, 178–82; Lee, *Punishment and Forgiveness*, 129–31.

19. Judith R. Baskin, *Pharaoh's Counselers: Job, Jethro, and Balaam in Rabbinic and Patristic Tradition* (BJS 47; Chico, Calif.: Scholars Press, 1983), 45–75.

20. See Milgrom, *Numbers*, 99–117; Levine, *Numbers 1–20*, 347–81; Knierim and Coats, *Numbers*, 183–94; Coats, *Rebellion in the Wilderness*, 137–56; Lee, *Punishment and Forgiveness*, 131–35; Olson, *The Death of the Old*, 129–52.

21. See Milgrom, *Numbers*, 117–63; Levine, *Numbers 1–20*, 385–479; Knierim and Coats, *Numbers*, 194–229; Coats, *Rebellion in the Wilderness*, 156–84; Lee, *Punishment and Forgiveness*, 135–52.

22. See Milgrom, *Numbers*, 169–72; Levine, *Numbers 1–20*, 494–95; Levine, *Numbers 21–36*, 79–85; Knierim and Coats, *Numbers*, 233–37; Lee, *Punishment and Forgiveness*, 156–58.

23. See Milgrom, *Numbers*, 173–84; Levine, *Numbers 21–36*, 85–133; Knierim and Coats, *Numbers*, 237–46; Lee, *Punishment and Forgiveness*, 158–66.

24. See Milgrom, *Numbers*, 211–18; Levine, *Numbers 21–36*, 279–303; Knierim and Coats, *Numbers*, 263–66; Lee, *Punishment and Forgiveness*, 173–75.

25. See Milgrom, *Numbers*, 233–36; Levine, *Numbers 21–36*, 348–61; Knierim and Coats, *Numbers*, 276–78; Lee, *Punishment and Forgiveness*, 179–81.

3. The Question of Theodicy in the Historical Books: Jeroboam, Manasseh, and Josiah

1. For introductions to the historical literature, see Richard D. Nelson, *The Historical Books* (IBT; Nashville: Abingdon, 1998); Antony F. Campbell, *Joshua to Chronicles: An Introduction* (Louisville: Westminster John Knox, 2004).

2. Martin Noth, *Überlieferungsgeschichtliche Studien* (3d ed.; Darmstadt: Wissenschaftliche Buchgesellschaft, 1967), 1–110; ET, *The Deuteronomistic History* (JSOTSup 15; Sheffield: JSOT Press, 1981).

3. For overviews of research, see especially, Marvin A. Sweeney, *King Josiah of Judah: The Lost Messiah of Israel* (New York: Oxford University Press, 2001),

3–32; Steven L. McKenzie, "Deuteronomistic History," *ABD* 2:160–68; Thomas Römer and Albert de Pury, "L'historiographie deutéronomiste (HD): Histoire de la recherché et enjeux du débat" in *Israël construit son histoire. L'historiographie deutéronomiste à la lumière des recherches récentes*, ed. A. de Pury et al. (Geneva: Labor et Fides, 1996), 9–120.

4. Rudolph Smend, "Die Gesetz und Völker: Ein Beitrag zur deuteronomistischen Redaktionsgeschichte," in *Probleme biblischer Theologie*, ed. H. W. Wolff (Munich: Chr. Kaiser, 1971), 494–509; Walter Dietrich, *Prophetie und Geschichte* (FRLANT 108; Göttingen: Vandenhoeck & Ruprecht, 1972).

5. Frank Moore Cross Jr., "The Themes of the Books of Kings and the Structure of the Deuteronomistic History," in *Canaanite Myth and Hebrew Epic* (Cambridge: Harvard University Press, 1973), 274–89; Richard D. Nelson, *The Double Redaction of the Deuteronomistic History* (JSOTSup 18; Sheffield: JSOT Press, 1981); Gary N. Knoppers, *Two Nations under G-d: The Deuteronomistic History of Solomon and the Dual Monarchies* (HSM 52–53; Atlanta: Scholars Press, 1993–94); Sweeney, *King Josiah of Judah*, 21–177.

6. Noth, *Überlieferungsgeshichtliche Studien*, 110–217; ET, *The Chronicler's History* (JSOTSup 50; Sheffield: JSOT Press, 1987).

7. H. G. M. Williamson, "Introduction," in Noth, *The Chronicler's History*, 11–26; Ralph W. Klein, "Chronicles, Book of 1–2," *ABD* 1:992–1002.

8. Sara Japhet, "The Supposed Common Authorship of Chronicles and Ezra-Nehemiah Investigated Anew," *VT* 18 (1968): 330–31; idem, *I & II Chronicles: A Commentary* (OTL; Louisville: Westminster John Knox, 1993), 3–7.

9. E.g., Andrew G. Vaughn, *Theology, History, and Archaeology in the Chronicler's Account of Hezekiah* (ABS 4; Atlanta: Scholars Press, 1999).

10. E.g., Sara Japhet, *The Ideology of the Book of Chronicles and Its Place in Biblical Thought* (BEATAJ; Frankfurt: Peter Lang, 1989); William M. Schniedewind, *The Word of G-d in Transition: From Prophet to Exegete in the Second Temple Period* (JSOTSup 197; Sheffield: Sheffield Academic Press, 1995).

11. E.g., Marvin A. Sweeney, "King Manasseh of Judah and the Problem of Theodicy in the Deuteronomistic History," in *Good Kings and Bad Kings*, ed. Lester L. Grabbe (JSOTSup 393; London and New York: T & T Clark, 2005), 264–78.

12. For discussion of the DtrH presentation of Jeroboam ben Nebat, see esp. Cross, "The Themes of the Books of Kings"; Werner Lemke, "The Way of Obedience: 1 Kings 13 and the Structure of the Deuteronomistic History," in *Magnalia Dei/The Mighty Acts of G-d*, ed. F. M. Cross et al. (Garden City, N.Y.: Doubleday, 1976), 301–26.

13. George W. Coats, *Genesis, with an Introduction to Narrative Literature* (FOTL 1; Grand Rapids: Eerdmans, 1983), 206–09.

14. Melanie Köhlmoos, *Bet-El—Erinnerungen an dine Stadt. Perspectiven der alttestamentlichen Bet-El Überleiferung* (FAT; Tübingen: Mohr Siebeck, 2006).

15. Yairah Amit, "Hidden Polemic in the Conquest of Dan: Judges xvii-xviii," *VT* 40 (1990): 4–20.

16. The MT inserts a *nun* into the name Moshe so that the name Jonathan ben Gershom ben Moshe/Moses becomes Jonathan ben Gershom ben Manasseh, apparently to identify Jonathan as a descendant of Judah's most wicked king (see

Tammi J. Schneider, *Judges* [Berit Olam; Collegeville, Minn.: Liturgical Press, 2000], 242–43).

17. Cf. Mordechai Cogan, *1 Kings* (AB 10; Garden City, N.Y.: Doubleday, 2001), 358.

18. Shmaryahu Talmon, "The Calendar Reckoning of the Sect from the Judaean Desert," in *Aspects of the Dead Sea Scrolls* (ScrHier 4; Jerusalem: Magnes, 1958), 162–99.

19. Moshe Elat, "The Economic Relations of the Neo-Assyrian Empire with Egypt," *JAOS* 98 (1978): 20–34.

20. In addition to Sweeney, "King Manasseh," see Lester L. Grabbe, "The Kingdom of Judah from Sennacherib's Invasion to the Fall of Jerusalem: If We Had Only the Bible . . ." in *Good Kings and Bad Kings*, 78–122, and Francesca Stavrakopoulou, "The Blackballing of Manasseh," in *Good Kings and Bad Kings*, 248-263.

21. For discussion of Josiah's reform, see Sweeney, *King Josiah of Judah*.

22. See Marvin A. Sweeney, *1 and 2 Kings: A Commentary* (OTL; Louisville: Westminster John Knox, forthcoming, 2007), 457; 469-70.

23. See Cross, "The Themes of the Books of Kings"; Nelson, *The Double Redaction*; Knoppers, *Two Kingdoms under G-d*; Sweeney, *King Josiah of Judah*.

24. For discussion of the ChrH account of Manasseh's reign, see esp. Japhet, *1 and 2 Chronicles*, 999–1014; Sweeney, "King Manasseh."

25. See Japhet, *1 and 2 Chronicles*, 1002.

26. E.g., Vaughn, *Theology, History, and Archaeology*.

27. For historical overview, see Amélie Kuhrt, *The Ancient Near East c. 3000-330 BC* (London and New York: Routledge, 1998) 2:499–501; A. K. Grayson, *Cambridge Ancient History 3/2*, ed. John Boardman, et al. (Cambridge: Cambridge University Press, 1991), 147–54.

28. For discussion of Josiah's reign, see Sweeney, *King Josiah of Judah*.

29. See Grayson, CAH 3/2, 142–61, 677–747, Kuhrt, *The Ancient Near East* 2:634–44.

30. Gerhard von Rad, *Old Testament Theology*, 2 vols. (New York: Harper & Row, 1962–65), 1:348–50.

4. Isaiah's Question to G-d

1. See esp. Craig A. Evans, "From Gospel to Gospel: The Function of Isaiah in the New Testament," *Writing and Reading the Scroll of Isaiah: Studies of an Interpretive Tradition*, ed. C. C. Broyles and C. A. Evans (VTSup 70/2; Leiden: Brill, 1997), 651–91.

2. For full discussion of the *haftarot*, see now Michael Fishbane, *Haftarot* (JPS Bible Commentary; Philadelphia: Jewish Publication Society, 2002).

3. For modern critical discussion on Isaiah, see Christopher R. Seitz, William Millar, and Richard J. Clifford, "Isaiah, Book of," in *ABD* 3:472–507; Marvin A. Sweeney, "The Book of Isaiah in Recent Research," *CR:BS* 1 (1993): 141–62; idem, "Reevaluating Isaiah 1-39 in Recent Critical Research," *CR:BS* 4 (1996): 79–113.

4. Marvin A. Sweeney, "On the Road to Duhm: Isaiah in Nineteenth-Century Critical Scholarship," in *As Those Who Are Taught: The Interpretation of Isaiah from the LXX to the SBL*, ed. C. M. McGinnis and P. K. Tull (SBLSym 27; Atlanta: Society of Biblical Literature, 2006), 243–61.

5. See esp. Peter R. Ackroyd, "Isaiah 36–39: Structure and Function," in *Studies in the Religious Tradition of the Old Testament* (London: SCM, 1987), 105–20; idem, "An Interpretation of the Babylonian Exile: A Study of II Kings 20 and Isaiah 38–39," in *Studies*, 152–71.

6. In addition to the works cited in Sweeney, "The Book of Isaiah," see H. G. M. Williamson, *The Book Called Isaiah: Deutero-Isaiah's Role in Composition and Redaction* (Oxford: Clarendon, 1994); Roy F. Melugin and Marvin A. Sweeney, eds., *New Visions of Isaiah* (JSOTSup 214; Sheffield: Sheffield Academic, 1996); Thomas L. LeClerc, *YHWH Is Exalted in Justice: Solidarity and Conflict in Isaiah* (Minneapolis: Fortress Press, 2001).

7. For discussion of the structure analysis presented here, see Marvin A. Sweeney, *Isaiah 1–39, with an Introduction to Prophetic Literature* (FOTL 16; Grand Rapids: Eerdmans, 1996), 31–62; idem, *The Prophetic Literature* (IBT; Nashville: Abingdon, 2005), 45–54.

8. Ronald E. Clements, "Beyond Tradition History: Deutero-Isaiah's Development of First Isaiah's Themes," in *Old Testament Prophecy: From Oracles to Canon* (Louisville: Westminster John Knox, 1996), 78–92; idem, "The Unity of the Book of Isaiah," in *Old Testament Prophecy*, 93–104; Odil Hannes Steck, *Bereitete Heimkehr. Jesaja 35 als redaktionelle Brücke zwischen dem Ersten und dem Zweiten Jesaja* (SBS 121; Stuttgart: Katholisches Bibelwerk, 1985).

9. Marvin A. Sweeney, "Isaiah and Theodicy after the Shoah," in *Strange Fire: Reading the Bible after the Holocaust*, ed. T. Linafelt (BibSem 71; Sheffield: Sheffield Academic Press, 2000), 208–19.

10. Eliezer Berkovits, *Faith After the Holocaust* (New York: KTAV, 1973).

11. Mordecai Kaplan, "Isaiah 6:1-11," *JBL* 45 (1926): 251–59; Rolf Knierim, "The Vocation of Isaiah," *VT* 18 (1968): 47–68; Rolf Rendtorff, "Isaiah 6 in the Framework of the Composition of the Book," in *Canon and Theology: Overtures to an Old Testament Theology* (OBT; Minneapolis: Fortress Press, 1993), 170–80; Sweeney, *Isaiah 1–39*, 132–42.

12. Victor Hurowitz, "Isaiah's Impure Lips and their Purification in Light of Akkadian Sources," *HUCA* 60 (1989): 39–89.

13. See esp. Ackroyd, "Isaiah 36–39."

14. Sweeney, *Isaiah 1–39*, 454–511.

15. Moshe Weinfeld, "Covenant, Davidic," in *IDBSup*, 188–92; idem, "Zion and Jerusalem as Religious and Political Capital: Ideology and Utopia," in *The Poet and the Historian: Essays in Literary and Historical Biblical Criticism*, ed. R. E. Friedman (HSS 26; Chico, Calif.: Scholars Press, 1983), 75–115.

16. See Marvin A. Sweeney, "The Reconceptualization of the Davidic Covenant in Isaiah," in *Studies in the Book of Isaiah. Festschrift for W. A. M. Beuken*, ed. J. van Ruiten and M. Vervenne (BETL 132; Leuven: Peeters, 1997), 41–61; idem, "On Multiple Settings in the Book of Isaiah," in *Form and Intertextuality in*

Prophetic and Apocalyptic Literature (FAT 45; Tübingen: Mohr Siebeck, 2005), 28–35.

17. Sweeney, *Isaiah 1–39*, 175–88.

18. Marvin A. Sweeney, "On *ûměśôś* in Isaiah 8:6," in *Form and Intertextuality*, 36–45; idem, "Prophetic Exegesis in Isaiah 65–66," *Form and Intertextuality*, 46–62.

19. Although many argue that Isa 66:18-24 indicates that priests and Levites will be chosen from among the nations that return Jewish exiles to Zion, Brooks Schramm, *The Opponents of Third Isaiah: Reconstructing the Cultic History of the Restoration* (JSOTSup 193; Sheffield: Sheffield Academic Press, 1995), 171–73, demonstrates that they are to be chosen from the returned exiles.

5. Jeremiah's Struggle with His Divine Commission

1. For discussion of Jeremiah, see Jack Lundbom, "Jeremiah, Book of," *ABD* 3:707–21; Joseph Blenkinsopp, *A History of Prophecy* (Louisville: Westminster John Knox, 1996), 129–47; David L. Petersen, *The Prophetic Literature* (Louisville: Westminster John Knox, 2002), 97–135; Marvin A. Sweeney, *The Prophetic Literature* (IBT; Nashville: Abingdon, 2005), 85–125.

2. E.g., Ronald E. Clements, "Jeremiah 1–25 and the Deuteronomistic History," *Old Testament Prophecy: From Oracles to Canon* (Louisville: Westminster John Knox, 1996), 107–22.

3. William L. Holladay, *The Architecture of Jeremiah 1–20* (Lewisburg, Pa.: Bucknell University Press, 1976); Winfried Thiel, *Die deuteronomistische Redaktion von Jeremia 1-25* (WMANT 41; Neukirchen-Vluyn: Neukirchener, 1973).

4. Claus Rietzschel, *Das Problem der Urrolle. Ein Beitrag zur Redaktionsgeschichte des Jeremiabuches* (Gütersloh: Gerd Mohn, 1966); E. W. Nicholson, *Preaching to the Exiles: A Study of the Prose Traditions in the Book of Jeremiah* (New York: Schocken, 1970); Winfried Thiel, *Die deuteronomistische Redaktion von Jeremia 26-45* (WMANT 52; Neukirchen-Vluyn: Neukirchener, 1981); Christopher R. Seitz, *Theology in Conflict* (BZAW 176; Berlin and New York: Walter de Gruyter, 1989); Carolyn J. Sharp, *Prophecy and Ideology in Jeremiah: Struggles for Authority in the Deutero-Jeremianic Prose* (London and New York: T. & T. Clark, 2003).

5. Christl Maier, *Jeremia als Lehrer der Tora. Soziale Gebote des Deuteronomiums in Fortschreibungen des Jeremiabuches* (FRLANT 196; Göttingen: Vandenhoeck & Ruprecht, 2002).

6. Cf. Thomas W. Overholt, *The Threat of Falsehood: A Study in the Theology of the Book of Jeremiah* (SBT 2/16; Naperville: Allenson, 1970).

7. For the following structure, see Sweeney, *The Prophetic Literature*, 85–95; cf. Louis Stuhlman, *Order Amid Chaos: Jeremiah as Symbolic Tapestry* (BibSem 57; Sheffield: Sheffield Academic Press, 1998).

8. Christopher R. Seitz, "The Prophet Moses and the Canonical Shape of Jeremiah," *ZAW* 101 (1989): 487–516.

9. For discussion of Jeremiah 2–6, see esp. Marvin A. Sweeney, "Structure and Redaction in Jeremiah 2–6," in *Form and Intertextuality in Prophetic and Apocalyptic Literature* (FAT 45; Tübingen: Mohr Siebeck, 2005), 94–108.

10. Cf. Ute Wendel, *Jesaja und Jeremia. Worte, Motive und Einsichten Jesajas in der Verkündigung Jeremias* (BibThS 25; Neukirchen-Vluyn: Neukirchner, 1995); Sweeney, "The Truth in True and False Prophecy," in *Form and Intertextuality*, 78–93.

11. See now Louis Stulman, *Jeremiah* (AOTC; Nashville: Abingdon, 2005), 86–113; Douglas Rawlinson Jones, *Jeremiah* (NCB; Grand Rapids: Eerdmans, 1992), 141–81; cf. Jack R. Lundbom, *Jeremiah 1–20* (AB 21A; Garden City, N.Y.: Doubleday, 1999), 446–613; cf. Helga Weippert, *Die Prosareden des Jeremiabuches* (BZAW 132; Berlin: Walter de Gruyter, 1973), 26–48; Maier, *Jeremia als Lehrer der Tora.*

12. For discussion of the ben Shaphan family and its support of the prophet Jeremiah, see Jay Wilcoxen, "The Political Background of Jeremiah's Temple Sermon," in *Scripture in History and Theology*, ed. A. Merrill and T. Overholt, Fest. J. C. Rylaarsdams; (Pittsburgh: Pickwick, 1977), 155–66.

13. For discussion of the Levitical sermon, see Gerhard von Rad, "The Levitical Sermon in the Books of Chronicles," in *The Problem of the Hexateuch and Other Essays* (London: SCM, 1966), 267–80; Rex Mason, *Preaching the Tradition* (Cambridge: Cambridge University Press, 1990).

14. Marvin A. Sweeney, *Isaiah 1–39, with an Introduction to Prophetic Literature* (FOTL 16; Grand Rapids: Eerdmans, 1996), 546–47.

15. Abraham Joshua Heschel, *The Prophets*, 2 vols. (New York: Harper & Row, 1969), 1:103–39, 2:1–11.

16. For discussion of Jeremiah's laments, see Kathleen O'Connor, *The Confessions of Jeremiah: Their Importance and Role in Chapters 1–25* (SBLDS 94; Atlanta: Scholars Press, 1988); Mark S. Smith, *The Laments of Jeremiah and Their Contexts* (SBLMS 42; Atlanta: Scholars Press, 1990).

17. See David L. Petersen, *Late Israelite Prophecy: Studies in Deutero-Prophetic Literature and in Chronicles* (SBLMS 23; Missoula: Scholars Press, 1977), 55–96.

18. For discussion of Jeremiah and the question of true and false prophecy, see Overholt, *The Threat of Falsehood*; Sweeney, "The Truth in True and False Prophecy"; cf. Armin Lange, *Vom prophetischen Wort zur prophetischen Tradition* (FAT 34; Tübingen: Mohr Siebeck, 2002).

19. Clements, "Jeremiah: Prophet of Hope," in *Old Testament Prophecy: From Oracles to Canon*, 123–41.

20. See Marvin A. Sweeney, "Jeremiah 30–31 and King Josiah's Program of National Restoration and Religious Reform," in *Form and Intertextuality*, 109–22.

21. Andrew G. Shead, *The Open and the Sealed Book: Jeremiah 32 in its Hebrew and Greek Recensions* (JSOTSup 347; London: Continuum, 2002), 114–24.

22. Yohanan Goldman, *Prophétie et royauté au retour de l'exil. Les origines littéraires de la forme massorétique du livre de Jérémie* (OBO 118; Göttingen: Vandenhoeck & Ruprecht, 1992), esp. 12–21.

6. Ezekiel and the Holiness of G-d

1. See, e.g., David J. Halpern, *The Faces of the Chariot: Early Jewish Responses to Ezekiel's Vision* (TSAJ 16; Tübingen: Mohr Siebeck, 1988).

2. See the comments on Ezek 40:1 by Rashi (R. Solomon ben Isaac, 1040–1105 C.E.) and to Ezek 40:2 by Radaq (R. David Kimḥi, 1160–1235 C.E.) in any standard edition of the Rabbinic Bible or Miqra'ot Gedolot; see also Nosson Scherman and Meir Zlotowitz, *Yechezkel/Ezekiel* (Art Scroll Tanach Series, vol. 3; Brooklyn: Mesorah, 1980), 603–07.

3. For discussion of the history of modern research on Ezekiel, see Henry McKeating, *Ezekiel* (OT Guides; Sheffield: Sheffield Academic Press, 1993); Katheryn Pfisterer Darr, "Ezekiel Among the Critics," *CR:BS* 2 (1994): 9–24; Risa Levitt Kohn, "Ezekiel at the Turn of the Century," *CBR* 2 (2003): 9–32; Daniel I. Block, "Ezekiel in Scholarship at the Turn of the Millennium," *Ezekiel's Hierarchical World: Wrestling with a Tiered Reality*, ed. S. L. Cook and C. L. Patton (SBLSym 31; Atlanta: Society of Biblical Literature, 2004), 227–39.

4. E.g., David J. Halpern, *Seeking Ezekiel: Text and Psychology* (University Park: Pennsylvania State University Press, 1993); Julie Galambush, *Jerusalem in the Book of Ezekiel: The City as YHWH's Wife* (SBLDS 130; Atlanta: Scholars Press, 1992).

5. For discussion of Ezekiel's identity as a Zadokite priest and its influence on the presentation of the prophet in the book, see Marvin A. Sweeney, "Ezekiel: Zadokite Priest and Visionary Prophet of the Exile," in *Form and Intertextuality in Prophetic and Apocalyptic Literature* (FAT 45; Tübingen: Mohr Siebeck, 2005), 125–43; cf. Margaret S. Odell, "You Are What You Eat: Ezekiel and the Scroll," *JBL* 117 (1998): 229–48; idem, *Ezekiel* (Smyth and Helwys Bible Commentary; Macon, Ga.: Smyth and Helwys, 2005), 14–16, who emphasizes Ezekiel's prophetic identity while recognizing his priestly background.

6. E.g., Gustav Hölscher, *Hesekiel: der Dichter und das Buch* (BZAW 39; Giessen: A. Töpelmann, 1924).

7. Sweeney, "Ezekiel: Zadokite Priest and Visionary Prophet of the Exile."

8. For discussion of the following formal structure of Ezekiel, see also Marvin A. Sweeney, *The Prophetic Literature* (IBT; Nashville: Abingdon, 2005), 127–32.

9. See esp. Odell, "You Are What You Eat."

10. For depictions of ancient cherubim as guardians of throne and gates, see *ANEP*, 534–36.

11. Jon D. Levenson, "The Temple and the World," *JR* 64 (1984): 275–98; idem, *Sinai and Zion: An Entry into the Jewish Bible* (Minneapolis: Winston, 1985).

12. See C. T. R. Hayward, *The Jewish Temple: A Non-Biblical Sourcebook* (London and New York: Routledge, 1996), who cites various Second-Temple-period texts (e.g., Aristeas, Philo, Jubilees, Josephus) to illustrate this point.

13. For discussion of the interrelationship between moral and ritual impurity in the Bible and postbiblical Judaism, see Jonathan Klawans, *Impurity and Sin in Ancient Judaism* (New York: Oxford University Press, 2000).

14. For detailed discussion of the following, see Marvin A. Sweeney, "The Destruction of Jerusalem as Purification in Ezekiel 8–11," in *Form and Intertextuality*, 144–55.

15. See the Egyptian examples of steles from Pharaoh Seti I at Beth Shean (*ANEP* 320–21) and Merneptah at Thebes (*ANEP* 342) as well as the Assyrian examples of Shalmaneser III (*ANEP* 351–55).

16. See Jay Wilcoxen, "The Political Background of Jeremiah's Temple Sermon," *Scripture in History and Theology: Essays in Honor of J. Coert Rylaarsdam*, ed. A. Merrill and T. Overholt (Pittsburgh: Pickwick, 1977), 151–66.

17. B. Alster, "Tammuz," *DDD²* 828–34.

18. See Moshe Greenberg, *Ezekiel 1–20* (AB 22; Garden City, N.Y.: Doubleday, 1983), 176–77; Walter Zimmerli, *Ezekiel 1: A Commentary on the Book of the Prophet Ezekiel Chapters 1–24*, trans. R. E. Clements; (Hermeneia; Philadelphia: Fortress Press, 1979), 248; Katheryn Pfisterer Darr, "Ezekiel," in *The New Interpreter's Bible*, ed. L. E. Keck, et al. (Nashville: Abingdon, 2001), 6:1179; Odell, *Ezekiel*, 115–16.

19. For detailed discussion of this material, see Marvin A. Sweeney, "The Assertion of Divine Power in Ezekiel 33:21—39:29," in *Form and Intertextuality*, 156–72.

20. Adrian Graffy, *A Prophet Confronts His People: The Disputation Speech in the Prophets* (AnBib 104; Rome: Biblical Institute Press, 1984), 78–82.

21. Contra Elie Assis, "Why Edom? On the Hostility toward Jacob's Brother in Prophetic Sources," *VT* 56 (2006): 1–20, who argues that Edom is targeted because of its representation in Pentateuchal tradition and because it occupied Judean lands in the postexilic period prompting questions that YHWH had rejected Judah and chosen Edom instead.

22. See Marvin A. Sweeney, "The Royal Oracle in Ezekiel 37:15-28: Ezekiel's Reflection on Josiah's Reform," in *Israel's Prophets and Israel's Past: Essays on the Relationship of Prophetic Texts and Israelite History in Honor of John H. Hayes*, ed. B. E. Kelle and M. B. Moore (LHBOTS 446; New York and London: T. & T. Clark, 2006), 239–53.

23. For recent critical discussion of Ezekiel 40–48, see esp., Jon D. Levenson, *Theology of the Program of Restoration of Ezekiel 40–48* (HSM 10; Missoula: Scholars Press, 1976); Steven Shawn Tuell, *The Law of the Temple in Ezekiel 40–48* (HSM 49; Atlanta: Scholars Press, 1992).

24. For discussion of the Temple structure and its parallels in the ancient world, see Carol L. Meyers, "Temple, Jerusalem," in *ABD* 6:350–69, esp. 355–58.

25. Levenson, *Sinai and Zion*, 139; cf. idem, *Theology*, 25–26"; idem, "The Temple and the World."

7. The Twelve Prophets and the Question of Shoah

1. See Ehud Ben Zvi, "Twelve Prophetic Books or 'The Twelve': A Few Preliminary Considerations," in *Forming Prophetic Literature: Essays on Isaiah and the*

Twelve in Honor of J. D. W. Watts, ed. J. W. Watts and P. R. House (JSOTSup 235; Sheffield: Sheffield Academic Press, 1996), 125–56; Barry A. Jones, *The Formation of the Book of the Twelve* (SBLDS 149; Atlanta: Scholars Press, 1995); Marvin A. Sweeney, *The Twelve Prophets* (Berit Olam; Collegeville, Minn.: Liturgical, 2000), 1:v–xlii.

2. See Marvin A. Sweeney, "Sequence and Interpretation in the Book of the Twelve," in *Reading and Hearing the Book of the Twelve,* ed. J. D. Nogalski and M. A. Sweeney (SBLSym 15; Atlanta: Society of Biblical Literature, 2000), 49–64.

3. For discussion of modern research on the Book of the Twelve Prophets, see Paul L. Redditt, "Recent Research on the Book of the Twelve as One Book," *CR: BS* 9 (2001): 47–80; idem, "The Formation of the Book of the Twelve: A Review of Research," in *Thematic Threads in the Book of the Twelve,* ed. P. L. Reddit and A. Schart (BZAW 325; Berlin: Walter de Gruyter, 2003), 1–26.

4. See John D. W. Watts, "A Frame for the Book of the Twelve: Hosea 1–3 and Malachi," in *Reading and Hearing the Book of the Twelve,* 209–17.

5. E.g., Hans Walter Wolff, *Hosea* (Hermeneia; Philadelphia: Fortress Press, 1974); idem, *Confrontations with Prophets: Discovering the Old Testament's New and Contemporary Significance* (Philadelphia: Fortress Press, 1983), 22–34.

6. For discussion of the marriage motif to portray the covenant relationship between YHWH and Israel as a marriage between husband and wife, see esp. Gerlinde Baumann, *Love and Violence: Marriage as Metaphor for the Relationship between YHWH and Israel in the Prophetic Books,* trans. L. Maloney (Collegeville, Minn.: Liturgical, 2003).

7. E.g., Wolff, *Confrontations with Prophets,* 22–34.

8. For discussion of Assyria's ambitions to control trade between Mesopotamia and Egypt, see Moshe Elat, "The Economic Relations of the Neo-Assyrian Empire with Egypt," *JAOS* 98 (1978): 20–34.

9. See Pritchard, *ANEP,* 100A.

10. Stephanie Page, "A Stele of Adad Nirari III and Nergal-ereš from Tell al Rimlah," *Iraq* 30 (1968): 139–53.

11. For discussion of Hosea 12, see Sweeney, *The Twelve Prophets,* 1:117–30.

12. Francis Landy, *Hosea* (Readings; Sheffield: Sheffield Academic Press, 1995), 21–52.

13. See also Yvonne Sherwood, *The Prostitute and the Prophet: Hosea's Marriage in Literary-Theological Perspective* (JSOTSup 212; GCT 2; Sheffield: Sheffield Academic Press, 1996).

14. For an overview of modern critical discussion of the book of Jonah, see R. B. Salters, *Jonah and Lamentations* (OTG; Sheffield: JSOT Press, 1994), 13–62.

15. Sweeney, *The Twelve Prophets,* 1:316–22.

16. E.g., Janet Howe Gaines, *Forgiveness in a Wounded World: Jonah's Dilemma* (SBL 5; Atlanta: Society of Biblical Literature, 2003); Daniel J. Simundson, *Hosea, Joel, Amos, Obadiah, Jonah, Micah* (ACOT; Nashville: Abingdon, 2005).

17. For discussion of the rhetorical dimensions of biblical literature and the book of Jonah in particular, see Phyllis Trible, *Rhetorical Criticism: Context, Method,*

and the Book of Jonah (Guides to Biblical Scholarship; Minneapolis: Fortress Press, 1994); idem, "The Book of Jonah," in *The New Interpreters' Bible,* ed. L. Keck, et al (Nashville: Abingdon, 1996), 7:461–529.

18. E.g., Julia M. O'Brien, *Nahum* (Readings; Sheffield: Sheffield Academic Press, 2002). For discussion of modern scholarship on Nahum, see Klaas Spronk, *Nahum* (HCOT; Kampen: Kok Pharos, 1997), 1–18.

19. Sweeney, *The Twelve Prophets,* 2:419–22; idem, "Concerning the Structure and Generic Character of the Book of Nahum," *ZAW* 104 (1992): 364–77.

20. Sweeney, *The Twelve Prophets,* 2:431.

21. Ibid., 2:432.

22. For discussion of modern critical scholarship on the book of Habakkuk, see M. A. Sweeney, "Habakkuk, Book of," *ABD* 3:1–6; Rex Mason, *Zephaniah, Habakkuk, Joel* (OTG; Sheffield: JSOT Press, 1994), 60–96.

23. Sweeney, *The Twelve Prophets,* 2:453–58; idem, "Structure, Genre, and Intent in the Book of Habakkuk," *VT* 41 (1991): 63–83.

24. For discussion of modern research on Malachi, see R. J. Coggins, *Haggai, Zechariah, Malachi* (OTG; Sheffield: JSPT Press, 1987), 73–80; Julia M. O'Brien, "Malachi in Recent Research," *CR:BS* 3 (1995): 81–94.

25. E. Pfeiffer, "Die Disputationsworte im Buch Maleachi," *EvT* 12 (1959): 546–68; cf. Sweeney, *The Twelve Prophets,* 2:715–17.

26. See D. F. Murray, "The Rhetoric of Disputation: Re-examination of a Prophetic Genre," *JSOT* 38 (1987): 95–121.

27. P. A. Verhoef, *Haggai and Malachi* (NICOT; Grand Rapids: Eerdmans, 1987), 160.

8. Complaints to G-d in Psalms and Lamentations: The Voice of the Victims

1. For orientation to modern research on Psalms and Lamentations, see esp. James Limburg, "Psalms, Book," in *ABD* 5:522–36; James L. Crenshaw, *The Psalms: An Introduction* (Grand Rapids; Eerdmans, 2001); Erhard S. Gerstenberger, *Psalms, Part 1, with an Introduction to Cultic Poetry* (FOTL 14; Grand Rapids: Eerdmans, 1988); idem, *Psalms, Part 2, and Lamentations* (FOTL 15; Grand Rapids: Eerdmans, 2001).

2. See, e.g., David R. Blumenthal, *Facing the Abusing G-d: A Theology of Protest* (Louisville: Westminster John Knox, 1993), 33–46, who examines the universes of discourse in the Psalms, particularly in relation to discourse between human beings and G-d. See also Jon D. Levenson, "The Jerusalem Temple in Devotional and Visionary Experience," *Jewish Spirituality, Volume 1: From the Bible through the Middle Ages,* ed. A. Green (New York: Crossroad, 1988), 32–61; Martin Buber, *I and Thou* (New York: Scribners, 1970).

3. E.g., James L. Mays, *The L-rd Reigns: A Theological Handbook to the Psalms* (Louisville: Westminster John Knox, 1994).

4. See Samuel E. Balentine, *The Hidden G-d: The Hiding of the Face of G-d in the Old Testament* (New York: Oxford University Press, 1983).

5. Ibid., 50–56.

6. See Meir Ydit, "Av, The Ninth of," in *EncJud* 3:936–40.

7. Blumenthal, *Facing the Abusing G-d*, passim.

8. For discussion, see esp. Crenshaw, *The Psalms*, 98–105.

9. Although modern Judaism follows the Babylonian practice of reading the entire Torah in an annual cycle of Shabbat Torah readings, practice in the land of Israel and Egypt through the twelfth century C.E. called for a three-year cycle for the reading of the entire Torah. For discussion, see Jacob Mann, *The Bible as Read and Preached in the Old Synagogue*, 2 vols. (New York: KTAV, 1971).

10. Gerald H. Wilson, *The Editing of the Hebrew Psalter* (SBLDS 76; Chico, Calif.: Scholars Press, 1985).

11. Crenshaw, *The Psalms*, 101.

12. For discussion of the individual types of psalms, see esp. Limburg, "Psalms, Book of," 5:531–34; Gerstenberger, *Psalms, Part 1*, 9–21; Crenshaw, *The Psalms*, 80–95; Hermann Gunkel, with Joachim Begrich, *An Introduction to the Psalms: The Genres of the Religious Lyric of Israel* (Macon, Ga.: Mercer University Press, 1998).

13. For discussion of Psalm 7, see esp. Gerstenberger, *Psalms, Part 1*, 63–67.

14. See Sigmund Mowinckel, *Psalmentstudien IV* (Kristiana: J. Dybwad, 1923), 7.

15. See the comments on Psalm 7 by Adele Berlin and Marc Brettler in *The Jewish Study Bible*, ed. A. Berlin and M. Brettler (New York: Oxford University Press, 2003), 1290.

16. For discussion of Psalm 94, see esp. Gerstenberger, *Psalms, Part 2*, 177–81.

17. For discussion of Psalm 22, see esp. Gerstenberger, *Psalms, Part 1*, 108–13.

18. For discussion of Psalm 83, see esp. Gerstenberger, *Psalms, Part 2*, 117–22.

19. For discussion of Psalm 44, see Gerstenberger, *Psalms, Part 1*, 182–86; Blumenthal, *Facing the Abusing G-d*, 85–110.

20. For discussion of the book of Lamentations, see Gerstenberger, *Psalms, Part 2, and Lamentations*, 465–76; Tod Linafelt, *Surviving Lamentations: Catastrophe, Lament, and Protest in the Afterlife of a Biblical Book* (Chicago: University of Chicago Press, 2000).

21. For discussion of the dirge, see esp. Gerstenberger, *Psalms, Part 1*, 10–11; idem, *Psalms, Part 2, and Lamentations*, 469–71. Note also the foundational study of dirge forms throughout the Hebrew Bible, Hedwig Jahnow, *Das hebräischen Leichenlied im Rahmen der Völkerdichtung* (BZAW 36; Giessen: A. Töpelmann, 1923). Jahnow, who wrote this work as a dissertation under the direction of Hermann Gunkel and later served on the faculty of Marburg University, was murdered by the Nazis at Theresienstadt because her father was Jewish.

22. Linafelt, *Surviving Lamentations*, esp. 1–34.

23. For discussion of Lamentations 1, see Gerstenberger, *Psalms, Part 2, and Lamentations*, 477–84.

24. For discussion of Lamentations 2, see ibid., 485–91.

25. For discussion of Lamentations 3, see ibid., 492–97.

26. See Linafelt, *Surviving Lamentations*, 5–18, for discussion.

27. See Gerstenberger, *Psalms, Part 2, and Lamentations,* 497–501.
28. See ibid., 501–05.
29. For discussion of the relationship between Lamentations and the Sumerian City-Lament genre, see esp. F. W. Dobbs-Allsopp, *Weep, O Daughter of Zion: A Study of the City-Lament Genre in the Hebrew Bible* (Bib Or 44; Rome: Pontifical Biblical Institute, 1993), esp. 30–96. See also Paul Wayne Ferris Jr., *The Genre of Communal Lament in the Bible and the Ancient Near East* (SBLDS 127; Atlanta: Scholars Press, 1992).

9. Divine Hiddenness and Human Initiative in the Wisdom Literature

1. For discussion of the role of wisdom in Old Testament theology, see Leo G. Perdue, *The Collapse of History: Reconstructing Old Testament Theology* (OBT; Minneapolis: Fortress Press, 1994), esp. 111–50; idem, *Wisdom and Creation: The Theology of the Wisdom Literature* (Nashville: Abingdon, 1994), 19–48.
2. For overviews concerning the study of wisdom literature, see Perdue, *Wisdom and Creation*; James L. Crenshaw, *Old Testament Wisdom: An Introduction* (Louisville: Westminster John Knox, 1998); Roland E. Murphy, *The Tree of Life: An Exploration of Biblical Wisdom Literature* (Winona Lake, Ind.: Eisenbrauns, 2002).
3. For discussion of education in ancient Israel and Judah as well as the ancient Near East, see James L. Crenshaw, *Education in Ancient Israel: Across the Deadening Silence* (Garden City, N.Y.: Doubleday, 1998); cf. David M. Carr, *Writing on the Tablet of the Heart: Origins of Scripture and Literature* (New York: Oxford University Press, 2005).
4. For introductory discussion of Proverbs, see esp. Crenshaw, *Old Testament Wisdom,* 55–88; Michael V. Fox, *Proverbs 1–9* (AnBib 18A; Garden City, N.Y.: Doubleday, 2000), 1–27; Richard J. Clifford, *Proverbs: A Commentary* (OTL; Louisville: Westminster John Knox, 1999), 1–33.
5. For discussion of the *māšāl* or "saying" as a fundamental genre of wisdom literature, see Roland E. Murphy, *Wisdom Literature: Job, Proverbs, Ruth, Canticles, Ecclesiastes, Esther* (FOTL 13; Grand Rapids: Eerdmans, 1981), 4–6.
6. E.g., Crenshaw, *Old Testament Wisdom,* 62; for a partial translation of the *Wisdom of Amenemope,* see *ANET* 421–25.
7. Contra Murphy, *Wisdom Literature,* 49, who employs a diachronic model for his assessment of the structure of Proverbs.
8. For discussion of the sequence of lectures in Proverbs 1–9, cf. Fox, *Proverbs 1–9,* esp. 44–49 and passim.
9. See Clifford, *Proverbs,* 259, 260.
10. For discussion of the book of Job, see Crenshaw, *Old Testament Wisdom,* 89–115; Carol A. Newsom, "The Book of Job," in *The New Interpreter's Bible,* ed. L. E. Keck et al (Nashville: Abingdon, 1996), 4:319–637; idem, *The Book of Job: A Contest of Moral Imaginations* (New York: Oxford University Press, 2003).

11. James L. Crenshaw, "Job, Book of," in *ABD* 3:858–68.

12. Cf. Gerhard von Rad, *Old Testament Theology*, 2 vols. (New York: Harper & Row, 1962–65), 1:408–18, emphasizes human naïveté and the limits of human reason when faced with the marvelous and incomprehensible character of the relationship between G-d and creation.

13. Martin Buber, *At the Turning: Three Addresses on Judaism* (New York: Farrar, Straus, and Young, 1952), 61.

14. Elie Wiesel, *Legends of Our Time* (New York: Holt, Rinehart and Winston, 1968), 181; Emil Fackenheim, *The Jewish Bible after the Holocaust: A Rereading* (Bloomington: Indiana University Press, 1990), 71–99; see also Richard Rubenstein, "Job and Auschwitz," in *Strange Fire: Reading the Bible after the Holocaust*, ed. T. Linafelt (Sheffield: Sheffield Academic Press, 2000), 233–51.

15. Cf. Murphy, *Wisdom Literature*, 15–16.

16. For discussion of the genre of Job, or more properly the interplay of genres within the book, see Murphy, *Wisdom Literature*, 16–20.

17. For discussion of Qoheleth, see Crenshaw, *Old Testament Wisdom*, 116–39; idem, *Ecclesiastes: A Commentary* (OTL; Philadelphia: Westminster, 1987); Michael V. Fox, *A Time to Tear Down and a Time to Build Up: A Rereading of Ecclesiastes* (Grand Rapids: Eerdmans, 1999); Choon-Leong Seow, *Ecclesiastes* (AnBib 18C; Garden City, N.Y.: Doubleday, 1997); Thomas Krüger, *Qoheleth* (Hermeneia; Minneapolis: Fortress Press, 2004); Norbert L. Lohfink, *Qoheleth* (ContCom; Minneapolis: Fortress Press, 2003).

18. Fox, *A Time to Tear Down*, 153–55; cf. the discussion of genre in Qoheleth by Murphy, *Wisdom Literature*, 129–31; Krüger, *Qoheleth*, 8–14.

19. For discussion of the unity and authorship of Qoheleth, see esp. Crenshaw, *Old Testament Wisdom*, 132–33; Krüger, *Qoheleth*, 14–27.

20. For discussion of the form and literary structure of Qoheleth, see esp. Fox, *A Time to Tear Down*, 147–53; Murphy, *Wisdom Literature*, 127–29; Crenshaw, *Old Testament Wisdom*, 128–32; Krüger, *Qoheleth*, 5–8.

21. A. Wright, "The Riddle of the Sphinx: The Structure of the Book of Qoheleth," *CBQ* 30 (1968): 313–34; idem, "The Riddle of the Sphinx Revisited: Numerical Patterns in the Book of Qoheleth," *CBQ* 42 (1980): 3851.

22. Murphy, *Wisdom Literature*, 128–29.

23. For discussion of the Song of Songs, see esp. Murphy, *Wisdom Literature*, 98–124; idem, *The Song of Songs* (Hermeneia; Minneapolis: Fortress Press, 1990); Marvin Pope, *Song of Songs* (AnBib 19; Garden City, N.Y.: Doubleday, 1977); Tremper Longman III, *The Song of Songs* (NICOT; Grand Rapids: Eerdmans, 2001); J. Cheryl Exum, *Song of Songs: A Commentary* (OTL: Louisville: Westminster John Knox, 2005).

24. Murphy, *Song of Songs*, 6–7.

25. Michael V. Fox, *Song of Songs and the Ancient Egyptian Love Songs* (Madison: University of Wisconsin Press, 1999).

26. Yitschak Sefati, *Love Songs in Sumerian Literature: Critical Edition of the Dumuzi-Inanna Songs* (Ramat Gan: Bar Ilan University Press, 1998).

27. Phyllis Trible, *G-d and the Rhetoric of Sexuality* (OBT; Philadelphia: For-

tress Press, 1978), 144–65; for discussion of the literary structure of Song of Songs, see esp. Exum, *Song of Songs*, 37–42.

28. See Longman, *Song of Songs*, 212–13; Murphy, *Song of Songs*, 191–92.

29. Cf. Trible, *G-d and the Rhetoric of Sexuality*, 144, who argues that Genesis 2–3 provides the key for reading Song of Songs. Her analysis of Genesis 2–3 appears in pp. 72–143.

30. Cf. Rolf P. Knierim, "Cosmos and History in Israel's Theology," in *The Task of Old Testament Theology: Substance, Method, and Cases* (Grand Rapids: Eerdmans, 1995), 171–224, who discusses the presumed cosmic and moral order of the world in biblical literature.

10. Lessons from the Didactic Narratives of the Writings

1. See, e.g., Gerhard von Rad, *Old Testament Theology*, 2 vols. (New York: Harper & Row, 1962–65), which tends to employ Ruth, Esther, and Ezra-Nehemiah as background for understanding the postexilic period. 1-2 Chronicles receives more substantial treatment due to its historical perspective and Daniel due to its prophetic perspective.

2. Cf. Leo G. Perdue, *The Collapse of History: Reconstructing Old Testament Theology* (OBT; Minneapolis: Fortress Press, 1994), who discusses the importance of narrative theology.

3. For discussion of issues in the interpretation of Ezra-Nehemiah, see esp. Ralph Klein, "Ezra-Nehemiah, Books of," in *ABD* 2:731–42; H. G. M. Williamson, *Ezra and Nehemiah* (OTG; Sheffield: Sheffield Academic Press, 1987).

4. In addition to Williamson, *Ezra and Nehemiah*, see also Joseph Blenkinsopp, *Ezra-Nehemiah: A Commentary* (OTL; Philadelphia: Westminster, 1988); David J. A. Clines, *Ezra, Nehemiah, and Esther* (NCB; Grand Rapids: Eerdmans; London: Marshall, Morgan, and Scott, 1984); Tamara Cohn Eskenazi, *In an Age of Prose: A Literary Approach to Ezra-Nehemiah* (SBLMS 36; Atlanta: Scholars Press, 1988); H. G. M. Williamson, *Ezra, Nehemiah* (WBC 16; Waco: Word, 1985).

5. See the summary discussion in Klein, "Ezra-Nehemiah, Books of," 2:735–37.

6. Cohn Eskenazi, *In an Age of Prose*.

7. E.g., Williamson, *Ezra, Nehemiah*, xxxiii–xxxv.

8. E.g., von Rad, *Old Testament Theology*, 1:89–92.

9. See esp. Blenkinsopp, *Ezra-Nehemiah*, 54–59.

10. Marvin A. Sweeney, "The Religious World of Ancient Israel to 586 B.C.E.," in *The Blackwell Companion to Judaism*, ed. Jacob Neusner and Alan Avery-Peck (Oxford: Blackwell, 2000), 20–36.

11. Anna L. Grant-Henderson, *Inclusive Voices in Post-Exilic Judah* (Collegeville, Minn.: Liturgical, 2002); cf. Walther Eichrodt, *Theology of the Old Testament*, 2 vols. (OTL; Philadelphia: Westminster, 1961-67), 2:337–49

12. Klaus Koch, "Ezra and the Origins of Judaism," *JSS* 19 (1974): 173–97.

13. For discussion of the role of Ruth in Judaism, see esp. Moshe Weinfeld and Alexander Rofé, "Ruth, Book of," in *EncJud* 14:518–24.

14. Kirsten Nielsen, *Ruth: A Commentary* (OTL; Louisville: Westminster John Knox, 1997), 5-8; Murphy, *Wisdom Literature*, 85-86; cf. Robert L. Hubbard Jr., *The Book of Ruth* (NICOT; Grand Rapids: Eerdmans, 1988), 47-48; Jack M. Sasson, *Ruth: A New Translation with a Philological Commentary and Formalist-Folklorist Interpretation* (BibSem 10; Sheffield: Sheffield Academic Press, 1995), 197-216.

15. Nielsen, *Ruth*, 1-5; contra Murphy, *Wisdom Literature*, 85.

16. E.g., Nielsen, *Ruth*, 8-17.

17. Ibid., 13-15.

18. E.g., Grant-Henderson, *Inclusive Voices*.

19. See Peter Schäfer, *Judeophobia: Attitudes toward the Jews in the Ancient World* (Cambridge: Harvard University Press, 1997); Aryeh Kasher, *The Jews in Hellenistic and Roman Egypt: The Struggle for Equal Rights* (TSAJ 7; Tübingen: Mohr Siebeck, 1985) for discussion of the origins of anti-semitism in Roman-period Egypt.

20. For discussion of the history of anti-semitism, see esp. the essays published in Shmuel Almog, ed., *Antisemitism through the Ages* (Oxford: Pergamon, 1988); cf. Daniel Jonah Goldhagen, *A Moral Reckoning: The Role of the Catholic Church in the Holocaust and Its Unfulfilled Duty of Repair* (New York: Knopf, 2002); James Carroll, *Constantine's Sword: The Church and the Jews: A History* (Boston and New York: Houghton Mifflin, 2001).

21. For treatments of Esther, see esp. Adele Berlin, *Esther* (JPS Bible Commentary; Philadelphia: Jewish Publication Society, 2001); Michael V. Fox, *Character and Ideology in the Book of Esther* (Grand Rapids: Eerdmans, 2001); Jon D. Levenson, *Esther: A Commentary* (OTL; Louisville: Westminster John Knox, 1997).

22. For the following, see Marvin A. Sweeney, "Absence of G-d and Human Responsibility in the Book of Esther," in *Reading the Hebrew Bible for a New Millennium: Form, Concept and Theological Perspective, vol. 2: Exegetical and Theological Studies*, ed. Wonil Kim, et al. (SAC; Harrisburg, Pa.: Trinity Press International, 2000), 264-75.

23. For discussion of the genre of Esther, see W. Lee Humphreys, "A Life-Style for Diaspora: A Study of the Tales of Esther and Daniel," *JBL* 92 (1973): 211-23; idem, "The Story of Esther and Mordecai: An Early Jewish Novella," in *Saga, Legend, Tale, Novella, Fable: Narrative Forms in Old Testament Literature*, ed. George W. Coats (JSOTSup 35; Sheffield: Sheffield Academic Press, 1985), 97-113; cf. Fox, *Character and Ideology*, 141-42; Murphy, *Wisdom Literature*, 154-56.

24. For discussion of Esther's literary character, plot, and narrative structure, see esp. Fox, *Character and Ideology*, 153-63; Berlin, *Esther*, xv-xxxii; Levenson, *Esther*, 1-23.

25. John J. Collins, *Daniel, with an Introduction to Apocalyptic Literature* (FOTL 20; Grand Rapids: Eerdmans, 1984), 4; idem, *Daniel* (Hermeneia; Minneapolis: Fortress Press, 1993), 54.

26. In addition to the commentaries on Daniel by Collins cited above, see Paul Hanson, *The Dawn of Apocalyptic* (Philadelphia: Fortress Press, 1975); Robert Carroll, *When Prophecy Failed: Cognitive Dissonance in the Prophetic Traditions of the Old Testament* (New York: Seabury, 1979).

27. E.g., Collins, *Daniel* (1993), 23–71.

28. For the following, see Marvin A. Sweeney, "The End of Eschatology in Daniel? Theological and Socio-Political Ramifications of the Changing Contexts of Interpretation," in *Form and Intertextuality*, 248–61.

29. E.g., Hanson, *The Dawn of Apocalyptic*.

30. E.g., Stephen L. Cook, *Prophecy and Apocalypticism: The Post-Exilic Social Setting* (Minneapolis: Fortress Press, 1995); Marvin A. Sweeney, "The Priesthood and the Proto-Apocalyptic Reading of Prophetic and Pentateuchal Texts," in *Form and Intertexutality*, 239–47.

31. See Jon D. Levenson, "The Temple and the World," *JR* 64 (1984): 275–98; idem, *Creation and the Persistence of Evil*; idem, *Sinai and Zion*.

Conclusion: What Have We Learned?

1. For discussion of the Gospel of Mark, see Luke Timothy Johnson, *The Writings of the New Testament: An Interpretation* (Minneapolis: Fortress Press, 1999), 159–84; Helmut Koester, *History and Literature of Early Christianity, vol. 2: Introduction to the New Testament* (Berlin: Walter de Gruyter, 2000), 2:169–75.

2. For discussion of the Gospel of Matthew, see Johnson, *The Writings*, 187–211; Koester, *History*, 2:176–82.

3. For discussion of Luke-Acts, see Johnson, *The Writings*, 213–57; Koester, *History*, 2:310–27.

4. For discussion of the Gospel of John, see Johnson, *The Writings*, 525–57; Koester, *History*, 2:183–99.

5. For discussion of rabbinic literature and thought, see esp. H. L. Strack and G. Stemberger, *Introduction to the Talmud and Midrash* (Minneapolis: Fortress Press, 1992); Ephraim E. Urbach, *The Sages: Their Concepts and Beliefs*, 2 vols. (Jerusalem: Magnes, 1979). For discussion of Roman rule of Judea and the three Jewish revolts against Rome, see Emil Schürer, *The History of the Jewish People in the Age of Jesus Christ*, rev. ed., ed. G. Vermes, et al.; (Edinburgh: T. & T. Clark, 1973), 1:243–557; E. M. Smallwood, *The Jews under Roman Rule* (Leiden: Brill, 1980); Seth Schwartz, "Political, Social, and Economic Life in the Land of Israel, 66-c235," in *Cambridge History of Judaism, vol. 4: The Late Roman-Rabbinic Period*, ed. S. Katz (Cambridge: Cambridge University Press, 2006), 23–52; Miriam Pucci Ben Zeev, "The Uprisings in the Jewish Diaspora," *CHJ*, 4:93–104; Hanan Eshel, "The Bar Kochba Revolt, 132–135," *CHJ*, 4:105–27.

6. For discussion of Elisha ben Abuyah or Aher, see esp. Alon Goshen-Gottstein, *The Sinner and the Amnesiac: The Rabbinic Invention of Elisha ben Abuya and Elazar ben Arach* (Stanford: Stanford University Press, 2000); see also Marvin A. Sweeney, "The Four Who Entered Pardes Reconsidered Once Again," in *Form and Intertextuality in Prophetic and Apocalyptic Literature* (FAT 45; Tübingen: Mohr Siebeck, 2005), 269–82.

7. For discussion of rabbinic mystical literature, see esp. Gershom Scholem, *Major Trends in Jewish Mysticism* (New York: Schocken, 1972); David R. Blumenthal,

Understanding Jewish Mysticism: A Source Reader: The Merkabah Tradition and the Zoharic Tradition (New York: KTAV, 1978); and Ithamar Gruenwald, *Apocalyptic and Merkavah Mysticism* (AGJU 14; Leiden: Brill, 1980).

8. For discussion of the *Heikhalot Rabbati*, see Gruenwald, *Apocalyptic*, 150–73; Scholem, *Major Trends*, 40–79; Blumenthal, *Understanding Jewish Mysticism*, 53–97.

9. *Heikhalot Rabbati*, 29; Blumenthal, *Understanding Jewish Mysticism*, 88–89.

10. For discussion of the Zohar, see Scholem, *Major Trends*, 156–243; Daniel Chanan Matt, *Zohar: The Book of Enlightenment* (New York: Paulist, 1983); for discussion of the Ten *Sefirot*, see also Marvin A. Sweeney, "Ten Sephirot," in *Dictionary of Deities and Demons in the Bible,* ed. K. Van Der Toorn, et al. (Leiden: Brill; Grand Rapids: Eerdmans, 1999), 837–43.

11. On Lurianic Kabbalah, see Scholem, *Major Trends*, 244–86.

Books and Monographs

Ackroyd, Peter R. *Studies in the Religious Tradition of the Old Testament*. London: SCM, 1987.

Almog, Shmuel, ed. *Antisemitism Through the Ages*. Oxford: Pergamon Press, 1988.

Alter, Robert. *The Art of Biblical Narrative*. New York: Basic, 1981.

Baeck, Leo. *This People Israel: The Meaning of Jewish Existence*. New York: Holt, Rinehart, and Winston, 1965.

Balentine, Samuel E. *The Hidden G-d: The Hiding of the Face of G-d in the Old Testament*. New York: Oxford University Press, 1983.

Baskin, Judith R. *Pharaoh's Counselers: Job, Jethro, and Balaam in Rabbinic and Patristic Tradition*. BJS 47. Chico, Calif.: Scholars Press, 1983.

Bauer, Yehuda. *A History of the Holocaust*. New York: F. Watts, 1982.

Baumann, Gerlinde. *Love and Violence: Marriage as Metaphor for the Relationship between YHWH and Israel in the Prophetic Books*. Trans. L. Maloney. Collegeville, Minn.: Liturgical, 2003.

Berkovits, Eliezer. *Faith after the Holocaust*. New York: KTAV, 1973.

Berlin, Adele. *Esther*. JPS Bible Commentary. Philadelphia: Jewish Publication Society, 2001.

Berlin, Adele, and Marc Brettler, eds. *The Jewish Study Bible*. New York: Oxford University Press, 2003.

Blenkinsopp, Joseph. *Ezra-Nehemiah: A Commentary*. OTL. Philadelphia: Westminster, 1988.

———. *A History of Prophecy in Israel*. Louisville: Westminster John Knox, 1996.

——. *The Pentateuch: An Introduction to the First Five Books of the Bible*. New York: Doubleday, 1992.

Blum, Erhard. *Die Komposition des Vätergeschichte*. WMANT 57. Neukirchen-Vluyn: Neukirchener Verlag, 1984.

Blumenthal, David R. *Facing the Abusing G-d: A Theology of Protest*. Louisville: Westminster John Knox, 1993.

——. *Understanding Jewish Mysticism: A Source Reader: The Merkabah Tradition and the Zoharic Tradition*. New York: KTAV, 1978.

Boorer, Suzanne. *The Promise of the Land as Oath: A Key to the Formation of the Pentateuch*. BZAW 205. Berlin: Walter de Gruyter, 1992.

Braiterman, Zachary. *(G-d) After Auschwitz: Tradition and Change in Post-Holocaust Jewish Thought*. Princeton: Princeton University Press, 1998.

Brueggemann, Walter. *Theology of the Old Testament: Testimony, Dispute, Advocacy*. Minneapolis: Fortress Press, 1997.

Buber, Martin. *At the Turning: Three Addresses on Judaism*. New York: Farrar, Straus, and Young, 1952.

——. *The Eclipse of G-d: Studies in the Relation between Religion and Philosophy*. New York: Harper & Row, 1952.

——. *I and Thou*. New York: Charles Scribner's, 1970.

Campbell, Antony F. *Joshua to Chronicles: An Introduction*. Louisville: Westminster John Knox, 2004.

——, and Mark A. O'Brien. *Sources of the Pentateuch: Texts, Introductions, Annotations*. Minneapolis: Fortress Press, 1993.

Carr, David M. *Reading the Fractures of Genesis: Historical and Literary Approaches*. Louisville: Westminster John Knox, 1996.

——. *Writing on the Tablet of the Heart: Origins of Scripture and Literature*. New York: Oxford University Press, 2005.

Carroll, James. *Constantine's Sword: The Church and the Jews*. New York: Houghton Mifflin, 2001.

Carroll, Robert. *When Prophecy Failed: Cognitive Dissonance in the Prophetic Traditions of the Old Testament*. New York: Seabury, 1979.

Cassuto, Umberto. *A Commentary on the Book of Exodus*. Jerusalem: Magnes, 1967.

Childs, Brevard S. *The Book of Exodus: A Critical, Theological Commentary*. OTL. Philadelphia: Westminster, 1974.

Clements, Ronald E. *Abraham and David*. SBT 2/5. London: SCM, 1967.

——. *Old Testament Prophecy: From Oracles to Canon*. Louisville: Westminster John Knox, 1996.

Clifford, Richard J. *Proverbs: A Commentary*. OTL. Louisville: Westminster John Knox, 1999.

Clines, David J. A. *Ezra, Nehemiah, and Esther*. NCB. Grand Rapids: Eerdmans; London: Marshall, Morgan, and Scott, 1984.

——. *The Theme of the Pentateuch*. JSOTSup 10. Sheffield: JSOT Press, 1982.

Coats, George W. *Exodus 1–18*. FOTL 2A. Grand Rapids: Eerdmans, 1999.

——. *Genesis, with an Introduction to Narrative Literature*. FOTL 1. Grand Rapids: Eerdmans, 1983.

——. *Moses: Heroic Man, Man of G-d.* JSOTSup 57. Sheffield: Sheffield Academic Press, 1988.

——. *Rebellion in the Wilderness: The Murmuring Motif in the Wilderness Traditions of the Old Testament.* Nashville: Abingdon, 1968.

Cogan, Mordechai. *1 Kings.* AB 10. New York: Doubleday, 2001.

Coggins, R. J. *Haggai, Zechariah, Malachi.* OTG. Sheffield: JSPT Press, 1987.

Cohen, Arthur A. *The Tremendum: A Theological Interpretation of the Holocaust.* New York: Crossroad, 1981.

Cohn-Sherbok, Dan. *Holocaust Theology.* London: Lamp Press, 1989.

Collins, John J. *Daniel.* Hermeneia. Minneapolis: Fortress Press, 1993.

——. *Daniel, with an Introduction to Apocalyptic Literature.* FOTL 20. Grand Rapids: Eerdmans, 1984.

Cook, Stephen L. *Prophecy and Apocalypticism: The Post-Exilic Social Setting.* Minneapolis: Fortress Press, 1995.

Crenshaw, James L. *Defending G-d: Biblical Responses to the Problem of Evil.* New York: Oxford University Press, 2005.

——. *Ecclesiastes: A Commentary.* OTL. Philadelphia: Westminster, 1987.

——. *Education in Ancient Israel: Across the Deadening Silence.* Garden City, N.Y.: Doubleday, 1998.

——. *Old Testament Wisdom: An Introduction.* Louisville: Westminster John Knox, 1998.

——. *The Psalms: An Introduction.* Grand Rapids: Eerdmans, 2001.

Cross, Frank Moore. *Canaanite Myth and Hebrew Epic.* Cambridge: Harvard University Press, 1973.

Dawidowicz, Lucy S. *The War Against the Jews, 1933–1945.* New York: Holt, Rinehart, and Winston; Philadelphia: Jewish Publication Society, 1975.

Dietrich, Walter. *Prophetie und Geschichte.* FRLANT 108. Göttingen: Vandenhoeck & Ruprecht, 1972.

Dobbs-Allsopp, F. W. *Weep, O Daughter of Zion: A Study of the City-Lament Genre in the Hebrew Bible.* BibOr 44. Rome: Pontifical Biblical Institute, 1993.

Eckardt, Alice L. and A. Roy Eckardt. *Long Night's Journey into Day: A Revised Retrospective on the Holocaust.* Detroit: Wayne State University Press, 1988.

Eichrodt, Walter. *Theology of the Old Testament.* 2 vols. OTL. Philadelphia: Westminster, 1961–67.

Eskenazi, Tamara Cohn. *In an Age of Prose: A Literary Approach to Ezra-Nehemiah.* SBLMS 36. Atlanta: Scholars Press, 1988.

Exum, J. Cheryl. *Song of Songs: A Commentary.* OTL: Louisville: Westminster John Knox, 2005.

Fackenheim, Emil L. *G-d's Presence in History: Jewish Affirmations and Philosophical Reflections.* New York: New York University Press, 1970.

——. *The Jewish Bible after the Holocaust: A Rereading.* Bloomington: Indiana University Press, 1990.

Ferris, Paul Wayne, Jr. *The Genre of Communal Lament in the Bible and the Ancient Near East.* SBLDS 127. Atlanta: Scholars Press, 1992.

270   Fishbane, Michael. *Haftarot*. JPS Bible Commentary. Philadelphia: Jewish Publication Society, 2002.

Fritz, Volkmar. *Israel in der Wüste. Traditionsgeschichtliche Untersuchung der Wüstenüberlieferung des J-hwisten*. Marburg: N. G. Elwert, 1970.

Fox, Michael V. *Character and Ideology in the Book of Esther*. Grand Rapids: Eerdmans, 2001.

———. *Proverbs 1–9*. AnBib 18A. Garden City, N.Y.: Doubleday, 2000.

———. *Song of Songs and the Ancient Egyptian Love Songs*. Madison: University of Wisconsin, 1999.

———. *A Time to Tear Down and a Time to Build Up: A Rereading of Ecclesiastes*. Grand Rapids: Eerdmans, 1999.

Gaines, Janet Howe. *Forgiveness in a Wounded World: Jonah's Dilemma*. SBL 5. Atlanta: Society of Biblical Literature, 2003.

Galambush, Julie. *Jerusalem in the Book of Ezekiel: The City as YHWH's Wife*. SBLDS 130. Atlanta: Scholars Press, 1992.

Gerstenberger, Erhard S. *Psalms, Part 1, with an Introduction to Cultic Poetry*. FOTL 14. Grand Rapids: Eerdmans, 1988.

———. *Psalms, Part 2, and Lamentations*. FOTL 15. Grand Rapids: Eerdmans, 2001.

Gilbert, Martin. *The Holocaust: A History of the Jews of Europe During the Second World War*. New York: Holt, Rinehart, and Winston, 1985.

———. *Israel: A History*. New York: William Morrow, 1998.

Goldhagen, Daniel Jonah. *A Moral Reckoning: The Role of the Catholic Church in the Holocaust and its Unfulfilled Duty of Repair*. New York: Knopf, 2002.

Goldman, Yohanan. *Prophétie et royauté au retour de l'exil. Les origines littéraires de la forme massorétique du livre de Jérémie*. OBO 118. Göttingen: Vandenhoeck & Ruprecht, 1992.

Goshen-Gottstein, Alon. *The Sinner and the Amnesiac: The Rabbinic Invention of Elisha ben Abuya and Eleazar ben Arach*. Stanford: Stanford University Press, 2000.

Graffy, Adrian. *A Prophet Confronts His People: The Disputation Speech in the Prophets*. AnBib 104. Rome: Biblical Institute Press, 1984.

Grant-Henderson, Anna L. *Inclusive Voices in Post-Exilic Judah*. Collegeville, Minn.: Liturgical, 2002.

Greenberg, Moshe. *Ezekiel 1–20*. AB 22. Garden City, N.Y.: Doubleday, 1983.

Gruenwald, Ithamar. *Apocalyptic and Merkavah Mysticism*. AGJU 14. Leiden: Brill, 1980.

Gunkel, Hermann. *Genesis*. Trans. M. Biddle. Macon, Ga.: Mercer University Press, 1997.

———, with Joachim Begrich. *An Introduction to the Psalms: The Genres of the Religious Lyric of Israel*. Macon, Ga.: Mercer University Press, 1998.

Halpern, David J. *The Faces of the Chariot: Early Jewish Responses to Ezekiel's Vision*. TSAJ 16. Tübingen: Mohr Siebeck, 1988.

———. *Seeking Ezekiel: Text and Psychology*. University Park: Pennsylvania State University Press, 1993.

Hanson, Paul. *The Dawn of Apocalyptic*. Philadelphia: Fortress Press, 1975.

Hasel, Gerhard. *Old Testament Theology: Basic Issues in the Current Debate*. Grand   271
Rapids: Eerdmans, 1991.

Hayes, John H., and Frederick Prussner. *Old Testament Theology: Its History and Its Development*. Atlanta: John Knox, 1985.

Haynes, Stephen R. *The Bonhoeffer Legacy: Post-Holocaust Perspectives*. Minneapolis: Fortress Press, 2006.

———. *Prospects for a Post-Holocaust Theology*. Atlanta: Scholars Press, 1991.

Hayward, C. T. R. *The Jewish Temple: A Non-Biblical Sourcebook*. London and New York: Routledge, 1996.

Heschel, Abraham Joshua. *Man Is Not Alone: A Philosophy of Religion*. Philadelphia: Jewish Publication Society, 1951.

———. *G-d in Search of Man: A Philosophy of Judaism*. New York: Meridian and Jewish Publication Society, 1955.

———. *Die Prophetie*. Krakow: Nakladem Polskiej Akademji Umiejetnosci, 1936.

———. *The Prophets*. Philadelphia: Jewish Publication Society, 1962 ; New York: Harper & Row, 1969.

Holladay, William L. *The Architecture of Jeremiah 1–20*. Lewisburg, Pa.: Bucknell University Press, 1976.

Hölscher, Gustav. *Hesekiel: der Dichter und das Buch*. BZAW 39. Giessen: A. Töpelmann, 1924.

Hubbard, Robert L., Jr. *The Book of Ruth*. NICOT. Grand Rapids: Eerdmans, 1988.

Humphreys, W. Lee. *The Character of G-d in the Book of Genesis: A Narrative Appraisal*. Louisville: Westminster John Knox, 2001.

Isaac, Jules. *The Teaching of Contempt: Christian Roots of Anti-Semitism*. New York: Holt, Rinehart, and Winston, 1964.

Jahnow, Hedwig. *Das hebräischen Leichenlied im Rahmen der Völkerdichtung*. BZAW 36. Giessen: A. Töpelmann, 1923.

Japhet, Sara. *I & II Chronicles: A Commentary*. OTL. Louisville: Westminster John Knox, 1993.

———. *The Ideology of the Book of Chronicles and Its Place in Biblical Thought*. BEATAJ. Frankfurt: Peter Lang, 1989.

Johnson, Luke Timothy. *The Writings of the New Testament: An Interpretation*. Minneapolis: Fortress Press, 1999.

Jones, Barry A. *The Formation of the Book of the Twelve*. SBLDS 149. Atlanta: Scholars Press, 1995.

Jones, Douglas Rawlinson. *Jeremiah*. NCB. Grand Rapids: Eerdmans, 1992.

Kaplan, Edward K., and Samuel H. Dresner. *Abraham Joshua Heschel: Prophetic Witness*. New Haven: Yale University Press, 1998.

Kasher, Aryeh. *The Jews in Hellenistic and Roman Egypt: The Struggle for Equal Rights*. TSAJ 7. Tübingen: Mohr Siebeck, 1985.

Katz, Steven T. *Post-Holocaust Dialogues: Critical Studies in Modern Jewish Thought*. New York and London: New York University Press, 1985.

Kellenbach, Katharina von. *Anti-Judaism in Feminist Religious Writings*. Atlanta: Scholars Press, 1994.

272   Klawans, Jonathan. *Impurity and Sin in Ancient Judaism*. New York: Oxford University Press, 2000.

Klein, Charlotte. *Anti-Judaism in Christian Theology*. Minneapolis: Fortress Press, 1978.

Knierim, Rolf P. *The Task of Old Testament Theology: Substance, Method, and Cases*. Grand Rapids: Eerdmans, 1995.

———, and George W. Coats. *Numbers*. FOTL 4. Grand Rapids: Eerdmans, 2005.

Knoppers, Gary N. *Two Nations under G-d: The Deuteronomistic History of Solomon and the Dual Monarchies*. HSM 52–53. Atlanta: Scholars Press, 1993–94.

Köhlmoos, Melanie. *Bet-El—Erinnerungen an die Stadt. Perspectiven der alttestamentlichen Bet-El Überlieferung*. FAT. Tübingen: Mohr Siebeck, 2006.

Koester, Helmut. *History and Literature of Early Christianity, vol. 2: Introduction to the New Testament*. Berlin: Walter de Gruyter, 2000.

Krüger, Thomas. *Qoheleth*. Hermeneia. Minneapolis: Fortress Press, 2004.

Kuhrt, Amélie. *The Ancient Near East c. 3000–330 BC*. 2 vols. London and New York: Routledge, 1998.

Landy, Francis. *Hosea*. Readings. Sheffield: Sheffield Academic Press, 1995.

Lange, Armin. *Vom prophetischen Wort zur prophetischen Tradition*. FAT 34. Tübingen: Mohr Siebeck, 2002.

LeClerc, Thomas L. *YHWH Is Exalted in Justice: Solidarity and Conflict in Isaiah*. Minneapolis: Fortress Press, 2001.

Lee, Won W. *Punishment and Forgiveness in Israel's Migratory Campaign*. Grand Rapids: Eerdmans, 2003.

Levenson, Jon. *Creation and the Persistence of Evil: The Jewish Drama of Divine Omnipotence*. New York: Harper & Row, 1988.

Levenson, Jon D. *Esther: A Commentary*. OTL. Louisville: Westminster John Knox, 1997.

———. *Sinai and Zion: An Entry into the Jewish Bible*. Minneapolis: Winston, 1985.

———. *Theology of the Program of Restoration of Ezekiel 40–48*. HSM 10. Missoula: Scholars Press, 1976.

Levine, Baruch A. *Numbers 1–20*. AB 4. Garden City, N.Y.: Doubleday, 1993.

Lewis, Bernard. *The Jews of Islam*. Princeton: Princeton University Press, 1984.

Linafelt, Tod. *Surviving Lamentations: Catastrophe, Lament, and Protest in the Afterlife of a Biblical Book*. Chicago: University of Chicago, 2000.

———, ed. *Strange Fire: Reading the Bible after the Holocaust*. New York: New York University Press; Sheffield: Sheffield Academic Press, 2000.

———, ed. *A Shadow of Glory: Reading the New Testament After the Holocaust*. New York and London: Routledge, 2002.

Littell, Franklin. *The Crucifixion of the Jews: The Failure of Christians to Understand The Jewish Experience*. Macon, Ga.: Mercer University Press, 1986.

Lohfink, Norbert L. *Qoheleth*. ContCom. Minneapolis: Fortress, 2003.

Longman, Tremper III. *The Song of Songs*. NICOT. Grand Rapids: Eerdmans, 2001.

Lundbom, Jack R. *Jeremiah 1–20*. AB 21A. Garden City, N.Y.: Doubleday, 1999.

Maier, Christl. *Jeremia als Lehrer der Tora. Soziale Gebote des Deuteronomiums in Fortschreibungen des Jeremiabuches.* FRLANT196. Göttingen: Vandenhoeck & Ruprecht, 2002.

Mann, Jacob. *The Bible as Read and Preached in the Old Synagogue.* 2 vols. New York: KTAV, 1971.

Mason, Rex. *Preaching the Tradition.* Cambridge: Cambridge University Press, 1990.

———. *Zephaniah, Habakkuk, Joel.* OT Guides. Sheffield: JSOT Press, 1994.

Matt, Daniel Chanan. *Zohar: The Book of Enlightenment.* New York: Paulist, 1983.

Maybaum, Ignaz. *The Face of G-d After Auschwitz.* Amsterdam: Polak and Van Glennep, 1965.

Mays, James L. *The L-rd Reigns: A Theological Handbook to the Psalms.* Louisville: Westminster John Knox, 1994.

McKeating, Henry. *Ezekiel.* OTG. Sheffield: Sheffield Academic Press, 1993.

Melugin, Roy F., and Marvin A. Sweeney, eds. *New Visions of Isaiah.* JSOTSup 214. Sheffield: Sheffield Academic Press, 1996.

Milgrom, Jacob. *Numbers.* JPS Torah Commentary. Philadelphia and New York: Jewish Publication Society, 1990.

Morgan, Michael L. *Beyond Auschwitz: Post-Holocaust Jewish Thought in America.* New York: Oxford University Press, 2001.

Mowinckel, Sigmund. *Psalmenstudien IV.* Kristiana: J. Dybwad, 1923.

Murphy, Roland E. *The Song of Songs.* Hermeneia. Minneapolis: Fortress Press, 1990.

———. *The Tree of Life: An Exploration of Biblical Wisdom Literature.* Winona Lake, Ind.: Eisenbrauns, 2002.

———. *Wisdom Literature: Job, Proverbs, Ruth, Canticles, Ecclesiastes, Esther.* FOTL 13. Grand Rapids: Eerdmans, 1981.

Nelson, Richard D. *The Double Redaction of the Deuteronomistic History.* JSOTSup 18. Sheffield: JSOT Press, 1981.

———. *The Historical Books.* IBT. Nashville: Abingdon, 1998.

Newsom, Carol A. *The Book of Job: A Contest of Moral Imaginations.* New York: Oxford University Press, 2003.

Nicholson, Ernest. *The Pentateuch in the Twentieth Century: The Legacy of Julius Wellhausen.* Oxford: Oxford University Press, 1998.

Nicholson, E. W. *Preaching to the Exiles: A Study of the Prose Traditions in the Book of Jeremiah.* New York: Schocken, 1970.

Nielsen, Kirsten. *Ruth: A Commentary.* OTL. Louisville: Westminster John Knox, 1997.

Noth, Martin. *Überlieferungsgeschichtliche Studien.* 3d ed. Darmstadt: Wissenschaftliche Buchgesellschaft, 1967. English eds.: *The Deuteronomistic History.* Trans. E. W. Nicholson. JSOTSup 15. Sheffield: JSOT Press, 1981; *Chronicler's History.* Trans. H. G. M. Williamson. JSOTSup 50. Sheffield: JSOT Press, 1987.

O'Brien, Julia M. *Nahum.* Readings. Sheffield: Sheffield Academic Press, 2002.

O'Connor, Kathleen. *The Confessions of Jeremiah: Their Importance and Role in Chapters 1–25.* SBLDS 94. Atlanta: Scholars Press, 1988.

274   Odell, Margaret S. *Ezekiel.* Smyth and Helwys Bible Commentary. Macon, Ga.: Smyth and Helwys, 2005.

Oldenhage, Tania. *Parables for Our Time: Rereading New Testament Scholarship after the Holocaust.* New York: Oxford University Press, 2002.

Olson, Dennis T. *The Death of the Old and the Birth of the New: The Framework of Numbers and the Pentateuch.* BJS 71. Chico, Calif.: Scholars Press, 1985.

———. *Deuteronomy and the Death of Moses: A Theological Reading.* OBT. Minneapolis: Fortress Press, 1994.

Otto, Rudolf. *The Idea of the Holy: An Inquiry into the Non-Rational Factor in the Idea of the Divine and its Relation to the Rational.* London: Oxford University Press, 1970.

Overholt, Thomas W. *The Threat of Falsehood: A Study in the Theology of the Book of Jeremiah.* SBT 2/16. Naperville, Ill.: Allenson, 1970.

Perdue, Leo G. *The Collapse of History: Reconstructing Old Testament Theology.* OBT. Minneapolis: Fortress Press, 1994.

———. *Reconstructing Old Testament Theology: After the Collapse of History.* OBT. Minneapolis: Fortress Press, 2005.

———. *Wisdom and Creation: The Theology of the Wisdom Literature.* Nashville: Abingdon, 1994.

Petersen, David L. *The Prophetic Literature.* Louisville: Westminster John Knox, 2002.

———. *Late Israelite Prophecy: Studies in Deutero-Prophetic Literature and in Chronicles.* SBLMS 23. Missoula: Scholars Press, 1977.

Pope, Marvin. *Song of Songs.* AnBib 19. Garden City, N.Y.: Doubleday, 1977.

Propp, William H. *Exodus 1–18.* AB 2. Garden City, N.Y.: Doubleday, 1999.

Pritchard, J. B. ed. *The Ancient Near East in Pictures Relating to the Old Testament.* Princeton: Princeton University Press, 1954.

———, ed. *Ancient Near Eastern Texts Relating to the Old Testament.* 3d ed. Princeton: Princeton University Press, 1969.

Rad, Gerhard von. *Old Testament Theology.* 2 vols. New York: Harper & Row, 1962–65.

Rendtorff, Rolf. *Canon and Theology: Overtures to an Old Testament Theology.* OBT. Minneapolis: Fortress Press, 1993.

———. *The Canonical Hebrew Bible: A Theology of the Old Testament.* Leiden: Deo, 2005.

———. *The Problem of the Process of Transmission in the Pentateuch.* JSOTSup 89. Trans. J. J. Scullion. Sheffield: JSOT Press, 1990.

———. *Theologie des Alten Testaments. Eine kanonischer Entwurf.* Neukirchen-Vluyn: Neukirchener, 1999–2001.

Rietzschel, Claus. *Das Problem der Urrolle. Ein Beitrag zur Redaktionsgeschichte des Jeremiabuches.* Gütersloh: Gerd Mohn, 1966.

Rubenstein, Richard L. *After Auschwitz: Radical Theology and Contemporary Judaism.* Indianapolis: Bobbs-Merrill, 1966.

Ruether, Rosemary Radford. *Faith and Fratricide: The Theological Roots of Anti-Semitism.* Eugene: Wipf & Stock, 1997.

———, and Herman J. Ruether. *The Wrath of Jonah: The Crisis of Religious Nationalism in the Israeli-Palestinian Conflict*. New York: Harper & Row, 1989.

Sachar, Howard M. *A History of Israel from the Rise of Zionism to Our Time*. New York: Knopf, 2003.

Sarna, Nahum. *Exodus*. JPS Torah Commentary. Philadelphia and New York: Jewish Publication Society, 1991.

———. *Understanding Genesis: The Heritage of Biblical Israel*. New York: Schocken, 1970.

Sasson, Jack M. *Ruth: A New Translation with a Philological Commentary and Formalist-Folklorist Interpretation*. BibSem 10. Sheffield: Sheffield Academic Press, 1995.

Schäfer, Peter. *Judeophobia: Attitudes toward the Jews in the Ancient World*. Cambridge: Harvard University Press, 1997.

Scherman, Nosson and Meir Zlotowitz. *Yechezkel/Ezekiel*. Art Scroll Tanach Series. Vol. 3. Brooklyn: Mesorah, 1980.

Schmid, H. H. *Der sogenannte J-hwist: Beobachtungen und Fragen zur Pentateuchforschung*. Zürich: Theologischer Verlag, 1976.

Schneider, Tammi J. *Judges*. Berit Olam. Collegeville, Minn.: Liturgical, 2000.

———. *Sarah: Mother of Nations*. New York and London: Continuum, 2004.

Schniedewind, William M. *The Word of G-d in Transition: From Prophet to Exegete in the Second Temple Period*. JSOTSup 197. Sheffield: Sheffield Academic Press, 1995.

Scholem, Gershom. *Major Trends in Jewish Mysticism*. New York: Schocken, 1972.

Schramm, Brooks. *The Opponents of Third Isaiah: Reconstructing the Cultic History of the Restoration*. JSOTSup 193. Sheffield: Sheffield Academic Press, 1995.

Schürer, Emil. *The History of the Jewish People in the Age of Jesus Christ*. Vol. 1. Rev. and ed. G. Vermes, et al. Edinburgh: T. & T. Clark, 1973.

Sefati, Yitschak. *Love Songs in Sumerian Literature: Critical Edition of the Dumuzi-Inanna Songs*. Ramat Gan: Bar Ilan University Press, 1998.

Seitz, Christopher R. *Theology in Conflict*. BZAW 176. Berlin: Walter de Gruyter, 1989.

Seow, Choon-Leong. *Ecclesiastes*. AnBib 18C. Garden City, N.Y.: Doubleday, 1997.

Sharp, Carolyn J. *Prophecy and Ideology in Jeremiah: Struggles for Authority in the Deutero-Jeremianic Prose*. London: T. & T. Clark, 2003.

Shead, Andrew G. *The Open and the Sealed Book: Jeremiah 32 in its Hebrew and Greek Recensions*. JSOTSup 347. London: Continuum, 2002.

Sherwood, Yvonne. *The Prostitute and the Prophet: Hosea's Marriage in Literary-Theological Perspective*. JSOTSup 212. GCT 2. Sheffield: Sheffield Academic Press, 1996.

Simundson, Daniel J. *Hosea, Joel, Amos, Obadiah, Jonah, Micah*. ACOT. Nashville: Abingdon, 2005.

Smallwood, E. M. *The Jews under Roman Rule*. Leiden: Brill, 1980.

Smith, Mark S. *The Laments of Jeremiah and Their Contexts*. SBLMS 42. Atlanta: Scholars Press, 1990.

Speiser, Ephraim A. *Genesis*. AB 1. Garden City, N.Y.: Doubleday, 1964.

Spronk, Klaas. *Nahum*. HCOT. Kampen: Kok Pharos, 1997.

276   Steck, Odil Hannes. *Bereitete Heimkehr. Jesaja 35 als redaktionelle Brücke zwischen dem Ersten und dem Zweiten Jesaja*. SBS 121. Stuttgart: Katholisches Bibelwerk, 1985.

Sternberg, Meir. *The Poetics of Biblical Narrative: Ideological Literature and the Drama of Reading*. Bloomington: Indiana University Press, 1985.

Stillman, Norman A. *Jews of Arab Lands in Modern Times*. Philadelphia: Jewish Publication Society, 2003.

Strack, H. L., and G. Stemberger. *Introduction to the Talmud and Midrash*. Minneapolis: Fortress Press, 1992.

Stuhlman, Louis. *Jeremiah*. AOTC. Nashville: Abingdon, 2005.

——. *Order Amid Chaos: Jeremiah as Symbolic Tapestry*. BibSem 57. Sheffield: Sheffield Academic Press, 1998.

Sweeney, Marvin A. *I and II Kings: A Commentary*. OTL. Louisville: Westminster John Knox, 2007.

——. *Form and Intertextuality in Prophetic and Apocalyptic Literature*. FAT 45. Tübingen: Mohr Siebeck, 2005.

——. *Isaiah 1–39, with an Introduction to Prophetic Literature*. FOTL 16. Grand Rapids: Eerdmans, 1996.

——. *King Josiah of Judah: The Lost Messiah of Israel*. New York: Oxford University Press, 2001.

——. *The Prophetic Literature*. IBT. Nashville: Abingdon, 2005.

——. *The Twelve Prophets*. 2 vols. Berit Olam. Collegeville, Minn.: Liturgical, 2000.

Tengström, Sven. *Die Toledotformel und die literarische Struktur der priesterlichen Erweiterungsschicht im Pentateuch*. ConBibOT 17. Uppsala: Gleerup, 1981.

Thiel, Winfried. *Die deuteronomistische Redaktion von Jeremia 1–25*. WMANT 41. Neukirchen-Vluyn: Neukirchener, 1973.

——. *Die deuteronomistische Redaktion von Jeremia 26–45*. WMANT 52. Neukirchen-Vluyn: Neukirchener, 1981.

Thomas, Matthew. *These are the Generations: Identity, Promise, and the Toledoth Formulae*. Ph.D. Dissertation. Claremont Graduate University, 2006.

Trible, Phyllis. *G-d and the Rhetoric of Sexuality*. OBT. Philadelphia: Fortress Press, 1978.

——. *Rhetorical Criticism: Context, Method, and the Book of Jonah*. Guides to Biblical Scholarship. Minneapolis: Fortress Press, 1994.

Tuell, Steven Shawn. *The Law of the Temple in Ezekiel 40–48*. HSM 49. Atlanta: Scholars Press, 1992.

Urbach, Ephraim E. *The Sages: Their Concepts and Beliefs*. 2 vols. Jerusalem: Magnes, 1979.

Van Seters, John. *Abraham in History and Tradition*. New Haven: Yale University Press, 1975.

Vaughn, Andrew G. *Theology, History, and Archaeology in the Chronicler's Account of Hezekiah*. ABS 4. Atlanta: Scholars Press, 1999.

Weinfeld, Moshe. *Deuteronomy*. AnBib 5. Garden City, N.Y.: Doubleday, 1991.

Wendel, Ute. *Jesaja und Jeremia. Worte, Motive und Einsichten Jesajas in der*
Verkündigung Jeremias. BibThS 25. Neukirchen-Vluyn: Neukirchner, 1995.

Weippert, Helga. *Die Prosareden des Jeremiabuches.* BZAW 132. Berlin: Walter de Gruyter, 1973.

Westermann, Claus. *The Promises to the Fathers: Studies on the Patriarchal Narratives.* Philadelphia: Fortress Press, 1980.

Whybray, R. Norman. *Introduction to the Pentateuch.* Grand Rapids: Eerdmans, 1995.

———. *The Making of the Pentateuch: A Methodological Study.* JSOTSup 53. Sheffield: JSOT Press, 1987.

Wiesel, Elie. *The Accident.* New York: Hill and Wang, 1962.

———. *Dawn.* New York: Hill and Wang, 1961.

———. *Legends of Our Time.* New York: Holt, Rinehart and Winston, 1968.

———. *Night.* New York: Random House, 1973.

———. *The Trial of G-d.* New York: Random House, 1977.

Williamson, Clark M. *A Guest in the House of Israel: Post-Holocaust Church Theology.* Louisville: Westminster John Knox, 1993.

Williamson, H. G. M. *The Book Called Isaiah: Deutero-Isaiah's Role in Composition and Redaction.* Oxford: Clarendon, 1994.

———. *Ezra, Nehemiah.* WBC 16. Waco: Word, 1985.

———. *Ezra and Nehemiah.* OTG. Sheffield: Sheffield Academic Press, 1987.

Wilson, Gerald H. *The Editing of the Hebrew Psalter.* SBLDS 76. Chico, Calif.: Scholars Press, 1985.

Wolff, Hans Walter. *Hosea.* Hermeneia. Philadelphia: Fortress Press, 1974.

———. *Confrontations with Prophets: Discovering the Old Testament's New and Contemporary Significance.* Philadelphia: Fortress Press, 1983.

Zimmerli, Walter. *Ezekiel 1: A Commentary on the Book of the Prophet Ezekiel, Chapters 1–24.* Hermeneia. Trans. R. E. Clements. Philadelphia: Fortress Press, 1979.

Articles and Chapters of Books

Alster, B. "Tammuz." 828–34. In *DDD²*.

Amit, Yairah. "Hidden Polemic in the Conquest of Dan: Judges xvii–xviii." *VT* 40 (1990): 4–20.

Assis, Elie. "Why Edom? On the Hostility toward Jacob's Brother in Prophetic Sources." *VT* 56 (2006): 1–20.

Beegle, D. M. "Moses." In *ABD* 4:909–18.

Ben Zeev, Miriam Pucci. "The Uprisings in the Jewish Diaspora," *CHJ* 4:93–104.

Ben Zvi, Ehud. "Twelve Prophetic Books or 'The Twelve': A Few Preliminary Considerations." In *Forming Prophetic Literature: Essays on Isaiah and the Twelve in Honor of J. D. W. Watts,* ed. J. W. Watts and P. R. House, 125–56. JSOTSup 235. Sheffield: Sheffield Academic Press, 1996.

278   Block, Daniel I. "Ezekiel in Scholarship at the Turn of the Millennium." In *Ezekiel's Hierarchical World: Wrestling with a Tiered Reality*, ed. S. L. Cook and C. L. Patton, 227–39. SBLSym 31. Atlanta: Society of Biblical Literature, 2004.

Crenshaw, James L. "Job, Book of." In *ABD* 3:858–68.

Darr, Katheryn Pfisterer. "Ezekiel." In *The New Interpreter's Bible*, ed. L. Keck, et al., 6:1073–607. Nashville: Abingdon, 2001.

———. "Ezekiel Among the Critics." *CR:BS* 2 (1994): 9–24.

De Pury, A., and T. Römer. "Le pentateuch en question. Position du problème et brève histoire de la recherché." In *Le Pentateuch en Question*, ed. A. De Pury and T. Römer, 9–80. Geneva: Labor et Fides, 1989.

Elat, Moshe. "The Economic Relations of the Neo-Assyrian Empire with Egypt." *JAOS* 98 (1978): 20–34.

Eshel, Hanan. "The Bar Kochba Revolt, 132–135." *CHJ* 4:105–27.

Evans, Craig A. "From Gospel to Gospel: The Function of Isaiah in the New Testament." In *Writing and Reading the Scroll of Isaiah: Studies of an Interpretive Tradition*, ed. C. C. Broyles and C. A. Evans, 651–91. VTSup 70/2. Leiden: Brill, 1997.

Garber, Zev, and Bruce Zuckerman. "Why Do We Call the Holocaust 'The Holocaust?' An Inquiry into the Psychology of Labels." *Modern Judaism* 9 (1989): 197–211. Reprinted in Zev Garber, *Shoah: The Paradigmatic Genocide: Essays in Exegesis and Eisegesis*, 51–67. Studies in the Shoah 8. Lanham, Md.: University Press of America, 1994.

Grabbe, Lester L. "The Kingdom of Judah from Sennacherib's Invasion to the Fall of Jerusalem: If We Had Only the Bible . . ." In *Good Kings and Bad Kings*, ed. Lester L. Grabbe, 78–122. JSOTSup 393. London and New York: T. & T. Clark, 2005.

Grayson, A. K. "Assyria 668–635 B.C.: The Reign of Ashurbanipal." In *The Cambridge Ancient History 3/2*, ed. John Boardman, et al., 142–61. Cambridge: Cambridge University Press, 1991.

Greenberg, Irving. "Cloud of Smoke, Pillar of Fire." In *Auschwitz: Beginning of a New Era?* 23. New York: KTAV, 1977.

Hendel, Ronald. "Genesis, Book of." In *ABD* 2:933–41.

Humphreys, W. Lee. "A Life-Style for Diaspora: A Study of the Tales of Esther and Daniel." *JBL* 92 (1973): 211–23.

———. "The Story of Esther and Mordecai: An Early Jewish Novella." In *Saga, Legend, Tale, Novella, Fable: Narrative Forms in Old Testament Literature*, ed. George W. Coats, 97–113. JSOTSup 35. Sheffield: Sheffield Academic Press, 1985.

Hurowitz, Victor. "Isaiah's Impure Lips and their Purification in Light of Akkadian Sources." *HUCA* 60 (1989): 39–89.

Japhet, Sara. "The Supposed Common Authorship of Chronicles and Ezra-Nehemiah Investigated Anew." *VT* 18 (1968): 330–31.

Kaplan, Mordecai. "Isaiah 6:1-11." *JBL* 45 (1926): 251–59.

Klein, Ralph W. "Chronicles, Book of 1-2." In *ABD* 1:992–1002.

————."Ezra-Nehemiah, Books of." In *ABD* 2:731–42.

Knierim. Rolf. "The Vocation of Isaiah." *VT* 18 (1968): 47–68.

Koch, Klaus. "Ezra and the Origins of Judaism." *JSS* 19 (1974): 173–97.

Kohn, Risa Levitt. "Ezekiel at the Turn of the Century." *CBR* 2 (2003): 9–32.

Lemke, Werner. "The Way of Obedience: 1 Kings 13 and the Structure of the Deuteronomistic History." In *Magnalia Dei/The Mighty Acts of G-d*, ed. F. M. Cross, et al., 301–26. Garden City, N.Y.: Doubleday, 1976.

Levenson, Jon D. "The Temple and the World." *JR* 64 (1984): 275–98.

————. "The Jerusalem Temple in Devotional and Visionary Experience." In *Jewish Spirituality, vol. 1: From the Bible through the Middle Ages,* ed. A. Green, 32–61. New York: Crossroad, 1988.

————. "Why Jews Are Not Interested in Biblical Theology." In *The Hebrew Bible, the Old Testament, and Historical Criticism: Jews and Christians in Biblical Studies,* 33–61, 165–70. Louisville: Westminster John Knox, 1993. Originally published in J. Neusner, et al, eds., *Judaic Perspectives on Ancient Israel.* Philadelphia: Fortress Press, 1987, 281–307.

Limburg, James. "Psalms, Book of." In *ABD* 5:522–36.

Lundbom, Jack. "Jeremiah, Book of." In *ABD* 3:707–21.

McKenzie, Steven L. "Deuteronomistic History." In *ABD* 2:160–68.

Meyers, Carol L. "Temple, Jerusalem." In *ABD* 6:350–69.

Murray, F. "The Rhetoric of Disputation: Re-examination of a Prophetic Genre." *JSOT* 38 (1987): 95–121.

Newsom, Carol A. "The Book of Job." In *The New Interpreter's Bible,* ed. L. E. Keck, et al. 4:319–637. Nashville: Abingdon, 1996.

O'Brien, Julia M. "Malachi in Recent Research." *CR:BS* 3 (1995): 81–94.

O'Connor, Kathleen M. "Lamentations." In *The New Interpreter's Bible,* ed. L. E. Keck, et al., 6:1011–72. Nashville: Abingdon, 2001.

Odell, Margaret S. "You Are What You Eat: Ezekiel and the Scroll." *JBL* 117 (1998): 229–48.

Orlinsky, Harry M. "The Biblical Concept of the Land of Israel: Cornerstone of the Covenant Between G-d and Israel." In *The Land of Israel: Jewish Perspectives,* ed. L. Hoffman, 27–64. Notre Dame, Ind.: University of Notre Dame Press, 1986.

Page, Stephanie. "A Stele of Adad Nirari III and Nergal-ereš from Tell al Rimlah." *Iraq* 30 (1968): 139–53.

Pfeiffer, E. "Die Disputationsworte im Buch Maleachi." *EvT* 12 (1959): 546–68.

Rad, Gerhard von. "The Levitical Sermon in the Books of Chronicles." In *The Problem of the Hexateuch and Other Essays,* 267–80. London: SCM, 1966.

Redditt, Paul L. "The Formation of the Book of the Twelve: A Review of Research." In *Thematic Threads in the Book of the Twelve,* ed. P. L. Reddit and A. Schart, 1–26. BZAW 325. Berlin: Walter de Gruyter, 2003.

————. "Recent Research on the Book of the Twelve as One Book." *CR:BS* 9 (2001): 47–80.

Römer, Thomas, and Albert de Pury. "L'historiographie deutéronomiste (HD): Histoire de la recherché et enjeux du débat." In *Israël construit son histoire. L'histo-*

riographie deutéronomiste à la lumière des recherches récentes, ed. A. de Pury, et al., 9–120. Geneva: Labor et Fides, 1996.

Rubenstein, Richard. "Job and Auschwitz." In *Strange Fire: Reading the Bible after the Holocaust*, ed. T. Linafelt, 233–51. Sheffield: Sheffield Academic Press, 2000.

Schwartz, Seth. "Political, Social, and Economic Life in the Land of Israel, 66–c. 235." In *Cambridge History of Judaism, vol. 4: The Late Roman-Rabbinic Period*, ed. S. Katz, 23–52. Cambridge: Cambridge University Press, 2006.

Scullion, John J. "Genesis, The Narrative of." In *ABD* 2:941–62.

Seitz, Christopher R, William Millar, and Richard J. Clifford. "Isaiah, Book of." In *ABD* 3:472–507.

Seitz, Christopher R. "The Prophet Moses and the Canonical Shape of Jeremiah." *ZAW* 101 (1989): 487–516.

Smend, Rudolph. "Die Gesetz und Völker: Ein Beitrag zur deuteronomistischen Redaktionsgeschichte." In *Probleme biblischer Theologie*, ed. H. W. Wolff, 494–509. Munich: Chr. Kaiser, 1971.

Stavrakopoulou, Francesca. "The Blackballing of Manasseh." In *Good Kings and Bad Kings*, ed. Lester L. Grabbe, 248–63. JSOTSup 393. London and New York: T. & T. Clark, 2005.

Sweeney, Marvin A. "Absence of G-d and Human Responsibility in the Book of Esther." In *Reading the Hebrew Bible for a New Millennium: Form, Concept, and Theological Perspective. Volume 2: Exegetical and Theological Studies*, ed. W. Kim et al., 264–75. Harrisburg: Trinity Press International, 2000.

———. "The Book of Isaiah in Recent Research," *CR:BS* 1 (1993): 141–62.

———. "Concerning the Structure and Generic Character of the Book of Nahum." *ZAW* 104 (1992): 364–77.

———. "The Emerging Field of Jewish Biblical Theology." In *Academic Approaches to Teaching Jewish Studies*, ed. Z. Garber, 84–105. Lanham, Md.: University Press of America, 2000.

———. "Form Criticism." In *To Each Its Own Meaning: Biblical Criticisms and Their Application*, ed. S. L. McKenzie and S. R. Haynes, 58–89. Louisville: Westminster John Knox, 1999.

———. "Isaiah and Theodicy after the Shoah." In *Strange Fire: Reading the Bible after the Holocaust*, ed. T. Linafelt, 208–19. Sheffield: Sheffield Academic Press, 2000.

———. "Habakkuk, Book of." *ABD* 3:1–6.

———. "King Manasseh of Judah and the Problem of Theodicy in the Deuteronomistic History." In *Good Kings and Bad Kings*, ed. Lester L. Grabbe, 264–78. JSOTSup 393. London and New York: T. & T. Clark, 2005.

———. "On the Road to Duhm: Isaiah in Nineteenth-Century Critical Scholarship." In *As Those Who Are Taught: The Interpretation of Isaiah from the LXX to the SBL*, ed. C. M. McGinnis and P. K. Tull, 243–61. SBLSym 27. Atlanta: Society of Biblical Literature, 2006.

———. "Reconceiving the Paradigms of Old Testament Theology in the Post-Shoah Period," *Biblical Interpretation* 6 (1998): 142–61.

———. "The Reconceptualization of the Davidic Covenant in Isaiah." In *Studies in the Book of Isaiah: Festschrift for W. A. M. Beuken*, ed. J. van Ruiten and M. Vervenne, 41–61. BETL 132. Leuven: Peeters, 1997.

———. "Reevaluating Isaiah 1-39 in Recent Critical Research," *CR:BS* 4 (1996): 79–113.

———. "The Religious World of Ancient Israel to 586 B.C.E." In *The Blackwell Companion to Judaism*, ed. Jacob Neusner and Alan Avery-Peck, 20–36. Oxford: Blackwell, 2000.

———. "The Royal Oracle in Ezekiel 37:15-28: Ezekiel's Reflection on Josiah's Reform." In *Israel's Prophets and Israel's Past: Essays on the Relationship of Prophetic Texts and Israelite History in Honor of John H. Hayes*, ed. B. E. Kelle and M. B. Moore, 239–53. LHBOTS 446. New York and London: T. & T. Clark, 2006.

———. "Sequence and Interpretation in the Book of the Twelve." In *Reading and Hearing the Book of the Twelve*, ed. J. D. Nogalski and M. A. Sweeney, 49–64. SBLSym 15. Atlanta: Society of Biblical Literature, 2000.

———. "Structure, Genre, and Intent in the Book of Habakkuk." *VT* 41 (1991): 63–83.

———. "Ten Sephirot." In *Dictionary of Deities and Demons in the Bible*, ed. K. Van Der Toorn, et al., 837–43. Leiden: Brill; Grand Rapids: Eerdmans, 1999.

———. "The Wilderness Traditions of the Pentateuch: A Reassessment of their Function and Intent in Relation to Exodus 32-34." In *Society of Biblical Literature 1989 Seminar Papers*, ed. David J. Lull, 291–99. Atlanta: Scholars Press, 1989.

Talmon, Shmaryahu. "The Calendar Reckoning of the Sect from the Judaean Desert." In *Aspects of the Dead Sea Scrolls*, 162–99. ScrHier 4. Jerusalem: Magnes, 1958.

Trible, Phyllis. "The Book of Jonah." In *The New Interpreters' Bible*, ed. L. E. Keck, et al., 7:461–529. Nashville: Abingdon, 1996.

Van Dijk-Hemmes, Fokkelien. "Sarai's Exile: A Gender-Motivated Reading of Genesis 12:10-13:2." In *A Feminist Companion to Genesis 2*, ed. A. Brenner, 222–34. Sheffield: Sheffield Academic Press, 1997.

Verhoef, P. A. *Haggai and Malachi*. NICOT. Grand Rapids: Eerdmans, 1987.

Watts, John D. W. "A Frame for the Book of the Twelve: Hosea 1-3 and Malachi." In *Reading and Hearing the Book of the Twelve*, ed. J. D. Nogalski and M. A. Sweeney, 209–17. SBLSym 15. Atlanta: Society of Biblical Literature, 2000.

Weinfeld, Moshe. "Covenant, Davidic." *IDBSup* 188–92.

———. "The Covenant of Grant in the OT and in the Ancient Near East." *JAOS* 90 (1970): 184–203.

———. "Deuteronomy, Book of." In *ABD* 2:168–83.

———. "Tithe." In *EncJud* 15:1156–62.

———. "Zion and Jerusalem as Religious and Political Capital: Ideology and Utopia." In *The Poet and the Historian: Essays in Literary and Historical Biblical Criticism*, ed. R. E. Friedman, 75–115. HSS 26. Chico, Calif.: Scholars Press, 1983.

———, and Alexander Rofé. "Ruth, Book of." In *EncJud* 14:518–24.

282   Wilcoxen, Jay. "The Political Background of Jeremiah's Temple Sermon." In *Scripture in History and Theology: Essays in Honor of J. Coert Rylaarsdam,* ed. A. Merrill and T. Overholt, 155–66. Pittsburgh: Pickwick, 1977.

Wright, A. "The Riddle of the Sphinx: The Structure of the Book of Qoheleth." *CBQ* 30 (1968): 313–34.

———. "The Riddle of the Sphinx Revisited: Numerical Patterns in the Book of Qoheleth." *CBQ* 42 (1980): 38–51.

Ydit, Meir. "Av, The Ninth of." In *EncJud* 3:936–40.

Theodicy — Vindication of the divine attributes particularly holiness & justice, in establishing or allowing the existence of physical & moral evil.

Printed in the United States
128283LV00004B/2/P